BICYCLE RIDES
San Diego County
and Imperial County

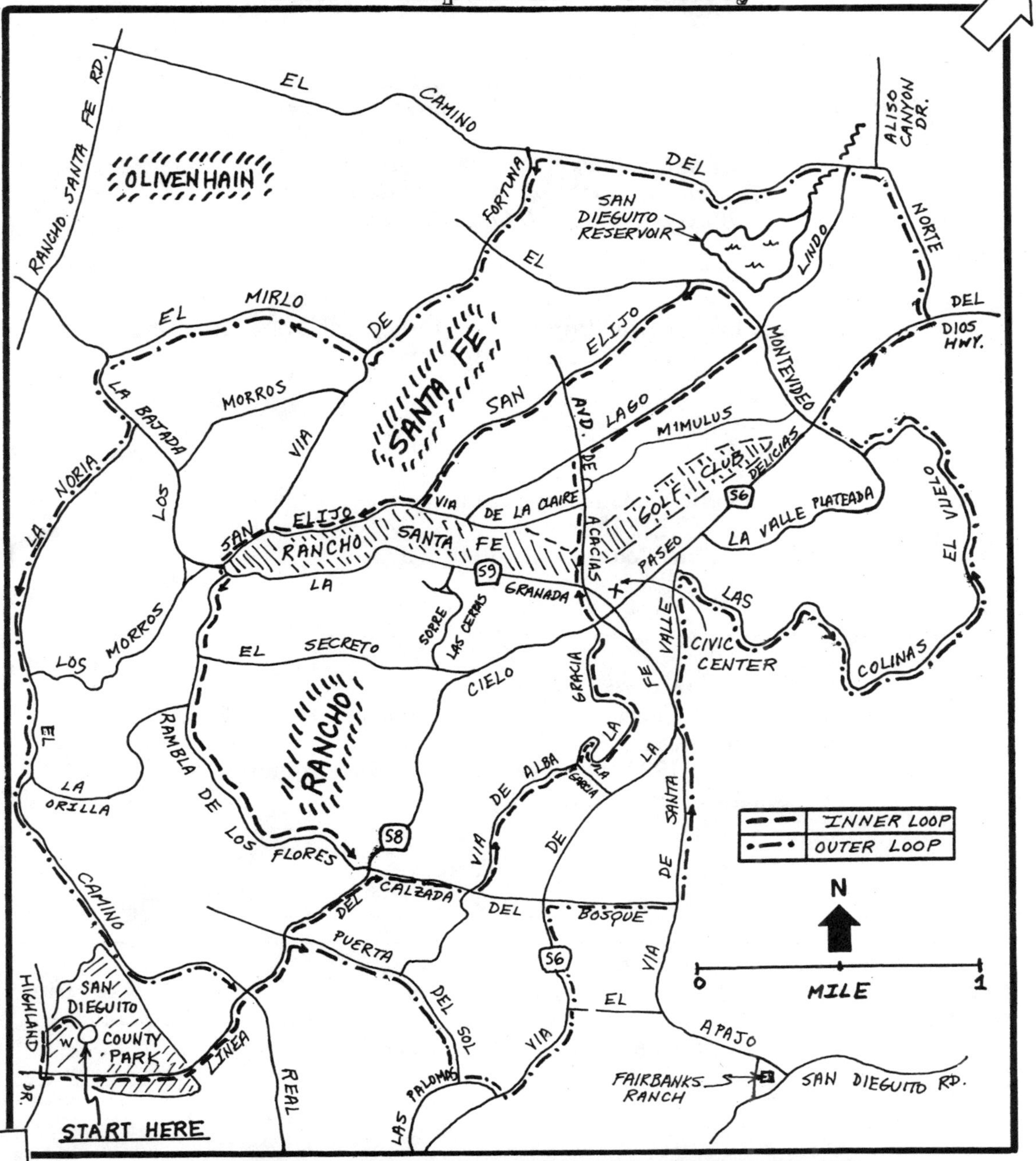

BY DON AND SHARRON BRUNDIGE

Disclaimer

These tour descriptions are provided as a guide. General comments are provided as to the safety and fitness of routes; however B-D Enterprises takes no responsibility for bicyclist's safety on the routes described.

Other Books by Don and Sharron Brundige:
Bicycle Rides: Los Angeles and Orange Counties (Out of Print)
Bicycle Rides: San Fernando Valley and Ventura County
Bicycle Rides: Orange County
Bicycle Rides: Los Angeles County
Bicycle Rides: Inland Empire

Printed by Griffin Printing & Lithograph Co., Inc.
Glendale, California

Published by B-D Enterprises
122 Mirabeau Ave.
San Pedro, California 90732

All rights reserved
Library of Congress Catalogue Number 90-093234
ISBN 0-9619151-5-3
Copyright © 1992 by Don and Sharron Brundige
Published in the United States of America

Limited Copyright Waiver

Book purchasers are granted permission to photocopy individual bike trips. However, transfer or sale of copies of any book portion to non-purchasers will be treated as an infringement of Copyright.

Corrections and updates will make this a better book and are gratefully appreciated. Publisher will reply to all such letters. Where information is used, submitter will be acknowledged in subsequent printing.

TABLE OF CONTENTS

	PAGE
INTRODUCTION	1
HOW TO USE THIS BOOK	2
TRIP ORGANIZATION	2
Master Trip Maps	3
Master Trip Matrices	5
TRIP DESCRIPTION/TERMINOLOGY	12
General Location	12
Level of Difficulty	12
Trip Mileage	12
Trip Elevation Gain	13
Bike Route Quality	13
Trip Characteristics	13
Trailhead	13
Water	14
Connecting Trips	14
Bike Trip Maps	14
GENERAL BIKING CONSIDERATIONS	15
Safety	15
Equipment	15
General Information	15
THE COAST	17
Metropolitan San Diego	
Trip #1 Mission Bay Loop	18
#2 Balboa Park	21
#3 Around San Diego Bay	24
#4 Seaport Village to Point Loma	29
#5 Marian Bear Park	32
#6 La Jolla Coastal Tour	36
#7 La Jolla Hillside Workout	39
#8 Heart O' the City	41
#9 Old Town Tour	44
#10 Overlooking Mission Valley	47
#11 San Diego 59-Mile Scenic Drive	50
#12 U. C. San Diego Campus Visit	53
#13 Techolote Canyon	55
#14 Run for the Border (Imperial Beach)	59
#15 Paradise Hills-Skyline Loop	63
#16 Lake Murray	65
#17 San Diego River Run	66
#18 Chula Vista Bikeway	71
#19 Sweetwater Park to Lower Otay Lake	74
#20 Lake Miramar Meander	77
#21 Coastal County Tour	78

	PAGE
North County	
#22 Riding "The Ranch" (Rancho Santa Fe)	85
#23 La Costa	88
#24 Lake San Marcos	91
#25 Vista City Tour	94
#26 Loop O' the Lagoons	97
#27 Ocean Hills-Vista Loop	100
#28 El Camino Real	102
#29 Oceanside City Tour	105
#30 Oceanside at Oceanside	108
INLAND	111
Urban	
#31 El Cajon Bikeway System	112
#32 Santee Lakes	114
#33 Rancho Bernardo	116
#34 Poway "Picnic"	118
#35 Escondido City Tour	121
#36 San Pasqual Valley	125
#37 Escondido to the Sea---and Back	129
#38 Old Hwy 395	133
#39 Fallbrook Countryside Tour	137
#40 Ramona/San Vicente Valley	141
#41 Eucalyptus Hills	144
#42 Lakeside-Lakeview Loop	146
#43 Tierrasanta Tour	148
#44 Mount Helix	150
#45 Hills and Dales (Blossom Valley)	153
Mountains/Backcountry	
#46 Palomar Mountain	155
#47 Julian "Junket"	159
#48 Laguna Mountains Crest	163
#49 Pala Mission Loop	166
#50 Jamul-Bratton Valley Loop	170
#51 Lake Morena-Live Oak Springs Loop	173
#52 Canyons N' Citrus	176
#53 Crest-Dehesa Valley Loop	179
#54 Wildcat Canyon	182
#55 Mussey Grade Road	186
#56 Bear Ridge Loop	188
Desert	
#57 El Centro City Tour	191
#58 Salton Sea Survey	193
#59 Borrego Springs	197
#60 Great Overland Stage Route	201
#61 Border Run	204
Colorado River	
#62 Winterhaven Workout	208
OTHER BICYCLING INFORMATION SOURCES	211
INDEX: San Diego County	213
Imperial County	217

DEDICATION

To Mom Brundige and John Flentz
Our two self-appointed researchers
For helping us stay current on the fast-moving world of cycling

ACKNOWLEDGEMENTS

We offer our thanks to family, friends and bicycling acquaintances who gave us ideas, advice and plenty of encouragement while developing this biking book. This includes a "thank you" to the state, county and city agencies and individuals who offered their services and publications. We show particular gratitude to the folks that were kind enough to review and comment to our manuscript: Jill Morales, Al Hook, Walt and Sally Bond, and Susan Cohen. Finally, we acknowledge Jackie Broom, who bailed us out of many computer-related difficulties.

We specifically wish to acknowledge the following individuals and/or organizations who also provided some excellent ideas for bicycle trips: COMMUTER COMPUTER (a cooperative effort between the City of San Diego, County of San Diego, SANDAG and CALTRANS) for their excellent (and free) "San Diego Regional Bicycling Map," E. C. Krulikowski of the El Cajon Department of Public Works, P. Joanne Watson of the El Centro Chamber of Commerce, Diane Willis of the Coronado Island Visitor Information Center, the Chambers of Commerce of Borrego Springs, Carlsbad, Escondido, La Jolla and Oceanside.

Finally, we acknowledge getting some nifty ride ideas from the following sources: *Gousha Weekend Guide to California Bike Tours* published by the H. M. Gousha Company, *Cycling San Diego* published by Centra Publications and *Southern California Bicycling* published by the Automobile Club of Southern California.

INTRODUCTION

One look at the COMMUTER COMPUTER "San Diego Regional Bicycling Map" convinced us that there were a host of San Diego County Bicycle tours that we had to try. The notes on the map relating to bus and trolley system support to bicyclists certainly indicated a county interest in biking activities. After testing a small fraction of the rides outlined, we decided to dive into this challenging bicycling project.

Again, we wanted to provide a trip guide that concentrates on trip navigation, contains a large number of well-documented trips, provides the necessary trip maps, and is reasonably priced. Hopefully we have succeeded!

This guide has been developed based on biking trips taken in 1990-1992. There are over 1500 one-way bike miles described! The document identifies 62 biking trips in San Diego and Imperial Counties. Each trip is written to be as complete and self-standing as possible. The authors used eighteen-speed bicycles (a touring bike and a mountain bike fitted with road tires), although a vast majority of the trips can easily be ridden with ten-speeds. Two off-road trips were included ("Marian Bear Park" and "Techolote Canyon"), which require fat-tire bikes.

A cross section of trips is provided. There are some short-length family trips on separated bike paths, many longer exploratory and workout trips for more experienced bikers on various quality bike routes, and a few "gut-buster" trips on open roadway for the most physically fit and motivated bikers. The trip domains include parks, rivers, lakes, mountains, valleys, canyons, basins and deserts. The trips vary from extremely scenic to somewhat monotonous (e.g., certain stretches of the desert roadways). There's a little something for everybody!

The strong emphasis in this book is "getting from here to there." This navigation is provided using detailed route descriptions in terms of landmarks, mileage and a quality set of trip maps. Scenery, vistas, scenic or historic landmarks, and sightseeing attractions are regularly noted for each trip, although detailed information about these features must be sought out in other publications. Public restrooms and sources of water are identified on trips where these facilities are scarce. Pleasant rest spots are also pointed out. Finally, "wine and dine" spots are noted for two specific circumstances: 1) where places to eat along the trip are scarce; and 2) where the establishment is too unique or exceptional not to mention.

HOW TO USE THIS BOOK

There are two ways to use this book, one way for the person who wants to enjoy the research along with enjoying the bike ride, and another way for the biker who is just anxious to get out there "amongst em" on a bike ride.

For the "anxious biker", follow Steps 1 through 5 below and split!

1. Use the "Master Trip Map" in the "TRIP ORGANIZATION" section to select areas of interest for the bike ride. Note the candidate trip numbers. (Another option is to select a trip based on landmarks and sightseeing attractions referenced in the "INDEX.")

2. Go to the "Master Trip Matrices" in the "TRIP ORGANIZATION" section and narrow down the number of candidate trips by reviewing their general features.

3. Read about the individual trips and select one.

4. Read and understand the safety rules described in the "GENERAL BIKING CONSIDERATIONS" section.

5. See you later. Enjoy the ride!

For the more methodical folks, continue reading the next chapter. By the time you're through, you'll understand the trip description and maps much better than the "anxious biker."

TRIP ORGANIZATION

This bike book is organized by trip number. Trip numbers are in a general sequence governed by whether the tours are in the coastal or inland areas. Refer back to the "TABLE OF CONTENTS" for the entire trip list.

The "Master Trip Maps" show the general location of trips by a circled reference number (i.e., ⑦ refers to Trip #7). Extended length trips are identified by circled numbers at both beginning and terminal points.

The "Master Trip Matrices" provide a quick reference for selecting candidate trips for more detailed reading evaluation. The matrices are organized by trip/number. The key trip descriptors provided in those matrices are briefly explained in the footnotes at the bottom of the last matrix (page 11). A more detailed explanation of those descriptors is provided in the "TRIP DESCRIPTION/TERMINOLOGY" section which follows.

TRIP ORGANIZATION

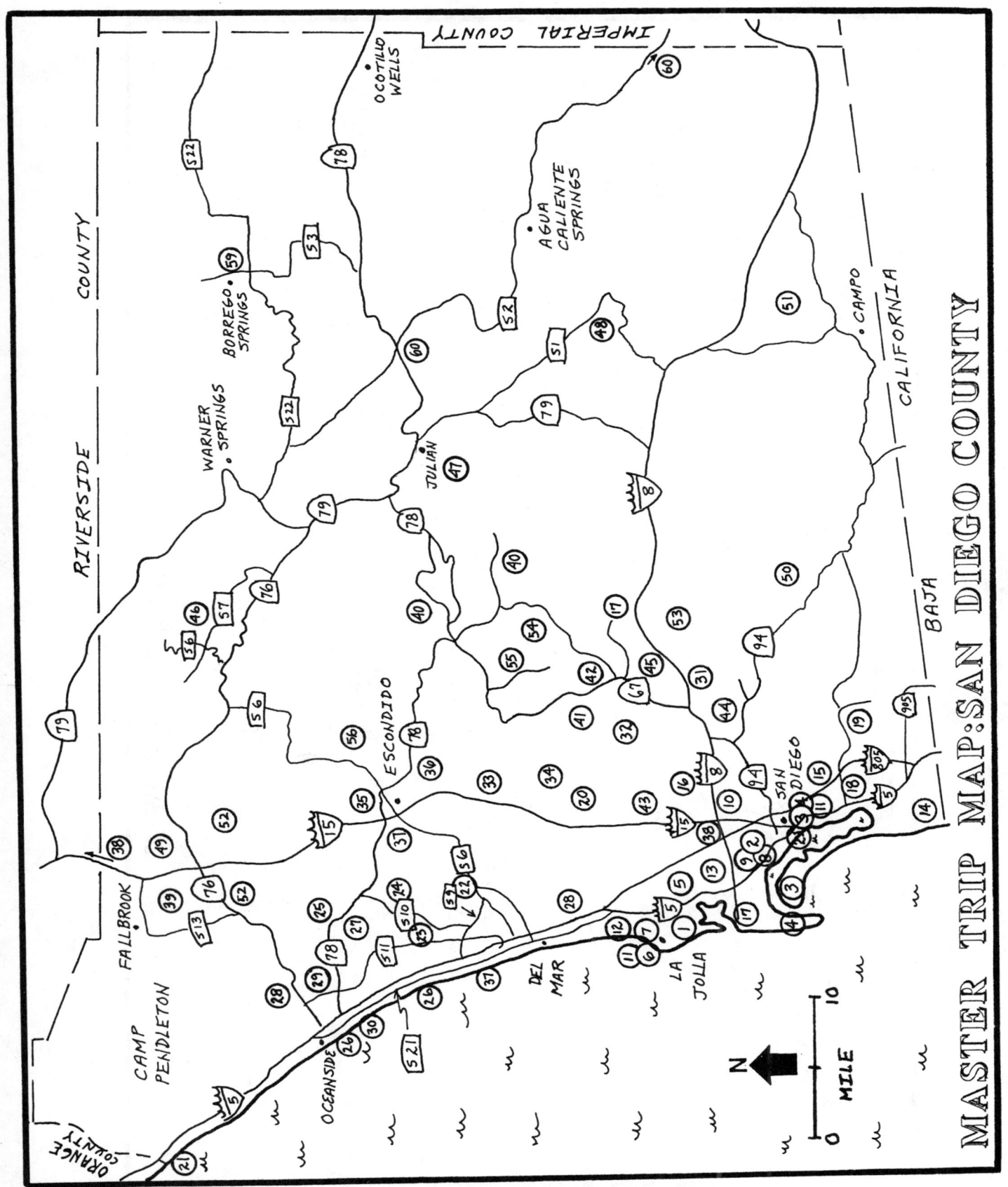

BICYCLE RIDES: SAN DIEGO COUNTY

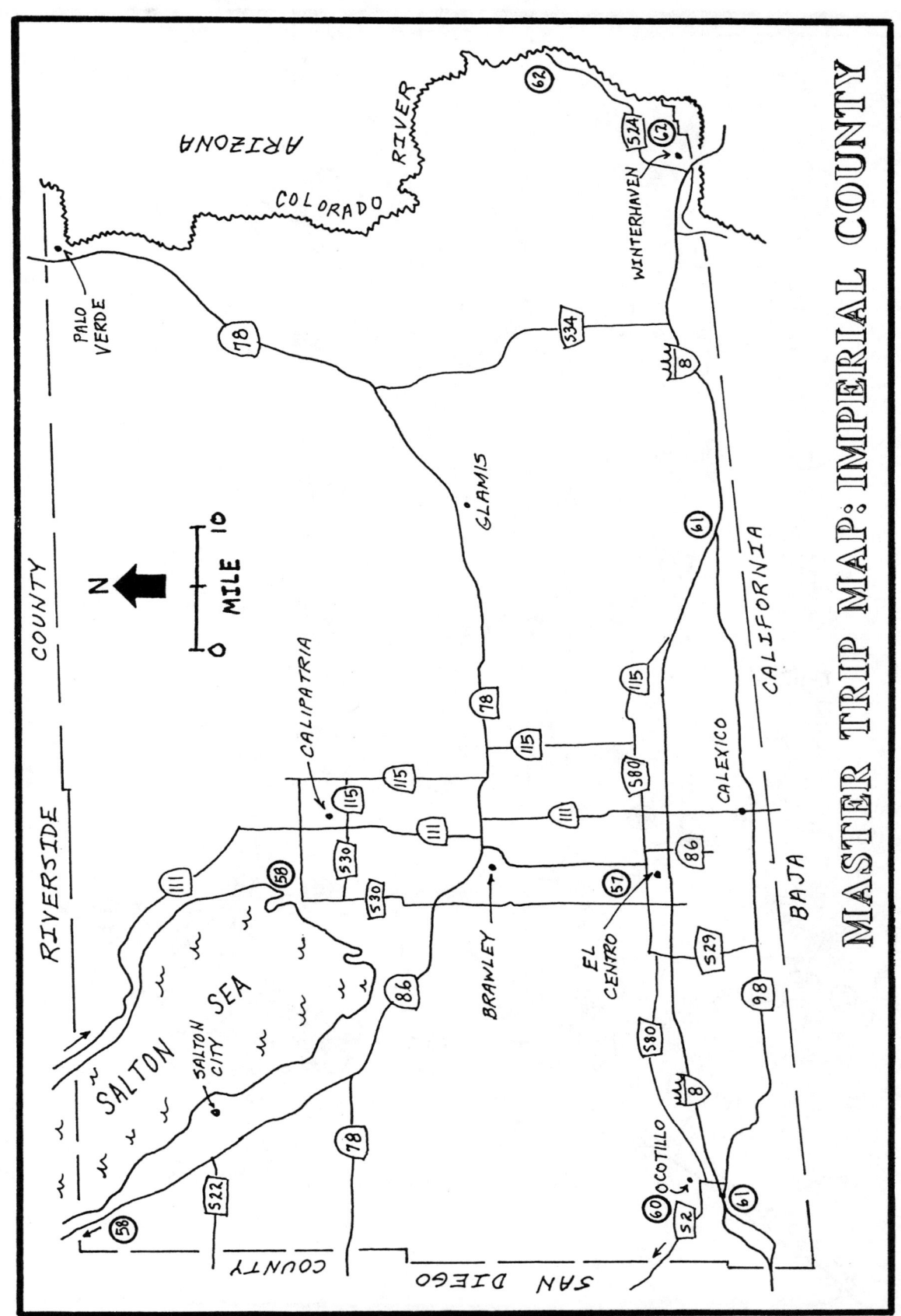

4

TRIP ORGANIZATION

MASTER TRIP MATRIX

TRIP NO.	GENERAL LOCATION	LEVEL OF DIFFICULTY			ROUTE QUALITY			TRIP CHARACT.[2]	COMMENTS
		L.O.D.[1]	MILES	ELEV.	BIKE TRAIL (%)	BIKE LANE (%)	OTHER (%)		
1	Mission Bay	E	13.9	Flat	60	40	-	S, N, L, S/A	Mission Bay (loop)
2	City of San Diego	M	8.8	Mod	20	80	10	S, N, L, S/A	Balboa Park (loop)
3	San Diego, Ocean Beach, Coronado	M	25.4	Flat	30	60	10	S, N, L, S/A	Southern San Diego Bay (loop) (plus Coronado)
4	San Diego, Point Loma	M-S	31.7	Mod-Steep	20	70	10	S, N, L, S/A	Northern San Diego Bay plus Point Loma (loop)
5	San Clemente Canyon	E(r/t)	7.0	Flat	100	-	-	S, N	Marian Bear Park (plus options) (off-road)
6	La Jolla	E(1-lp) M(2-lp)	16.0 (2-lp)	Mod	5	90	5	S, N, L, S/A	La Jolla Coastal Tour (2 loops)
7	La Jolla	S	11.8	Steep	-	60	40	S, N, L, S/A, E	La Jolla Interior (hills) Tour (loop)
8	City of San Diego	E	7.2	Flat	10	20	70	S, L, S/A	Downtown San Diego (Skyscraper Tour)
9	Old Town, Hillcrest	M	7.1	Flat-Steep	-	70	30	S, N, L, S/A	Old Town and old Banker's Hill (loop)
10	Mission Hills-Kensington Park	M	21.2	Flat-Mod	-	10	90	S, N, L, S/A	Mesa Tour above Mission Valley

1,2 See footnotes on page 11

BICYCLE RIDES: SAN DIEGO COUNTY

MASTER TRIP MATRIX

TRIP NO.	GENERAL LOCATION	LEVEL OF DIFFICULTY			ROUTE QUALITY			TRIP CHARACT.[2]	COMMENTS
		L.O.D.[1]	MILES	ELEV.	BIKE TRAIL (%)	BIKE LANE (%)	OTHER (%)		
11	San Diego, Pt. Loma, La Jolla	S	59+ (1-w)	Mod-Steep	10	30	60	S, N, L, S/A, M	San Diego 59-Mile Scenic Drive (loop)
12	North La Jolla	E	4.0	Mod	20	80	-	S, N, L	U. C. San Diego Campus Tour (loop)
13	Clairemont, Linda Vista	M	5.7	Mod	95	5	-	S, N	Techolote Canyon Park (plus option) (off-road)
14	Imperial Beach	E	16.3 (2-1p)	Flat	-	40	60	S, N, L, S/A	Mexican Border and Imperial Beach (2 loops)
15	Paradise Hills, Skyline	M	13.7	Mod	-	20	80	S, N	Paradise Hills-Skyline Loop
16	La Mesa	E	6.0	Flat	100	-	-	S, N	Lake Murray (loop)
17	Ocean Beach-Santee -El Capitan Lake	M	30.2	Mod	10	40	50	S, N, L, S/A, M	San Diego River (Sea to Foothills)
18	Chula Vista	M	12.0	Mod	-	90	10	S, N	Chula Vista Bikeway (loop)
19	Chula Vista, Lower Otay Lake	M	9.4	Mod	-	70	30	S, N	Sweetwater River Park to Lower Otay Lake
20	Scripps Miramar Ranch	E	4.8	Flat	100	-	-	S, N	Lake Miramar (loop)

1,2 See footnotes on page 11

TRIP ORGANIZATION

MASTER TRIP MATRIX

TRIP NO.	GENERAL LOCATION	LEVEL OF DIFFICULTY			ROUTE QUALITY			TRIP CHARACT.[2]	COMMENTS
		L.O.D.[1]	MILES	ELEV.	BIKE TRAIL (%)	BIKE LANE (%)	OTHER (%)		
21	San Diego–San Clemente	S	67.2 (1-w)	Mod-Sheer	20	80	–	S, N, L, S/A, E, M	San Diego to San Clemente Coastal Tour
22	Rancho Santa Fe	S	25.7 (2-1p)	Mod-Steep	–	10	90	S, N, M	Rancho Santa Fe (2 loops)
23	La Costa	M-S	18.1	Mod-Sheer	–	30	70	S, N, S/A, E	La Costa Residential Tour (2 loops)
24	Lake San Marcos	M	7.9	Mod	–	–	100	S, N, S/A	Lake San Marcos (loop)
25	Vista	M-S	18.8	Mod	–	40	60	S, N	Vista City Tour (2 loops)
26	Carlsbad	M	25.5	Mod	–	95	5	S, N	Carlsbad City Tour (three-lagoon loop)
27	Ocean Hills, Vista	M	9.7	Mod	–	85	15	S, N	Ocean Hills-Vista Loop
28	San Diego-Encinitas-Carlsbad-Oceanside	M-S (1-w)	28.6	Mod-Steep	–	60	40	S, N, L, M, E	El Camino Real (The King's Highway)
29	Oceanside	M	20.6	Mod	–	75	25	S, N, L, S/A	Inland City Loop
30	Oceanside	E	7.6	Flat	–	75	25	S, N, L, S/A	Coastal City Loop

1,2 See footnotes on page 11

7

BICYCLE RIDES: SAN DIEGO COUNTY

MASTER TRIP MATRIX

TRIP NO.	GENERAL LOCATION	LEVEL OF DIFFICULTY			ROUTE QUALITY			TRIP CHARACT.[2]	COMMENTS
		L.O.D.[1]	MILES	ELEV.	BIKE TRAIL (%)	BIKE LANE (%)	OTHER (%)		
31	El Cajon	M	14.6	Mod	-	100	-	S, M	El Cajon Tour (loop)
32	Santee	E	3.8	Flat	-	-	100	S, N	Santee Lakes (loop)
33	Rancho Bernardo	M	20.5	Mod	-	100	-	S, N	Rancho Bernardo (2 loops)
34	Poway	E-M	14.1	Mod	-	100	-	S, N	Poway City Tour (loop)
35	Escondido	M-S	29.5	Mod	-	50	50	S, N, M	Escondido City Tour (peripheral loop)
36	Escondido, Rancho Bernardo	M	22.9	Mod-Steep	-	25	75	S, N, L, S/A, E, M	San Pasqual Valley (loop)
37	Escondido-Encinitas-Rancho Santa Fe	S	39.4	Mod-Steep	-	40	60	S, N, L, S/A, E, M	Escondido to the Sea ---and Back! (loop)
38	San Diego-Escondido-Temecula	S	56.7	Mod-Steep	5	90	5	S, N, L, S/A, E, M	Old Highway 395 (San Diego to Temecula)
39	Fallbrook	M-S	23.8	Mod-Steep	-	10	90	S, N	Fallbrook Countryside Tour (loop)
40	Ramona	M-S	17.5	Mod-Steep	-	-	100	S, N, L	Ramona Loop (plus San Vicente Valley Option)

1,2 See footnotes on page 11

MASTER TRIP MATRIX

TRIP NO.	GENERAL LOCATION	LEVEL OF DIFFICULTY			ROUTE QUALITY			TRIP CHARACT.²	COMMENTS
		L.O.D.¹	MILES	ELEV.	BIKE TRAIL (%)	BIKE LANE (%)	OTHER (%)		
41	Eucalyptus Hills	M	5.2	Mod	-	-	100	S, N	Eucalyptus Hills Rural Loop
42	Lakeside, Lakeview	M	7.3	Mod	-	30	70	S, N	Lakeside-Lakeview Loop
43	Tierrasanta	M	5.0	Mod	-	70	30	S, N	Tierrasanta City Loop
44	La Mesa, Mt. Helix	S	6.1	Steep-Sheer	-	10	90	S, N, L	Mt. Helix City and Mountain Loop
45	Blossom Valley Live Oak Springs	M	11.6	Mod	-	30	70	S, N	Blossom Valley Loop
46	Palomar Mountain	M (VS)	22.0 (27.0)	M-S (Sheer)	- (-)	- (-)	100 (100)	S, N, L, S/A (S,N,L,S/A,E)	Palomar Mtn. Crest (Palomar Mtn. Loop)
47	Julian	M-S	19.7	Mod-Steep	-	-	100	S, N, L, S/A	Julian Countryside Tour (loop)
48	Mt. Laguna	M-S	10.2 (1-w)	Mod-Steep	-	-	100	S, N, L	Mt. Laguna Crest (up and back)
49	Rainbow-Temecula-Pala	S	25.0	Mod-Steep	-	-	100	S, N, L, S/A, E	Pala Mission Loop
50	Jamul-Brayton Valley-Lyons Valley	VS	25.1	Steep-Sheer	-	-	100	S, N, E	Jamul-Brayton Valley Loop

1,2 See footnotes on page 11

BICYCLE RIDES: SAN DIEGO COUNTY

MASTER TRIP MATRIX

TRIP NO.	GENERAL LOCATION	LEVEL OF DIFFICULTY			ROUTE QUALITY			TRIP CHARACT.[2]	COMMENTS
		L.O.D.[1]	MILES	ELEV.	BIKE TRAIL (%)	BIKE LANE (%)	OTHER (%)		
51	Lake Morena, Live Oak Springs	S	41.7	Mod-Steep	-	-	100	S, L, S/A, M, E	Lake Morena-Live Oak Springs Loop
52	Bonsall	S	24.5	Mod-Steep	-	-	100	S, L, E	Bonsall-Gopher Cyn.-W. Lilac Rd. (loop)
53	Alpine, El Cajon	S	26.7	Steep	-	15	85	S, N, E	Crest-Dehesa Valley Loop
54	Lakeside, San Vicente Canyon	S	15.1 (1-w)	Steep	-	5	95	S, N, L, S/A, E	Wildcat Canyon (incl. Barona Valley)
55	Ramona, San Vicente Reservoir	M	5.1 (1-w)	Mod	-	-	100	S, N	Mussey Grade Road
56	Escondido, Lake Wohlford	S	14.3	Steep	-	-	100	S, N	Bear Ridge Loop
57	El Centro	E	5.6	Flat	-	-	100	S, L, S/A	El Centro City Tour (loop)
58	Salton Sea	M-S (2 day)	118	Flat	-	-	100	S, N, L, M	Salton Sea Loop
59	Borrego Springs	M (S)	35.0 (24.7)	Mod (Steep)	- (-)	- (-)	100 (100)	S, N, L, M (S, N, E)	Borrego Springs Loop (Yaqui Pass Loop)
60	Shelter Valley-Ocotillo	S	46.6	Mod-Steep	-	-	100	S, N, L, M	Great Overland Stage Route (segment)

1,2 See footnotes on page 11

TRIP ORGANIZATION

MASTER TRIP MATRIX

TRIP NO.	GENERAL LOCATION	LEVEL OF DIFFICULTY			ROUTE QUALITY			TRIP CHARACT.2	COMMENTS
		L.O.D.1	MILES	ELEV.	BIKE TRAIL (%)	BIKE LANE (%)	OTHER (%)		
61	Ocotillo, Calexico	M-S (VS)	55.2 (110)	Mod (Mod)	- (-)	- (-)	100 (100)	S, N, L, M (S, N, L, M)	St. Hwy. 98/Mexico Brdr. (+Evan Hewes Hwy.)(loop)
62	Winterhaven, Bard (Colorado River)	M (M)	21.9 (22.6)	Flat (Mod)	- (-)	- (-)	100 (100)	S, N, L, M (S, N, L, M)	Winterhaven-Bard Loop (Senator Wash Reservoir)

1 **L.O.D.** - Overall trip level of difficulty: **VS**-very strenuous; **S**-strenuous; **M**-Moderate; **E**-easy; **1-w**-one way; **r/t**-round trip

2 **TRIP CHARACTERISTICS** - General trip features and highlights: **S**-scenic; **N**-nature trail or natural setting; **L**-landmarks; **S/A**-sight-seeing attractions; **E**-elevation workout; **M**-mileage workout

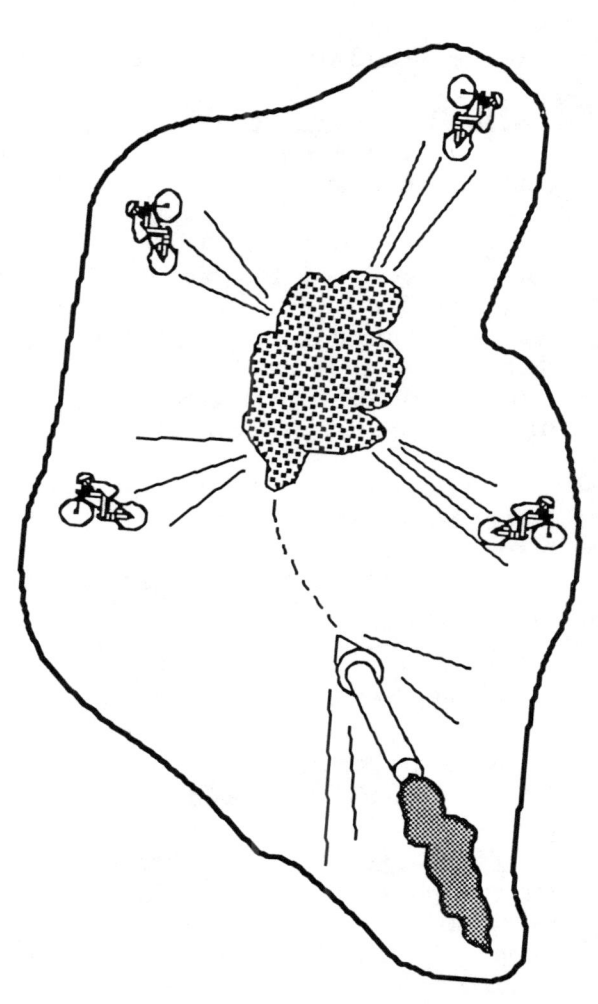

11

BICYCLE RIDES: SAN DIEGO COUNTY

TRIP DESCRIPTION/TERMINOLOGY

The trip descriptors in the "Master Trip Matrices" are described below in further detail. Several of these same descriptors are also used in the individual trip writeups.

GENERAL LOCATION: The general location of the bike trail is provided in terms of a city, landmark or general area description, as applicable. The "Master Trip Map" may be useful in conjunction with this general locator.

LEVEL OF DIFFICULTY: The rides are rated on an overall basis as *very strenuous*, *strenuous*, *moderate* and *easy*, based on elevation gain, trip distance and condition of the bike route.

A *very strenuous* trip can be of any length, has very steep grades and is generally designed for bikers in excellent physical condition. It should be noted that even on the most strenuous trip, the bike can be walked uphill for bikers in reasonably good condition. However, rather than suffer this fate, it is recommended that bikers start with the easier trips and work up. Alternately, trips are well enough described such that the biker might plan to ride the easier part of a stressing trip and link up with other easier trips.

A *strenuous* trip has some steep grades and/or relatively long mileage (on the order of 50 miles total). The trip is of sufficiently long duration to require trip planning and strong consideration of weather, water, food and bike spare parts. Some portions of the trip may be on surfaces in poor condition or on shared roadway.

A *moderate* trip may have mild grades and moderate mileage, on the order of 15-30 miles. The trip is typically of several hours duration and is generally on well-maintained bike route.

An *easy* trip is on the order of 10 miles or less, is relatively flat and is generally on well maintained bike trails or bike paths.

TRIP MILEAGE: Trip mileage is generally computed for the one-way trip length for *up and back* trips and full-trip length for *loop* trips. *Up and back* is specifically used for trips that share a common route in both outgoing and return directions. *Loop* specifically means that the outgoing and return trip segments are on predominantly different routes. *Round trip* is used without distinction as to whether the trip is an *up and back* or *loop* trip. <u>In the trip writeups, the mileage from the starting point or "trailhead" is noted in parentheses to the nearest tenth mile, for example, (6.3).</u>

Obviously, the one-way trips listed can be exercised with a planned car shuttle, ridden as an *up and back* trip, or biked in connection with another bicycle trip listed in this book. For convenience, connections with other trips are noted in the trip writeups or in a separate subsection for that trip titled, "Connecting Trips."

TRIP DESCRIPTION/TERMINOLOGY

TRIP ELEVATION GAIN: The overall trip elevation gain is described in a qualitative fashion. *Flat* indicates that there are no grades of any consequence. Steepness of upgrades is loosely defined as follows: 1) *light* indicates limited slope and very little elevation gain; 2) *moderate* means more significant slope requiring use of low gears and may be tens of feet of upgrade; 3) *steep* indicates workout-type grades that require low gears and high physical exertion; 4) *sheer* indicates gut-buster grades that require extreme physical exertion (and a strong will to live!).

The frequency of upgrades is divided into the following categories: 1) *single* for flat rides with a single significant upgrade; 2) *periodic* for flat rides where uphill segments are widely spaced; 3) *frequent* where narrowly spaced upgrades are encountered (e.g., rolling hills).

Elevation contour maps are provided for trips with significant elevation change. A reference 5% (*steep*) grade is shown on all such maps.

BIKE ROUTE QUALITY: The trip is summarized with respect to route quality in the "Master Trip Matrices" and a more detailed description is given in the individual trip writeups. The following route terminology (which is similar to that used by CALTRANS) is used:

. *Class I* - off-roadway bike paths or bike trails

. *Class II* - on-roadway, separated (striped) bike lanes

. *Class III* - on-roadway, signed (but not separated) bike lanes

If the route is on-roadway and not signed (i.e., not marked as a bike route), it is arbitrarily referred to as *Class X*. All routes are paved unless otherwise noted.

TRIP CHARACTERISTICS: The overall highlights of the bike trip are provided in the "Master Trip Matrices" to assist in general trip selection. The trip may be scenic (*S*), with sweeping vistas, exciting overlooks or generally provide views of natural or man-made attractions such as cities. Alternatively, the trip may be a nature trail (*N*) or a path through areas which have an abundance of trees, flowers and other flora. The nature trips or portions thereof are generally on Class I bike routes. The trip may highlight historical or well-known landmarks (*L*) or may have one or more sightseeing attractions (*S/A*). An example of the former is Mission San Luis Rey in San Luis Rey (Trip #29) while the latter might be Seaworld in Mission Bay (Trip #1). Finally, some trips are potentially good workout trips in that there is significant elevation change (*E*) or lengthy mileage (*M*) if the entire trip is taken. Some trips may provide a mix of these characteristics and are so noted.

Several descriptors are unique to the individual trip writeups. Those descriptors are defined below.

TRAILHEAD: The general location of the start of the bike path is provided for a single starting point. Driving directions to that trailhead and/or directions for parking are included where there is a possibility of confusion. Always check to ensure that parking is consistent with current laws.

BICYCLE RIDES: SAN DIEGO COUNTY

Note that for most trails, there are multiple points of entry beyond the primary point listed. For some of the trips in this book (particularly the river routes), alternate bicycle entry points are noted on maps by arrows (↗) along the bike route. Alternate trailheads may be found using information obtained from other bikers, or from state or local publications for more popular routes.

WATER: In the "Trailhead" description, general statements are provided about water availability. In the "Trip Description," available water along the route is noted where water is scarce, although the trip should be planned to assume that water stops may not be operational. Particular emphasis is placed on public facilities for water and use of restrooms. Stores, shopping centers, and gas stations are sometimes noted, although the availability of water or other facilities in these instances is subject to the policies of those establishments.

CONNECTING TRIPS: Where bike trips can be linked, they are so noted. *Continuation* trips are those where there is direct linkage at the beginning or end of the trip being described. *Connection* trips are either not directly linked (i.e., a Class X connector is required) or the linkage occurs at the interior of the trip being described. A brief "connector" route description is provided.

BIKE TRIP MAPS: Each ride in the book has an accompanying detailed bike map. A summary of symbols and features used in those maps is provided below.

Symbol	Description	Symbol	Description	Symbol	Description
— — — —	Bike trail in trip description (unless otherwise noted).				
･････	Alternate bike route (unless otherwise noted).				
SAN DIEGO RIVER ∼∼∼	River or creek when it is a point of interest.	MAIN ST.	Roadway.		
1-SEA WORLD 2-CRYSTAL PIER	Key trip features. Numbers in key correspond to numbers marked along the mapped route.				
DEL MAR	Nearby City	🝰	Park	☐ 5 ▨ 5	Landmark #5
W	Public Water Source	P	Parking	→	Entry Point to Trail
•—•	Locked Gate/ Limited Entry	✗✗✗	Railroad Crossing or Overcrossing	)(	Pass or Trip Summit
⌹	Mission	△5%	Reference 5% Grade	Mt. Laguna (5975)	Mountain & Elev. (feet)

MAP SYMBOLS AND FEATURES

GENERAL BIKING CONSIDERATIONS

The following is a collection of the thoughts that we've had in the thousands of miles of biking that we have done:

SAFETY: Use common sense when you are biking. Common sense when combined with courtesy should cover most of the safety-related issues. But just to be on the safe side, write to CALTRANS (see the chapter on "OTHER BICYCLING INFORMATION SOURCES") for any of their publications and you will get some excellent safety information along with it. The four safety "biggies" are: 1) understand bike riding laws; 2) keep your bicycle in safe operating order; 3) wear personal safety equipment as required (helmet is a must, bright or reflective clothes, sunglasses); 4) ride defensively--always assume that moving and parked car inhabitants are not aware that you are there.

Common courtesy is to offer assistance to bikers stopped because of breakdowns. Point out ruts, obstructions and glass to bikers behind you.

EQUIPMENT: Necessary biking equipment includes a water bottle or two, tire pump, tool kit (typically tire irons, wrench(es), and a screwdriver), patch kit and (sorry to say) bike lock. For longer trips, add a spare tube and bike repair manual as well as a light first-aid kit. Bring sunblock and lip salve for extended tours on sunny days. We recommend a bike light even if there are no plans for night biking.

Necessary biking apparel includes a helmet, sunglasses and clothes which will fit pessimistic weather conditions (particularly for longer trips). On all-day, cool or wet winter outings, we carry a layered set of clothes (this includes long pants, undershirt, long-sleeve shirt, sweater and a two-piece nylon rain suit). Padded cycling pants and biking gloves are a must for long trips. Lycra clothes are light and extremely functional. For cool and dry days, we may drop the rain suit for a windbreaker (look for a windbreaker that folds up into a fanny pack). For other conditions, our outfits are normally shorts, undershirt, long-sleeve shirt and windbreaker. Add a set of long pants as a backup for extended tours, even on sunny days.

If you are going to get your money out of this book, get an automobile bike rack! The cost of bike racks is cheap compared to most bikes. Besides, it just doesn't make sense to bike fifty miles to take the planned twenty-mile bike trip.

GENERAL INFORMATION: A collection of seemingly random, unconnected, and useless comments are provided which we actually think are "gems of wisdom" based on hard experience:

o Develop and follow a checkoff list for a pre-trip bike examination (tires, brakes, cables, etc.) and equipment (water, food, clothing, tools, spare parts, etc.). A brake check is particularly vital for steep hilly rides. It's embarrassing to start a trip and realize that you've forgotten your bicycle!

BICYCLE RIDES: SAN DIEGO COUNTY

o Check the weather before going on an extended trip. Select trips and plan clothing accordingly.

o Plan the trip timing to ensure that there is a "pad" of daylight. Night biking just isn't as fun when it wasn't in the original plans. Night biking without the proper equipment is dangerous!

o Trip timing should include allowances for finding parking, trailheads or connector routes. You never can fully trust authors of bike books!

o Trip conditions and routing are subject to change because of weather damage, building and highway construction, bikepath rerouting, etc. Especially for long trips, research these key elements before departing.

o Stay out of riverbeds, even concrete ones, unless it is marked part of the route. It may be a very long way to the next exit and it may also rain.

o Some river and creek trails flood out during heavy rains, particularly at river crossings and underpasses. Don't take these trips after heavy rains unless you are willing to plan on many route detours.

o Always take some water, no matter how short the trip. Having water available provides a feeling of security. Being thirsty creates a bad attitude. Bring enough water to provide for the contingency that "guaranteed" water spots may be dry.

o The best time of day for most trips on busy thoroughfares is before the rush-hour morning traffic. Morning is also best for rides on narrow country roads. With few exceptions, the best time of the week is the weekend, particularly Sunday.

o The best season for some trips depends on the person. If you want comradery, ride the popular routes in the on-season. If your pleasure is free-wheeling and wide-open spaces, save these routes for the off-season.

o Bring snacks for longer trips. Snacks provide needed energy and attitude improvement when the going gets tough. Having snacks available also allows more flexibility in selecting a "dining out" stop.

o Walk your bike through heavy glass-strewn areas. Lift your bike onto and off of curbs. Trips are more fun when you can _ride_ your bike!

o Bring a map for trips that are not on well-marked bike routes. Once off the prescribed route, it is amazingly easy to lose the sense of direction.

o Maintain a steady pace when taking a long bike ride. For pleasure trips, the pace is too fast if you cannot carry on conversation while biking.

o **Desert biking has its own set of ground rules.** Save desert trips for the cool seasons. Overload on water supplies. Bring a full repair kit. Bring a biking buddy! Stay out of the desert if the forecast is for heavy rain. (Flash floods can be dangerous to a biker's health!)

THE COAST

Civic Center from Coronado Island

BICYCLE RIDES: SAN DIEGO COUNTY

TRIP #1 - MISSION BAY LOOP

GENERAL LOCATION: Mission Bay

LEVEL OF DIFFICULTY: Loop - easy
Distance - 13.9 miles
Elevation gain - essentially flat

GENERAL DESCRIPTION: This scenic, predominantly Class I tour circumnavigates the delightful playground of Mission Bay. Once a large marsh, Mission Bay was created through a massive dredging operation, which also created several of the bay islands. The highlight of this trip is the variety of attractions scattered around the bay, including Mission Point, Ocean Front Walk ("hard-body heaven"), the scenic East Mission Bay bikeway, and the isolated tour along the San Diego River. There are numerous interesting diversions off the described tour that include visits to Crystal Pier, Rose Inlet, Fiesta Island, Seaworld and Quivera Basin.

TRAILHEAD: From Interstate Hwy. 5 southbound, exit at Mission Bay Dr. and drive 1/2 mile southbound to Garnet Ave. Continue two miles to Mission Blvd. (just short of the beach) and turn left (south). In another 1-3/4 miles at West Mission Bay Dr. is the northern edge of Bonita Cove Park. There is plentiful parking scattered across the park reaches. For northbound traffic, exit west at Interstate Hwy. 8 and drive 1-1/4 miles to the W. Mission Bay Dr. turnoff. Turn northwest, cross the San Diego River, and follow the W. Mission Bay Dr. markers another 1-1/2 miles to the Bonita Cove Park entry.

This dandy palm tree-covered piece of real estate has restrooms, 180-degree view, grass-a-plenty, barbecue pits and even an amusement park (with a brand new roller coaster) just beyond the park boundary.

TRIP DESCRIPTION: Mission Beach. Find the Class I bikeway on the west edge of Mariner's Basin and pedal 0.7 mile past a cozy cluster of beach homes. The bikeway veers left and follows a 1/2-mile loop around Mission Point, a serene spot from which to examine the basin, the San Diego skyline and the air traffic leaving San Diego International Airport. Bike west another 0.3 mile to South Mission Beach Park and the ocean's edge, enjoying views north to the rugged La Jolla coastline and south to Ocean Beach and the Ocean Beach Pier.

Return to Class I Ocean Front Walk (1.6) and begin a two-mile stretch of generally dead-slow weaving past beachfront homes and eateries. Natural barriers to orderly progress include pedestrians skaters, and skate-boarders (best to share our attitude of enjoying the excellent coastal views and display of "hunks" and "hunkesses" at the expense of speed). Key landmarks along the way are the fire pits/benches at the western edge of Bonita Cove Park (San Fernando Pl.), the shopping and rooftop dining areas at Ventura Pl., and the sunbather's mecca near the foot of Pacific Beach Dr. (An alternate to the busy route is to cross Mission Blvd. at Ventura Pl. and follow the lesser-used basin-side Class I route which parallels the former road.). This is one of the many segments of the 1000-mile Pacific Coast Bicentennial Bike Route in the book.

North Shore. Follow Pacific Beach Dr. inland (the Class I beach path continues north 3/4 mile), pass through the bayside residential area and turn toward the bay at

E. Briarfield Dr. Pedal on the Class I path along Riviera Shores 0.8 mile, then follow a switchback asphalt pathway a short distance to Class III Riviera Dr. In 0.4 mile is Ingraham St. and an overlook of Vacation Isle (4.8). Just beyond, on what is now Class II Crown Point Dr., is a vista point with a spectacular view of the distant San Diego city skyline.

View South from Crown Point Drive

Pass above delightful Crown Point Shores Park (palm trees, picnic facilities, recreation fields, grass, restrooms) and bike alongside a marsh estuary just before returning to Pacific Beach Dr. (6.0). (Most of Mission Bay used to look like this.) Snake through an adjoining residential area and turn right (east) on busy Grand Ave. In 0.3 mile, just beyond a small inlet, is a set of motorized vehicle guard posts which lead to a southbound Class I trail (6.7).

East Mission Bay. Bike the narrow bikepath to its terminus at N. Mission Bay Dr. and turn left. Follow the meandering route to the Class I bikeway alongside De Anza Cove and prepare for a 2.8-mile Class I cruise along East Mission Bay. On De Anza Cove is a large grassy park with restrooms, playgrounds, palm trees, sand beaches, volley ball courts and a sweeping Mission Bay view. On this segment, the biker passes the Mission Bay Visitor Center (8.3), the developed Hilton Hotel area (complete with a large paddlewheel boat), and the roadway entry to Fiesta Island before reaching Sea World Dr. (10.2). Note that the four miles of paved roadway on flat and relatively undeveloped Fiesta Island is a nice mileage addition to the trip. Also, the island is an interesting locale to get a different visual perspective of Mission Bay.

Southern Return Segment. Bike 0.2 mile to Friars Rd., turn left onto that road, follow the Class II path 1/4 mile, then turn sharply right onto the Class I road which parallels the San Diego River channel. Follow the unshaded path under the Mission Bay Dr. bridge (note the Sea World spire to the right), the Sunset Class Blvd. bridge, and buck the off-shore ocean breeze up to the path's end at Quivera Wy. (12.1).

A left turn here leads to the waterfront haven of Quivera Basin and Hospitality Point, sailor's heaven! However, our base route bears right and continues past a small auto/bike access to the Sunset Cliffs Blvd. bridge, then meets a small access road to W. Mission Bay Dr. Follow that access and turn left onto the latter street, passing over the Mission Bay Channel. There is a dandy 360-degree view of Mission Bay from the center of the bridge. Bike another 0.4 mile and reenter Bonita Cove Park, then bike the Class I park path back to the origin (13.9).

BICYCLE RIDES: SAN DIEGO COUNTY

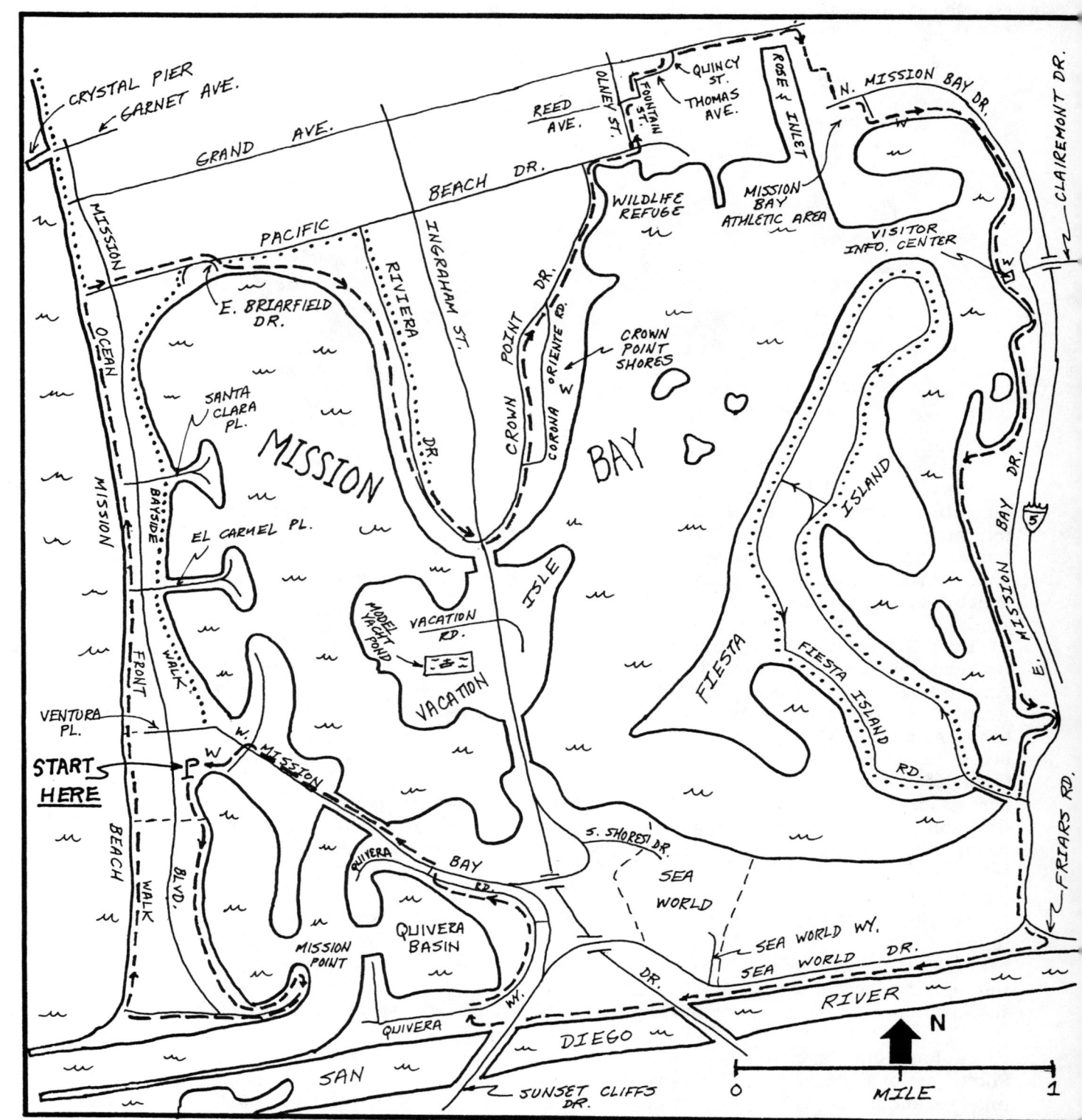

TRIP #1 - MISSION BAY LOOP

CONNECTING TRIPS: 1) Connection with the La Jolla Coastal Tour (Trip #6) and the La Jolla Hillside Workout (Trip #7) - at Pacific Beach Dr. and Mission Blvd., bike north on Mission Blvd. to Turquoise St.; 2) connection with the San Diego River Run (Trip # 17) - at Sea World Dr. and Friars Rd., bike east on the latter road.

 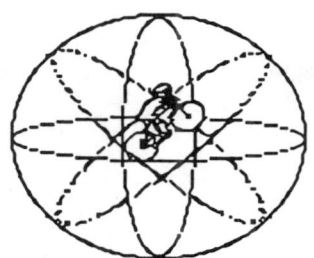

TRIP #2 - BALBOA PARK

GENERAL LOCATION: San Diego

LEVEL OF DIFFICULTY: Loop - moderate
Distance - 8.8 miles
Elevation gain - short, steep grades in Florida Canyon and above Cabrillo Fwy.

GENERAL DESCRIPTION: This is a "must" tour for bicyclists ranging from the inexperienced "lightweight" to the ultra-serious. Though moderate in terms of workout distance and elevation gain, this is an experience worth setting aside an entire day. Most of the route is within the 1100-plus acre recreation and cultural area that is nationally known Balboa Park. A lush landscaped oasis in the middle of the San Diego metropolis, the park offers the walker or cyclist one series of sensual delights after another. Start with a meander through the roadways and plazas of the western park, passing by the galleries, museums, displays and performing hawkers. Next, enjoy a tour down Florida Canyon, followed by a workout upgrade on Pershing Dr., which leads the biker to the massive Morley Field Sports Complex on the park's east side. The return segment includes a roller coaster revisit to the canyon, a cozy off-road segment which crosses the Cabrillo Fwy. on a narrow bridge and a pleasant pedal through the shaded glen on Balboa Dr.

TRAILHEAD: From State Hwy. 163 northbound, exit at Quince Dr. Cross over Hwy. 163 (Cabrillo Fwy.) and turn left (south) at Balboa Dr. Continue south and find parking anywhere within the loop south of Juniper Rd. This lush western edge of the park has tree-studded grassy knolls, restrooms and bikeways/walkways scattered throughout. From the southbound direction, take the 6th Ave. offramp and continue 1-1/4 mile to Quince Dr. Turn left (east) and then right, in a short distance, at Balboa Dr. From other area freeways, use Interstate Hwys. 5 or 8 to gain access to Hwy. 163.

TRIP DESCRIPTION: Westside Park. Bike south for a pleasant warm-up loop through the lightly-developed western park edge. This is the Pine Grove Area. Use the road or one of many bikeway/walkway paths. Also stop and enjoy the scenic city panorama from the parking area at the southern edge of the loop. Return north to Laurel St. and follow what soon becomes El Prado on the stately Cabrillo Bridge. This landmark sits astride a deep canyon which holds the Cabrillo Fwy. Dead ahead is a cluster of buildings housing several museums and galleries, all dwarfed by the imposing 200-foot tall California Tower. In a half mile from the bridge, after passing a continuing series of gardens, plazas and cultural centers, is the Plaza De Panama.

Cabrillo Bridge

Auto traffic is steered right (south) at this point, past the Organ Pavilion, and onto Pan American Rd. West; we follow and make a loop through another group of museums and galleries. At the loop's southern edge is the Aerospace Historical Center, with an awe-inspiring SR-71 "Blackbird" reconnaissance aircraft mounted on stilts at its entrance (1.8). Our route follows through the parking lot, then loops around the Starlight Bowl, returning to Pan American Rd. East. We divert from the loop at President's Wy. and follow a freewheeling downhill on Ford Bowl Dr. At the shaded canyon bottom is an equally steep Class I uphill path (no free rides in this book!) that lets out near the Fleet Space Theater. Continue north on a path closed to traffic, pass the Natural Science Museum, and pedal on a street now called Village Pl. Where Village Pl. bends east, continue north toward the world-famous San Diego Zoo, biking a path with the zoo fence to the left and parking lot to the right. Pass the miniature railroad near Zoo Pl. and continue pedaling north alongside Zoo Dr. until it bends east and meets Park Blvd.

Eastside Park. Follow Class II Park Blvd. to Zoo Pl., enjoying the view into Florida Canyon and the mesa further to the east; the eastside park route will transit that mesa. A steep downhill on Zoo Pl. puts the biker in the bowels of the canyon from which there is an additional 3/4-mile coast past the massive Naval Hospital grounds. At the Pershing Dr./26th St. Rd. intersection (4.9), follow the former street hard left and pay for the prior downhill "sins" with a tough 3/4-mile pedal which moderates, then nearly flattens during a passage through the plush Balboa Park Municipal Golf Course. At Jacurunda Dr., veer left and bike past the large Morley Field Sports Complex (swimming pool, velodrome, tennis courts and a vast manicured grassland).

The Return Segment. At Alabama St., veer left, then follow Morley Field Dr. as it gradually bears west and returns to the steep "bath-tub" entry and exit of Florida Canyon. At Park Blvd., jog north to Upas St. and follow that road 1/2 mile to its terminus at Vermont St. Just beyond is an asphalt trail which enters a lush forested area, drops down about 100 feet to a small bikeway/walkway bridge over the Cabrillo Fwy., then veers right and returns steeply up to the west bank. Work over to Balboa Dr., cruise south 1-1/4 miles on this scenic shaded byway through the Cyprus Grove Picnic Area, and return to the trip origin (8.8).

METROPOLITAN SAN DIEGO

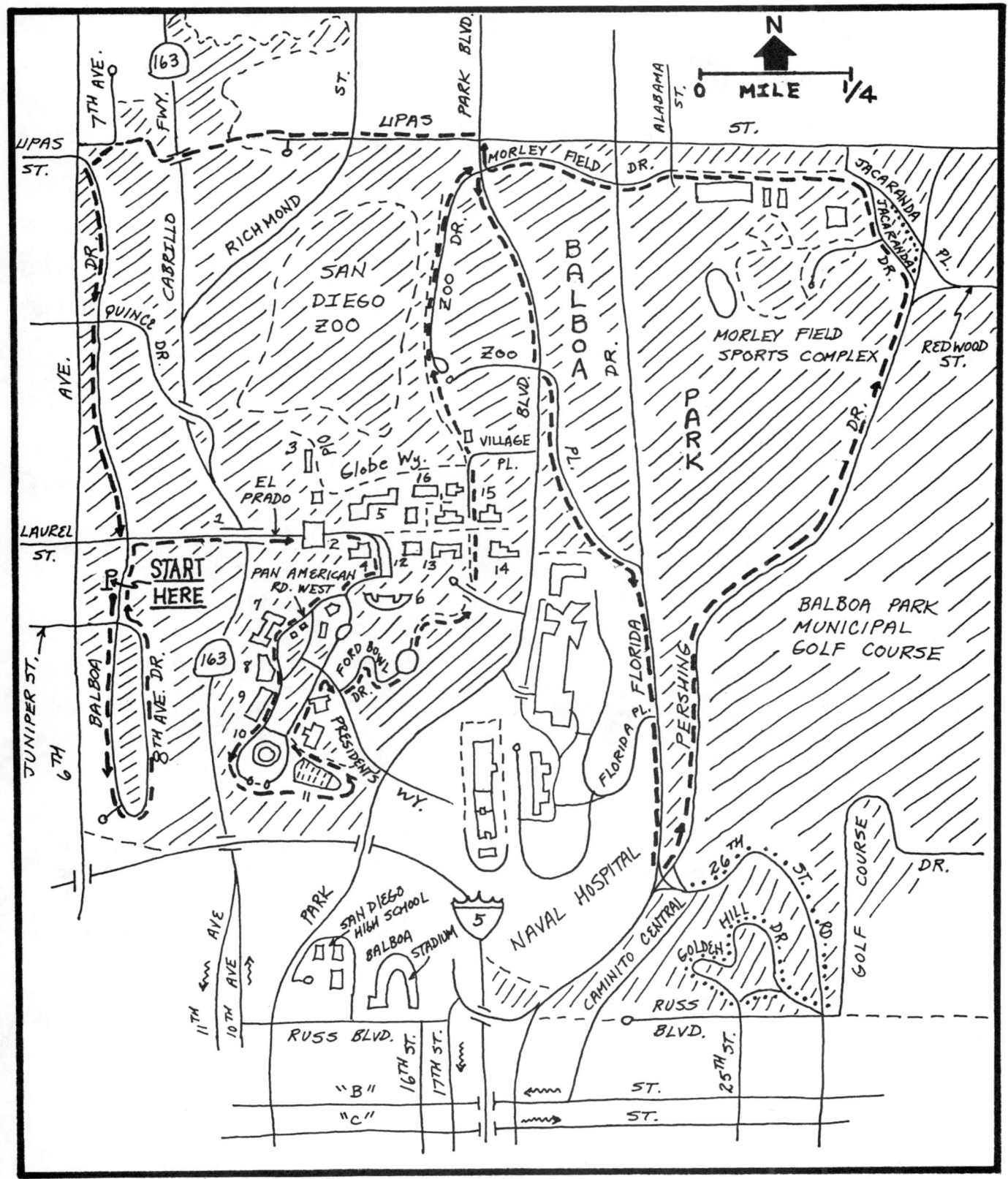

TRIP #2 - BALBOA PARK

BICYCLE RIDES: SAN DIEGO COUNTY

Number References for Trip #2 Tour Map:	
1. Cabrillo Bridge	9. San Diego Automotive Museum
2. Museum of Man	10. Aerospace Historical Center
3. Old Globe Theater	11. Starlight Bowl
4. House of Charm	12. House of Hospitality
5. Medical Arts Building	13. Casa De Balboa
6. Organ Pavilion	14. R. H. Fleet Space Theater & Science Center
7. Balboa Park Building	15. Natural History Museum
8. Palisades Building	16. Botanical Building

Trip Options. A diversion off Pershing Dr. on 26th St. Rd. (figure that one out!) takes the biker to a loop on Golden Hill Dr., the Golden Hill section of Balboa Park. There are unique views of the civic center and San Diego Bay from this scenic perch.

SR-71 "Blackbird"

<u>**CONNECTING TRIPS**</u>: 1) Connection with the Heart O' the City Tour (Trip #8) - at Park Blvd. and Zoo Pl., continue south on the former street; 2) continuation with the Old Town Tour (Trip #9) - at the trip origin, bike west out of the park on Laurel St.

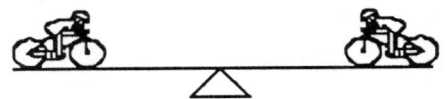

TRIP #3 - AROUND SAN DIEGO BAY

<u>**GENERAL LOCATION:**</u> San Diego, Chula Vista, Imperial Beach, Coronado

<u>**LEVEL OF DIFFICULTY:**</u> Loop - moderate
Distance - 25.4 miles
Elevation gain - essentially flat

METROPOLITAN SAN DIEGO

GENERAL DESCRIPTION: Cyclists are treated to eye-catching harbor scenes on the heavy-industrial east bay, a seven-mile Class I Silver Strand spin on the west bay, and a ferry ride to tie this tour into a grand loop. Though bikeable any day of the week, the east-side segment is most enjoyable on the weekend, early in the morning. The route is relatively flat and predominantly on marked bikeway. Tour highlights include Seaport Village, the ship-building and ship-berthing facilities near 32nd St., Marina View Park, the Silver Strand, the Hotel Del Coronado, Tidelands Park and the Coronado Ferry. (Be still my heart!) A five-mile Coronado loop tour is also provided for bikers wishing to further investigate this interesting community.

TRAILHEAD: From Interstate Hwy. 5 southbound, exit south at Sassafras St. Turn right towards the harbor, then left onto Pacific Hwy., following that road south 1-3/4 miles to Broadway. Turn left (west) and follow that street to its end near the Broadway Pier. Find parking in a nearby pay lot. From I-5 northbound, exit at Market St. (State Hwy. 163) and make a left turn (west). Continue 1-1/2 miles to its end and turn onto Harbor Dr., then follow that street north to Broadway. Park as described above.

TRIP DESCRIPTION: **Broadway Pier to Silver Strand.** Pedal south on N. Harbor Dr. past the Navy Pier, the "G" St. Pier ("Tuna Harbor," with commercial fishing boats), and veer left (east) just beyond. Pass Kettner Blvd. and an entrance to two dandy attractions -- Seaport Village and Embarcadero Marina Park. "The Village" offers varied tourist shopping treats, while the park provides an excellent and comfortable vantage point for viewing the transits of the U.S.N.'s biggest and best. Just beyond Kettner Blvd., what is now called Harbor Blvd. veers to the right. The cyclist passes First St. (1.3) and the beginning of a mixed Class II and Class III path, then cruises by the massive San Diego Convention Center.

Marina View Park

Soon is the 5th St. entry to the southern portion of Embarcadero Marine Park. For the next roughly four miles, the biker travels through an old heavy-industrial waterfront setting. Take extreme care in crossing the myriad of railroad tracks in this segment. Treats along the way are the San Diego Trolly yard, Coronado Bridge undercrossing, the National Steel and Shipbuilding Company yard and the U.S. Naval Station (Don's old haunt and the home to a wide variety of naval ships). When Harbor Dr. veers east to meet the Interstate, take the Civic Center Dr. spur to Cleveland Ave. (5.5). At road's end, turn left at 24th St. and pass a small shopping center.

BICYCLE RIDES: SAN DIEGO COUNTY

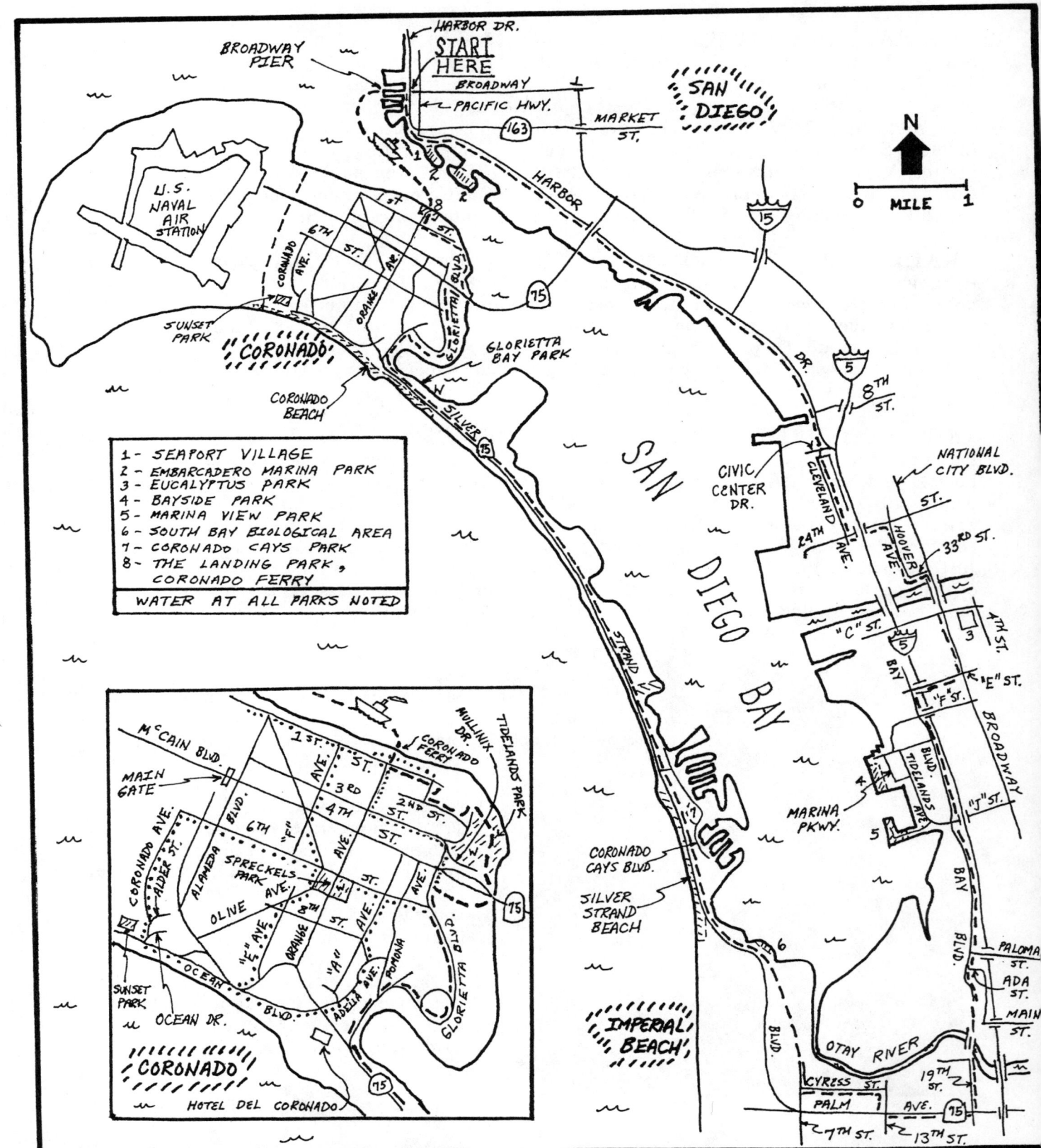

TRIP #3 - AROUND SAN DIEGO BAY

METROPOLITAN SAN DIEGO

Using Hoover St. and 33rd St. delays the inevitable, a busy one-mile Class X segment on National City Blvd. and "E" St., which returns the cyclist to the harbor area. Once on Bay Blvd., our reference route diverts right (west) on "F" St. in order to visit pleasant and scenic Bayside and Marina View Parks along the bay (the straight-through route on Bay Blvd. saves a mile). Also located near the parks are the Chula Vista Marina and a deli shop on Marina Pkwy. Returning to Class II Bay Blvd. (10.7), the route passes the salt evaporators and large Western Salt mounds before reaching the road's terminus at the Main St. overcrossing.

At road's end is a signed Class I bikepath which crosses a small bridge over the Otay River and dumps out at Palm Ave. After 0.6 mile of marked bikeway, the cyclist leaves busy Palm Ave. and follows a meandering 0.7-mile course through residential areas to the 7th St. terminus in Imperial Beach (15.3).

Silver Strand to Coronado. The traffic dodging and railroad track crossings of the industrial east bay give way to a Class I tour through the more lightly-developed Silver Strand. With Silver Strand Beach to the left and San Diego Bay right, the biker has roughly seven blissful miles (except for several crossings of small access streets) to observe the interesting surroundings and wildlife. A mile from the path entry is the South Bay Ecological Study Area and, in two more miles, the entrance to both Silver Strand Beach and the Coronado Cayes. In about six miles is the gateway to the U.S. Naval Amphibious Base. (Don has <u>fond</u> memories of night seaside practice landings nearby. They cheated and used Hotel Del Coronado lights as position locators on black nights!) Near Glorietta Bay Park is the end of the Class I path.

San Diego-Coronado Bay Bridge from Glorietta Bay Park

Turn onto paralleling Strand Wy. and follow this road to Glorietta Blvd., pass the Coronado Yacht Club, then stay to the right alongside the Coronado Golf Course. Glorietta Blvd. ends at an entry road to the Coronado Bridge; just before that entry, follow the Class I path on the north edge of the golf course. The path leads under the bridge and onto the periphery of super-scenic, well-equipped Tidelands Park. At the park's northern edge, turn onto the walkway/bikeway to Glorietta Blvd. (the bayside peripheral path dead ends about 0.3 mile beyond the turnoff). After this road veers left and becomes 2nd St., bike to 1st St. via "A" Ave. and follow the first entry to

BICYCLE RIDES: SAN DIEGO COUNTY

Centennial Park, a small bayside park surrounded by a cozy complex of shops and restaurants (25.4).

All that remains is to visit the ticket booth at the Coronado Ferry Landing and wait for the every-hour-on-the-half-hour pedestrian/bikeway ferry. Sit back and enjoy the dramatic San Diego city skyline view or browse around the shops before returning on the ferry. In about ten minutes from departure, the ferry will return you to the trip's origin.

Stars and Stripes

Coronado. A flat tour of Coronado is worthy in its own right. The mix of wide thoroughfares and smaller residential streets allows the biker to travel anywhere on the island in relative safety. One suggested route starts from the ferry landing (see the Coronado Insert Map and note that the dots represent bicycle routes recommended by the Coronado Visitor Center). The tour up 1st St. passes Harbor View Park and "I" Ave. Park; the carrier berths on North Island are clearly visible from the latter point. Ride the periphery of the U.S. Naval Air Station on Alameda Blvd. and Coronado Ave. to Ocean Blvd. (stay to the right after Alder St.); enjoy the varied aircraft traffic along the way.

A turn right leads to North Beach with its firepits, as well as Sunset Park. Our route turns left (south) and cruises along this broad western-facing beach, veering left and becoming Dana Pl. alongside the historic "Hotel Del." Cross busy Orange Ave. at the traffic light, continue on Adella Ave., then follow the zig-zag path to Glorietta Blvd. as noted in the map. From this junction, turn left and follow the route described in the "Around San Diego Bay" tour. Total loop distance is about five miles.

<u>**CONNECTING TRIPS**</u>: 1) Continuation with the Seaport Village to Point Loma ride (Trip #4)- at the trip origin, bike north on Harbor Dr.; 2) connection with the Heart O' the City tour (Trip #8), the San Diego 59-Mile Scenic Dr. (Trip #11), and the Coastal County Tour (Trip #21) - the trips share a common segment on Harbor Dr.; 3) connection with the Run for the Border (Trip #14) - the trips share a common segment in the Cherry Ave. area.

METROPOLITAN SAN DIEGO

TRIP #4 - SEAPORT VILLAGE TO POINT LOMA

GENERAL LOCATION: San Diego, Point Loma, Ocean Beach

LEVEL OF DIFFICULTY: Loop - moderate to strenuous
Distance - 31.7 miles
Elevation gain - mostly flat; steep upgrade on Canon Dr., periodic moderate grades on Pt. Loma

GENERAL DESCRIPTION: This coastal junket is really a collection of three individual tours: 1) a bayside tour which explores the waterfront from Seaport Village through Spanish Landing Park, ending at Shelter Island; 2) a ride to Point Loma starting at Fiesta Island, visiting the Cabrillo National Monument, and concluding at Sunset Cliffs Park; and 3) a general visit of the Ocean Beach area beginning at Sunset Cliffs Park, touring the western peninsula shoreline, and winding up at the Ocean Beach Athletic area. For less aggressive cyclists, the tours can be ridden separately. The scenery on this 30-plus mile mixed-class tour is exceptional. Most of the trip is on marked bikeway with limited exposure to high-density traffic; the area of exception is the Rosecrans St. - Canon St. segment.

TRAILHEAD: From Interstate Hwy. 5 southbound, exit at Front St. and drive south. Turn right at any convenient cross street and drive five blocks to Kettner Blvd. Continue south, cross Harbor Dr. and follow to road's end at Embarcadero Marina Park. For northbound traffic, take the "J" St. off-ramp and drive west on that road one mile to Harbor Dr. Turn right (northwest) and continue 1/3 mile to Kettner Blvd. Turn left and drive to road's end. Park in one of the local pay lots if you cannot arrange for a start/finish point shuttle. The park has restrooms, tree cover, benches and great vantage points for watching the U.S. Navy sail the harbor.

Ships and Suntans (Embarcadero Marina Park)

TRIP DESCRIPTION: **North San Diego Bay.** Pedal on the bayside Class I walkway/bikeway past Seaport Village and an array of piers containing commercial fishing boats, U.S. Navy ships, cruise ships and the old classic sailing craft, the Star of India. This is the exciting first mile of a grand tour! In 0.3 mile, the path bends left 90 degrees and continues its bayside passage. At Laurel St. is the U.S. Coast Guard

BICYCLE RIDES: SAN DIEGO COUNTY

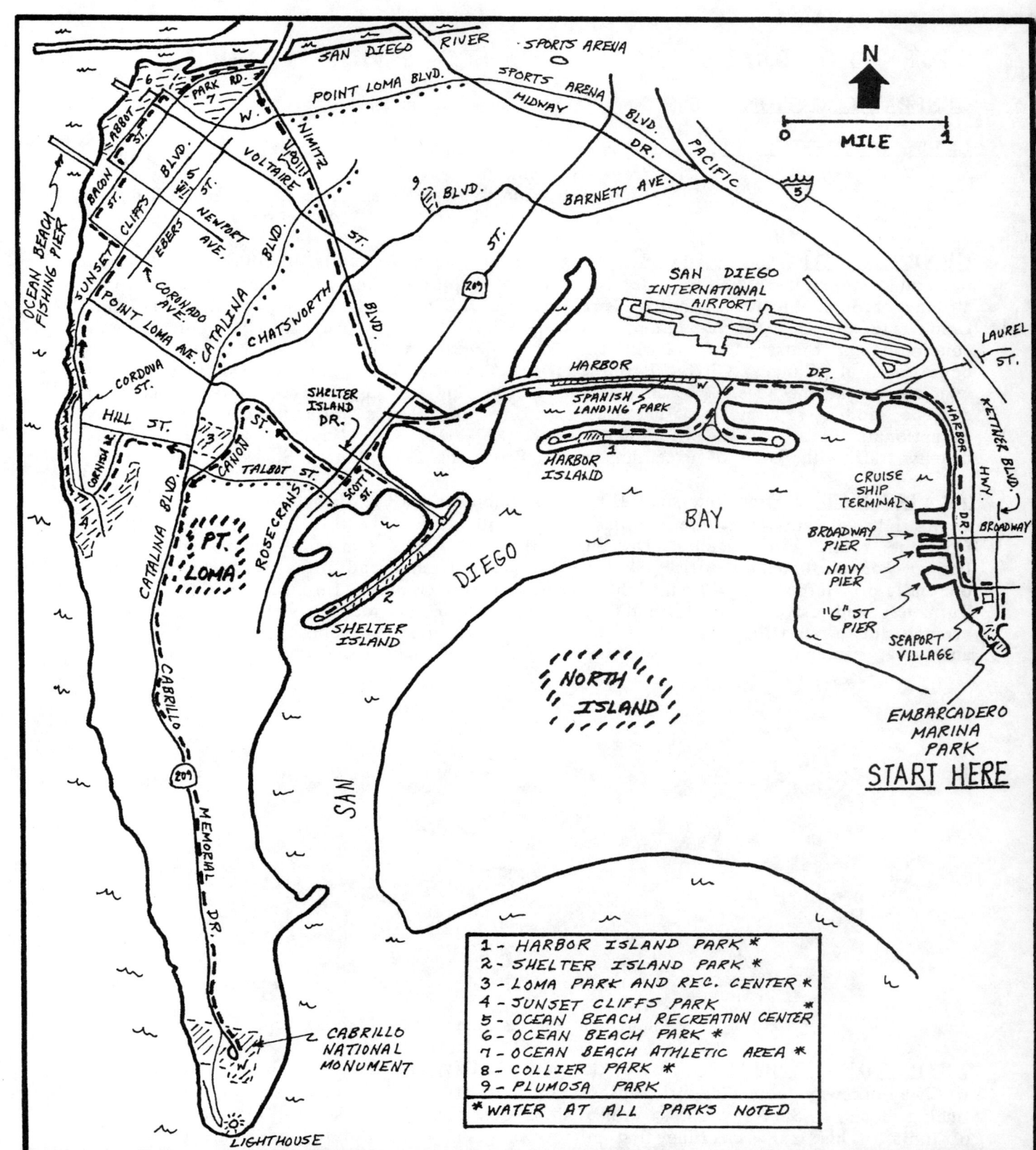

TRIP #4 - SEAPORT VILLAGE TO POINT LOMA

METROPOLITAN SAN DIEGO

Station. With some luck, the cyclist might observe seaplane operations. The views of San Diego Bay are many and varied from the trip start to the Cabrillo National Monument -- in this area, there is an excellent perspective across the bay to North Island/Coronado and back to the downtown piers.

At Air Ln., the route turns south for a tour of Harbor Island. Before returning to the bayside path 3.6 miles later, the biker is treated to a spin alongside the numerous bayside hotels, the East and West Yacht Basins, and Harbor Island Park. There is mucho money here, as attested by some of the sailing behemoths in the marina. Back alongside Harbor Dr. (6.4), the Class I path meanders through long, thin and grassy Spanish Landing Park, dotted with palm trees. Beyond the park, the trail passes on a bridge over the concrete-bound training ship U.S.S. Recruit, then meets the Fleet Anti Submarine Warfare School (where Don learned how to "drive" boats) at the foot of Nimitz Blvd.

A left at Scott St. and a right on Shelter Island Dr. leads the cyclist onto Shelter Island with its boatworks and drydocks interspersed with restaurants and hotels. Turning right at the main circle leads the biker down a lane with the yacht basin on one side and the bay on the other. The inviting Shelter Island Park, with its long grassy strip, scattered trees, picnic tables and gazebos, is a pleasant place for a rest. While there, we saw a couple of aircraft carriers steam by that seemed close enough to touch. After a visit to the Friendship Bell (from sister city Yokohama) at lands end, the biker reverses direction and finds his way to Rosecrans St. and Canon St.

Point Loma. A 1.3 mile, 225-foot workout upgrade on busy and winding Canon St. takes the cyclist past Point Loma Park and Recreation Center to Catalina Blvd. Follow this Class II highway on the spine of the peninsula 3.6 miles past a residential area, military reservations and Fort Rosecrans National Cemetery before reaching the Cabrillo National Monument. (16.4). Pay the entrance fee ($1.00 for cyclists in late 1991) and take in the Old Point Loma Lighthouse, Cabrillo Statue and Whale Observation Building. The bay view from the statue area will take your breath away!

San Diego Bay from Point Loma

Backtrack to Canon St. and continue beyond to Hill St. After a short uphill, the cyclist looks down the steep road to the Pacific, then descends 0.4 mile through residential environs to Cornish Dr. A half-mile pedal on the Class III road leads to lightly-developed Sunset Cliffs Park with a tree-surrounded dirt parking area and an

BICYCLE RIDES: SAN DIEGO COUNTY

array of ocean vistas. This is the southern end of a two-mile thread of park along the Sunset Cliffs.

Ocean Beach. Upon leaving the park, turn left and bike to seaside Sunset Cliffs Blvd. A scenic mile-plus undulating cliff-side ride transitions to a business-commercial environment as the road turns away from the beach at Pt. Loma Ave. A 1.6-mile zig-zag path through Ocean Beach on mixed Class II, III and X roadways leads past the Ocean Beach Pier (great fishing) and places the cyclist at Ocean Beach Park (north of Abbot St. via Voltaire St) (23.9). Continuing on Abbot St. northwest to W. Pt. Loma Blvd., the biker turns left (north) at Bacon St. and enters the Ocean Beach Athletic Area at Mission Bay Park. The grassy, tree-shaded park has about every type of athletic facility that one could ask for.

Follow the road now named Park Rd. north to the San Diego River levee. Next access the Class I path on the levee, enjoying the views across the river to Mission Bay. Turn right (south) onto busy Sunset Cliffs Dr., carefully work across the complex intersection to Class II Nimitz Blvd., then follow that road through residential areas 2.1 miles to Rosecrans St. From this junction, turn left and backtrack 4.8 miles to the starting point (31.7).

CONNECTING TRIPS: 1) Continuation with Around San Diego Bay (Trip #3) and the Coastal County Tour (Trip #21) - from the trip origin, return to Harbor Dr. and turn east; 2) connection with Heart O' the City (Trip #8) - bike north on Kettner Blvd.; 3) connection with the San Diego 59-Mile Scenic Dr. (Trip #11) - the trips have a common segment on Harbor Dr.; 4) connection with the San Diego River Run (Trip #17) - from the Ocean Beach Athletic Area, bike across the river on Sunset Cliffs Blvd. (see Trip #17 for detailed connector information).

TRIP #5 - MARIAN BEAR PARK

GENERAL LOCATION: San Clemente Canyon

LEVEL OF DIFFICULTY: Up and back - easy
Distance - 7.0 miles
Elevation gain - flat

GENERAL DESCRIPTION: Surrounded by three major freeways, it is difficult to believe that the natural riparian environment of San Clemente Canyon has survived, much less that it is a favorite nature trail for off-road bicyclists, walkers and joggers. Even with State Hwy. 52 above and along its entire flat 3-1/2-mile length, Marian Bear Park is an oak-, sycamore- and brush-lined strip threaded by a mix of dirt roadway, narrow dirt path and meandering San Clemente Creek. Bring a fat-tire bike and plan a leisurely cruise through the canyon.

TRAILHEAD: From Interstate Hwy. 5, transition east onto State Hwy. 52, take the first exit (Clairemont Mesa Blvd.) south and turn right at the next exit into Marian Bear Park. Follow the packed dirt road a few hundred yards to the picnic area. The park has abundant tree shade, picnic tables, restrooms and water fountains.

TRIP DESCRIPTION: **Eastbound.** The reference route leaves the picnic area and heads east, passing through a large road gate, then wandering through an extended dense stand of vegetation. Almost immediately, the main route passes an array of side trails leading into the surrounding finger canyons. (To stay on the main trail, follow the "most well-used path rule."). These side trails criss-cross our path throughout the tour.

Workout at the Park's Western Edge

In about 2-3/4 miles is a diversion path that leads 1/2-mile steeply north under Hwy. 52 to the eucalyptus groves of Standley Park and Recreation Center. Look for a 3-4 foot high redwood post which is marked "Standley Trail." The trail cuts sharply westward and uphill and is easy to miss for eastbound cyclists. However, our route continues eastward and crosses the creek about a half-dozen times. (There were 2 or 3-foot pools and several inches of running water in the creek when we passed through during February of '92.). The route passes under Genesee Ave., then transits another 1-1/2 miles on a mix of packed dirt, sand and rocky surfaces. There are rest and observation benches scattered alongside the path. Below the Hwy. 52 transition road to Interstate Hwy. 805, the path ends just above the creek near an asphalt drainway (2.5).

Westbound. Return to the parking area (5.0) and read the posted park information on the side of the restroom. The postings announce a wide variety of flora and fauna, including poison oak (we didn't see any on the main route). Westbound cyclists have the immediate option to bike the hillside route (left at the first major junction) or the creekside route (right), or in very low water, to bike in the creek itself. Try the "high road" in high water, as we encountered at least one crossing area with creek pools up to five feet deep on the creekside tour. We particularly liked the elevated route, which takes the cyclist through a meadow, onto a narrow, steep roller-coaster trail, and lets out steeply downhill into Marian Bear Creek within view of Rose Canyon near Interstate Hwy. 5 (6.5). For variety (in low water), return via the flatter and better quality creekside path (7.0).

BICYCLE RIDES: SAN DIEGO COUNTY

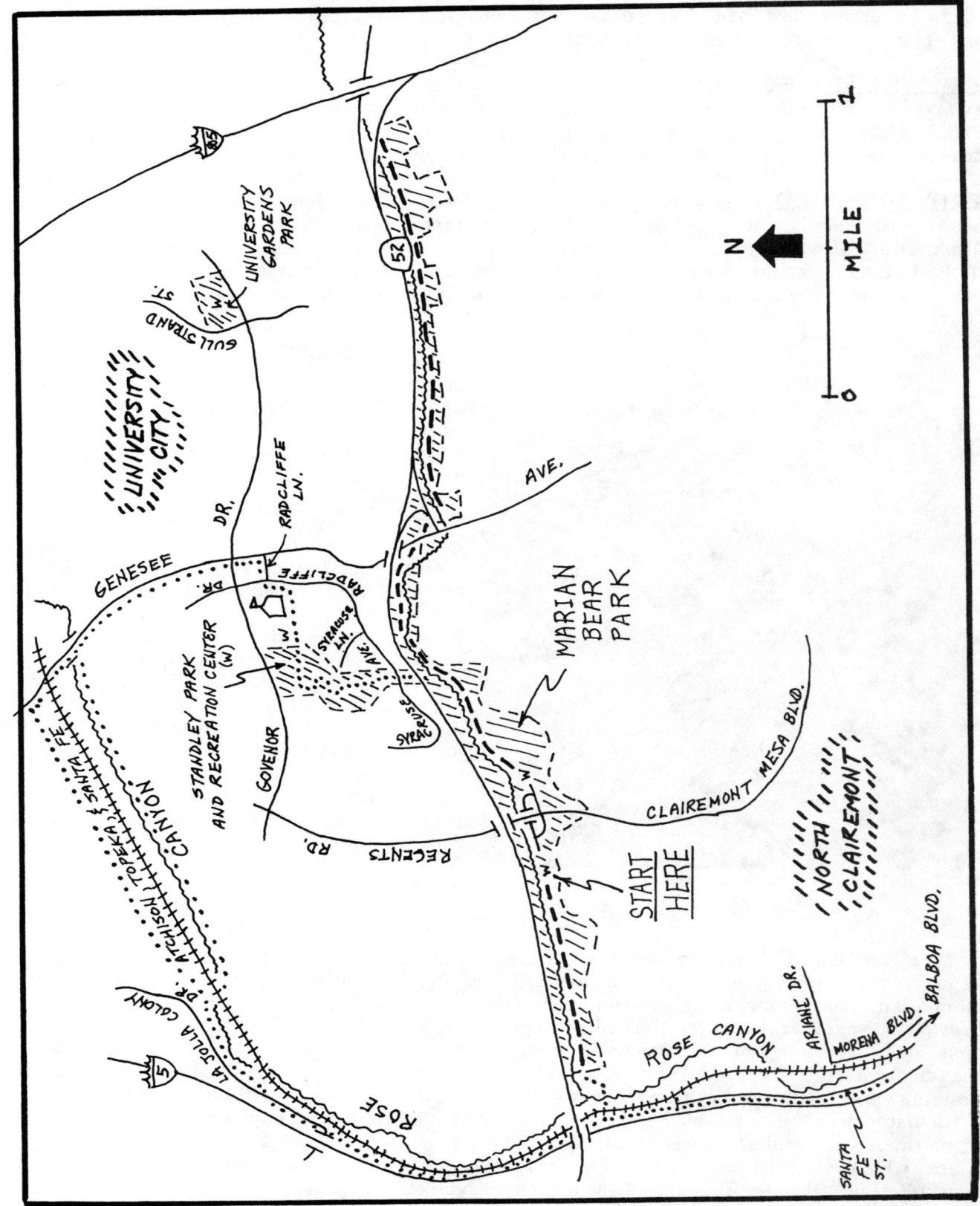

TRIP #5 - MARIAN BEAR PARK

METROPOLITAN SAN DIEGO

Trip Options: From the western edge of the tour, bike south and west on the canted dirt trail on the hillside. The trail dumps back down into Marian Bear Creek via several spur paths. Cross the railroad tracks below the concrete freeway overpasses and look for a fenced, Class I, asphalt bike trail. There are two basic alternatives: 1) **A turn south** leads to the head of Santa Fe St. This is a frontage road along I-5 which continues three miles to it's terminus at Balboa Blvd; 2) **A turn north** leads to a tour of Rose Canyon (fat-tire bikes only). Follow that asphalt path alongside I-5 one mile to La Jolla Colony Dr. Cycle north a few hundred yards on the marked bikeway and look for a dirt trail which leaves the roadway on a downhill diagonal to the railroad tracks below. The cyclist can bike on the roller-coaster dirt trail on the west side of the tracks for an elevated view of Rose Canyon. The trail is rough in spots and has some short, sheer upgrades, where Don and two "adopted" bike buddies had difficulty even maintaining traction in spots. The main, relatively flat trail is on the east side of the tracks. Both follow the canyon 1.8 miles to an exit at Genessee Ave.

Off-road above Rose Canyon

To return to Marian Bear Park, bike south on Genesee Ave. Pump a steep, 0.6-mile upgrade to Govenor Ave., then turn right at Radcliffe Ln. In a short distance is Radcliffe Dr. and Standley Jr. High School. Bike between the southern edge of the school and the two eastern baseball diamonds and continue beyond the westernmost diamond, staying near the canyon edge. The signed entry here leads to a series of steep switchbacks (walking only), followed by a shallower downhill transit on a narrow, overgrown (Spring 1992) trail. (This section made Don think of Humphery Bogart's "workout" in *The African Queen*.)

The trail dumps out at Syracuse Wy. (Cyclists can substitute a less adventurous segment from Standley Jr. High School down Radcliffe Dr./Syracuse Ave.) Just to the east is a rough trail connector that leads down 0.1 mile, passes below Hwy. 52, then branches left before fusing with the Marian Bear Park trail. The total length for the (moderate) segment from the park's west edge to the park trail junction is 5.7 miles.

<u>**CONNECTING TRIPS**</u>: Connection with Techolote Canyon (Trip #13) - continue south and east from the park on Clairemont Mesa Blvd.

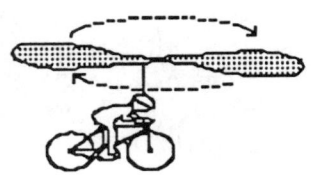

BICYCLE RIDES: SAN DIEGO COUNTY

TRIP #6 - LA JOLLA COASTAL TOUR

GENERAL LOCATION: La Jolla

LEVEL OF DIFFICULTY: Two loops - moderate
Distance - 16.0 miles (two loops)
Elevation gain - essentially flat southern loop; two short moderate-to-steep grades on northern loop

GENERAL DESCRIPTION: Want to see the La Jolla that we've all heard about? This double loop provides the cyclist with a chance to ply four miles of coastal cliffs south of the snazzy La Jolla commercial (shopping) district. A zig-zag route northward through a quiet residential area leads the biker to a dandy northern loop along N. La Jolla Scenic Dr. After traversing this naturally scenic road, the grand tour is topped off with a passby of the Scripps Institute of Oceanography and La Jolla Shores Beach/Kellogg Park and a return to Scripps Park just beyond the La Jolla Caves.

TRAILHEAD: Heading southbound on Interstate Hwy. 5, exit west at La Jolla Village Dr. Drive one mile to Torrey Pines Rd. and follow this road south 3-1/2 miles to Prospect Pl. Turn right and, after 1/4 mile, veer to the right at small, steep Coast Blvd. Next, continue around the bend to beach-side Ellen Scripps Park. For northbound traffic, exit west at Ardath Rd. Follow this road 1-1/2 miles to where it fuses with Torrey Pines Rd. In another mile is Prospect Pl. Continue as above. The park has scattered tree cover, grass, restrooms, benches, gazebos, long-distance coastline vistas and waves crashing over the nearly rocks.

P.S. Bring an automobile roadmap in case you stray from the designated route.

TRIP DESCRIPTION: **Southern Loop.** From the park, the four-mile zig-zag path to the southern edge of the loop passes through a vintage La Jolla residential area on relatively flat, lightly-traveled road. The initial stretch passes below the commercial heart of La Jolla with its scattered high-rise buildings and smaller shopping stores. There are numerous classic ocean vistas and parks along this route, which is generally on the low cliffs above the rugged coastline. A favorite of ours is Coast Blvd. Park, a thin 1/2-mile stretch of cliff-side park which includes several separate beach accesses. Several of the parks tempt the biker with benches from which to take in the pounding surf, seagulls and enticing coastal views. Follow the bike route signs and, if in doubt, stay to the right (nearest the ocean) -- the worst that can happen is to bike some short dead-end segments.

At the southern edge of the loop at Calumet Ave. and Chelsea Ave., there is an option to follow a patchwork 0.9-mile route to the head of the Mission Beach Class I beachside bikeway. (See the "Mission Bay Connector" described later.) However, our reference route follows Calumet Ave. as it becomes Sea Ridge Dr. and meets La Jolla Blvd. A slight jog south to Carla Wy. takes the cyclist east to La Jolla Hermosa Ave. and a 1.2-mile residential cruise. This leads to a Class I path entry just west of the Beaumont Ave. terminus off Via Del Norte. The next one-mile spin is a delightful respite from traffic, buried within the hillside neighborhood and surrounded by greenery. Following another of the on-road, zig-zag paths (designed to keep the tourist off heavily-traveled roads) brings the biker to Torrey Pines Rd. at Prospect Pl. in 1.4 miles (7.6). (Note that the strip route from La Jolla Hermosa Ave. northward is part of the "1976 Bicentennial Bike Route.")

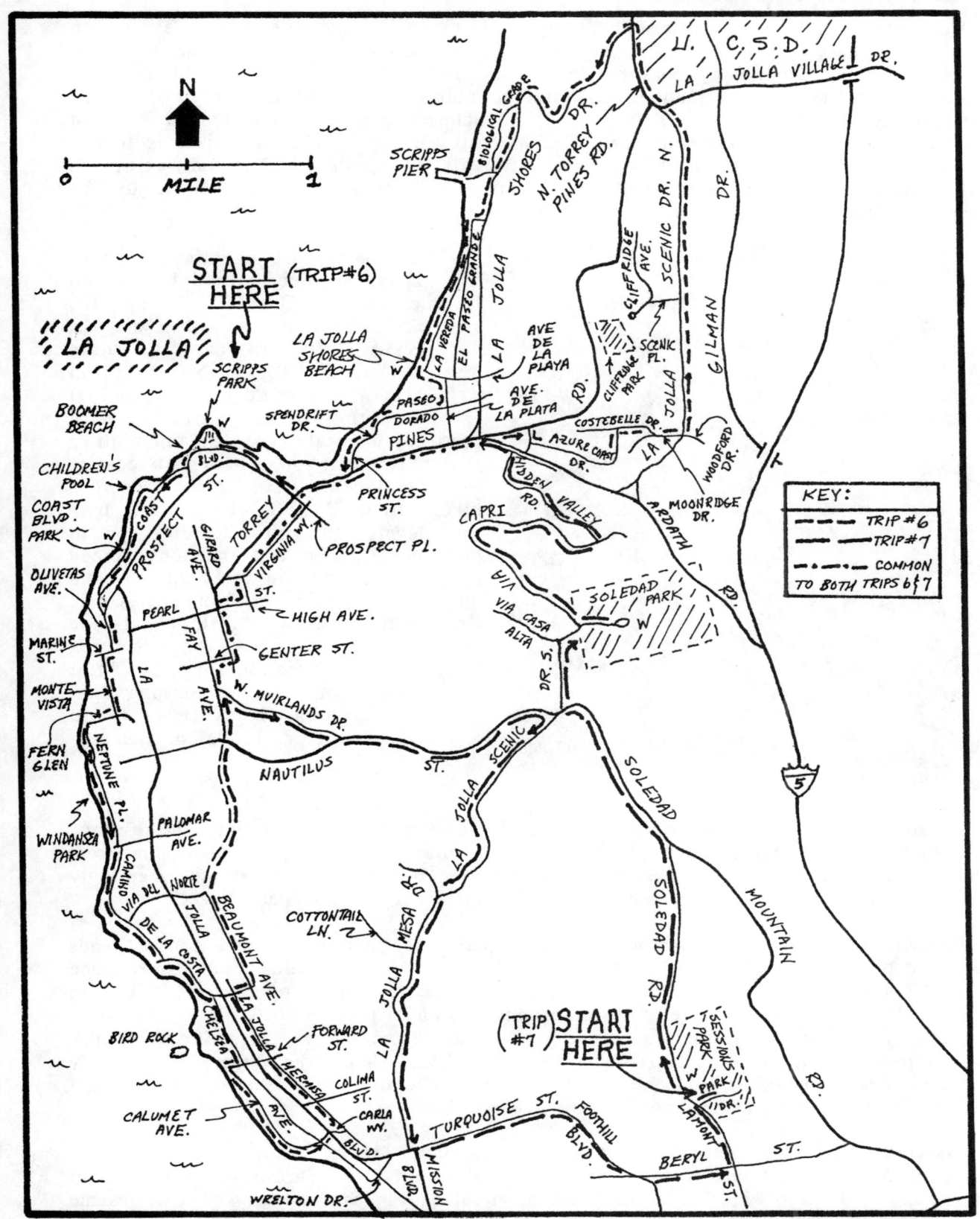

TRIPS #6 & #7 – LA JOLLA COASTAL TOUR & HILLSIDE WORKOUT

BICYCLE RIDES: SAN DIEGO COUNTY

Northern Loop. By proceeding westward along Prospect Pl., the biker can complete an easy 8.1-mile loop. However, for the more adventurous, the moderate northern loop is accessed by coasting down busy Torrey Pines Rd. across the La Jolla Shores Dr./Ardath Dr. intersection and turning south on easy-to-miss Ardath Ln. (the next right turn). Beyond is a stiff 1/4-mile strenuous upgrade on Azure Coast Dr. just prior to dead-ending at Costabelle Dr. The hardest work is over as the biker is treated to a refreshing ride on N. La Jolla Scenic Dr. This is a posh neighborhood, well-treed, well-manicured, with a landscaped center strip and sporadic views down to the shores of North La Jolla. Traffic is delightfully light.

Ellen Scripps Park

The biker must negotiate a short and busy segment (though marked for bicycling) on La Jolla Village Dr. and N. Torrey Pines Rd., then make a very sharp left turn onto La Jolla Shores Dr. (11.9). Next is an exhilarating, winding downhill through the dense pines with scattered coastal views, leading to a real "eye-catcher" near Discovery Wy. Follow the lead of the numerous bikers from U.C.S.D. above and bike this downgrade with a careful eye to both auto traffic and the long thread of parked cars along the road. In 0.8 mile is a diversion at Biological Grade Rd., which allows a look at the "working side" of the Scripps Institute of Oceanography. After passing the entry to the Scripps Pier, return to La Jolla Shores Dr. and turn towards the coast at El Paseo Grande.

By hugging the roads nearest the ocean, the cyclist runs directly into the Kellogg Park entry and the super-scenic expanses of La Jolla Shores Beach. The palm-treed, shaded park has grass and restrooms, while the broad, lengthy strand seemingly stretches from the cliffs of the south northward to Torrey Pines State Beach.

A fiendishly clever route through rows of expensive apartments and condos leads the biker past the Spindrift Golf Course and the swanky Grand Champions Hotel, then rejoins Torrey Pines Rd. at Princess St. A 1/4-mile uphill returns the biker to Prospect Pl. Turn right, bike a short distance through the outskirts of the "Tourist Quarter" of La Jolla and make a hard right at the "Scenic Drive" sign (Coast Blvd.). This narrow thoroughfare leads past the La Jolla Caves Shop, where there is an entry to shell-collectors paradise and the La Jolla Caves via a beach walkway. In a short distance around the point is Scripps Park (16.0).

Mission Bay Connector. This is the "backdoor" route! Follow Chelsea Ave. southbound. The road curves east and becomes Wrelton Dr. Turn south for a minor stretch on La Jolla Blvd., then toward the ocean at Loring St. At Crystal Dr., resume the southbound cruise on the road which soon becomes Ocean Blvd, then look for the Class I Ocean Front Walk entry near where the road bends east and becomes Law St.

METROPOLITAN SAN DIEGO

CONNECTING TRIPS: 1) Connection with the Mission Bay Loop (Trip #1) - proceed south from the most southerly point of the tour to Law St. as described in the write-up; 2) connection with the La Jolla Hillside Workout (Trip #7) - the two tours share a common segment from W. Muirlands Dr. to Ardath Dr.; 3) connection with the San Diego 59-Mile Scenic Dr. (Trip #11) and Coastal County Tour (Trip #21) - the trips share a common segment on La Jolla Shores Dr.; 4) connection with the U. C. San Diego Campus Visit (Trip #12) - at N. Torrey Pines Rd. and La Jolla Shores Dr., turn north on the former street.

TRIP #7 - LA JOLLA HILLSIDE WORKOUT

GENERAL LOCATION: La Jolla

LEVEL OF DIFFICULTY: Two loops - strenuous
Distance - 11.8 miles
Elevation gain - steep grades on Soledad Rd. and Nautilus St.

GENERAL DESCRIPTION: This hillside tour east of La Jolla provides the cyclist with several scenic viewpoints, each with a markedly different perspective of the San Diego city area and beyond. Early highlights are Sessions Park and a visit to the Mt. Soledad Easter Cross, from which spectacular views into the San Diego metropolis can be had. The downhill segment from Mt. Soledad provides several grand looks to the northern and eastern areas. Finally, the La Jolla Scenic Dr./La Jolla Mesa segment has several vistas into the Mission Bay/Ocean Beach area. Much of the route is Class II with generally lightly-traveled Class X segments. There are several scenic routes down Mt. Soledad should the cyclist be seeking variety.

TRAILHEAD: From Interstate Hwy. 5, exit west at Mission Bay Dr. From either direction, continue a short distance to Garnet Ave./Balboa Ave. Turn west and continue 0.3 mile (southbound traffic from Hwy. 5) or 0.6 mile (northbound) to Lamont St. Turn right (north) and in 3/4 mile, turn right again at Park Dr., the entry to Kate O. Sessions Park. The park is on a grassy hillside with sweeping views to the south towards Mission Bay that continue into Mexico. Park perquisites include restrooms, tree cover, children's playground, picnic tables and a bikeway/walkway on the park's periphery.

TRIP DESCRIPTION: Sessions Park to Soledad Park. After exploring the park, start a two-mile, 400-foot pumpathon on what is now Soledad Rd. The upgrade is through a well-manicured, hilly-residential community. Part of the uphill includes a left turn onto Class II Soledad Mountain Rd. and a right at La Jolla Scenic Dr., where the grade lessens. To the left are the radio towers of Soledad Mountain, while directly ahead, the Mt. Soledad Easter Cross dominates the horizon. In 0.6 mile from the La Jolla Scenic Dr. entry, the cyclist is at the base of the cross within Soledad Nature

BICYCLE RIDES: SAN DIEGO COUNTY

Park. The sweeping views of San Diego, La Jolla and the inland areas are breathtaking. This is a well-established rest spot for bikers who have managed the climb from one of many directions (although we did see one serious athlete doing push-ups as part of his "break").

View North from Mount Soledad

Soledad Park to La Jolla Country Club. As shown on the detail map, there are several routes down the mountain, all very scenic. Our reference path follows a northward steep, winding descent on Via Capri and Hidden Valley Rd. through elegant residential areas. The sweeping views from La Jolla Shores to the inland hills and mesas are real "grabbers." At Ardath Rd. (4.4), cross the busy roadway and follow it as it fuses into Torrey Pines Rd., then pump uphill on Class II road to Prospect Pl. A 1.2-mile zig-zag path beyond that intersection leads to a scenic spin to the border of the La Jolla Country Club on W. Muirlands Dr., which ends at Nautilus St. The 3/4-mile segment on W. Muirlands Dr. is a challenging upgrade.

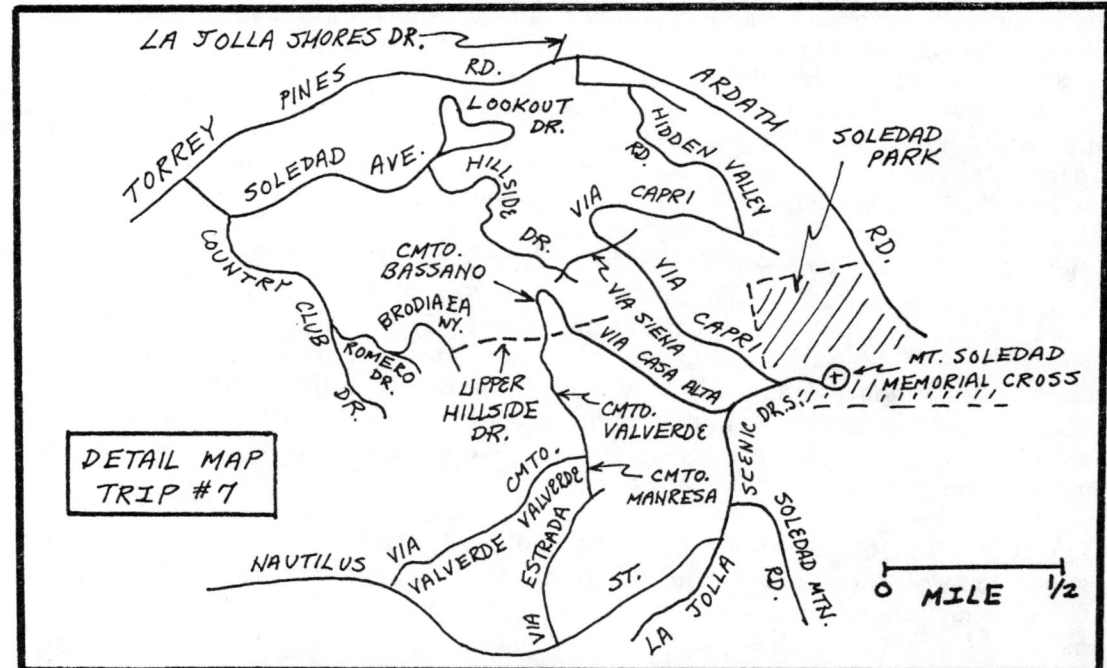

The Return Leg. The next 0.7 mile on Nautilus St. is on a varying, but generally very steep, upgrade on Class II bikeway. The reward on reaching S. La Jolla Scenic Dr. is a 2.1-mile downgrade through posh residential neighborhoods. Stay to the

METROPOLITAN SAN DIEGO

right at Rutgers Rd. and continue south just beyond on what is now Class II La Jolla Mesa Dr. (9.1). The views of Mission Bay and the San Diego city skyline complete the total four points of the compass on this tour. A particularly fine view of Mission Bay can be enjoyed from Cottontail Ln.

At Turquoise St., the cyclist returns to a short stretch of busy commercial area, then follows a Class II route through a northern Pacific Beach residential area to Lamont St. All that remains is a workout 0.4-mile, 150-foot upgrade which levels near the park entrance at Park Dr. (11.8).

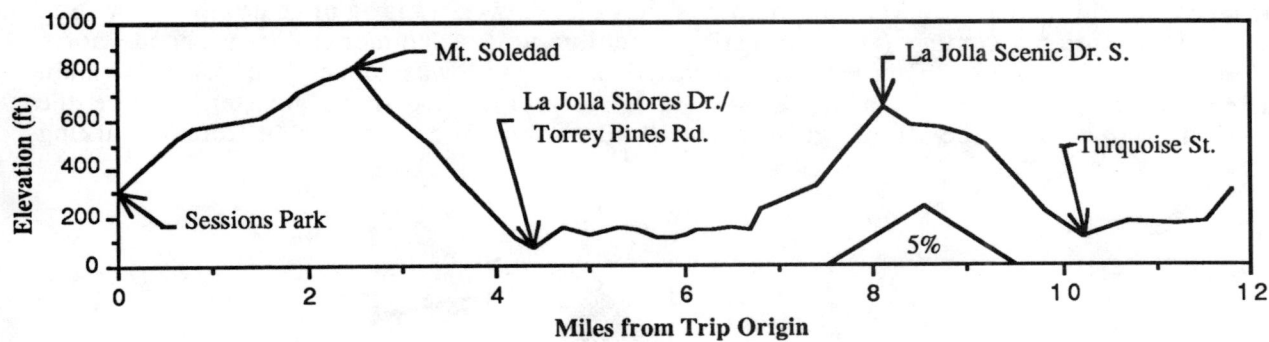

CONNECTING TRIPS: 1) Connection with the Mission Bay Loop (Trip #1) - at Turquoise St. and Mission Blvd., bike south on the latter road to Loring St. and turn left in a short distance at Crystal Dr. Follow the directions for the trip extension to Ocean Front Walk in Trip #6; 2) connection with the La Jolla Coastal Tour (Trip #6) - the trips share a common segment from Prospect Pl. to W. Muirlands Dr.; 3) connection with the San Diego 59-Mile Scenic Dr. (Trip #11) - the trips share a common segment on Torrey Pines Rd.; 4) connection with the U. C. San Diego Campus Visit (Trip #12) - at Torrey Pines Rd. and La Jolla Shores Dr., bike north on the latter road.

TRIP #8 - HEART O' THE CITY

GENERAL LOCATION: Downtown San Diego

LEVEL OF DIFFICULTY: Loop - easy
　　　　　　　　　　　　　Distance - 7.2 miles
　　　　　　　　　　　　　Elevation gain - essentially flat

BICYCLE RIDES: SAN DIEGO COUNTY

GENERAL DESCRIPTION: A tour through the commercial heart of the City of San Diego, this land was originally the site of Alonzo Horton's "New Town," a development begun in 1867. The ensuing twentieth-century development has resulted in an interesting quiltwork of restored Victorian buildings nestled amongst the central city's numerous skyscrapers. Most of the bicycle route described is on the San Diego 59-mile Scenic Drive.

This early Sunday morning neck-craning cycle tour starts from bayside Embarcadero Marina Park, transits Seaport Village, then bursts onto the edge of the commercial scene on Harbor Dr. With luck, you'll see one of the horse-drawn tour carriages in this area. We cycle below several skytowers and alongside the new San Diego Convention Center (all interesting architectural specimens), then head north to visit the Gas Lamp Quarter, the restored area that was once San Diego's main business district. At "F" St. and 4th Ave. is a view of the "parking monster." Here the bicyclist stares into the front grilles of 30-40 automobiles on the different parking levels - an eerie sight.

Gas Lamps and Skyscrapers

The route works west and visits the numerous sight-seeing attractions, gift shops and eateries alongside the Class I harbor side northern Harbor Dr. segment. For those that are lovers of the nautical, the military dreadnoughts, cruise liners and the Star of India (old sailing ship) are particularly nice distractions. The route turns east beyond the County Health Center Building (3.3), then south, passing the Firehouse Museum, a home to antique fire equipment, including a steamer. An eastward cruise on "A" St. takes the biker past the modern Convention and Performing Arts Centers, leading to a spin around San Diego City College, and a return to the business/shopping district north of Broadway near 4th Ave. The Broadway tour segment passes the Horton Plaza Center (known for its imaginatively designed, multi-level mall), and the other major redevelopment projects to the south. At Pacific Hwy., the biker turns south along the Naval Supply Center and, in a short distance, returns to the Kettner Blvd. entry to Seaport Village. A short stint of car dodging returns the cyclist to the starting point (7.2).

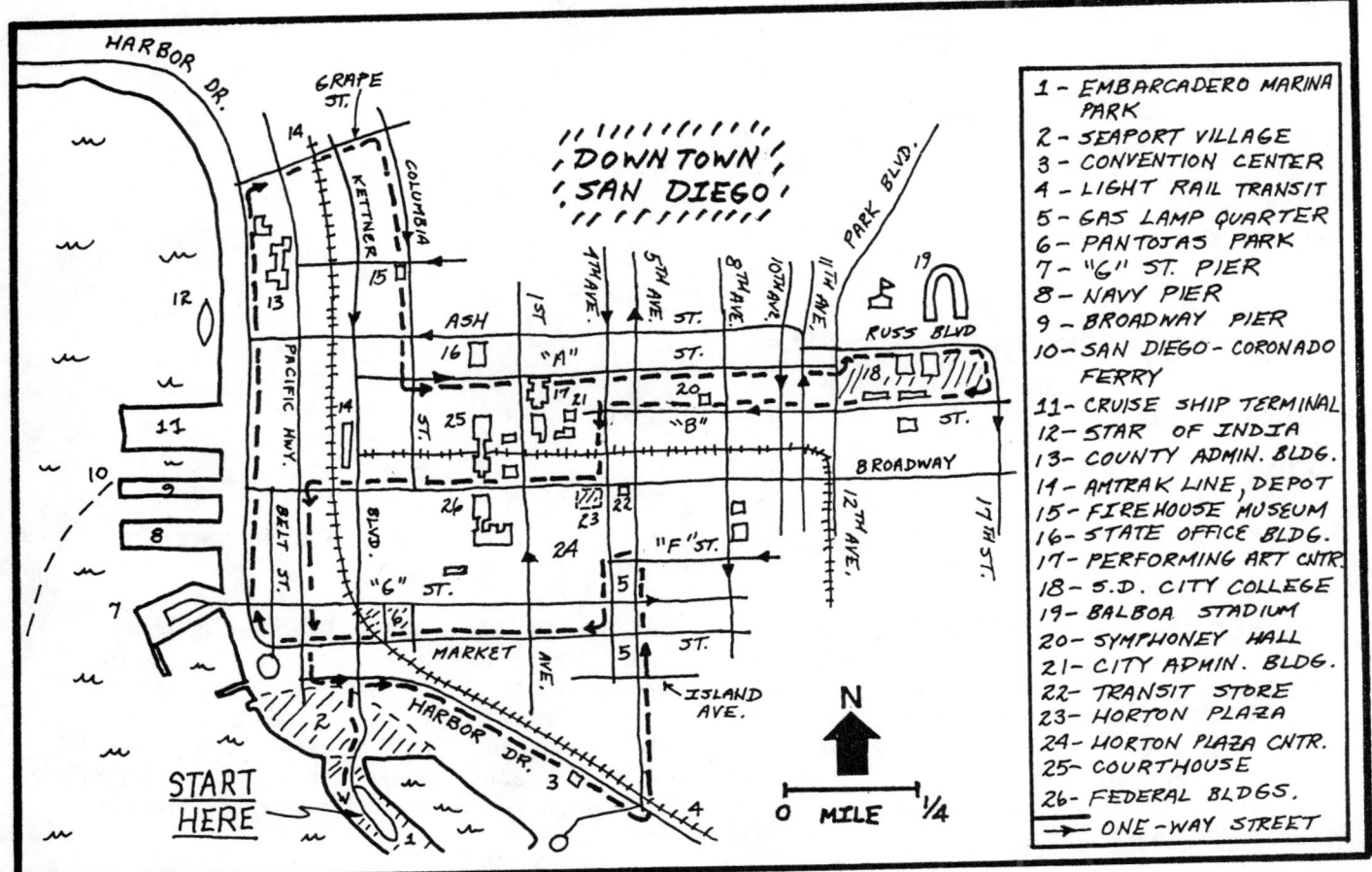

TRIP #8 - HEART O' THE CITY

TRAILHEAD: From Interstate Hwy. 5 southbound, take the Sassafras St. exit south. Turn right towards the harbor, then left on Pacific Hwy., continuing southbound to its terminus at Harbor Dr. Turn left, then right in a short distance at Kettner Blvd. into Seaport Village. Drive directly south to Embarcadero Marina Park. For northbound traffic, exit at the Market St. turnoff. Follow 19th St. north to Market St., turn left and drive 1-1/3 miles to Kettner Blvd. Proceed as described above. Park in one of the local pay lots if a start/finish point shuttle cannot be arranged.

The park has restrooms, shade trees, grass, picnic areas, and is a great location for watching the comings and goings of the aircraft carriers from Coronado Island and other warships from the U.S. Naval Station to the south. Seaport Village offers numerous specialty shops within a harborside village setting, with special attractions such as a New England lighthouse, a 100-year old carousel and a Victorian clock tower.

CONNECTING TRIPS: 1) Connection with the Balboa Park ride (Trip #2) - at Park Blvd. and Russ Blvd., bike north on the former road; 2) connection with the Around San Diego Bay (Trip #3) and Seaport Village to Point Loma (Trip #4) tours - the trips

BICYCLE RIDES: SAN DIEGO COUNTY

share a common segment on Harbor Dr.; 3) connection with the Old Town Tour (Trip #9) - at 5th Ave. and "A" St., turn north on the former road.

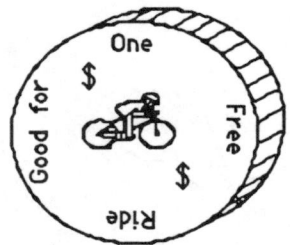

TRIP #9 - OLD TOWN TOUR

GENERAL LOCATION: Hillcrest, Old Town, Mission Hills

LEVEL OF DIFFICULTY: Loop - moderate
Distance - 7.1 miles
Elevation gain - steep grade from Jackson St. intersection to Presidio Park

GENERAL DESCRIPTION: Though Old Town is certainly a major trip highlight, this is actually a double-loop tour of older San Diego. The route starts from Mission Hills Park, travels westward to Old Town State Historical Park, then climbs up to visit the Serra Museum and Fort Stockton of Presidio Park, the original City of San Diego building site. After returning to Mission Hills, the tour heads east through the Hillcrest and old Banker's Hill areas, then crosses two canyons via suspended walking bridges. The bikeway wends its way north through a broad canyon on Class II bikeway, then returns to plush little Mission Hills Park.

San Diego Presidio Site

METROPOLITAN SAN DIEGO

TRAILHEAD: From Interstate Hwy. 5, exit west at Washington St. and drive 3/4 mile to Hawk St. (just beyond University Ave.). Make a hard left at Washington Pl. and continue 1/3 mile to Mission Hills Park. From State Hwy. 163, exit west at Washington St. and drive one mile to Washington Pl. Continue straight ahead to the park. From Interstate Hwy. 8, transition to either I-5 or Hwy. 163 and continue as described above. Mission Hills Park has abundant tree shade, grassy rest areas, children's playground, tennis courts and restrooms. There is also a paved bikeway/walkway around the pocket park.

TRIP DESCRIPTION: **Mission Hills Park to Presidio Park.** Bike a short distance north to Fort Stockton Dr., then enjoy a 0.7-mile ride through a palm tree-lined residential area. Near Witherby St. on Sunset Blvd. is an overlook of the I-8/I-5 freeway complex and a steep downgrade just ahead. (Note: to take the "easy" tour without the upgrade to Presidio Park, take Witherby St., work over to Presidio Dr., and turn right.) A 0.3-mile coast on what is now Juan St. leads the biker past Heritage Park, a hillside complex of restored Victorian houses which includes a doll shop and a bed-and-breakfast establishment. Pedal alongside Old Town, then turn right and bike the modest Mason St. upgrade.

Suspension Bridge Over Canyon

Turn left on Jackson St., pass the Presidio Hill Golf Course and Casa de Carillo (the oldest standing adobe structure in San Diego, now used as a clubhouse). Near Chestnut St. is steep, narrow Presidio Dr. which circuits the Presidio Park periphery, providing Mission Valley views. At 0.3 mile on the upgrade is the stately Serra Museum (museum galleries focusing on early San Diego history; panoramic viewpoint), followed by the Fort Stockton ruins. After a 0.5-uphill mile is the lovely glen enclosed by Cosoy Wy. and, a few hundred feet later, the end of the upgrade at Altimirano Wy.

Presidio Park to Hillcrest. The route works its way over to Fort Stockton Dr. near the bluffs overlooking Mission Valley (see Trip #10). As is characteristic of the residential area, there are highly mixed architectural styles of tightly-packed, well-groomed residences. Our now Class III bike route veers left at Lewis St. (3.2) and negotiates a 0.6-mile stretch of small, well-restored old business establishments. A short meandering Class III route through the edge of Hillcrest's main shopping district leads to the intersection of University Ave. and 3rd Ave.

BICYCLE RIDES: SAN DIEGO COUNTY

TRIP #9 - OLD TOWN TOUR

METROPOLITAN SAN DIEGO

Canyon Crossings. A pleasant 0.8-mile stint on 3rd. and 4th Aves. through a district of well-tended apartments and homes leads to Quince St. Here on the west side of 4th Ave. is a small, short wooded bridge that takes the cyclist across a small canyon (using the bridge requires lifting bikes up several steps). A short tour to the north on 1st. Ave. and a left turn on Spruce St. leads, at road's end, to a second bridge. Walk your bike across the couple hundred feet of this metal suspension bridge, enjoying the wooded canyon almost one hundred feet below. While Don was photographing the scene, a half-dozen hard-at-work walkers surprised him by setting the bridge into very noticeable motion. (The bridge was designed for this and is quite safe!)

The Return Segment. A 3/4-mile maze leads the cyclist to Class II Reynard Wy. from Eagle St. At the intersection with the northern branch of Curlew St., cycle a testy uphill on Goldfinch St. Bike 0.7 mile on continued Class II bikeway through an increasingly commercial area, to reach Washington St. Turn left and cruise Washington Pl. back to the trip origin.

Trip Option. An alternate for the Mission Hills Park to Old Town segment is to bicycle west from the park following residential Pringle St. There is an excellent view of San Diego International Airport above Guy St. and an exciting steep-to-sheer 0.2-mile downhill which flattens near San Diego Ave. A one-mile flat return through a mixed commercial/residential area leads the cyclist past the southern edge of Old Town to the Harney St./Juan St. intersection (1.6 miles total segment).

<u>CONNECTING TRIPS</u>: 1) Connection with the Balboa Park ride (Trip #2) - at 4th Ave. and Upas St., bike west on the latter street; 2) connection with the Heart O' the City tour (Trip #8) - at Quince St., continue south on 4th Ave.; 3) connection with the Overlooking Mission Valley tour (Trip #10) - at Arista St. and Fort Stockton Dr., continue northeast on the former road; 4) connection with the San Diego River Run (Trip #17) - follow Taylor St. east to the first freeway overcrossing, which leads to Hotel Circle N.

TRIP #10 - OVERLOOKING MISSION VALLEY

<u>GENERAL LOCATION</u>: Mission Hills, Normal Heights, Kensington Park

<u>LEVEL OF DIFFICULTY</u>: One way - moderate
Distance - 21.2 miles
Elevation gain - periodic moderate grades

<u>GENERAL DESCRIPTION</u>: For the "meander of the mesas," talk a friend into dropping you off at Presidio Park and picking you back up about ten miles east (shortest driving distance) in Kensington Park. The mesas above Mission Valley are

BICYCLE RIDES: SAN DIEGO COUNTY

laced with finger canyons from the Old Town area to the point where the San Diego River and Mission Valley swing north towards Mission Gorge. This tour explores the generally-secluded or lightly-used roadways along the mesa/canyon boundaries. There are views-a-plenty of the valley floor and beyond. We have highlighted a few favorite off-shoot routes, but encourage the bicyclist to explore at his/her whim; there are two key suggestions: 1) bring an auto road map, and 2) if in doubt, turn left at every opportunity where there is not an immediate dead end.

TRAILHEAD: From Interstate Hwy. 8, exit south at the Taylor St. off-ramp and follow that road west, paralleling and south of I-8. At Chestnut St., turn left and follow Presidio Dr. into beautifully-landscaped Presidio Park. From other freeways, transition onto I-8 and take the off-ramp noted.

The park is on a restful grass-covered, tree-studded hill with a picnic area, restrooms and such noted attractions as the Serra Museum and Fort Stockton. Peruse the entire park before taking off on this eastbound adventure.

TRIP DESCRIPTION: Presidio Park to Hillcrest. Bike through Presidio Park to Arista St. and follow that road northeast to Pine St. This begins the canyon-side adventure. Follow Pine St. to its end, then return to Fort Stockton Dr. via Pine St. Two clear observations can be made which will be characteristic of the remaining canyon overlook side tours: 1) these diversions are in quiet neighborhoods where people actually walk and play in the street; and 2) in many places, canyon overlooks are found by peeking between homes or at dead-end street barriers.

Looking Northeast from the Mesa

After Pine St. is a succession of three of the most serene and scenic routes in quiet residential neighborhoods, the Sierra Vista-, Randolph St.-, and Jackdaw St.- diversions. There is a particularly nice overlook at Hawk St. and Arcadia Dr. Our route works its way over to Eagle St. and Washington St. (4.6), then follows that road to the Front St. and Third Ave. diversions. These latter two off-shoot tours are on

METROPOLITAN SAN DIEGO

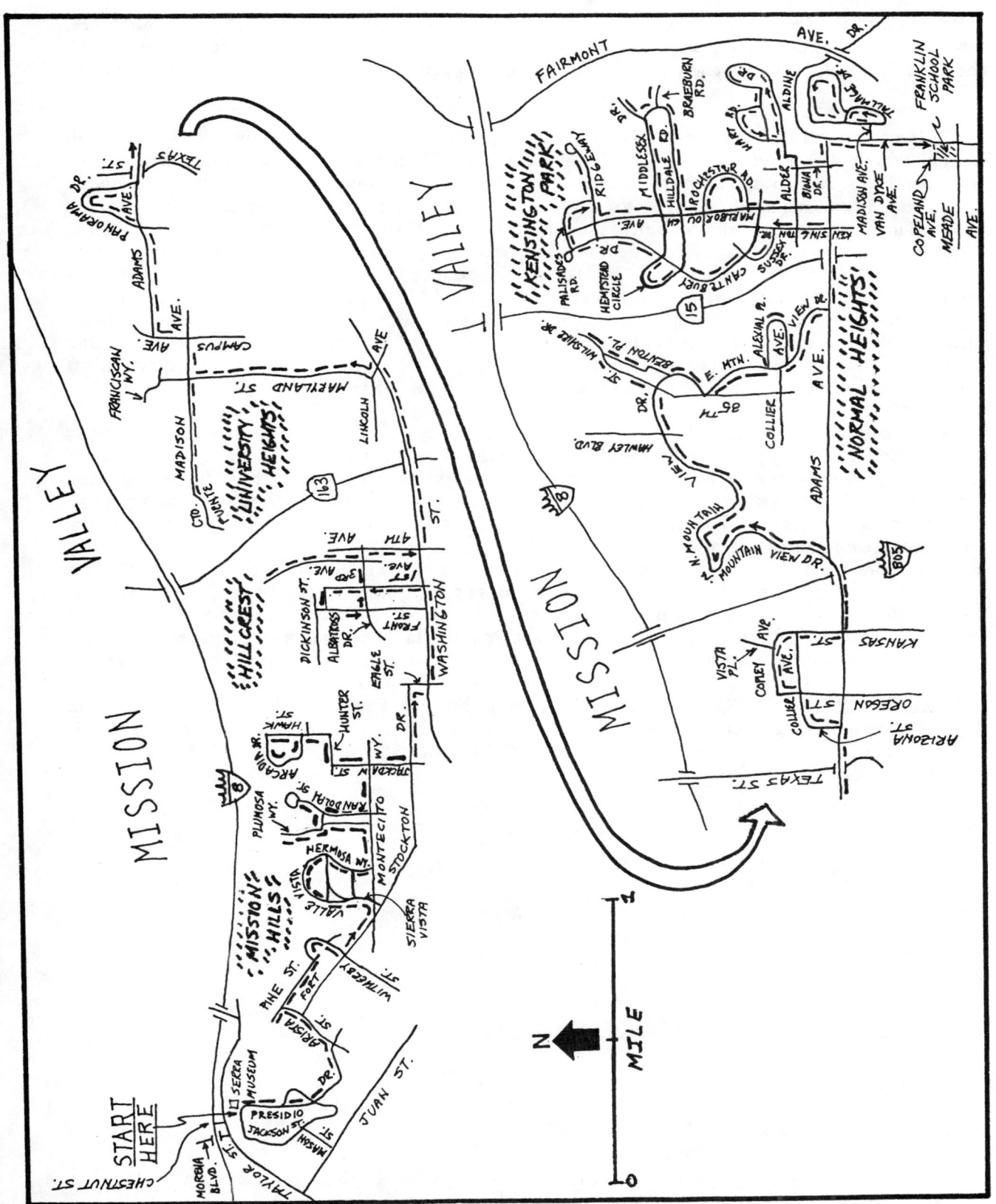

TRIP #10 - OVERLOOKING MISSION VALLEY

BICYCLE RIDES: SAN DIEGO COUNTY

well-traveled roads due to the heavy traffic flows into the University of California, San Diego Medical Center, and the many rest homes and medical facilities in the area. There is a particularly open view to the western edge of Mission Valley at the end of Third Ave.

University Heights and Normal Heights. The tour returns to Washington St. and travels 0.6 mile of busy Class X road across State Hwy. 163 to University Heights (we found no easy way to bypass this stretch). A hard left at the first street beyond Hwy. 163 introduces the cyclist to a pleasant residential segment leading to Madison Ave. Turn left (west) and explore the short dead-end streets scattered along this mesa finger, enjoying views on both sides of the street. Backtrack east and work your way to Adams Ave. (9.9), which will be the main connecting artery for the remainder of the trip. Pass the cozy park near Georgia St. just before plying the Panorama Dr. and Arizona St. diversions. Across Texas St. in Normal Heights is the outstanding three-mile Mountain View Dr. segment, again lightly-traveled residential roads along the bluffs. Don't miss the Hawley Blvd. and 35th St. rides out onto two adjacent bluff fingers, each with a splendid view to the other, and of Mission Valley below.

Kensington Park. A return to Adams Ave. (14.1) and subsequent freeway crossing places the cyclist into what we thought was the most posh and desirable of these delightful mesa towns. The route follows the tried-and-true left-hand rule (right-hand rule if biking west), following a sequence of streets along the mesa edge. This is a well-maintained residential area with a mixed variety of expensive, but not exorbitant residences. Traffic is light -- the streets were spotted with bikers, skaters, skateboarders and even baseballers. Ridgeway is the last look at Mission Valley before it heads north and the tour route proceeds south. The southbound follows several diversionary loops, crosses Adams Ave., then makes a final salute on the Tallmage Dr. excursion. A short distance south is the asphalt playground called Franklin School Park, a place to gulp down some water and meet your bike courier.

<u>CONNECTING TRIPS</u>: 1) Continuation with the Old Town Tour (Trip #9) - the trips share a common segment at the route origin; 2) connection with the San Diego River Run (Trip #17) - return via Chestnut St. to Taylor St. and take the Morena Blvd. underpass to Hotel Circle Dr.

TRIP #11 - SAN DIEGO 59-MILE SCENIC DRIVE

GENERAL LOCATION: San Diego, Pt. Loma, La Jolla

LEVEL OF DIFFICULTY: Loop - strenuous
Distance - 59+ miles
Elevation gain - steep grades in Scripps Institute and Soledad Mountain Areas

METROPOLITAN SAN DIEGO

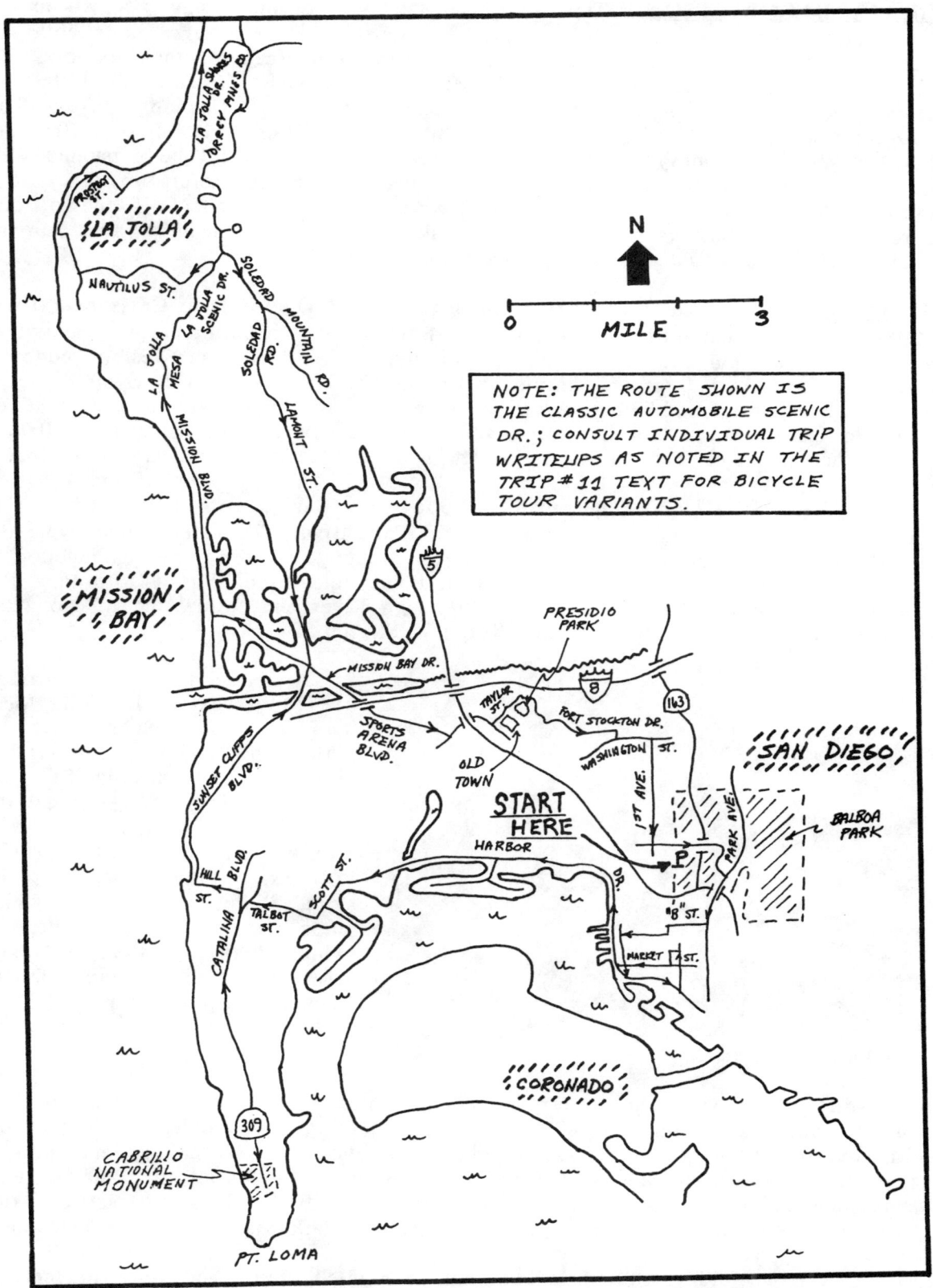

TRIP #11 - SAN DIEGO 59-MILE SCENIC DRIVE

BICYCLE RIDES: SAN DIEGO COUNTY

GENERAL DESCRIPTION: This is a "short-cut" way of introducing yourself to the San Diego area. The marked 59-mile scenic tour starts at Balboa Park, visits both the new and old San Diego Metropolis, passes along the Embarcadero, then explores Pt. Loma. The route continues north through Mission Bay, visits upscale La Jolla and reaches its northernmost point near the Scripps Institute of Oceanography. The southerly return climbs to Mt. Soledad, then returns to the origin via Mission Bay and Old Town. With exploratory stops along the way, this easily could be expanded well beyond a one-day tour. Note that the route described below refers to other tour descriptions; these tours have some variants which take the cyclist off the official scenic route. These variants are provided to take the biker off heavily-traveled roads and/or to provide scenic side routes not accessible to auto traffic.

TRAILHEAD: From State Hwy. 163 northbound, exit at Quince Dr. Cross over Hwy. 163 (Cabrillo Fwy.) and turn left (south) at Balboa Dr. Continue south and find parking anywhere within the loop south of Juniper Rd. This lush western edge of the park has tree-studded grassy knolls, restrooms and bikeways/walkways scattered throughout. From the southbound direction, take the 6th Ave. offramp and continue 1-1/4 mile to Quince Dr. Turn left (east) and then right, in a short distance, at Balboa Dr. From other area freeways, use Interstate Hwys. 5 or 8 to gain access to Hwy. 163.

TRIP DESCRIPTION: **Northbound.** Follow the Balboa Park tour (Trip #2) to President's Wy. and bike southeast on that road to Park Blvd. Turn south and cycle 0.6 mile to "B" St. (1.9). Follow the Heart O' the City route (Trip #8) from this junction to Grape St. (7.2), then continue on the Seaport to Point Loma ride (Trip #4) to Park Rd. and Sunset Cliffs Blvd. (24.3). Cross the San Diego River and follow the Mission Bay ride (Trip #1) north to Mission Blvd. and Turquois St. (30.5).

La Jolla Shores Beach

A rugged climb through the Muirlands on La Jolla Mesa and La Jolla Scenic Dr. is balanced by a hang-it-out downhill on Nautilus St. (see map for Trip #7 -- note the direction reversal). A tour along the La Jolla cliffs follows, giving way to a La Jolla Shores Dr. segment which ends, after a steep upgrade, which leads to the University of California, San Diego campus (Trip #6 map) (41.1).

Southbound. A southward return on Torrey Pines Rd. leads to a strenuous-sheer climb up to Soledad Mountain, followed by a refreshing downgrade which lets out above Mission Bay (Trip #1 map). A southbound alternate crosses the bay and a quilt-work path through the Midway area leads to Old Town. A climb to Presidio Park follows a segment of the Old Town Tour (Trip #9). It involves an eastward ride through Mission Hills and a southerly return to Balboa Park via Banker's Hill (59+).

CONNECTING TRIPS: See the individual trips cited above and refer to the trip connectors in those individual write-ups.

METROPOLITAN SAN DIEGO

TRIP #12 - U.C.S.D. CAMPUS VISIT

GENERAL LOCATION: La Jolla

LEVEL OF DIFFICULTY: Loop - easy
Distance - 4.0 miles
Elevation gain - periodic easy-to-moderate grades

DESCRIPTION. Save this campus tour for the weekend. Surrounded by several busy streets, this is essentially a walker and biker sanctuary. Although a reference route is provided, the cyclist might consider freewheeling the entire campus. The reference trip has a 2-1/2-mile Class II road tour which passes such landmarks as the tree-studded Natural Reserve, the futuristic new Central Library, and the scenic Myers Dr./Hutchison Wy./S. Gilman Dr. segment. Near the Mandeville Center, the tour shifts over to a 3/4-mile Class I tour on shared walkway/bikeway. Just before reaching the southwestern campus parking area, the pathway crosses through the striking and beautifully-landscaped Revelle College foyer, surrounded by no less than seven buildings! The described route proceeds north alongside a sports/recreation area before returning to automobile roadway at Scholars Dr. near the La Jolla Shores entry. A 3/4-mile spin on that peripheral road returns the biker to the starting point (4.0).

New U.C.S.D. Library

Options. There are several interesting spur trips off the campus, including the posh La Jolla Farms Rd. residential loop, the Torrey Pines Scenic Dr. entry to spectacular Torrey Pines City Park, and the Tower Rd. access to Soledad Valley.

BICYCLE RIDES: SAN DIEGO COUNTY

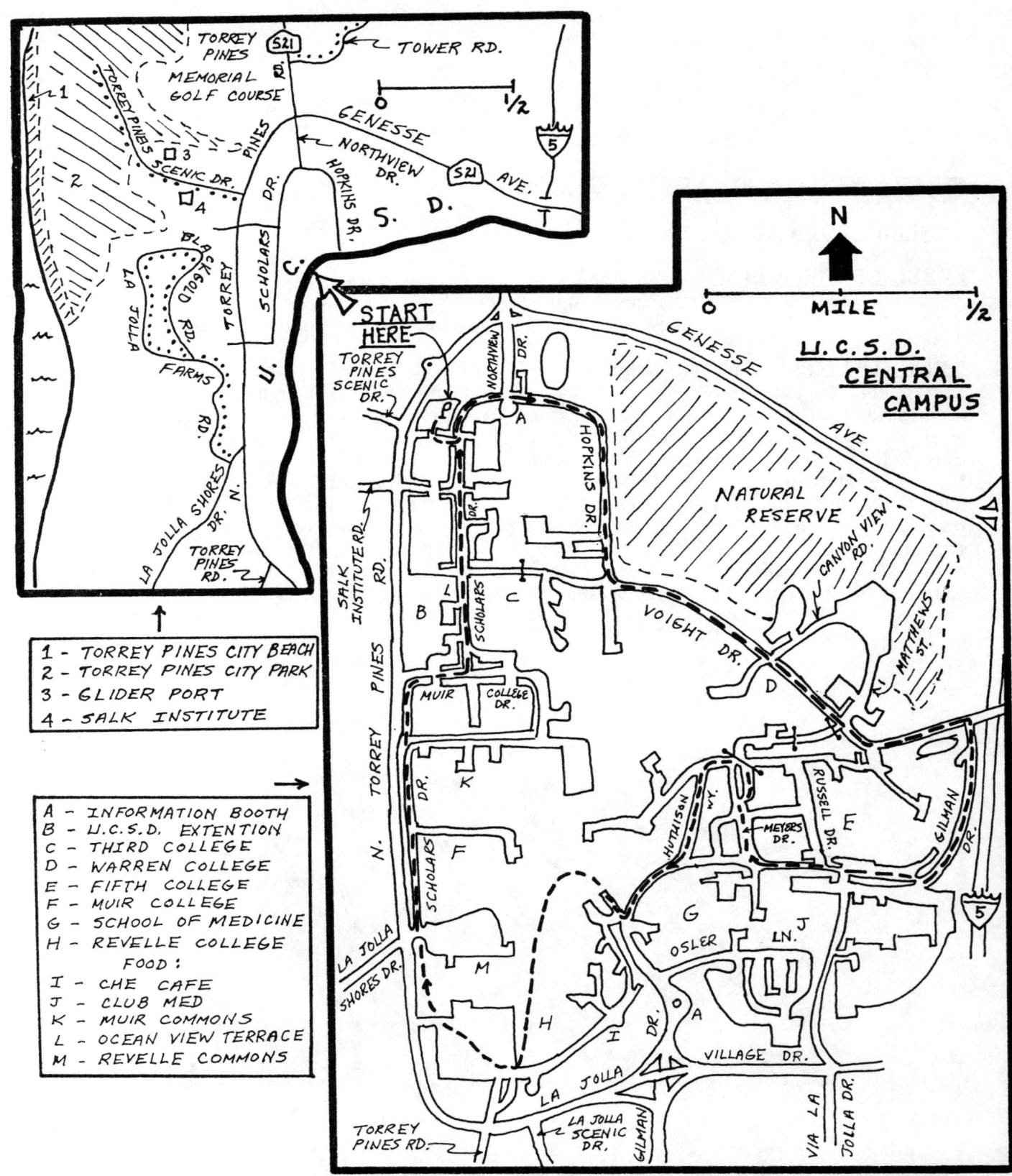

TRIP #12 - U.C.S.D. CAMPUS VISIT

METROPOLITAN SAN DIEGO

Torrey Pines City Park

TRAILHEAD: From Interstate Hwy. 5, exit west at Genesee Ave. and drive about one mile to the intersection of Genesee Ave., North Torrey Pines Rd. and Northview Dr. Turn sharply left onto the latter road and drive 1/2-mile to the roads end (there is an information booth in the cul-de-sac across the street). Turn right onto Scholars Dr. and find parking in any of the lots. (Do not park in reserved slots!)

CONNECTING TRIPS: 1) Connection with the La Jolla Coastal Tour (Trip #6) - at the southern campus edge, continue south at either Torrey Pines Rd. or La Jolla Scenic Dr.; 2) connection with the San Diego 59-Mile Scenic Drive (Trip #11) - at N. Torrey Pines Rd. and La Jolla Shores Dr., bike south on either road; 3) connection with the Coastal County Tour (Trip #21) - at La Jolla Shores Dr., bike to N. Torrey Pines Blvd.

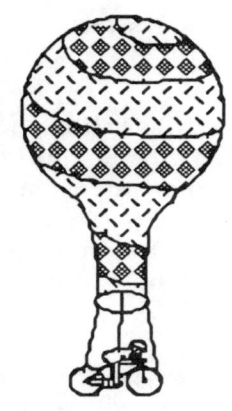
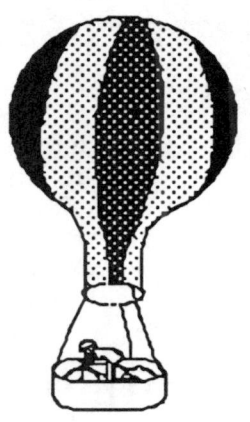

TRIP #13 - TECHOLOTE CANYON

GENERAL LOCATION: Clairemont, Linda Vista

LEVEL OF DIFFICULTY: One way - moderate (strenuous for Poopout Hill option)
Distance - 5.7 miles (one way)
Elevation gain - periodic moderate-to-steep grades
(short, sheer grades at Poopout Hill)

GENERAL DESCRIPTION: Smack dab in the middle of San Diego is Techolote Canyon Natural Park, an off-road bikers delight. Buried in the brush- and tree- filled canyon are a maize of dirt trails plying the Techolote Creek drainage and the finger canyons spread along the route. Unfortunately, the bicyclist has to do some heroics to connect the three segments, which are broken off by the Techolote Canyon Golf Course and Balboa Ave. But a few hours of exploring the canyon, starting from

BICYCLE RIDES: SAN DIEGO COUNTY

Techolote Park and Recreation Center and ending at the N. Clairemont Park and Recreation Center will definitely "make your day." Bring a street map, topographic map and compass if you plan to take the Poopout Hill option, as it is very easy to get disoriented in the southern canyon segment. Note that there is a less heroic option to bike an up and back on the southern segment, then do the other segments separately.

University of San Diego Campus from the Canyon

TRAILHEAD: From Interstate Hwy. 5, exit at Sea World Dr./Techolote Rd. and drive east on Techolote Rd. to its terminus within Techolote Park and Recreation Center. The park has baseball fields, snack bar and restrooms. Note that there are other entries to the canyon beyond those noted here, generally from about any of the developments on the less-steep eastern slopes. Specific methods for handling trip logistics are left to the cyclist for this tour. Bring a quart or two of water, as there are no public sources near the route.

TRIP DESCRIPTION: **Southern Segment - Techolote Park to Mt. Acadia Blvd.** At the end of Techolote Rd. is the signed dirt entry to the southern section (most entries have a large sign denoting "Techolote Canyon Natural Park, Hiking and Golf"). In 0.4 mile, on a wide dirt path with periodic sand patches, are views of the magnificent older and ornate buildings of the University of San Diego above. Everywhere along the path, wild flowers were in full bloom in May 1992. In another 0.4 mile of relative solitude, the route veers left (northeast). The periodic diet of residences creeping up to the park boundary does limit the feel of isolation, however.

In 1.3 miles from the entrance point, the biker is alongside the Techolote Canyon Golf Course with Techolote Creek flowing through on the left. Ahead is "Poopout Hill" (our name) and a major decision. The nominal choices would be to turn around and return (2.6), climb Poopout Hill and then return, or to follow a challenging cross-country route beyond Poopout Hill which connects with the middle segment. For the cross-country challenge, bike and hike the sheer (170-foot elevation gain) hill to a plateau, following the power lines on the way up. Enjoy the sweeping views of canyon and golf course, then drop into a small canyon in order to enjoy the pleasure of a 120-foot gain repeat performance.

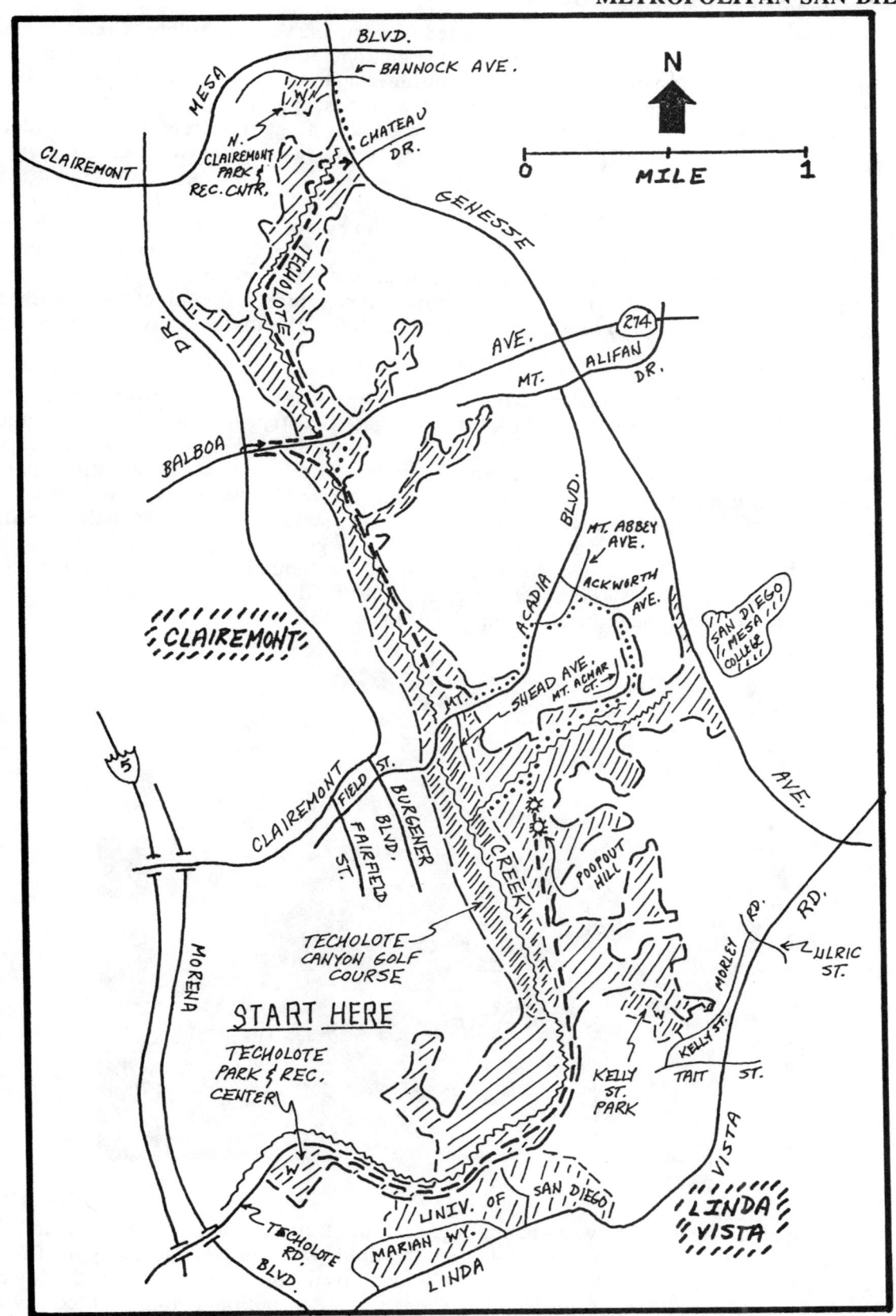

TRIP #13 - TECHOLOTE CANYON

BICYCLE RIDES: SAN DIEGO COUNTY

A very steep downhill leads to an unnamed feeder creek (Techolote Creek remains to the left or west). At the first major trail junction, turn east, cross the rock-filled creek under a tree-shaded awning, then continue about a half mile on variable-quality dirt trail to a large canyon outlet (the landscape is highly eroded at the outlet). Follow a small trail left (north) as it passes a large concrete structure (debris basin?) and winds steeply uphill. (If you miss the trail, the worst you can do is pedal another 0.3 mile to Genesee Ave.)

The trail hugs the west canyon wall as it continues to the edge of a finger mesa just below Mt. Acmar Ct. Bike along the mesa edge 1/4 mile to a small turnout/park on Acworth Ave. What now remains is to connect with the middle segment on paved road. Follow Acworth Ave. 0.3 mile to Mt. Abbey Ave., turn left and connect with Mt. Acadia Blvd. in 0.3 mile. Turn left again and coast 0.6 mile to the canyon bottom (2.6-mile segment).

Middle Segment - Mt. Acadia Blvd. to Balboa Ave. Just above Snead Ave. on the north side of Mt. Acadia Blvd. is the gated entry to the middle segment. Immediately, the cyclist is treated to a short downhill followed soon by a short, very steep uphill. In this brush-filled area are mounds of dirt (great observation points) and a meandering mesa trail which stays east and above Techolote Creek. Much of the tour in this relatively-flat area is spent flushing jackrabbits. Just below Balboa Ave. is a key trail fork. The right fork leads to a large roadside drainage ditch, from which the cyclist can gain access to Balboa Ave. eastbound (where the ditch turns away from the road is an access up an asphalt run-off ditch). Our route follows the left fork, crosses the creek and heads steeply up to Balboa Ave.

Poopout Hill

Here the cyclist must bike westbound, against the traffic, since there is a tall lane divider in place. One quarter-mile and one hundred feet above the canyon floor is Clairemont Dr., where the biker must cross and now bike eastward and downhill against traffic to the northern segment gated entry. (An optional route noted by one biker we met was to follow the overhead water culvert under Balboa Ave. -- we were not at all comfortable with that option.) (1.7-mile segment).

Northern Segment - Balboa Ave. to North Clairemont Park and Recreation Center. At the signed entry, pass around the metal guard gate and cycle along a two-track path (slightly overgrown in May 1992). Cross a small creek on the narrowing path in a well-treed area, then ease up alongside Techolote Creek in 0.9 mile. Proceed along the tree-studded creek, then make three successive crossings before encountering a single short, steep upgrade that lets out at the signed entry at Genesee Ave. (1.4-mile segment).

N. Clairemont Park and Recreation Center is 0.3 mile further north on Genesee Ave., at the corner of Bannock Ave. The park has scattered picnic benches and barbecue grills, basketball courts and bikeways/walkways throughout. There is a particularly nice loop on the small flat on the south side of the park which looks into Techolote Canyon. Families with young bikers should consider visiting the park.

<u>**CONNECTING TRIPS**</u>: 1) Connection with the Mission Bay Loop (Trip #1) - at the trip origin, return south and west on Techolote Rd./Mission Bay Dr.; 2) connection with the Marian Bear Park tour (Trip #5) - at Clairemont Mesa Blvd., bike west.

TRIP #14 - RUN FOR THE BORDER

<u>**GENERAL LOCATION**</u>:   Imperial Beach

<u>**LEVEL OF DIFFICULTY**</u>: East and west loops - easy
Distance - 6.2 (east loop); 16.3 (east and west loops)
Elevation gain - essentially flat

<u>**GENERAL DESCRIPTION**</u>: Two very different Imperial Beach loop tours are provided. The eastern loop is through rural landscape on generally Class II or III, lightly-used roads -- this is a route for cyclists who want to chart little-known pathways. The tour passes within 1/4 mile of the U.S.A./Mexico Border on rural Monument Rd., where there are interesting views of hillside Tijuana. The longer and equally scenic western loop plys the more developed portions of the city. The jigsaw puzzle route visits the Imperial Beach Naval Air Station, the Imperial Beach strand and the Tijuana Slough National Wildlife Refuge. The westside tour is generally Class X through lightly traveled neighborhoods.

BICYCLE RIDES: SAN DIEGO COUNTY

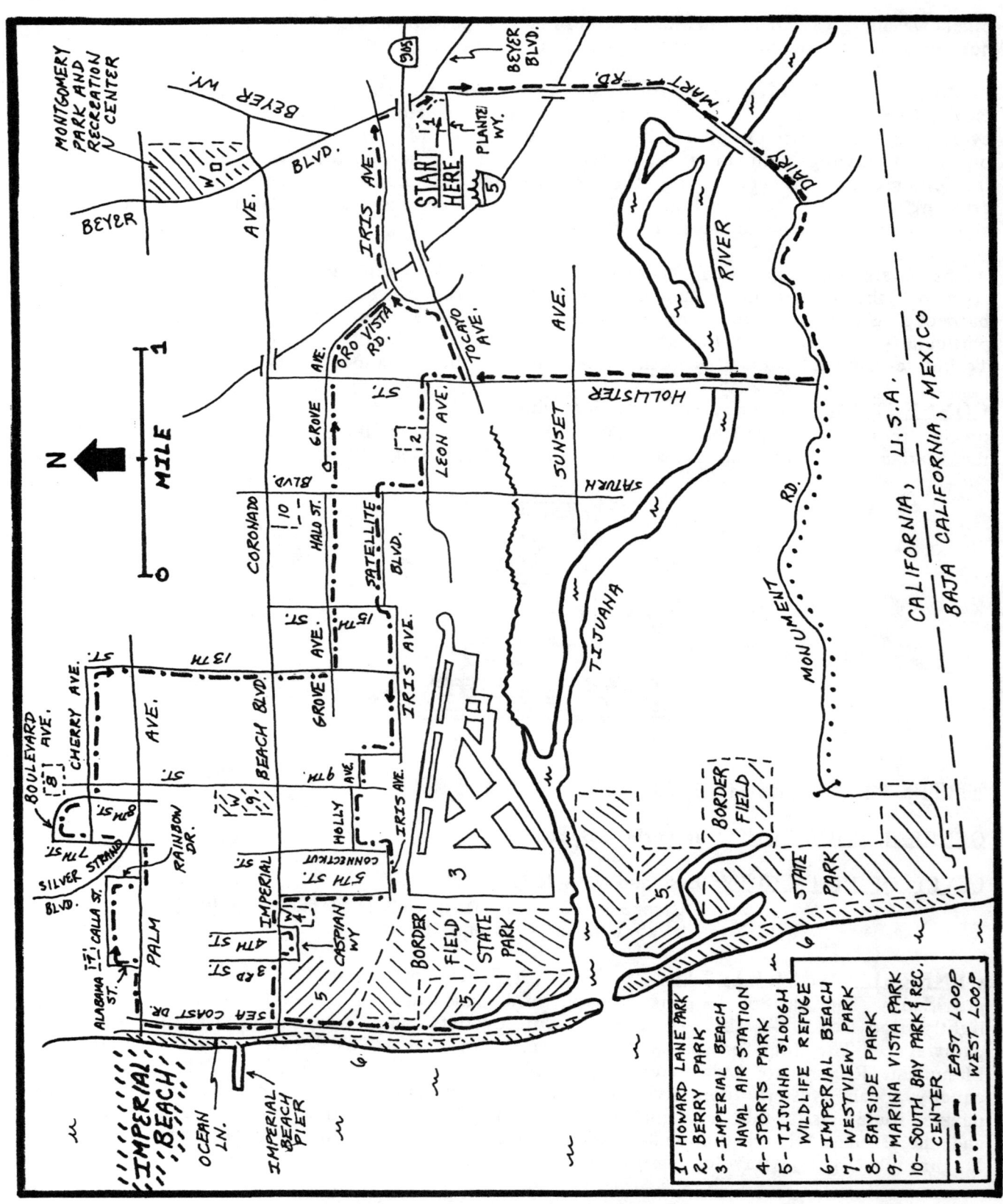

TRIP #14 - RUN FOR THE BORDER

METROPOLITAN SAN DIEGO

TRAILHEAD: From Interstate Hwy. 5, exit north at Dairy Mart Rd. and continue 1/2 mile to Tequila Wy. Turn left and follow that road a short distance as it curves north and meets Howard Lane Park at Plantel Wy. The park has children's playgrounds, basketball courts, picnic benches, open fields and a water fountain.

TRIP DESCRIPTION: **East Loop.** The smaller of the two loops is primarily through rural landscape, with numerous dairy farms and some croplands to the west of the Interstate. The primarily Class III route crosses the Tijuana River, then follows Monument Rd., which parallels the Mexican Border at about 1/4 mile-distance. The views of densely-developed hillside Tijuana are outstanding. Bikers can continue westbound two miles on Monument Rd. beyond Hollister St. to the gated eastern edge of Border Field State Park; the road is little used (this area might be described as secluded) and provides some extra workout mileage.

However, our reference tour heads north on Hollister St., recrosses the river and returns to civilization near Sunset Ave. By following Tocayo Ave. eastward, the biker returns to the park via a freeway overcrossing and a short journey through a predominantly residential area on Iris Ave. At Beyer Blvd., turn right and proceed under State Hwy. 905 (6.2).

Famous Book Reviewer at South Imperial Beach

West Loop. Continue north just beyond Tocayo Ave. and turn left (west) at Leon Ave. In a short distance is Berry Park (asphalt playground, water); this is one of several parks which could be used as a starting point if the biker prefers to do just the western loop. The cyclist proceeds west on a zig-zag route through 1950's vintage residential territory alongside ghostly Imperial Beach Naval Station. Just to the southeast, the Tijuana Bullring-by-the Sea comes into view. At 5th St. (7.3), the route skirts the expansive wetlands of the Tijuana Slough National Wildlife Refuge (walk touring only) and proceeds west to Seacoast Dr.

BICYCLE RIDES: SAN DIEGO COUNTY

Follow the road south 3/4 mile alongside a thread of beachfront homes sandwiched between the mighty Pacific and the slough (take the time to visit inviting and lightly-used Imperial Beach in this area). Return north on this street and visit the Imperial Beach metropolis, a throwback to our youthful days in a smaller, less-developed Newport Beach. The route passes the large local fishing pier and turns west at Palm Ave., then snakes alongside the U.S. Naval Communications Station on the north border of Imperial Beach. At the head of 7th St. (11.6), the biker passes the entry to the Silver Strand bikepath, then follows a 1.9 mile, general southeasterly residential route to Grove Ave. The early portion of this segment is on the signed "Bay Route Bikeway."

Imperial Beach Municipal Pier

About one mile east, cross Saturn Blvd., pass to the right of a large chain-link fence and continue east on the Grove Ave. extension to Hollister St. If returning to Berry Park, turn south and then west on Leon Ave. If the destination is Howard Lane Park, continue across Hollister St. as it becomes Oro Vista Rd. At Iris Rd., follow the freeway overcrossing east as described for the east loop (16.3).

CONNECTING TRIPS: Connection with the Around San Diego Bay tour (Trip #3) - at the north terminus of 7th St., follow the Silver Strand Bikeway north or the Bay Route Bikeway east.

METROPOLITAN SAN DIEGO

TRIP #15 - PARADISE HILLS-SKYLINE LOOP

GENERAL LOCATION: Paradise Hills, Skyline

LEVEL OF DIFFICULTY: Loop - moderate
Distance - 13.7 miles
Elevation gain - continuous moderate grades

DESCRIPTION: You want hills! We got hills! The tour described is on a roller-coaster route through two cities with a steady diet of small hills. The tour starts from Paradise Hills Park and Recreation Center, drops to the edge of National City, then climbs to Skyline Dr. and cruises that ridge route 2-1/2 miles. The road plunges down Briarwood Rd. below Paradise Valley Rd., descends further and less steeply along the southern edge of Paradise Hills, then makes up about 330 feet from Reo Rd. to Bougainville Rd. The trip finale is a short, steep downhill which lets out at the starting point.

The route is predominantly Class X, though most of the pedaling is done on residential streets with modest traffic. There are Pacific Ocean views from the upper western edge of Paradise Hills and looks down into Paradise Valley from Skyline Dr. Best of all, however, is a super view south into the Sweetwater River plain and beyond into Mexico from Briarwood Rd. For easily entertained bikers, track the location of the hard-to-miss Skyline and Paradise Hills water towers on either side of Paradise Valley as you bike the circuit. There are parks scattered along the route and shopping plazas near Skyline Dr./Meadowbrook Dr., Alta View Rd./Woodman St., and above Cumberland St. on Reo Dr.

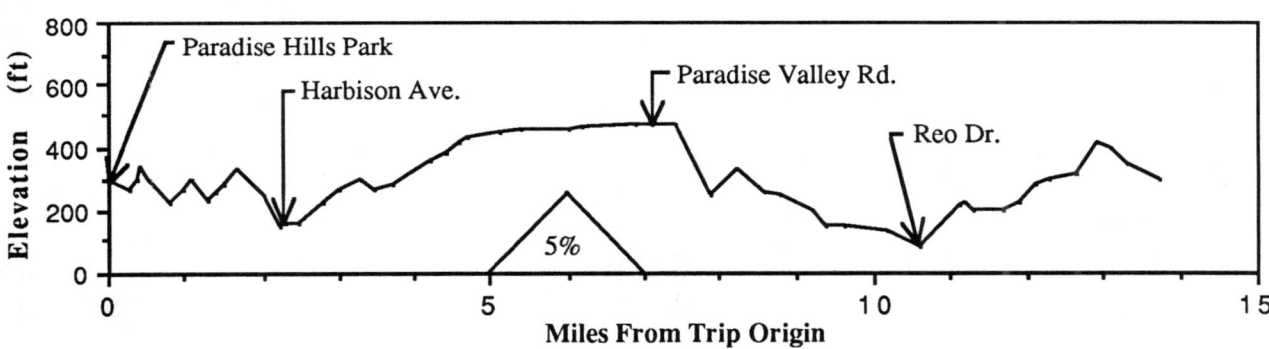

TRAILHEAD: From Interstate Hwy. 805, exit east at Plaza Blvd. and proceed as the road fuses with, and becomes, Paradise Valley Rd. in 1-1/4 miles. In 1-1/2 miles is Potomac St. and the Paradise Hills Park and Recreation Center. The park has picnic benches placed on the grassy slope, scattered tree cover, and walking/bikeway paths, with restrooms and other facilities at the recreation center near the hilltop (just below Alta View Dr.). The large west end of the park is undeveloped grass-covered, tree-studded terrain.

CONNECTING TRIPS: 1) Connection with the Chula Vista Bikeway (Trip #18) - at Tonawanda Dr. and Reo Dr., cross Reo Dr. and follow what is now Valley Rd. to Sweetwater Rd.; turn left, cross over County Hwy. S17, then turn right at Plaza Bonita

BICYCLE RIDES: SAN DIEGO COUNTY

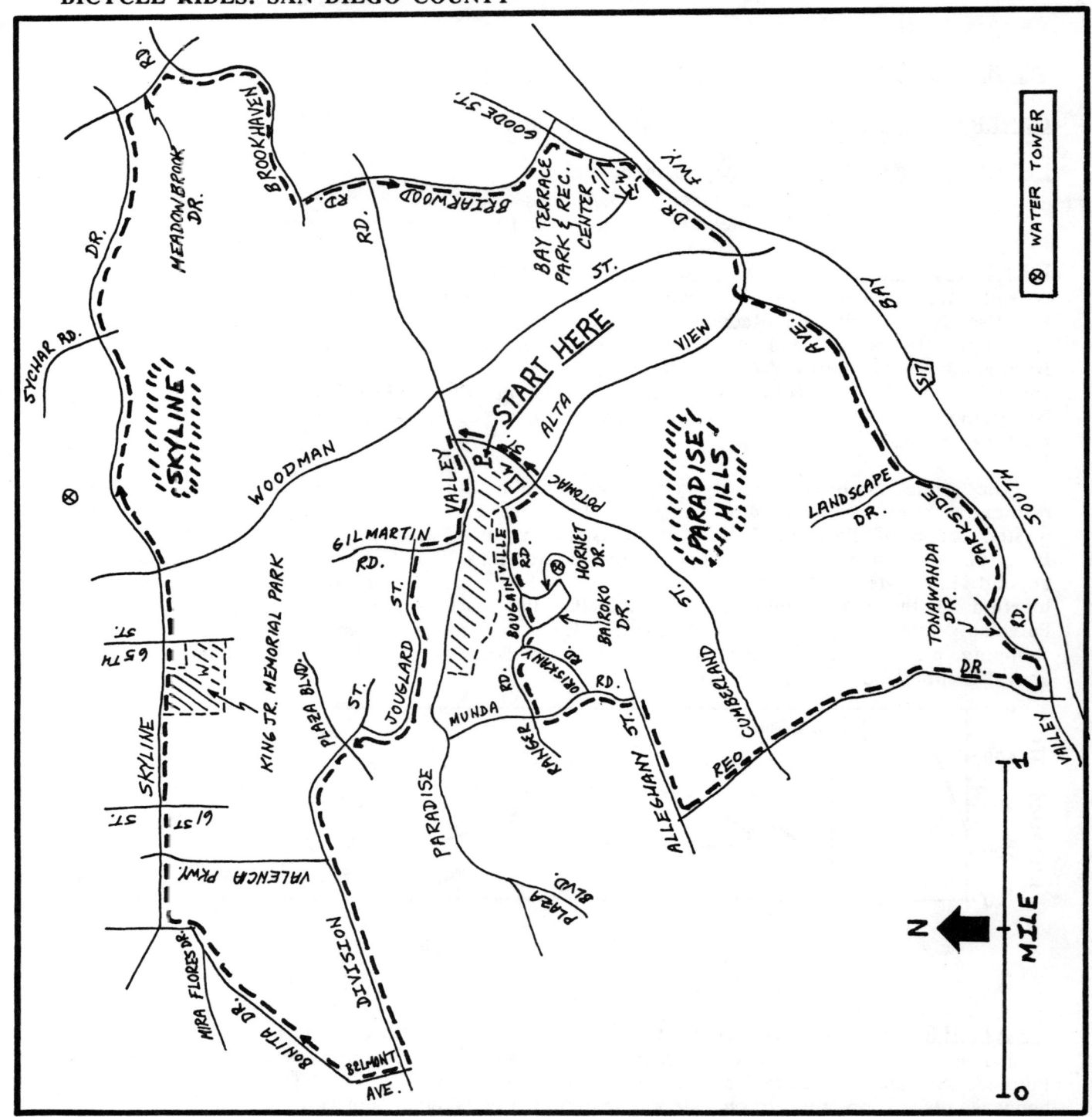

TRIP #15 - PARADISE HILLS-SKYLINE LOOP

Rd.; 2) connection with the Sweetwater River to Lower Otay Lake ride (Trip #19) - same as for Trip #18, except continue on Sweetwater Rd. beyond Plaza Bonita Rd.

METROPOLITAN SAN DIEGO

TRIP #16 - LAKE MURRAY

GENERAL LOCATION: La Mesa

LEVEL OF DIFFICULTY: Up and back - easy
Distance - 6.0 miles (up and back)
Elevation gain - essentially flat

DESCRIPTION Lake Murray and the Lake Murray Park and Recreation Center are the developed southern edge of the expansive Mission Trails Regional Park. The northern section consists of a relatively natural area dominated by boulder-strewn Cowles and Fortuna Mountains. From the parking area near the entrance, the tour proceeds counterclockwise 2.8 miles before reaching a locked gate just short of the dam on the west side. Hitch a boat ride (ha!) or cycle back to the trip origin.

The pleasant lakeside tour transits the five main lake fingers on asphalt path that is closed to auto traffic. Along the way are both chaparral and tree-covered segments, short walking-paths along the lakes and under the scattered tree cover, and the designated fishing areas occupied by America's most laid-back sportsmen. Take time to enjoy the water fowl spread around the lake -- we particularly enjoyed the egrets and ducks within the fifth finger.

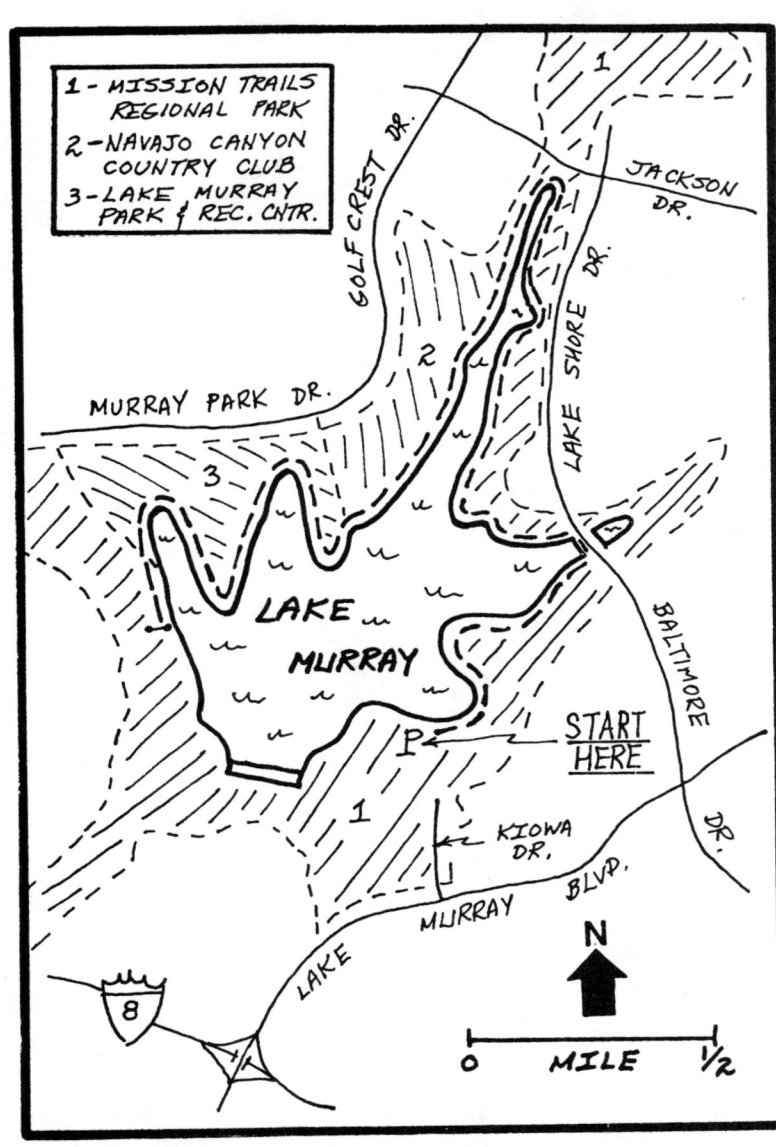

TRIP #16 - LAKE MURRAY

BICYCLE RIDES: SAN DIEGO COUNTY

TRAILHEAD: From Interstate Hwy. 8, exit north at Lake Murray Blvd. and drive 3/4 mile to Kiowa Dr. Turn left and continue into the main parking area. The park area has picnic facilities, boat rentals, sparse tree cover and restrooms.

"Mellow" Lake Murray

CONNECTING TRIPS: 1) Connection with the El Cajon Bikeway System (Trip #31) - return to Lake Murray Blvd. and follow that road to Navajo Rd., continue east and turn left at Fletcher Pkwy.; 2) connection with the San Diego River Run (Trip #17) - near the Lake Murray Park and Recreation Center, follow Murray Park Dr. as it becomes Golfcrest Dr.

TRIP #17 - SAN DIEGO RIVER RUN

GENERAL LOCATION: Ocean Beach, Santee, El Capitan Reservoir

LEVEL OF DIFFICULTY: One way - moderate
Distance - 30.2 miles
Elevation gain - periodic moderate grades, single steep grade south of Mission Gorge

GENERAL DESCRIPTION: This generally flat tour follows the San Diego River from its ocean outlet to the mountain-surrounded El Capitan Reservoir 30 miles distant. In between, the cyclist navigates the Mission Valley commercial centers before returning to a less-developed area just south of Mission Trails Regional Park. In this park is a super-scenic tour of Mission Gorge. A subsequent spin through the cities of

METROPOLITAN SAN DIEGO

Santee and Lakeview leads to the El Monte Rd. segment, another of the trip's highlights. Six miles of pedaling on this scenic rural road leads from a farming valley in the foothills to a narrow tree-filled canyon terminus at the reservoir.

Families not interested in the 30-miler can explore the Ocean Beach area near the trip's origin. The 2-1/2-mile spin visits North Ocean Beach, Dog Beach and provides a short Class I cruise alongside the San Diego River.

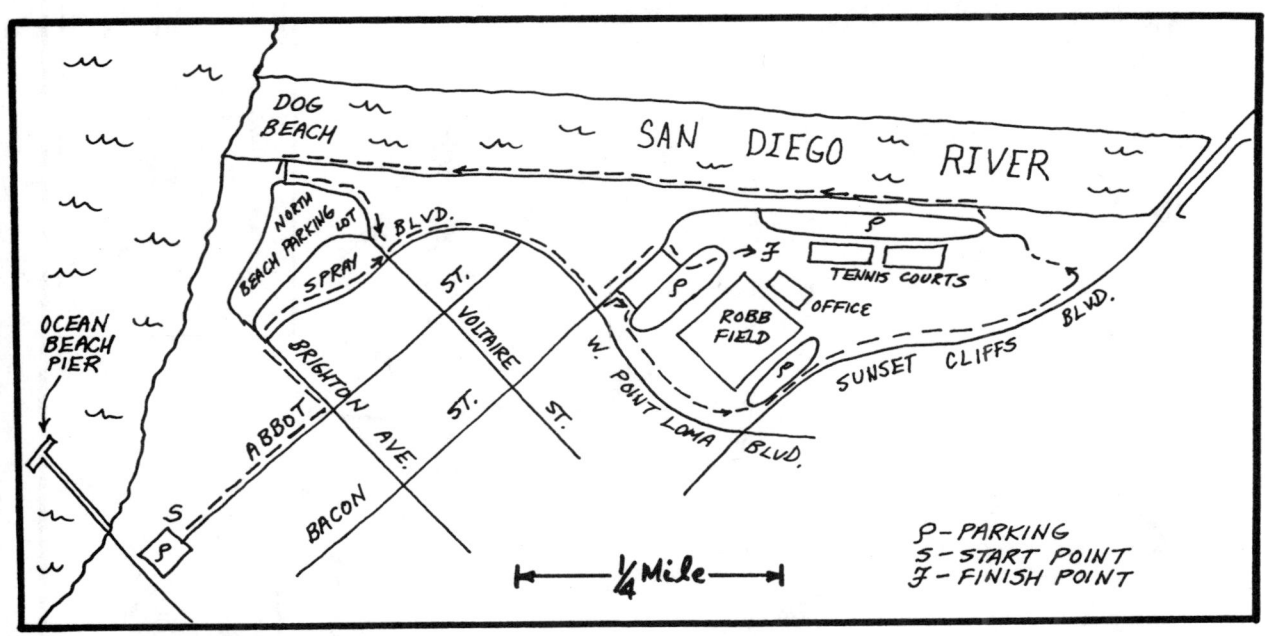

Ocean Beach: A Local Favorite Path (Compliments of the Ocean Beach Athletic Area Staff)

TRAILHEAD: From Interstate 5 northbound, exit at Interstate Hwy. 8 west. Continue to the freeway terminus at Sunset Cliffs Blvd. Turn left (southwest), drive 1/4 mile to West Point Loma Blvd. and turn right in 1/4 mile at the entrance (across from Bacon St.) to the Ocean Beach Athletic Area. From I-5 southbound, exit at Rosecrans St., proceeding southeast 3/4 mile to Sports Arena Blvd. Turn right and continue to the intersection of Sports Arena Blvd., Midway Dr., and West Point Loma Blvd. Veer slightly left on the latter road and continue 1-3/4 mile to the park entrance. This large park has a wide array of athletic fields/courts, children's play area, water and restrooms.

TRIP DESCRIPTION: Ocean Beach to Mission Gorge. Follow the Class I path along the San Diego River to Sunset Cliffs Blvd., then take the <u>westside</u> bikeway/walkway on the bridge. Cross the river, against traffic, on the Class I path and exit at the next <u>on</u>-ramp; keep to the left. At Quivera Wy., turn left again and look for a small southward-heading Class I access path. The connecting Class I bikeway/roadway leads east under the Sunset Cliffs Dr. and Mission Bay Dr. bridges, then passes alongside the eye-catching Sea World spire. The road cruises 1.3 miles alongside the San Diego River to Friars Rd. on a stretch where there are excellent views southeast of the San Diego skyline and north to the coastal mountains and mesas. Turn right onto Friars Rd. and enjoy a 2-1/4 mile Class II spin through the land of condominiums and golf courses. At Fashion Valley Rd., the route crosses Mission Valley and the river plain on the eastern edge of the Stardust Country Club.

BICYCLE RIDES: SAN DIEGO COUNTY

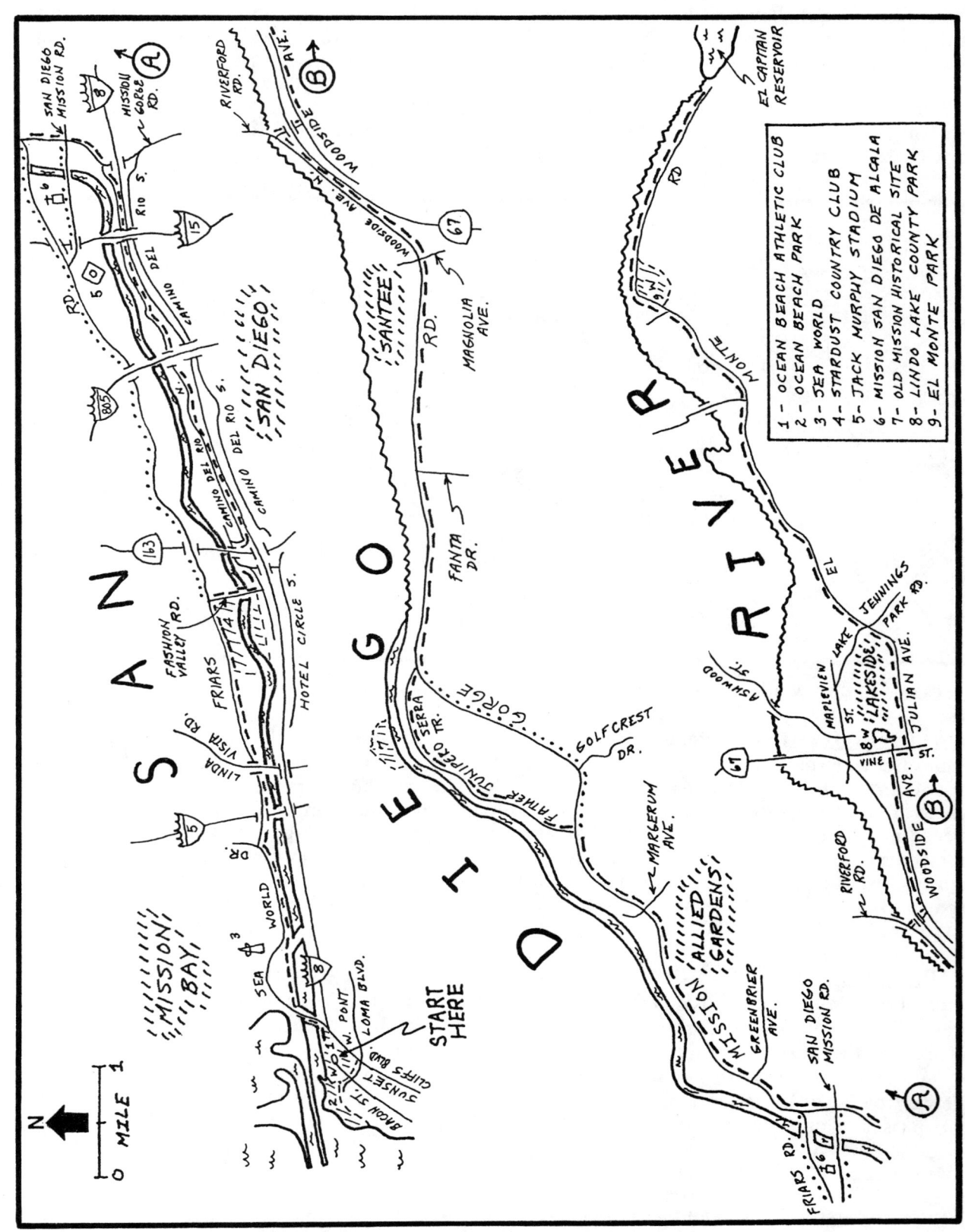

TRIP #17 - SAN DIEGO RIVER RUN

METROPOLITAN SAN DIEGO

Where the San Diego River Meets the Ocean

A left turn onto Hotel Circle N./Camino De La Reina takes the cyclist on a five-mile variable Class X/Class II tour alongside shopping centers, fast-food meccas and condominiums. In this stretch, turn right just past the State Hwy. 163 undercrossing on Camino De La Siesta to reach Camino Del Rio N. Keep an eye peeled for traffic pulling out from the shopping areas in this stretch. There are interesting looks at the long, continuous mesa which borders Mission Valley to the south, a passby of Jack Murphy Stadium, and a fine neck-straining view of the elevated I-805 structures from directly below. The route turns north onto busy Mission Gorge Rd., navigates about a mile through heavy commercial territory, then weaves right (east) after swallowing up Friars Rd. The path then transitions to Class II. After a two-mile flat stretch, the biker is greeted with a 300-foot upgrade which peaks just north of Margerum Ave. While doing this workout, there are views to the left into the quarries at the north of Mission Gorge and directly ahead to undeveloped Mission Trail Regional Park. In another one-half mile is the turnoff to Mission Gorge at Father Junipero Serra Trail (13.7). Note that there is an option to continue on Mission Gorge Rd.; however, the route is far less scenic and involves another 350-foot of climb.

Mission Gorge to Lakeside. The less-traveled Class X road sinks slowly into the narrowing gorge. The neck-craning views of the unnamed peaks on either side provides a sharp contrast to the prior valley segments. In 1-3/4 miles is the earthen Old Mission Dam and the Old Mission Dam Historical site -- a throwback to some of Father Serra's earliest efforts to settle Southern California. In another 3/4 mile, the cyclist emerges from the gorge and returns to the San Diego River plain, smack at the edge of the City of Santee. The now Class II path cruises 4.5 miles through a scattered mix of commercial/light industrial establishments (including numerous mini-markets and eateries).

Near Mesa Rd., the biker gets an initial look at distant El Cajon Mountain. This is a dominant peak almost due east with a sheer south face, reminiscent of Yosemite's El Capitan. The mountain just happens to overlook El Capitan Reservoir, our trip

BICYCLE RIDES: SAN DIEGO COUNTY

destination. At Magnolia Ave. on the east side of Santee, the route veers northeast and follows Woodside Ave., a frontage road alongside State Hwy. 62. The three-mile segment on this road leads the biker into the hamlet of Lakeside near Lindo Lake County Park (22.7).

Lakeside to El Capitan Reservoir. Just beyond Lakeview Rd., Julian Ave. veers sharply left and becomes El Monte Rd. The remaining six-mile tour is on this two-lane rural roadway. The route crosses Lake Jennings Park Rd., with its mini-mart and gas station, then heads directly towards the local mountains. The road follows the San Diego River on the south edge of a wide valley, replete with numerous small farms and ranches. Four miles of pedaling in this serene surrounding leads the cyclist by the El Monte Park (tree cover, barbecue facilities, sports fields, general store). Here the wide valley begins to compress and the biker navigates an uphill in an ever-narrowing tree-covered canyon. The fall tree foliage is gorgeous here! El Cajon Mountain dominates the northern landscape. Just a quarter-mile before reaching the El Capitan Dam is the first sighting of the landmark. The winding path continues to the dam, open for boating and fishing on weekends (30.2).

Trip Option. A trip generally confined to the trails and less traveled streets of Ocean Beach is provided in the Ocean Beach detail map above. This is an excellent family short tour.

Friends along El Monte Road

CONNECTING TRIPS: See connector trips for detailed connection information. Connection with: 1) Mission Bay Loop (Trip #1); 2) Seaport Village to Point Loma (Trip #4); 3) Old Town Tour (Trip #9); 4) Overlooking Mission Valley (Trip #10); 5) San Diego 59-Mile Scenic Dr. (Trip #11); 6) Lake Murray (Trip #16); 7) Coastal County Tour (Trip #21); 8) El Cajon Bikeway System (Trip #31); 9) Santee Lakes (Trip #32); 10) Old Hwy. 395 (Trip #38); 11) Eucalyptus Hills (Trip #41); 12) Lakeside-Lakeview Loop (Trip #42); 13) Wildcat Canyon (Trip #54).

METROPOLITAN SAN DIEGO

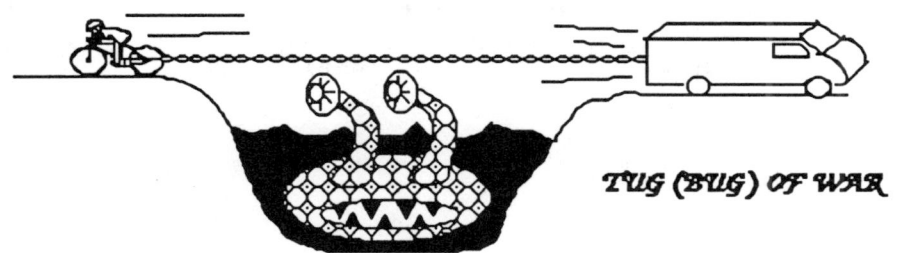

TUG (BUG) OF WAR

TRIP #18 - CHULA VISTA BIKEWAY

GENERAL LOCATION: Chula Vista

LEVEL OF DIFFICULTY: Loop - moderate
Distance - 12.0 miles
Elevation gain - steady moderate grade on Telegraph Canyon Rd.

DESCRIPTION: This Class II loop gives the cyclist a chance to observe the transition of Chula Vista from a small pocket development surrounded by rural environs to a spreading urban center. At 0.4 mile from Hilltop Park, the route turns east at Telegraph Canyon Rd. From this junction, the cyclist is treated to a steady four-mile modest upgrade (250-foot climb) which is equally split between developed residential areas and still underdeveloped rolling hillsides. The transition occurs near Paseo Ladera; the illusion of being in the country is mildly dampened by the wide separated roadway, built in anticipation of future traffic needs (4.9).

Sweetwater River Trail

At Otay Lakes Rd., there are scattered views of both Mother Miguel and San Miguel Mountains to the northeast in this and several other areas of the trip. The route turns north and proceeds uphill, reaching a trip crest near the Southwestern Community College campus. In this area are new housing tracts and shopping

BICYCLE RIDES: SAN DIEGO COUNTY

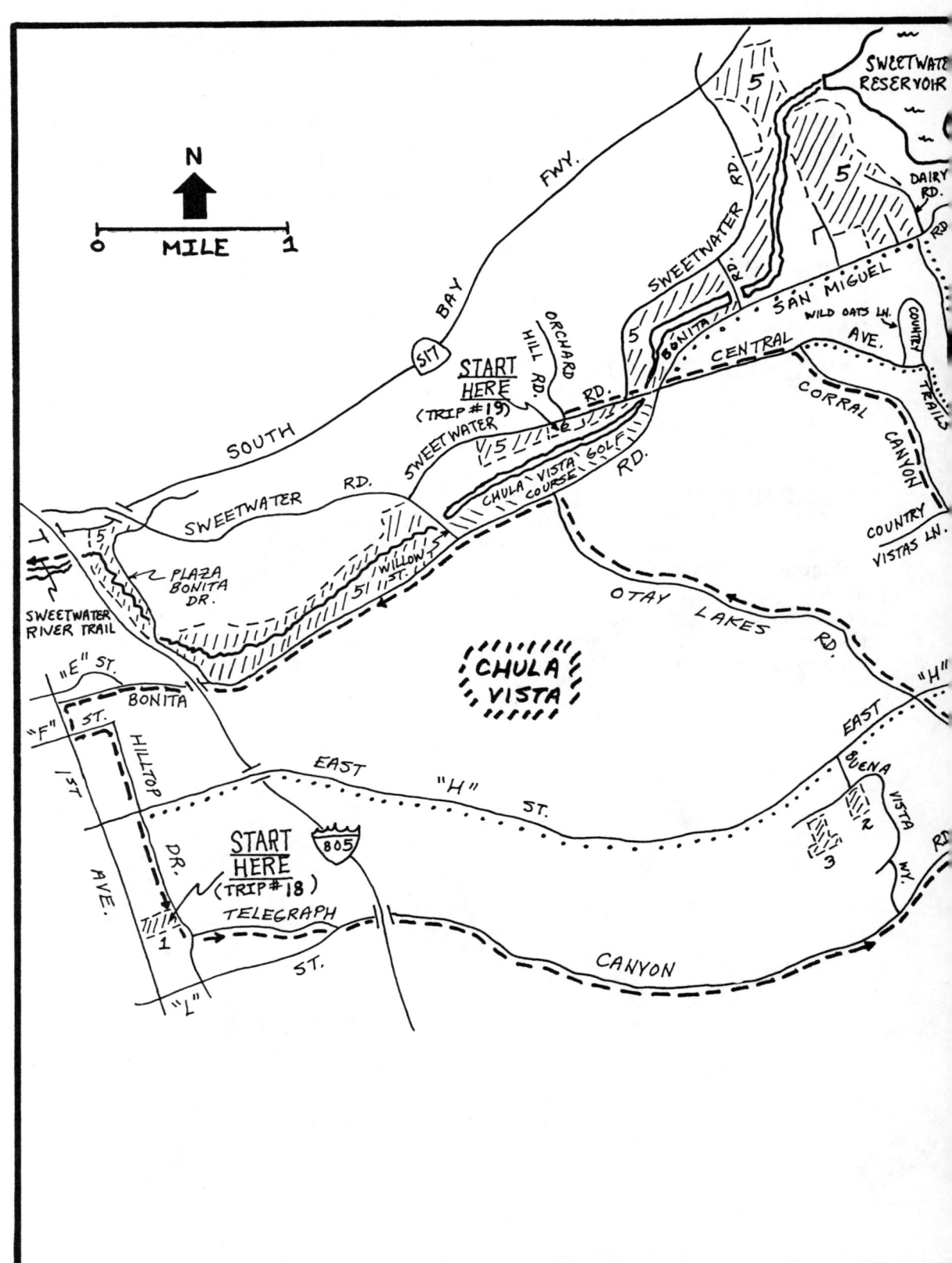

TRIPS #18 and #19 - CHULA VISTA BIKEWAY and

METROPOLITAN SAN DIEGO

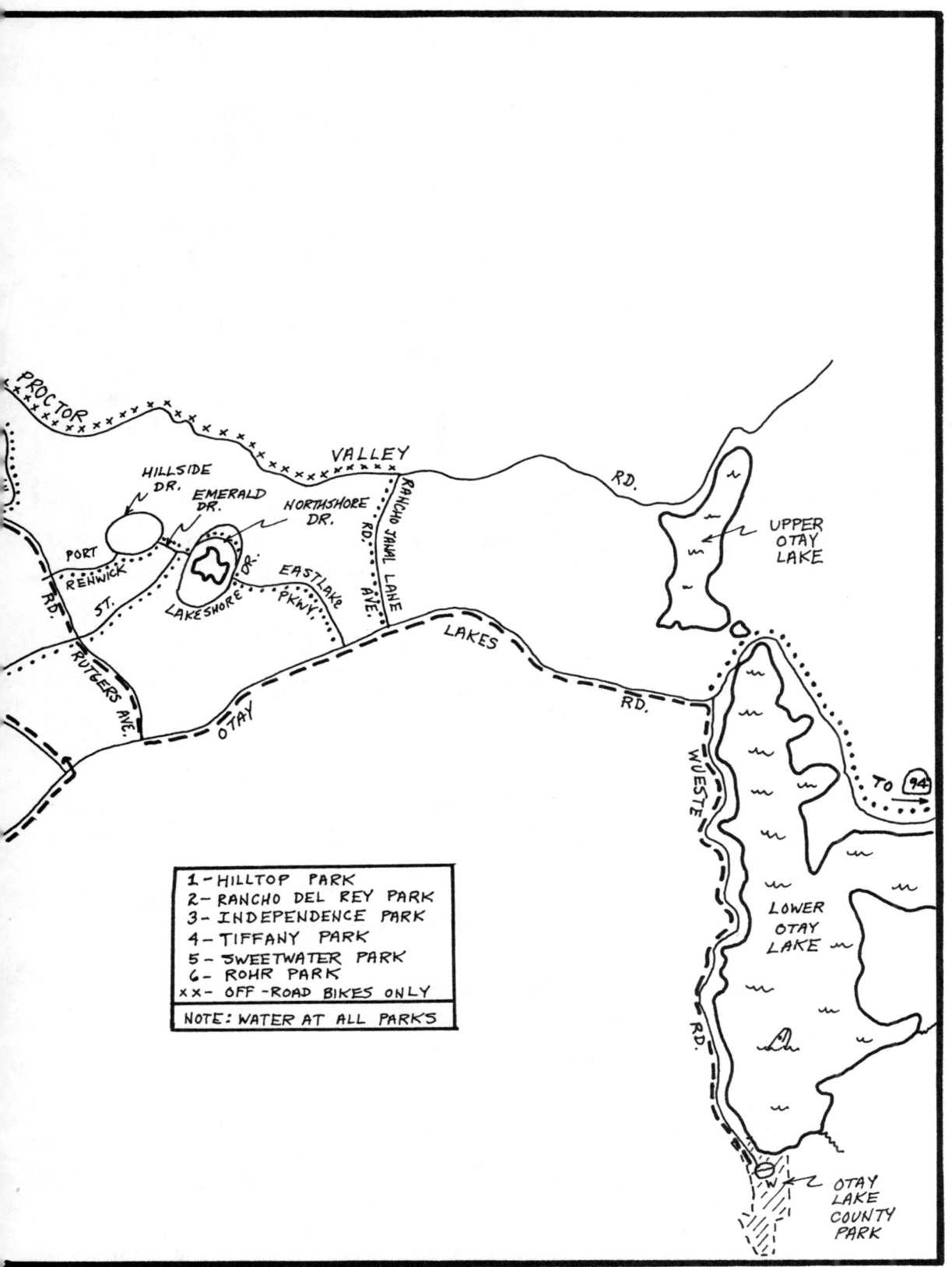

SWEETWATER PARK TO LOWER OTAY LAKE

BICYCLE RIDES: SAN DIEGO COUNTY

centers, as well as the beginning of a rewarding three-mile downhill through scattered dense developments built on the surrounding bluffs and hillsides. At Bonita Rd. is one of several shopping centers/mini-malls in an area seemingly dominated to the south by condominiums and apartments. For the three-mile return to Chula Vista proper, the segment highlight is Sweetwater Park to the north, where scenery ranges from golf courses to the lush Sweetwater River bottomlands. Just west of the Interstate Hwy. 805 undercrossing, the cyclist turns south on First Ave. and follows a weaving route back to Hilltop Park (12.0).

Sweetwater River Trail. Just west of the Plaza Bonita Shopping Center, roughly 300 yards from Sweetwater Rd., is the unmarked eastern entry to the river trail. Look for a light dirt trail that leads, in about 50 yards, to a group of sunken posts which block off motorized traffic. The asphalt path, on the river's north edge, takes the biker along a tree-rich riverbottom, under the Interstate Hwy. 805 overpasses, then onto a 1-1/2 mile stretch alongside the now water-filled river. Along the way, enjoy the wide variety of waterfowl. The path ends near the intersection of Hoover Ave. and 33rd St. in National City. Unless your plans are to link up with the Around San Diego Bay tour (Trip #3), return the way you came (4-1/2 mile round trip).

<u>**TRAILHEAD**</u>: From I-805, exit west at Telegraph Canyon Rd. In 1/4 mile, turn right to stay on that road (continuing straight ahead places you on E. "L" St.), and drive one mile to Hilltop Dr. Turn right and drive into the Hilltop Park entrance. From I-5, exit east at "J" St. Drive two miles to Hilltop Dr., turn right and continue 1/4 mile to the park.

<u>**CONNECTING TRIPS**</u>: 1) Connection with the Sweetwater Park to Lower Otay Lake (Trip #19) - bike east from the Lower Otay Lakes Rd./Bonita Rd. intersection on the latter street; 2) connection with the Paradise Hills-Skyline Loop (Trip #15) - from Plaza Bonita Dr., take Sweetwater Rd. over County Hwy. S17.

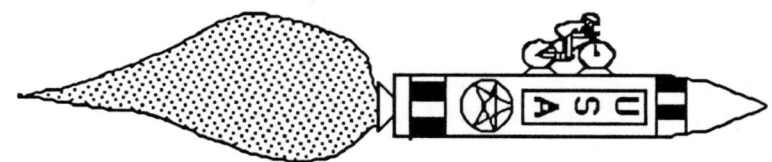

TRIP #19 - SWEETWATER PARK TO LOWER OTAY LAKE

<u>**GENERAL LOCATION**</u>:   Chula Vista, Lower Otay Lake

<u>**LEVEL OF DIFFICULTY**</u>: One way - moderate
Distance - 9.4 miles
Elevation gain - periodic moderate grades

<u>**GENERAL DESCRIPTION**</u>: The primary tour leaves Rohr Park within Sweetwater Park, then follows Corral Canyon Rd. on the newly built-up rolling hills of eastern Chula Vista to Otay Lakes Rd. A three-mile easterly tour on this road leads the cyclist into lightly-developed rolling hills where there are dandy views of the Jamul Mountains (east) and the more imposing San Ysidro Mountains (southeast). At road's end is Lower Otay Lake County Park. The return leg repeats the incoming route for

METROPOLITAN SAN DIEGO

about five miles, then turns into the residential East Lake and Country Trails areas (21.6 miles for up and back tour).

Two alternate or add-on tours are also provided. One eight-mile (one-way) pedal examines the full length of Sweetwater Park from the western edge near Plaza Bonita to the eastern edge below the Sweetwater Reservoir. The other travels 2-1/2 miles (one-way) on a Class I stretch of bikeway along the Sweetwater River west of the park.

TRAILHEAD: From Interstate Hwy. 805, exit east at Bonita Rd., drive 1-3/4 miles to Willow St. and turn left. Proceed 1/4 mile to Sweetwater Rd. and turn right. In about one mile near Orchard Hill Rd. is the entrance to Fred H. Rohr Park. From I-5, exit at "E" St. (County Hwy. S17) and continue east to I-805, where the street is now called Bonita Rd. Continue as described above. The park has restrooms, grassy fields, scattered tree cover and picnic facilities.

TRIP DESCRIPTION: Sweetwater Park to Lower Otay Lake County Park. Follow Sweetwater Rd. eastward, continuing straight ahead at the junction with Class X Central Ave., which puts you onto that road. In 0.7 mile from the Bonita Rd. junction is Corral Canyon Rd. For the next 2-1/2 miles, the cyclist follows that Class II road on a general upgrade (almost 400-foot gain) through scattered dense residential pockets. The road becomes Rutgers Ave. beyond E. "H" St. After cresting near Ithaca St., the biker is treated to a 0.3-mile steep downgrade which ends at Otay Lakes Rd. Turning east onto this street, the pedaler stares head-on into the Jamul Mountains. The subsequent three-mile Class II spin to the Lower Otay Lake entry at Wueste Rd. (6.3) passes through rolling, grassy countryside, where there were numerous subtle signs of impending development.

Lower Otay Lake

At Wueste Rd. is a spectacular distant view of the immense, dominant peak of the San Ysidro Mountains, Otay Mountain. This range separates San Diego from Mexico in this area of the county. From the entry, the route follows the undulating lake contour on generally barren slopes, in constant view of this water storage basin. At

BICYCLE RIDES: SAN DIEGO COUNTY

the lake's southern edge is a dense tree stand and Lower Otay Lake County Park (9.4). The park has family and group picnic and camping sites, as well as boating and fishing in season.

Extended Country Tour. The cyclist can add sixteen excellent (round-trip) biking miles on Lower Otay Rd. beyond Wueste Rd. This is cycling through relatively undeveloped scenic wonderland. The road crosses between Lower and Upper Otay Lakes, then follows the general contour of the lower lake's eastern arm, tracking Dulzura Creek beneath the Jamul Mountains. Otay Mountain looms to the south as the route passes a glider/skydiving center, then reaches the Thousand Trails Resort, where there is a general store. The road narrows just beyond, breaks into a wide, flat flood plain then reaches State Hwy. 94 in two miles beyond the resort.

Return Options. Enjoy the park and thank your patient friend who will shuttle you back to the starting point, if desired. If this option is not available, there are two return alternatives: **One route** is pedal back about 4.8 miles to East Lake Pkwy. and follow both the Lakeshore Dr. and Hillside Dr. loops before returning to Corral Canyon Rd. at Port Renwick/Thorton Rd. One mile further north on Corral Canyon Dr., turn east onto Country Vistas Ln. At the next intersection, a left turn places the cyclist on Country Trails Ln. which leads to a turn west at the origin of Central Ave. A beeline route on Central Ave. returns the cyclist to the trip origin (10.2-mile return). The **second alternative** (off-road bikes only) is to return 4.5 miles and turn north at Lane Ave., then bike 0.8 mile to unpaved Proctor Valley Rd. Turn left and wheel along this packed dirt roadway in open countryside, enjoying the view and the sounds of silence. In several miles, Proctor Valley Rd. returns to pavement and residential development, then meets San Miguel Rd. in 3.3 miles. Another 1.6 miles on San Miguel Rd./Bonita Rd. and a right turn at Central Ave. returns the cyclist to the starting point (10.9-mile return).

Sweetwater Park. There are two ways to bike the park: one is to ride on the peripheral streets, and the other more exciting option is to visit off-road by following the Sweetwater River channel (in low water periods only!). From Rohr Park, bike west on Sweetwater Rd. to the intersection with Willow St. Just across Willow St. is the unmarked dirt path entry into the river bed. For on-roaders, follow Willow St. south to Bonita Rd. and bike that Class II road 1-1/2 miles to Plaza Bonita Rd., then follow that street another one mile to Plaza Bonita. The loop can be closed by following Sweetwater Rd. 2-3/4 miles back to the park on Class II roadway. The cyclist can also cycle Sweetwater Rd. east and north, following the river edge 2-1/2 miles to Quarry Rd. A 1-1/2-mile pedal on that road, followed by a 1/2-mile direction reversal on Lakeview Ave., leads to the foot of the Sweetwater Reservoir Dam.

<u>**CONNECTING TRIPS**</u>: 1) Connection with the Chula Vista Bikeway (Trip #18) - at the intersection of Central Ave. and Bonita Rd., bike west on the latter road ; 2) connection with the Paradise Hills-Skyline Loop (Trip #15) - from Rohr Park, bike east on Sweetwater Rd.

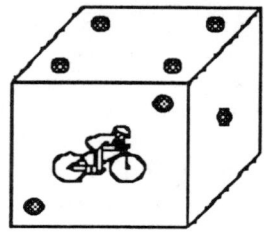

76

TRIP #20 - LAKE MIRAMAR MEANDER

GENERAL LOCATION: Scripps Miramar Ranch

LEVEL OF DIFFICULTY: Loop - easy
Distance - 4.8 miles
Elevation gain - essentially flat

Patient Fishermen and Cyclists' Reflections

DESCRIPTION: Lake Miramar is equally popular amongst bikers, walkers and joggers -- all anxious to work out on this almost five-mile lakeside loop. From the south shore, the route looks deceptively short, but the asphalt path meanders along the many lake fingers, thus extending the mileage. An easy counter-clockwise tour will take the biker 3.8 miles on a road shared with limited traffic, restricted to a 10-m.p.h. limit. Stop and enjoy the flora and waterfowl along the scenic route, particularly at the lake fingers. At 3.8 miles, a barricade filters out the auto traffic and the biker is left to cycle atop the western-side earthen dam before returning the to start point. Mileage addicts can circumnavigate the lake as many times as their hearts desire.

Scripps-Miramar Option. Take some additional time to explore the roads off Scripps Lake Dr. further east. This is a pleasant, low-key neighborhood cycling area with moderate elevation change. Bring an auto road map.

TRAILHEAD: From Interstate Hwy. 15, exit east at Mira Mesa Blvd. Continue 1/4 mile to the street's terminus, turn right on Scripps Ranch Blvd., and drive 1/3 mile to Scripps Lake Dr. In another 1/2 mile is the marked entrance to the lake; however, a solid double line and lack of a turn lane suggests that the driver should continue east and make a U-turn to gain access. The park has picnic/barbecue facilities on the south shore, where there is scattered tree cover, restrooms, boat rentals and a concession stand near the boat ramp. A couple of intense fisherman we met touted the lake for its fine Florida bass and trout.

CONNECTING TRIPS: 1) Connection with Old. Hwy. 395 (Trip #38) - return to Scripps Ranch Blvd. and bike beyond Mira Mesa Blvd. to Erma Rd.; 2) connection with the Rancho Bernardo (Trip #33) - follow the Old Hwy. 395 connector above to Poway Rd.

BICYCLE RIDES: SAN DIEGO COUNTY

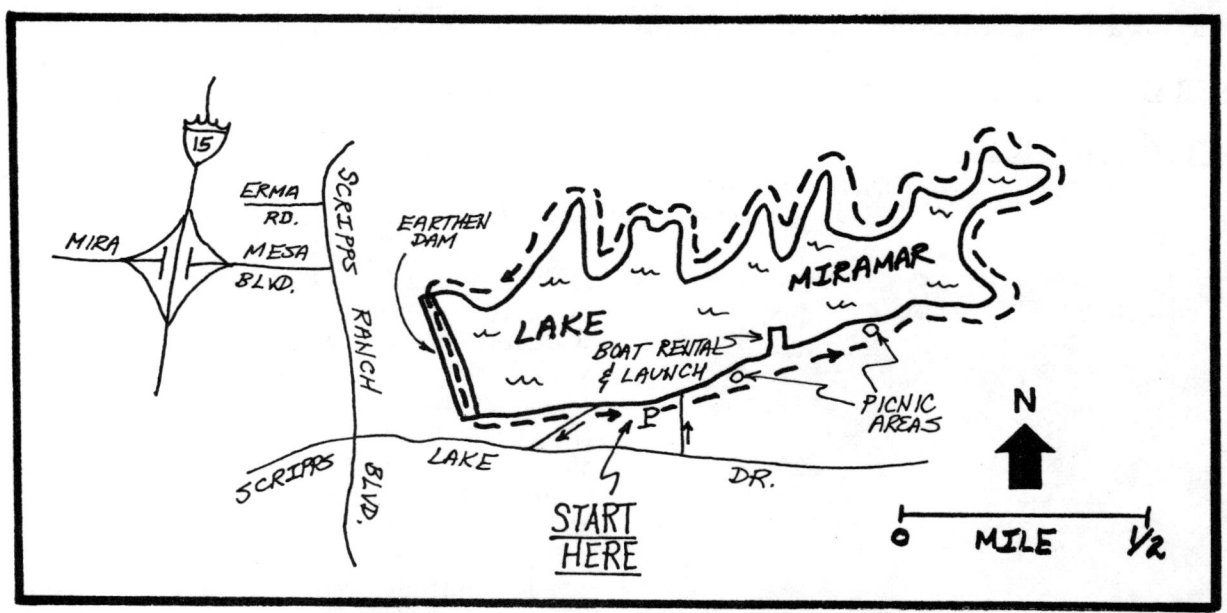

TRIP #20 - LAKE MIRAMAR MEANDER

TRIP #21 - COASTAL COUNTY TOUR

GENERAL LOCATION: San Diego-Carlsbad-Oceanside-Camp Pendleton-San Clemente

LEVEL OF DIFFICULTY: One way - strenuous
Distance - 67.2 miles (one way)
Elevation gain - periodic moderate-to-steep grades; steep grades at La Jolla Shores Dr. (San Diego) and S21 south of Del Mar

GENERAL DESCRIPTION: A perennial favorite of ours, this odyssey follows the Pacific Coast Bicentennial Bike Route. Few trips that we've ridden have the variety and natural scenic beauty of this coastal tour. This classic starts by visiting the Embarcadero, plies the periphery of San Diego Bay and Mission Bay, then visits La Jolla. After a testy climb above La Jolla Shores, the route skirts U.C.S.D., then visits Torrey Pines State Reserve, and provides a super-scenic downhill run to Torrey Pines State Beach. Next is a 23-mile segment which tours the beaches and lagoons from Del Mar to Oceanside. A Camp Pendleton roller coaster tour of the mesas is next, followed by a ride along the bluffs of San Onofre and trip's end near the Orange County Line.

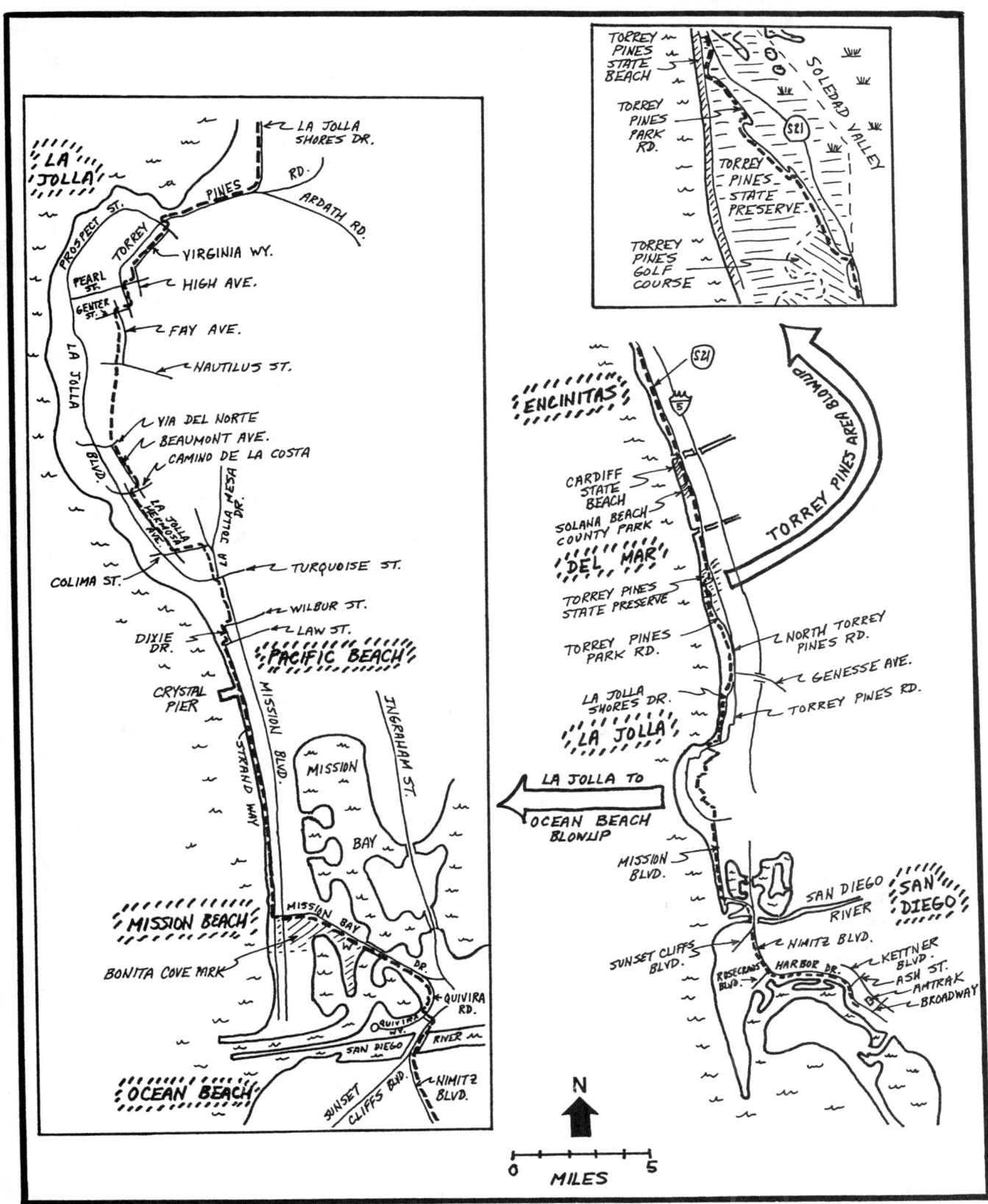

TRIP #21 - COASTAL COUNTY TOUR (SOUTHERN SEGMENT)

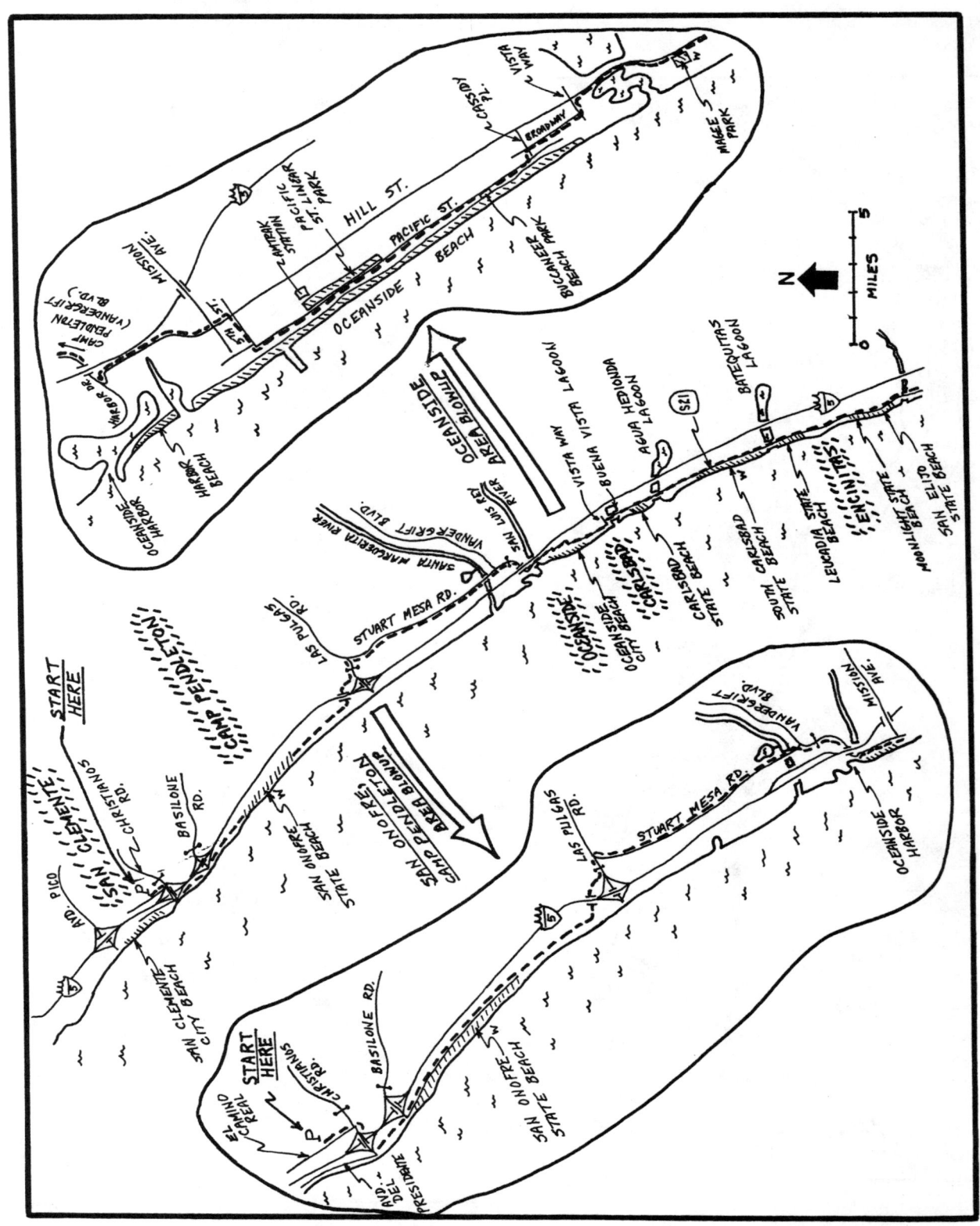

TRIP #21 - COASTAL COUNTY TOUR (NORTHERN SEGMENT)

METROPOLITAN SAN DIEGO

There is an option to end the trip at Oceanside or Santa Ana and take the AMTRAK on the return leg. Refer to the detailed trip description and information.

TRAILHEAD: From Interstate Hwy. 5 southbound, exit at Front St. and drive south. Turn right at any convenient cross street and drive five blocks to Kettner Blvd. Continue south, cross Harbor Dr. and follow to road's end at Embarcadero Marina Park. The park has restrooms, tree cover, benches and great vantage points for watching the U.S. Navy sail the harbor. If a start/finish point shuttle cannot be arranged, park instead in a pay parking lot.

TRIP DESCRIPTION: **San Diego Bay.** (See Trip #4 for additional details.) Leave Embarcadero Marina Park and pedal on the bay periphery on a Class I bikeway/walkway. Cruise the Embarcadero and continue on the bayside path as it turns north, passes alongside the San Diego International Airport and crosses Harbor Island Dr. near the landmark Sheraton Hotel (2.0). Just beyond is the continuation of the Class I path which meanders through the cozy mile-long thread of Spanish Landing Park. Pass on a bridge over an inlet alongside the U.S. Naval Training Center and observe the cement-bound U.S.S. Recruit "floating" majestically directly ahead. The distant backdrop is the long, high spine of Point Loma.

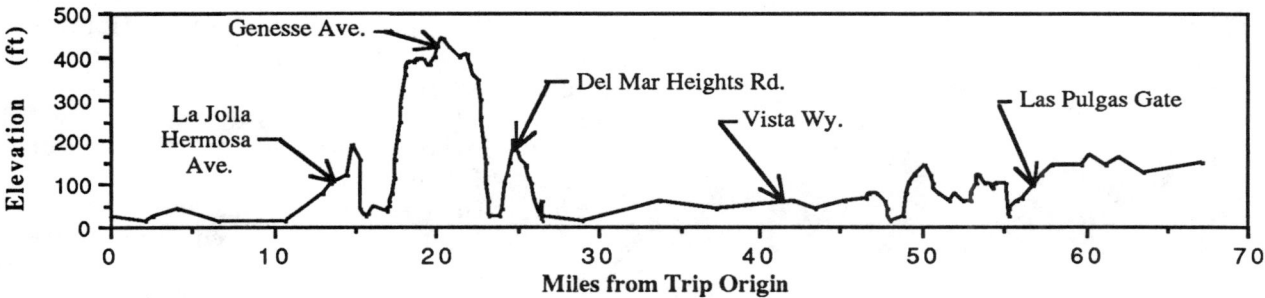

Point Loma to Mission Bay. At the Fleet Anti-Submarine Warfare School, turn northwest onto busy Class II Nimitz Blvd., which jogs north and beelines through primarily residential neighborhoods. Pass expansive Collier Park (baseball and other recreation fields, water on the east side) and cycle onward to the Ocean Beach Athletic Area near the Sunset Cliffs Blvd. intersection (6.5). Carefully cross to the opposite (west) side of Sunset Cliffs Blvd. and cross the bridge over the San Diego River (keep a close watch for on-coming cyclists).

Mission Bay to La Jolla. (See Trip #1 for additional details.) Exit the first on-ramp (remember that the route is going against traffic) and take the first left which places the cyclist on Quivera Rd. Turn at the next right, then left (northwest) at Mission Bay Dr., biking onto the bridge over the Mission Bay Channel. Stop and enjoy the spectacular 360-degree view from this open structure.

Follow Mission Bay Dr. as it veers left alongside Bonita Cove Park and becomes Ventura Pl. Here is a recently refurbished amusement park and an entry to the strand walkway/bikeway (Ocean Front Walk). A 1.9-mile cruise on this scenic and frequently-crowded path (an option is to use the Bayside Walk and return to the beach via Pacific Beach Dr.) leads through Pacific Beach, where the cyclist reaches the north end of the strand path near Law St. (10.8). A subsequent patchwork of turns leads the biker north to the intersection of Colima St. and La Jolla Hermosa Ave.

BICYCLE RIDES: SAN DIEGO COUNTY

Blowup of La Jolla to Del Mar segment.

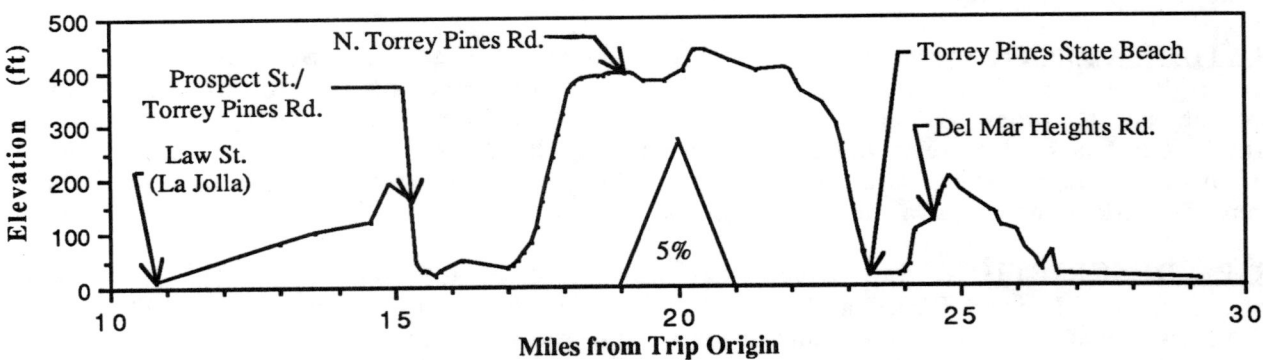

Bicycling Break at Torrey Pines State Beach

La Jolla to Torrey Pines State Beach. (See Trips #6 and 12 for additional details.) The cyclist is treated to a refreshing Class II downhill on Torrey Pines Rd., with enjoyable views of La Jolla Heights closeup and to the right and the La Jolla Shores/La Jolla Bay area to the left. In 0.9 mile is a very complex and busy intersection, where the biker turns left (north) onto La Jolla Shores Dr. A mile of flat gives way to a mild upgrade, which gets downright nasty (steep) near the Scripps Institute of Oceanography (17.5). A "mere" 0.6 mile and a switch-back-plus later, the cyclist has pumped 250 feet (8% grade) through a nicely wooded area to reach Azul St. The route maintains a steady, mild upgrade as it follows N. Torrey Pines Rd. alongside U.C.S.D., passes Torrey Pines Scenic Dr., and bends east just before returning north after the busy Genesee Ave. (20.2) intersection.

Just beyond, the route reaches a summit and begins a mild 0.7-mile downgrade through tree-lined streets before turning left on Callans Rd. The next 1.9-mile exhilarating stretch takes the cyclist along the plush Torrey Pines Golf Course, into the natural beauty of the Torrey Pines State Preserve, and onto a super-scenic, one-mile, 350-foot downgrade which lets the biker out at Torrey Pines State Beach.

Del Mar to Carlsbad. The tour route returns to Class II County Hwy. S21 and crosses a giant seaside lagoon play area, then follows a steady upgrade into the southern outskirts of Del Mar. In 1-1/2 miles from the bridge over the lagoon, this

METROPOLITAN SAN DIEGO

segment reaches a crest, passes Del Mar Heights Rd. (24.5) and begins a slow-paced downgrade through a pleasant commercial area with several upscale hotels. Beyond 14th St., the downhill pitch increases, then dumps out steeply to almost sea level near 27th St. Cross over the lagoon created by the San Dieguito River and enjoy the post-card view of the Del Mar Racetrack just inland.

Class II S21 pulls inland into Solana Beach and passes a more commercialized area, including the Coast Carbo Station (where we have now enjoyed "Power Sandwiches" and "Energy Drinks" several times). Return to the coast and cross the expansive San Elijo Lagoon, entering Cardiff-by-the-Sea. The route passes scenic Cardiff State Beach and San Elijo State Beach in this area. The road cuts inland near the palacial Indian grounds of Swamis City Park, then enters more-developed Encinitas, with its Kipling's Restaurant in the Lumberyard (with a delightful band playing outdoors on the Saturday that we passed through). Pass the Moonlight State Beach entry at Encinitas Blvd. and then enter Leucadia. In order, the route passes Leucadia Park (water), Leucadia Blvd. (33.6), and a series of inviting lunch stops and delis. The tree-lined road then veers back near the ocean just below picturesque Batiquitos Lagoon.

Carlsbad through Oceanside. (See Trip #26 for further details.) After crossing the lagoon, S21 soon passes Poinsettia Ln., the main entry to beautiful, 2-1/2-mile South Carlsbad State Beach (water, restrooms, campsites). The road crosses Palomar Airport Rd., Cannon Park at Cannon Rd., then cruises a two-mile seaside highway segment alongside the fisherman-filled Agua Hedionda Lagoon and the sun-god-filled Carlsbad State Beach. Beyond, in a more commercialized area, are several popular, but contrasting, dining establishments: Norby's (Danish bakers with outdoor dining), quaint Ollie's Oyster Bar and ritzy Neimans. Pass Magee Park (water) and make an inland crossing of Buena Vista Lagoon, the last of these scenic inlets on this tour.

Across the lagoon is the City of Oceanside, where S21 disappears and is now named Hill St. At Vista Wy. (42.1), we begin a series of maneuvers through a residential area that avoids busy Hill St. and places us on scenic Class III Pacific St. (see Trip #30 for additional detail). There are scattered ocean views from this road, which passes by such attractions as cozy Buccaneer Beach Park within a coastal residential community. In two miles at 5th St., the bike route returns to Hill St. Follow that road a short distance north where it curves downhill and terminates at Harbor Dr. (46.5).

Camp Pendleton North of Las Pulgas Gate

BICYCLE RIDES: SAN DIEGO COUNTY

Camp Pendleton. Bike under Interstate Hwy. 5, cross San Rafael Dr. and check in at the main entrance gate (bikers are generally waved through -- bring identification as a precaution). Pedal on Vandergrift Blvd. past Wire Mountain Rd., then follow a variable level one-mile downgrade to Stuart Mesa Rd. Turn left (northwest) and continue steeply downhill into the Santa Marguerita River drainage, before paying the piper on an equally steep uphill. Pedal past the large fields of cultivated flowers and cross both Hammond Rd. (51.1) and the road to the Cook overcrossing.

The next three miles is a roller-coaster ride through the mesas. In the middle section, the road passes the main Los Flores area at Nelson Dr., the site of a permanently-parked U. S. Marine tank. Continue on Stuart Mesa Rd., veer left, pass by the Boy Scouts of America's Camp Flores, and just beyond, turn left at Las Pulgas Rd. Clear the entrance gate and turn right a couple hundred yards down the road, pedaling northwest through flat, arid terrain on a wide paved Class I path. The 1-1/2-mile path heads toward I-5, then follows a tunnel underneath it (57.9), placing the biker at Old Hwy. 101 on the coast side of the freeway.

San Onofre. In a short distance, pass through a motorized vehicle barricade and begin a 3-1/2-mile beeline through San Onofre State Beach on paved road, passing RV's, tent campers, canyon-hiking trails to the beach and numerous water and restroom stops. Leaving the park, the route passes the main entrance to the San Onofre power generating station, follows an overcrossing of the railroad tracks and continues as an I-5 frontage road. The roadway then crosses over Basilone Rd., the northernmost entry to Camp Pendleton. Just beyond is a fenced Class I bike entry, and the biker travels another one mile along the rolling terrain of the oceanside bluffs before reaching the Orange Country Line at Christianos Rd. (67.2).

Trestle Beach/San Mateo Point. Just south of Christianos Rd. is a junction path which leads 0.4 mile west to lovely and lightly-used Trestle Beach with a nice overlook/vista near San Mateo Point. If your timing is right, you may be treated to an AMTRAK passenger train passing by on the elevated railway near the beach.

The AMTRAK Option. Park at the San Diego AMTRAK station, bike to Oceanside or Santa Ana (these have bicycle baggage stops) and take the train on the return trip. The San Diego station is near the intersection of Kettner Blvd. and "C" St. The biker's "specials" presently leave at 11:45 am, 1:38 pm and 9:58 pm from Santa Ana and 12:41 pm, 2:30 pm and 10:48 pm from Oceanside on the weekend. Call AMTRAK at 1-800-872-7245 for the latest information before starting the trip.

<u>**CONNECTING TRIPS**</u>: This route connects with almost every tour listed in "THE COAST" section of this book. Refer to individual trips for these connectors.

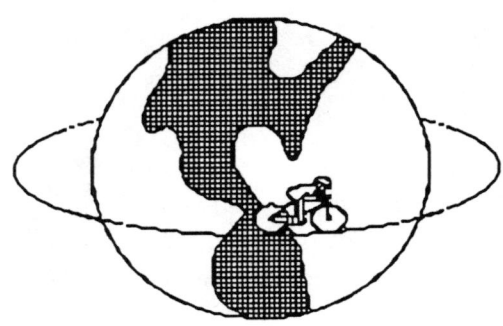

NORTH COUNTY

TRIP #22 - RIDING "THE RANCH"

GENERAL LOCATION: Rancho Santa Fe

LEVEL OF DIFFICULTY: Outer loop and inner loop - moderate to strenuous
Distance - 15.1 miles (outer loop); 9.6 miles (inner loop)
Elevation gain - periodic moderate-to-steep grades

GENERAL DESCRIPTION: This dandy Class X Rancho Santa Fe tour meanders through rolling hills covered with citrus and eucalyptus groves. Scenic vistas are scattered throughout this terrific ride. Traffic is light, the moderate workout through this secluded and rural area is refreshing, and the tour through one of the ten wealthiest communities in the nation is captivating. "The Ranch," as it is affectionately known, is studded with equestrian trails, tennis courts, golf courses and even hosts a polo field. The area was originally developed by the Santa Fe Railroad to grow eucalyptus trees for railroad ties. However, the wood proved unsuitable and the project was abandoned. The city was left with a lovely cover of several million trees.

From San Dieguito Park, the described route proceeds up rustic Linea Del Cielo, then follows a set of roughly counterclockwise patterns through the Rancho Santa Fe area. The outer loop examines the periphery of Rancho Santa Fe, while the inner loop concentrates on the area surrounding the civic center. The route provided is a base reference; however, bikers should explore other options as the trip unfolds -- there is not a bad street in the area! Key areas that free-form cruisers should visit as a minimum include the town proper, Osuna Valley and the San Dieguito Reservoir area.

Classic Rancho Santa Fe

TRAILHEAD: From Interstate Hwy. 5, exit east at Lomas Santa Fe (County Hwy. S8) and drive one mile to Highland Dr. Turn left (north) and continue a short distance to the San Dieguito Park entrance. The upper park has abundant tree cover, restrooms, picnic facilities, children's playgrounds, nature trails and scenic vistas. From Interstate 15, exit west at Del Dios Hwy. (County Hwy. S6) and drive ten miles to Linea Del Cielo (County Hwy. S8) near the center of Rancho Santa Fe. Turn onto the latter roadway and continue two miles to Highland Dr.

BICYCLE RIDES: SAN DIEGO COUNTY

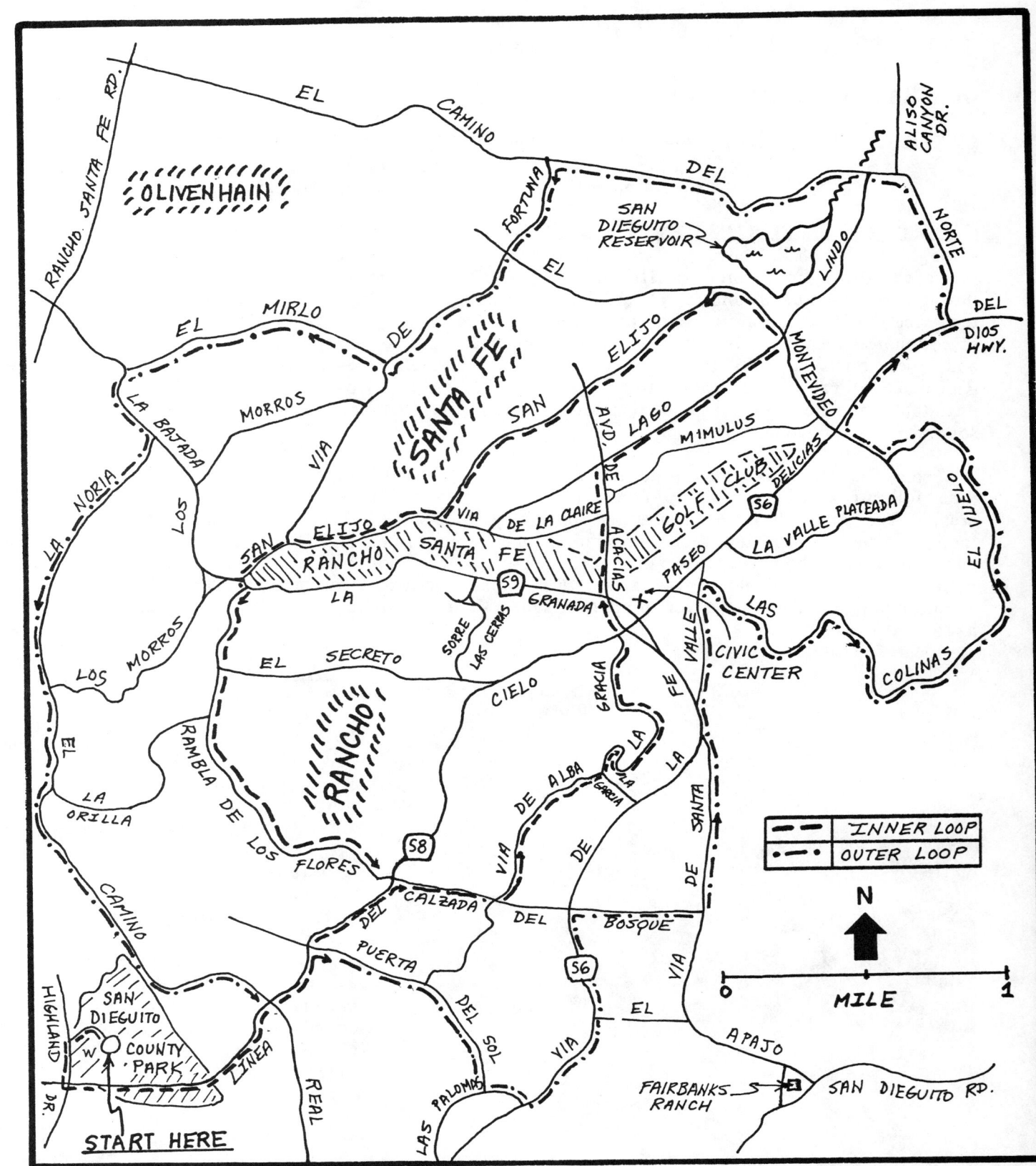

TRIP #22 - RIDING "THE RANCH"

Bring a quart or two of thirst quencher, unless plans are to "sweet talk" for water in the central Rancho Santa Fe area. Also, bikers who do not appreciate being lost for short periods of time should bring a road map.

TRIP DESCRIPTION: Outer Loop. Bike to Class II Linea Del Cielo, turn north and enjoy the periodic views into Osuna Valley southward and the hills of Rancho Santa Fe northward. A turn at Puerta Del Sol leads the biker through the first of many stretches which provide a little two-lane road meandering through the trees, amidst scattered exclusive residences. A nifty downhill lets out on the floor of Osuna Valley and is followed by a set of turns which take the biker over to Via De Santa Fe. Bike uphill through this farming/ranch land and veer right on Via De La Valle, continuing one-half mile to Las Colinas (4.6).

A right turn here takes the biker around a 2.9-mile winding, hilly loop even further embedded in the local serenity. This light residential loop lets out at Class II Paseo Delicias, where the pedaler turns right (north) and rides a short distance to El Camino Del Norte. On this 1-1/2-mile segment, there are varied views into the San Dieguito Reservoir, more of the ever-present citrus groves, and a pleasant spin through tree-lined roadways. The route follows Via De Fortuna (10.0) and El Mirlo to the outskirts of Olivenhain, dropping several hundred feet to a low point near La Bajada. There are several excellent vista points just above and below the Via De Fortuna/El Mirlo intersection.

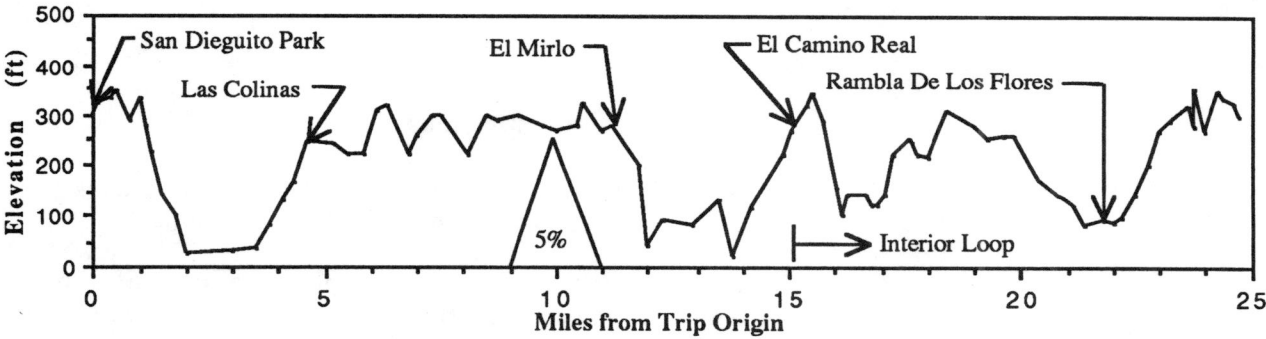

In a short distance is La Noria, where the biker begins a 2.8-mile uphill return to County Hwy. S8 (15.1). The road changes name to El Camino Real in this segment, passing through a sparsely-populated wooded area. Stay to the right at La Orilla unless you plan to leave El Camino Real. We spotted a small fox near Via Gaviota while touring this area!

Inner Loop. Bike north on Linea Del Cielo, this time continuing further uphill and turning right onto Calzada Del Bosque. In 0.4 downhill and tree-shaded mile, turn left (north) at Via De Alba and enjoy more of this wooded wonderland. Beyond La Garcia (stay to the left at this intersection) is a winding, steep uphill with an outlet at Linea Del Cielo. Turn right, then left in a short distance onto Avd. De Acacias. This is an abbreviated tour of the "big city," the Rancho Santa Fe Civic Center. Here are a limited number of small businesses, including a drug store, housed within unassuming (but obviously in good taste) structures.

The route crosses the beautiful Rancho Santa Fe Golf Club at La Granada, then proceeds up a short workout upgrade which peaks near Lago Lindo (3.1). Follow a counterclockwise course, turning left on El Montevideo. There are sweeping distant views directly ahead with San Dieguito Reservoir in the foreground. Turn left again

BICYCLE RIDES: SAN DIEGO COUNTY

at San Elijo. Near Avd. De Acacias is a refreshing downhill which levels in about 1.9 miles at La Granada. Turn left, and in a short distance, turn right onto Rambla De Las Flores. (Keep your eyes peeled for these road names, as there are several intersections in the area.) In 1/2-mile near La Orilla, begin a steady upgrade which tops out near Linea Del Cielo (7.9). From here, return 1.7 miles to the trip origin.

CONNECTING TRIPS: 1) Connection with the El Camino Real tour (Trip# 28) - continue north or south on El Camino Real beyond the Rancho Santa Fe city limits; 2) connection with the Escondido to the Sea---and Back tour (Trip #37) - proceed north or south on County Hwy. S6 outside of Rancho Santa Fe.

TRIP #23 - LA COSTA

GENERAL LOCATION: La Costa

LEVEL OF DIFFICULTY: Two loops - moderate to strenuous
Distance - 18.1 miles
Elevation gain - frequent moderate grades; sheer grades on Bolero St. and El Fuerte St.

GENERAL DESCRIPTION: This challenging hillside tour explores a pair of loops which sandwich the San Marcos Creek drainage and the La Costa Country Club. Almost entirely confined to newly-built residential areas with light traffic, this mixed Class II/Class X ride provides a steady series of short workout grades, with a single severe one-mile upgrade on the northern loop. There are excellent views of Batiquitos Lagoon, the San Marcos Creek canyon area, plus other undeveloped hillside and valley vistas scattered throughout both loops.

TRAILHEAD: From Interstate Hwy. 5, exit at La Costa Ave. Continue east four miles to Cadencia St. Follow this road 3/4 mile north to Cadencia Park. From the east, follow County Hwy. S-10 (Rancho Santa Fe Rd.) to Cadencia St. Turn right and continue 1/4 mile to the park. Bring one or two filled water bottles as the only park offerings are grass, very limited shade, children's play area and scenic vistas down the San Marcos Creek drainage to the ocean.

TRIP DESCRIPTION: Southern Loop. There is an immediate downhill after leaving the park, with the first of many views of Batiquitos Lagoon and the San Marcos Creek canyon. We take a diversionary loop tour on Piragua St., just one of many semi-circular residential paths nestled on the bluffs over the canyon on this southern loop. A light roller-coaster route leads to the "main drag" of the southern loop, Levante St. After a turn to the west, the cyclist continues 1.3 miles through a nicely-manicured residential area on this street. A short loop tour off Reposado Dr.

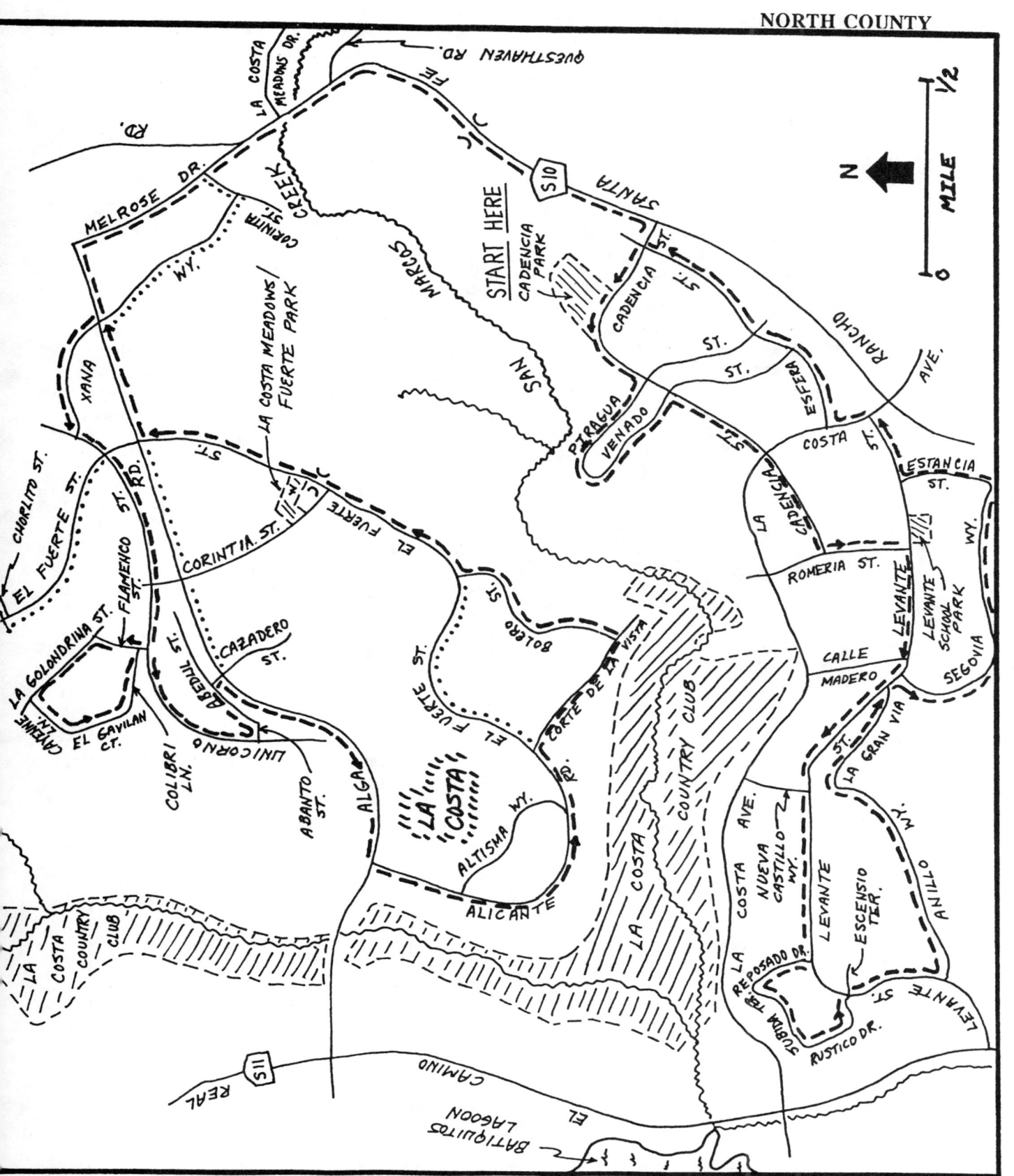

TRIP #23 - LA COSTA

BICYCLE RIDES: SAN DIEGO COUNTY

dumps the biker back onto Levante St., which continues downhill to El Camino Real. However, we take an earlier turn left on Anillo Wy. in an area of eroded bluffs and very scattered tree cover.

Melrose Drive Upgrade

From this low point on the southern loop, our tour treats the cyclist to a 420-foot net elevation gain, 2.8-mile return to the intersection of Esfera St. and Cadencia St. (most of that gain occuring on Anillo Wy. and Esfera St.). Most of the return route is through a residential area with light traffic, the exception being the side tour on Sequoia Wy. Here the biker is provided with a pastoral view into untouched hillsides and deep valleys to the southwest. At Cadenia St. is a short segment which takes the rider to busy Rancho Santa Fe Rd. (6.6).

To the North Loop -- and Return. A 1.3-mile ride on this Class II road leads to Melrose Dr. (note that there is an outstanding view westward from the near-midpoint crest of this segment). From here we follow a mostly uphill Class II path through a mix of new single-family houses and condominiums to El Fuerte St.

Next is a short, steep downhill (and deadend) at Charlito St., where there is a view of a lightly-developed valley to the north, Rancho Agua Hedionda. The westward swing on Unicorno St. surveys a pleasant residential loop off Flamenco St., then returns to busier Class II Alga Rd. via Cazadero St. (12.1). A steep two-mile downhill on Alga Rd. and Alicante Rd. drops the cyclist to the level of the renowned La Costa Country Club lying in a beautiful meadow with La Costa Creek passing through.

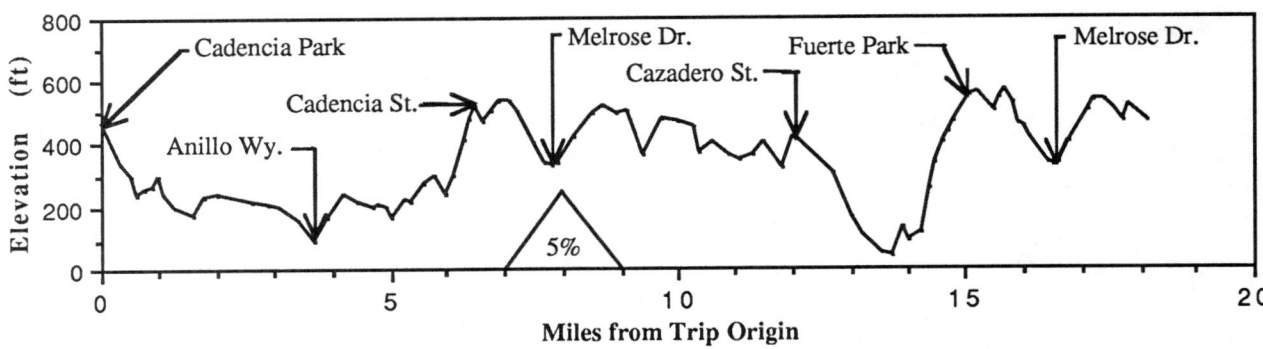

Soon is a sheer one-mile (average 8%) upgrade on Bolero St. and El Fuerte St., which peaks near La Costa Meadows/Fuerte Park. This stretch offers more than one opportunity to "stretch your legs" and enjoy the views of the hills to the southeast and the deep San Marcos Creek canyon (or like bike book authors, multiple opportunities for "note taking"). Beyond the crest is a relatively easy return to Rancho Santa Fe Rd. and a one-hill climb return to Cadencia Park. (18.1).

CONNECTING TRIPS: 1) Connection with the Coastal County Tour (Trip #21) - continue west beyond El Camino Real on La Costa Ave. or Alga Rd.; 2) connection with the Lake San Marcos tour (Trip #24) - continue northeast on Rancho Santa Fe Rd. beyond Melrose Dr.; 3) connection with the Loop O' the Lagoons (Trip #26) or El Camino Real (Trip #28) tours - follow Alga Rd. west beyond Alicante Rd.; 4) connection with the Escondido to the Sea---and Back ride (Trip #37) - the two trips share a common segment on Rancho Santa Fe Rd.

TRIP #24 - LAKE SAN MARCOS

GENERAL LOCATION: Lake San Marcos

LEVEL OF DIFFICULTY: Loop - moderate
Distance - 7.9 miles
Elevation gain - periodic moderate grades

GENERAL DESCRIPTION: This Class X mini-tour visits the Lake San Marcos community environs with the cyclist dodging golf carts and Rolls Royce convertibles along the way (poetic license taken, of course!). A southern loop into the residential Hermosita Dr. hill area is followed by the crossing of Lake San Marcos and a second larger loop generally on the periphery of the elegant Lake San Marcos Country Club. The La Plaza Dr. segment is in the hills above the lake, providing interesting looks of both the community below and the mini-mansions along the road.

TRAILHEAD: From State Hwy. 78, exit south at San Marcos Blvd. (County Hwy. S12) and drive two miles to Rancho Santa Fe Rd. Turn left and continue 1/2 mile to Lake San Marcos Dr. Turn left onto that road and then right immediately into a parking area.

TRIP DESCRIPTION: From Lake San Marcos Dr., observe the panoramic view of the residence-covered hills, including the mansions tucked into a massive hillside to the south. We coined the term "Sea of Roof Tiles" to describe the view. Pass the gas station and turn right onto San Marino Dr., cycling past the small shopping center and the many private, gated residential enclaves. A right on Hermosita Dr. takes the biker on an uphill which peaks near the southernmost Camino Del Arroyo junction, then on a steep downhill return to Hermosita Dr. To the right at our return to San Marino Dr. is a short and scenic diversion to the west side of Lake San Marcos at Camino De Vela.

BICYCLE RIDES: SAN DIEGO COUNTY

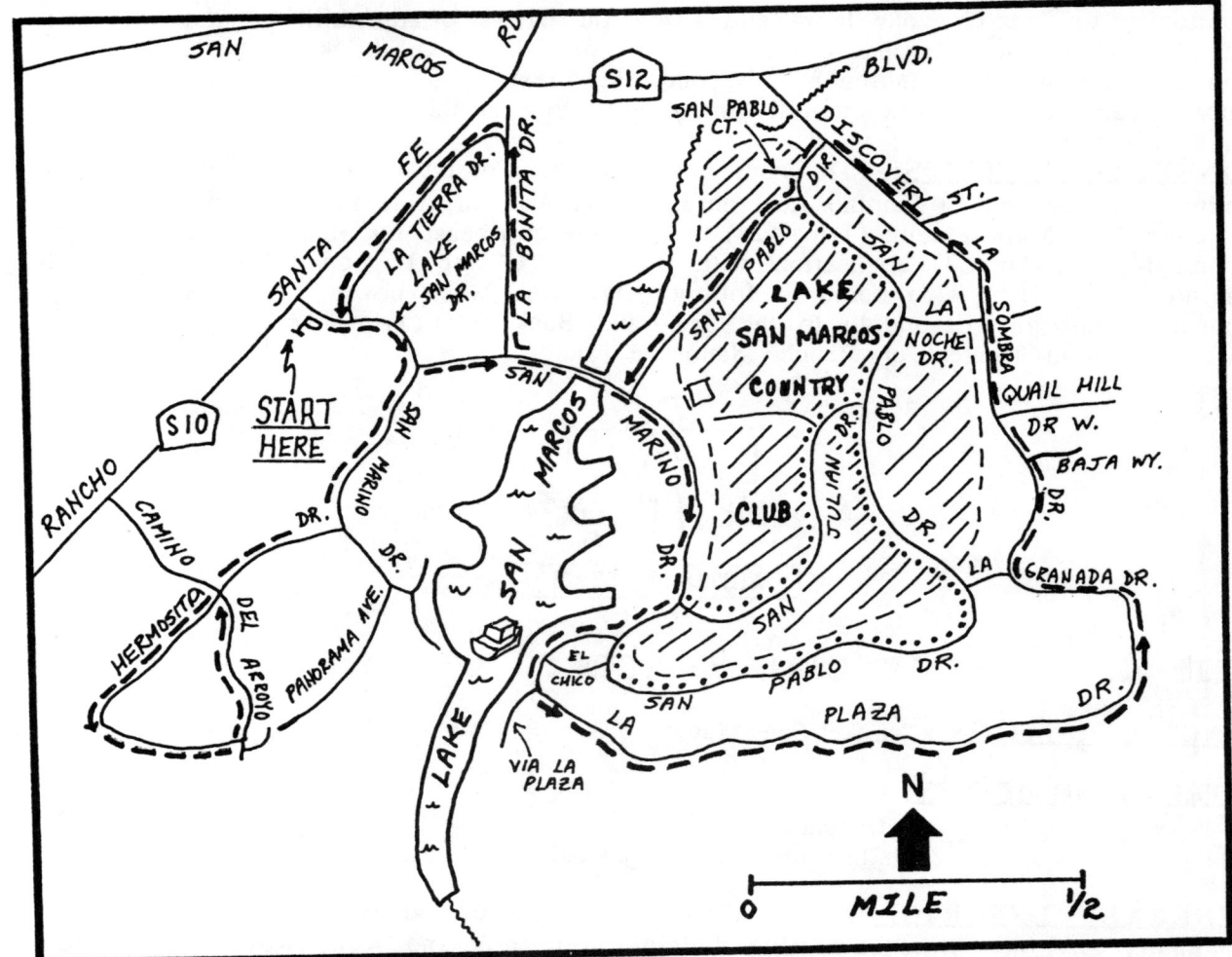

TRIP #24 - LAKE SAN MARCOS

The route returns to Lake San Marcos Dr., passes Lake Village Center and crosses the lake (2.6). Stop and enjoy the serenity of the tree-studded, residence- and boat-lined, wildlife-filled lake. San Marino Dr. passes the Lake San Marcos Country Club and Dining Room near La Habra Dr. The tour transitions onto La Plaza Dr., then follows a short workout upgrade which passes behind and above the previously mentioned mansions. There are exceptional Lake San Marcos vistas from this area. The road winds along the hillside before veering left onto La Granada Dr. and dropping down to a flat near La Sombra Dr. A 0.3-mile upgrade on this street reaches a crest near Baja Wy., then passes the northern edge of the San Marcos Club Golf Course near La Noche Dr. The roadway becomes Discovery St. and continues on the golf course periphery, passing through a well-maintained, but less opulent residential area.

Our tour turns west at San Pablo Dr. (6.4), enters the lush golf course proper and passes San Pablo Ct. Just beyond, San Pablo Dr. splits, with each fork maintaining this singular name. Turn a hard right and continue 0.4 mile back to San Marino Dr. A second lake crossing and a partial loop on La Bonita Dr./La Tierra Dr. returns the cyclist to the starting point (7.9).

NORTH COUNTY

"Backyard" Lake San Marcos

Lake San Marcos Country Club. An option is to extend the tour to include the inner San Pablo Dr./San Julian Dr. loop.

<u>**CONNECTING TRIPS**</u>: 1) Connection with the La Costa tour (Trip #23) and the Escondido to the Sea---and Back ride (Trip #37) - bike southwest on Rancho Santa Fe Rd.; 2) connection with the Ocean Hills-Vista Loop (Trip #27) - at the trip origin, bike northeast on Rancho Santa Fe Rd.

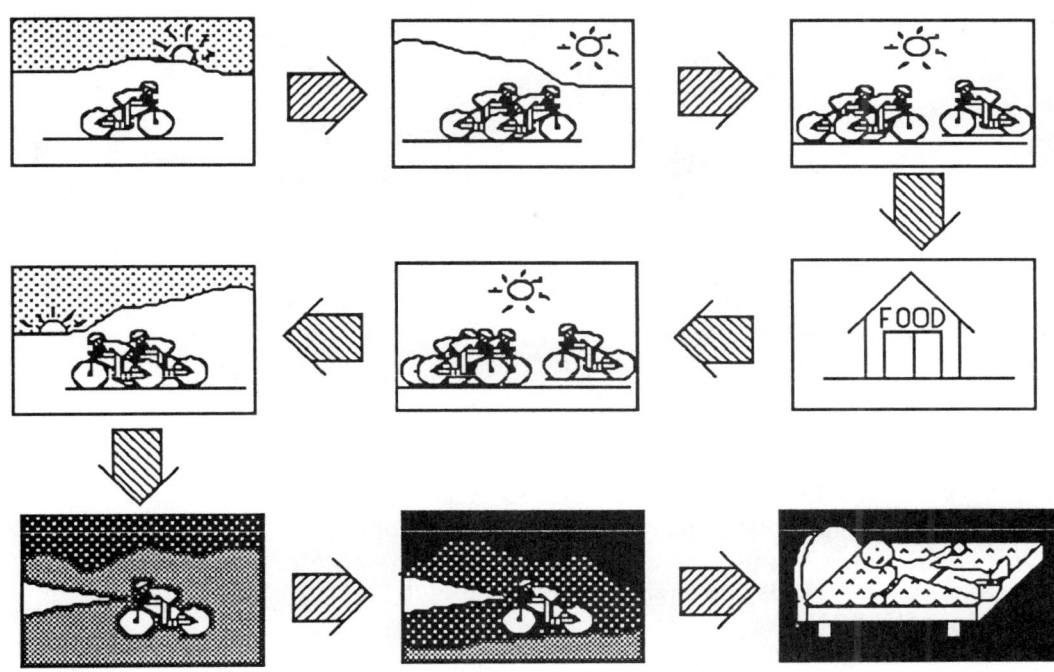

BICYCLE RIDES: SAN DIEGO COUNTY

TRIP #25 - VISTA CITY TOUR

GENERAL LOCATION: Vista

LEVEL OF DIFFICULTY: Double loop - moderate to strenuous
Distance - 18.8 miles (two loops)
Elevation gain - periodic moderate grades

GENERAL DESCRIPTION: This interesting double-looper tours the city center, as well as the lightly-developed outskirts. Vista, incorporated in 1963, is a young and well-planned city criss-crossed by bicycle paths and lightly-traveled roadways. The 8.8-mile eastern loop departs Wildwood Park near the civic center, then follows a clockwise loop on Class II Vista Wy. before plying the less-populated and hilly north eastern edge. The return segment is a general downhill via busier Class II South Santa Fe Ave. The western loop transits the lightly developed southern city section along country-like Mar Vista Ave. and Sunset Dr. before crossing State Hwy. 78. The return route follows rolling hills through a residential area above, and with views of, the Alta Vista Creek drainage.

Rural Sunset Drive

TRAILHEAD: From State Hwy. 78, exit north at Escondido Ave. Drive 1-1/4 miles to Vista Wy. and turn right. The entry to Wildwood Park is just beyond the intersection. From State Hwy. 76, turn south onto North Santa Fe Ave. (County Hwy. S14), continuing 4-1/2 miles to the north branch of Vista Wy. Turn left and drive 1/2 mile to the park's entrance. The park has plentiful tree cover, restrooms, a children's playground and picnic facilities.

Bring a roadmap if you are not a confident navigator.

TRIP DESCRIPTION: Eastern Loop. Follow Vista Wy. 2.2 miles on Class II bikeway on a light general upgrade. The busy road passes shopping centers at Foothill Dr. and Arcadia Ave., then turns right at Class X Warmlands Ave. near the city outskirts. Follow that street as it winds through lightly-populated rolling hills at the base of the San Marcos Mountains.

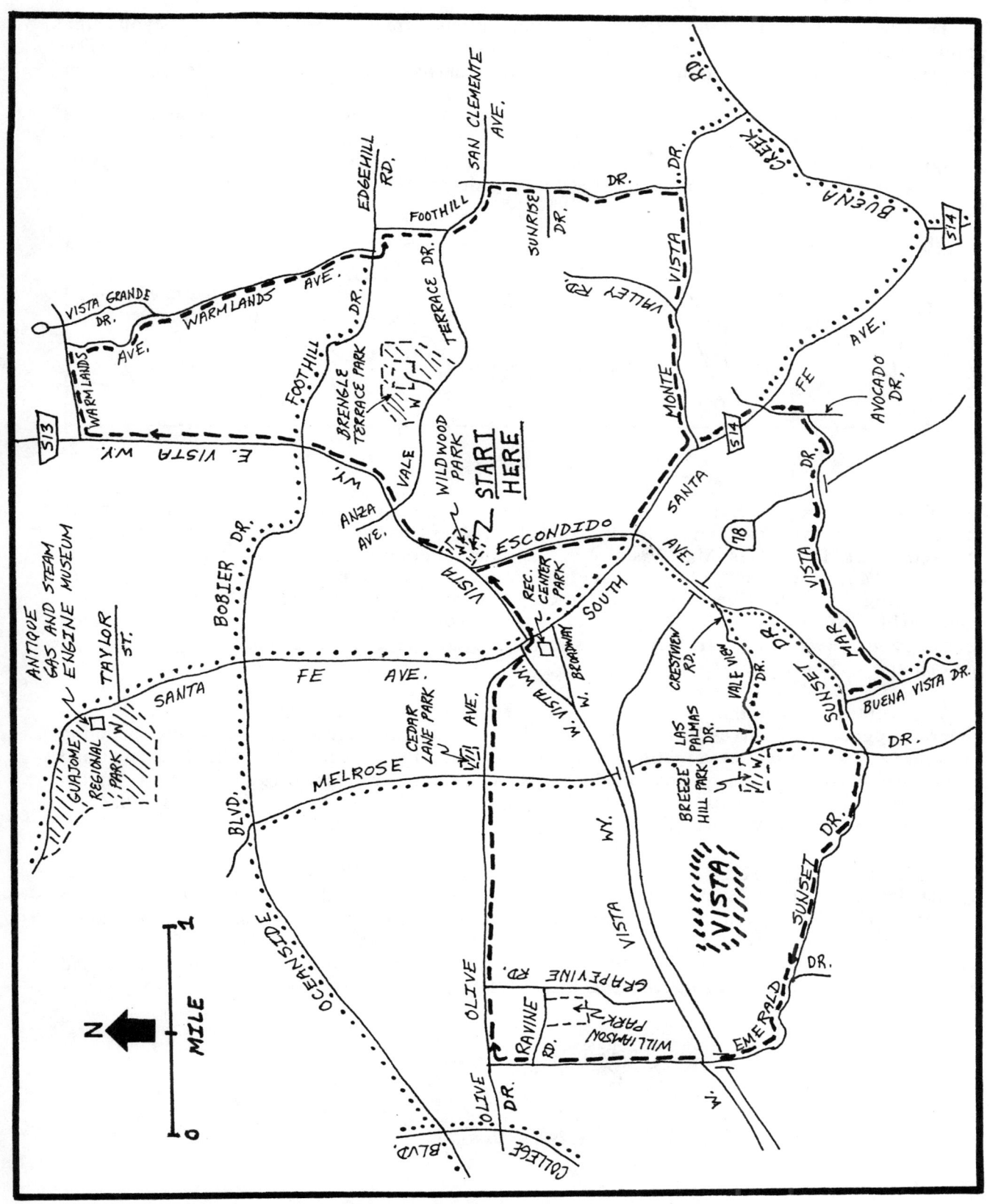

TRIP #25 - VISTA CITY TOUR

BICYCLE RIDES: SAN DIEGO COUNTY

Turn at Foothill Dr. and stay on this circuitous street. Just 0.4 mile beyond the point where Foothill Dr. veers south at Edgehill Rd. is Vale Terrace Dr. (5.7). The unique Brengle Terrace Park, with its architecturally-varied picnic kiosks located at the park's upper reaches, is a 3/4-mile diversion to the right. However, our reference tour follows Foothill Dr. on a general downgrade through scattered residences and citrus groves before dropping back into civilization at Monte Vista Dr. A right turn takes the biker on an easy Class II pedal 1.3 miles to South Santa Fe Ave. All that remains is a 1/2-mile transit, with a single hill to navigate, to complete this loop (8.8).

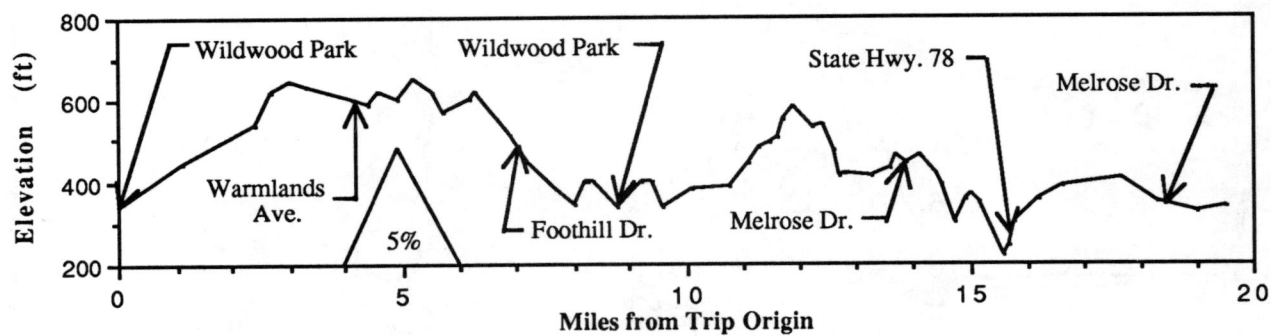

Western Loop. Exit Wildwood Park and follow Class II Escondido Ave. for 0.8 mile, then turn southeast onto South Santa Fe Ave. In another 1.2 miles on this well-traveled Class II road is Mar Vista Ave., a quiet alternative to the prior two miles. A 3/4-mile upgrade on a less-traveled, curving residential road leads to an overcrossing of State Hwy. 78. The next 3.5 miles are on a series of what seem like countryside roadways on rolling hills with a net 300-foot elevation loss between crossings of Hwy. 78. In between are residential areas nestled between garden- and hot- house complexes.

The route crosses the freeway on a street now named Emerald Dr. and follows a general upgrade to Olive Village Ave. (7.4). Turn right (east) and continue pedaling through a residential area with views north into the Loma Alta Creek basin and Oceanside Blvd. An easy downgrade leads the biker past Melrose Dr. with a market and small Cedar Lane Park. At road's end, the route follows W. Vista Wy. another 1/2 mile and returns to Wildwood Park.

CONNECTING TRIPS: 1) Connection with the Ocean Hills-Vista Loop (Trip #27) - at Sunset Dr. and Buena Vista Dr., turn south on the latter road; 2) Connection with the Oceanside City Tour (Trip #29) - at Emerald Dr. and Olive Ave., turn left onto the latter street; 3) connection with Canyon's N' Citrus route (Trip #52) - at Warmlands Ave. and Vista Wy., turn north on Vista Wy. and continue to State Hwy. 76. Turn right and right again in a short distance at Old River Rd.

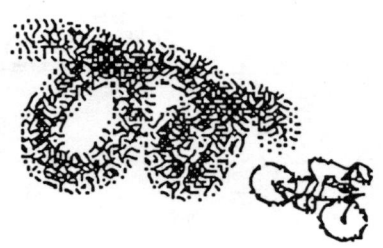

NORTH COUNTY

TRIP #26 - LOOP O' THE LAGOONS

GENERAL LOCATION: Carlsbad

LEVEL OF DIFFICULTY: Round trip - moderate
Distance - 25.5 miles
Elevation gain - periodic moderate grades

GENERAL DESCRIPTION: This 25-mile plus scenic loop is essentially a Carlsbad city tour. As a highlight, the route explores the shores of three beautiful lagoons, Buena Vista, Agua Hedionda and Batiquitos. Bikers are treated to a tour through varied environments, including seaside, coastal hills and the lagoons. The route is predominantly on Class II and Class III roads.

TRAILHEAD: From Interstate Hwy. 5, exit east at State Hwy. 78 and take the first turnoff (Jefferson Rd./Marron) south to Jefferson St. Turn left on Marron Rd. and park in the spacious Plaza Camino Real Shopping Center lot. From Interstate Hwy. 15, exit west at State Hwy. 76 and continue into Oceanside. At Interstate Hwy. 5, take the on-ramp south and follow the instructions above.

Overlooking Buena Vista Lagoon

TRIP DESCRIPTION: **Coastal Segment.** At the Jefferson St. intersection, bike west on that road. Immediately to the right is a parking area with a sweeping view of the Buena Vista Lagoon Ecological Reserve. Follow the narrow, two-lane road over Interstate Hwy. 5, pass Los Flores Dr. and continue south through the residential area to Elm St. Turn right and pedal past little Rotary Park before reaching Class II Hwy. S21, the mainline coastal bike route (refer to Trip #21). Continue south, passing the Daily News Cafe, Baking and Catering establishment and the Carlsbad Inn (two personal favorites).

Meanwhile, enjoy the spectacular views of the county coastline. Next, the route passes Tamarack Ave. and the inviting Tamarack Beach Resort. (Honest, we don't own stock in this area!) In 0.6 mile, the coastal highway passes the Encina Public Fishing Area, the outlet of the Aqua Hedionda Lagoon. After enjoying continuous coastal views in both directions, the biker turns left at Cannon Rd. (5.6), crosses under Interstate Hwy. 5 and turns again in 1/4-mile at Paseo Del Norte. For the next 2-1/2 miles, the rider cruises on Class II bikeway past Car Country (the highest density of

BICYCLE RIDES: SAN DIEGO COUNTY

car dealers we've seen), Anderson's Pea Soup Restaurant, Palomar Airport Rd. (gas station, Hadley's Fruits and Nuts), a massive new housing development with periodic views to the ocean, and reaches Poinsettia Ln.

In times past, bikers could turn left and follow a route via Batiquitos Dr., which skirted the quiet northern Batiquitos Lagoon shore. However, new construction has caused that scenic stretch to be closed, hopefully to be reopened in the near-future. Thus, the reference route returns to Hwy. S21 and proceeds across the lagoon to La Costa Ave. (10.0), The rider joins heavier traffic on this Class II roadway, but is compensated by the interesting north shore lagoon vistas.

Trail along the Batiquitos Lagoon

Inland Loop. A 2-1/2 mile flat ride on La Costa Ave. brings the biker to very busy El Camino Real. The pedaler passes a shopping plaza and gas station after turning north onto the Class II road and cruises alongside the La Costa Country Club. In about 0.6 mile after the turn, the route heads uphill, passes another shopping center near Alga Rd., and continues uphill for a total 1.3-mile gradual upgrade. In the vicinity of Swallow Ln., the payoff is a refreshing downhill with sweeping views into the hills to the east and of the Hedionda Creek drainage.

A left at Camino Vida Roble (15.0) takes the tour through a light-industrial area. In 0.9 mile, the route turns on Palomar Airport Rd. and passes through barren rolling hills. The hilly tour continues as the biker turns north on Class II College Blvd. and continues to a crest in 0.7 mile, from which there is an interesting view of several surrounding mesas. After a steep downhill and left turn on El Camino Real, the biker passes the tempting Moncone's Country Village Restaurant and turns right in 1-1/2 miles at Kelly Dr. (20.6).

In a short distance, the route passes Laguna Riviera Park (water, trees, grassy playground area and wood "sculptured" picnic tables). After a right turn on Park Dr., the tour continues one mile on flat road through a residential area to Adams St. Follow this little two-lane Class X road alongside the north shore of Aqua Hedionda Lagoon, then continue to Class II Tamarack Ave. Bike uphill to Highland Dr. and turn left, continuing 1.2 miles through a residential area on a coastal bluff. Pedal a short segment on the Las Flores Dr. continuation segment to Jefferson St. and backtrack to the trip origin (25.5).

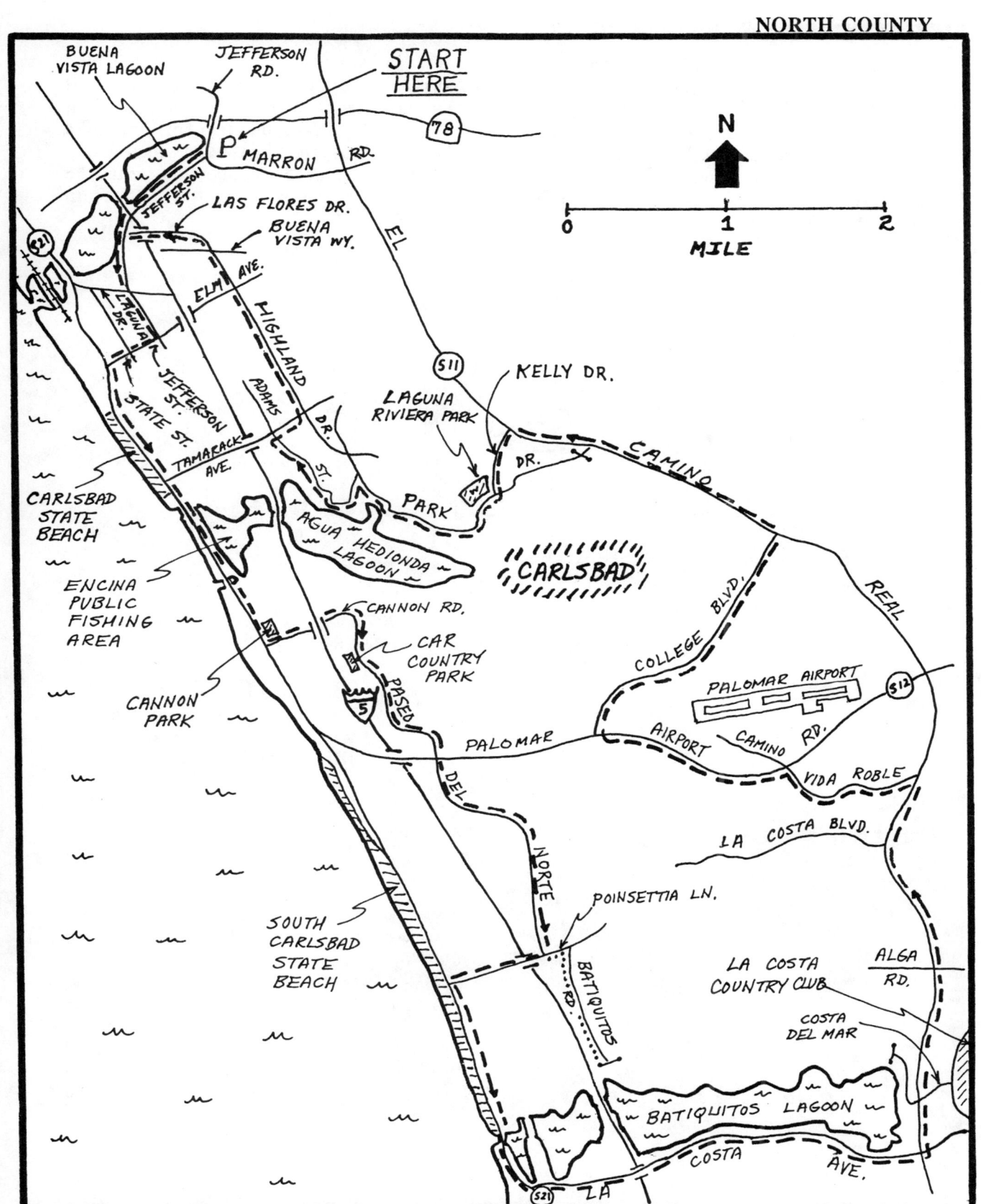

TRIP #26 - LOOP O' THE LAGOONS

BICYCLE RIDES: SAN DIEGO COUNTY

CONNECTING TRIPS: 1) Connection with the Coastal County Tour (Trip #21) - bike north or south on common County Hwy. S21 road segments; 2) connection with the El Camino Real tour (Trip #28) - the trips share a common segment in the Carlsbad area; 3) continuation with the Oceanside City Tour (Trip #29) - at the trip origin, bike north on Jefferson St.; 4) connection with the Escondido to the Sea---and Back loop (Trip #37) - continue south on Hwy. S21 below La Costa Ave; 5) connection with the La Costa ride (Trip #23) - at El Camino Real and either La Costa Ave. or Alga Rd., turn east on either of the latter streets.

TRIP #27 - OCEAN HILLS-VISTA LOOP

GENERAL LOCATION: Ocean Hills, Vista

LEVEL OF DIFFICULTY: Loop - moderate
Distance - 9.7 miles
Elevation gain - periodic moderate grades

Ocean Hills Development

DESCRIPTION: Within 5 to 6 miles of the ocean is a recently-discovered hillside-dotted area which is now falling under the developers' machinery. The charm of the out-of-the-way area is that it is still isolated from the major roadways. The cyclist is treated to a continuous checkerboard of developed and undeveloped sectors on primarily Class II bikeway. With the exception of the older, more rural areas along Mar Vista Dr., most of the residential areas are new and pleasantly landscaped.

This clockwise tour described leaves Thibodo Park and transits the southern Vista city segment, cutting through the lush Shadowridge Golf Club, passing a mining operation just east of La Mirada Dr., and visiting several scattered segments of Buena Vista Park along Melrose Dr. This tour slice involves crossing the drainage of several meandering small waterways, including Agua Hedionda Creek. The route passes on the Ocean Hills periphery in the Cannon Rd. area, then follows a 1.7-mile winding cruise through the older and more serene section of Vista along Buena Vista Dr. and Mar Vista Dr. The end of the reference tour involves an easy cruise on the Thibodo Rd. frontage road and a short workout uphill return to the park.

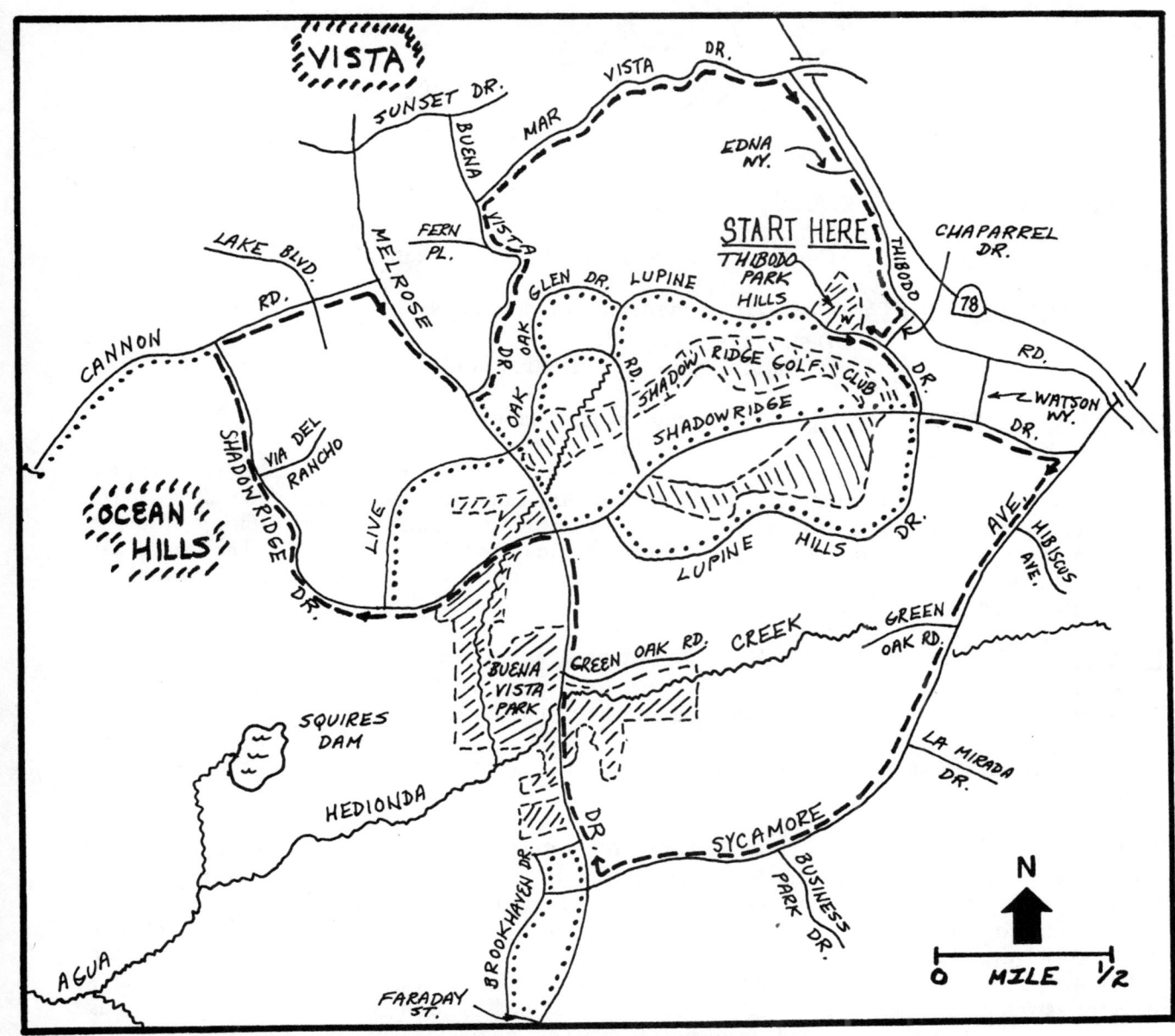

TRIP #27 - OCEAN HILLS-VISTA LOOP

TRAILHEAD: From State Hwy. 78, exit west at Sycamore Ave. Turn left, then right just beyond, at Lupine Hills Dr. Several hundred yards up the hill is the entrance to Thibodo Park. The lower park section has restrooms, tennis and basketball courts and

BICYCLE RIDES: SAN DIEGO COUNTY

tree cover, while the equally treed upper section has the community center, nature working paths and several vista points.

CONNECTING TRIPS: 1) Connection with the Vista City Tour (Trip #25) - at Buena Vista Dr. and Mar Vista Dr., continue north on the former street; 2) connection with the Lake San Marcos ride (Trip #24) - bike south on Business Park Dr.

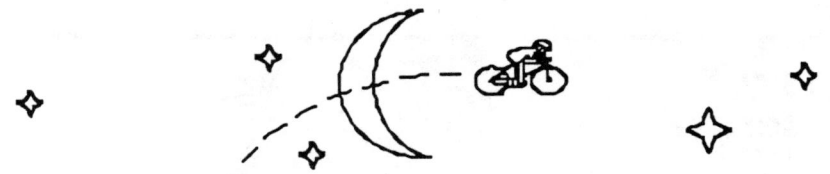

TRIP #28 - EL CAMINO REAL

GENERAL LOCATION: Cardiff-by-the-Sea, Carlsbad, Oceanside

LEVEL OF DIFFICULTY: One way - moderate to strenuous
Distance - 28.6 miles
Elevation gain - periodic moderate-to-strenuous grades

GENERAL DESCRIPTION: This dandy, predominantly Class II ride of El Camino Real or "The Kings Highway," is an alternate to the Hwy. S21 coastal tour. Though less scenic than the coast route, the biker is treated to several interesting vistas, specifically in the still relatively undeveloped hill and canyon areas. The first 9-1/2 miles on generally rural roads is serene with a particularly eye-catching Rancho Santa Fe segment. Bike this "beauty" before the area is fully developed. The route can also be linked with one segment of the Coastal County Tour (Trip #21) to provide a challenging and varied 55-mile loop.

TRAILHEAD: From Interstate Hwy. 5, exit west at Carmel Valley Rd. and turn south at the first unsigned street. Continue 3/4 mile to a gate -- this is the current "origin" of El Camino Real. Have a friend drop you off here and meet you in San Luis Rey.

There is a roughly ten-mile waterless stretch north of Encinitas Blvd. Bring a filled water bottle or two for hot days.

TRIP DESCRIPTION: Carmel Valley to Encinitas. Bike north through Carmel Valley and continue four miles on Class II path through the scattered new developments. In this section, the route rises to Half-mile Dr., where there are views west to the ocean, before dropping into San Dieguito Valley. After crossing the San Dieguito River, the cyclist passes a small shopping center on Via De La Valle, then pedals for about 5-1/2 miles along the rustic western edge of Rancho Santa Fe. This pleasant stretch through tree-studded rolling hills passes San Dieguito Park (6.5), as well as groomed properties and mini-horse ranches characteristic of "The Ranch." El Camino Real becomes La Noria, then the route turns north at La Bajada This road continues into Encinitas to a four-way intersection with four different street names and a shopping center.

Encinitas to Rancho La Costa. A turn west puts the biker onto a 1-1/2 mile stretch on Manchester Ave. alongside Escondido Creek and the marshy San Elijo

NORTH COUNTY

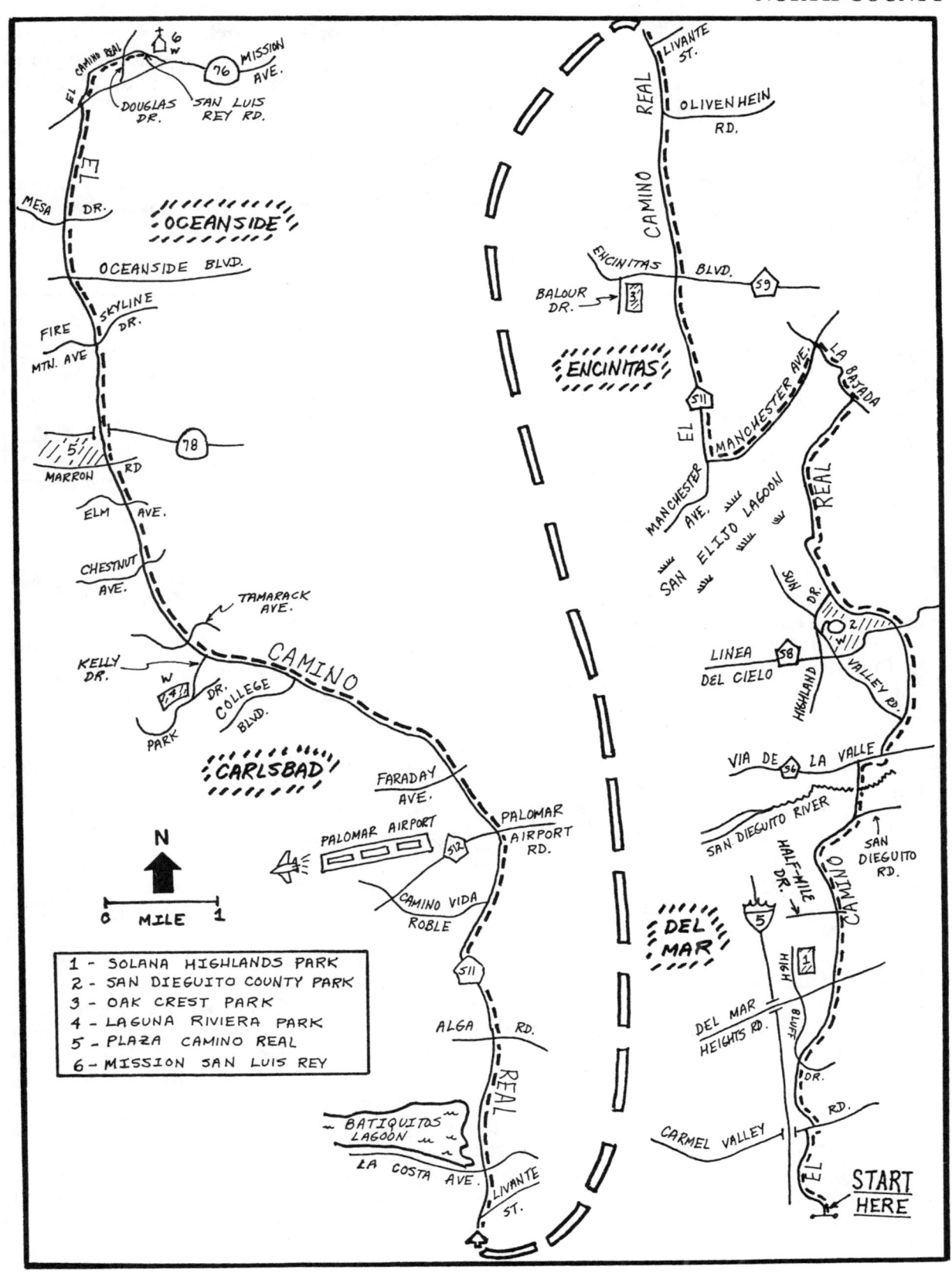

TRIP #28 - EL CAMINO REAL

BICYCLE RIDES: SAN DIEGO COUNTY

Lagoon. The route comes into view of a stately gold-domed church, then turns north onto the continuation of El Camino Real. The road transitions from quiet and rural roadway to a busier four-laner (the latter characteristic of the remainder of the trip) and follows a workout grade to a crest near Encinitas Blvd. (12.6).

The tour returns to Class II bikeway and proceeds through a highly-developed commercial area. In another mile, El Camino Real returns to a rural setting in an area sandwiched between barren, rolling hills. The biker reaches La Costa Ave. and skirts the western edge of La Costa, one of golfdom's favorite cities. In this area, the roadway also grazes the eastern edge of the Batiquitos Lagoon.

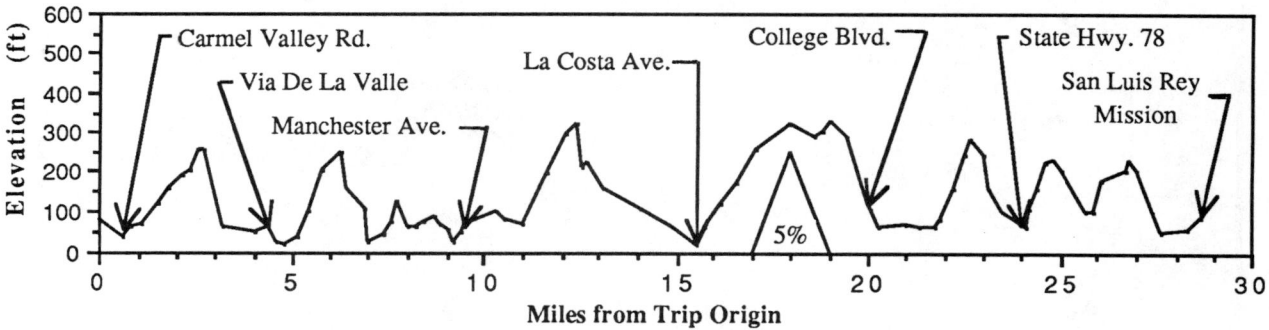

La Costa to Oceanside. In 1/2 mile, cyclists are greeted by a stairstep upgrade which levels near Camino Vida Roble on a bluff containing the Mc Clellan/Palomar airport. Pass Palomar Airport Rd. (18.6) and enjoy the one-mile downgrade which follows, including a sweeping view of the canyon areas to the east. Continue past Tony's Country Villa Restaurant and tackle the 1-1/4 mile testy upgrade which peaks near Chestnut Ave. (22.7). An invigorating downhill past Marron Rd. leads to the immense Plaza Camino Real Shopping Center.

Cross State Hwy. 78 and, at Vista Hwy., pump up an imposing 3/4-mile upgrade, which bikers navigate on Class X roadway with a wide shoulder. The route crests at Skyline Dr./Fire Mountain Dr., then follows a long downhill where both marked bike path and bike shoulder disappear. For the next 2-1/4 miles until reaching Mission Ave. in Oceanside (27.6), the road continues through a rural area of rolling hills. Continue across busy Mission Ave. to the El Camino Real terminus at Douglas Dr., cross that street to San Luis Rey Rd. and bike 1/4 mile to the trip's end at the San Luis Rey Mission (28.6).

CONNECTING TRIPS: 1) Continuation with the Coastal County Tour (Trip #21) - bike Hwy. 78 west to the intersection with County Hwy. S21 in Oceanside, then turn north towards San Clemente or south toward Cardiff-by-the-Sea (the latter option to turn this into a loop trip); 2) connection with the Riding The Ranch tour (Trip #22) - the trips share a common segment in Rancho Santa Fe; 3) connection with the La Costa ride (Trip #23) - at El Camino Real and La Costa Ave. or Alga Rd., turn east on either of the latter two streets; 4) connection with the Loop O' the Lagoons (Trip #26) - the trips share a common segment in the Carlsbad area; 5) connection with the Oceanside City Tour (Trip #29) - at Vista Wy. or Mesa Dr. in Oceanside, turn east onto either street.; 6) connection with the Escondido to the Sea---and Back tour (Trip #37) - at El Camino Real and La Costa Ave., bike east or west on the latter street.

NORTH COUNTY

TRIP #29 - OCEANSIDE CITY TOUR

GENERAL LOCATION: Oceanside

LEVEL OF DIFFICULTY: Round trip - moderate
Distance - 20.6 miles
Elevation gain - periodic moderate-to-steep grades

GENERAL DESCRIPTION: This twenty-miler is a pleasant loop through the modest hillsides of the City of Oceanside. There are numerous and varied views of Oceanside and the mountains in the distance. Most of the route is in residential areas, although there are brushes with undeveloped regions of the city. The tour is primarily on Class II or Class III bikeways with some Class X on lightly-traveled roads. Bikers have the opportunity to visit Mission San Luis Rey early in the tour, as well as to enjoy two outstanding parks, Guajome Park at the trip origin and Buddy Todd Memorial Park near the midpoint of the trip.

Mission San Luis Rey

TRAILHEAD: From Interstate Hwy. 5, exit east on Mission Ave. (State Hwy. 76) and drive about eight miles to North Santa Fe Ave. (Hwy. S14). Continue another 1/2 mile and turn right at Guajome Lake Rd. Turn right again in a short distance at the entry to Guajome Regional Park. The grassy park has water, restrooms, shade trees, picnic tables, children's playground and sports a lovely overlook of Guajome Lake.

From Interstate Hwy. 15, exit west on Pala Rd. and proceed about 11 miles to Guajome Lake Rd. Continue as described above.

BICYCLE RIDES: SAN DIEGO COUNTY

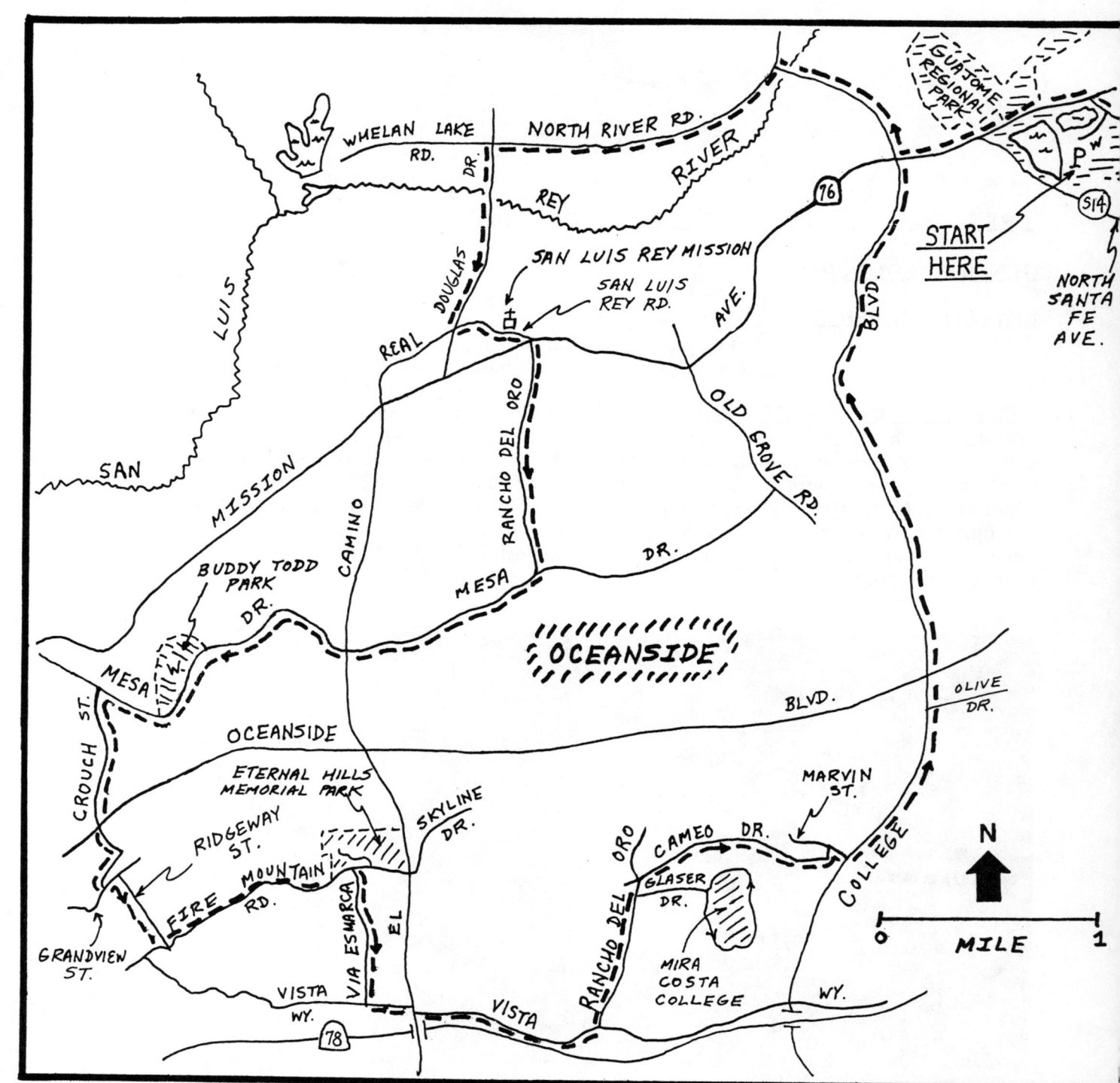

TRIP #29 - OCEANSIDE CITY TOUR

NORTH COUNTY

TRIP DESCRIPTION: North Segment. Exit the park and turn left (west) onto busy Class III Mission Ave., then continue 1.1 miles uphill to Class II College Blvd. Cross over the San Luis Rey River toll bridge and, in a short distance, bike into the northern reaches of Oceanside at N. River Rd. Turn left and follow the flat road through a mixed area of open space and new construction, passing Calle Montecito and a small convenience store. A left turn at Douglas Dr. takes the biker past a shopping center, and in another 1-1/4 miles is El Camino Real (4.1).

Turn left onto San Luis Rey Rd. and pedal past Mission San Luis Rey. This grand example of old Spanish architecture was once the home of almost 3000 Indians and is still used as a place of worship. Cross Mission Ave. and follow a steep, curving uphill on Class II Rancho Del Oro. In 0.9 mile at the high point is the Heritage Reservoir, with a water tank painted in Spanish mission decor. Just beyond, follow a mild downhill to Mesa Dr. For the next mile before recrossing El Camino Real, the biker is on a mesa (surprise!) with dense condominium developments to the north and still undeveloped and barren hills southward.

Cross "The King's Highway" and follow a steep, winding upgrade on the Class II road to a summit with an outstanding view to the north. After a short span of rolling hills, pass Buddy Todd Memorial Park, an inviting oasis with restrooms, tree cover, grassy fields, playground areas, picnic facilities and Oceanside views to boot! Follow Mesa Dr. to Crouch St., then bike a steep downgrade through a residential area to the Loma Alta Creek bottomlands at Oceanside Blvd. There is a gas station and food market here (10.1).

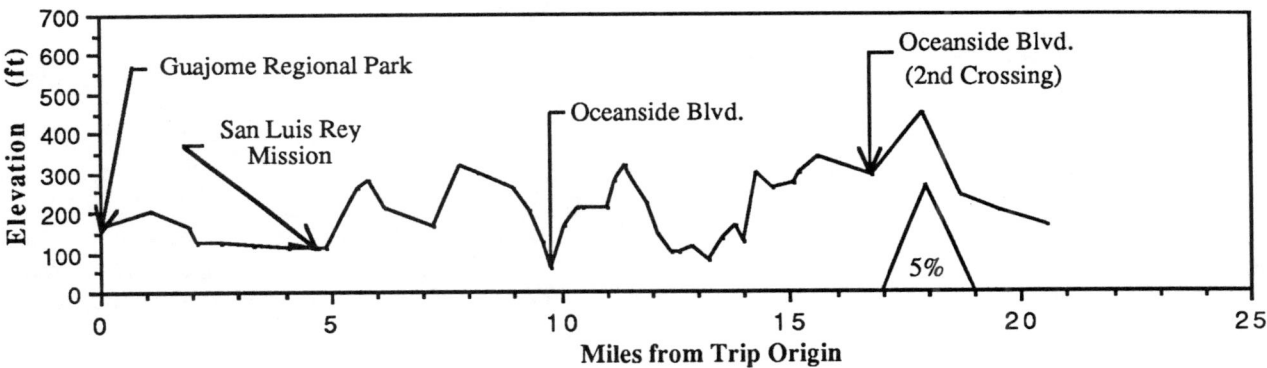

Southern Segment. After an immediate 1/2-mile testy upgrade, the biker follows a circuitous route through a mix of Class I and Class X roadways in residential rolling hills. On Fire Mountain Rd. near the stately Eternal Hills Memorial Park (cemetery), there are grand views into the eastern Oceanside area. At Via Esmarca, turn south and follow a downgrade before turning left (east) on Vista Wy. This Class II freeway frontage road follows the Buena Vista Creek bottomland 1-1/4 miles before the tour turns north and heads back into the foothills at Rancho Del Oro (13.8).

Next, the pedaler faces a steady workout upgrade which crests in one-half mile near Glaser Dr. Our Class III road is surrounded by developed tracts which envelope the hillsides. After a right turn on Cameo Dr., the biker cruises the rolling hills with Mira Costa College above on the bluffs and to the right. Upon reaching busy Class II College Blvd., the biker is treated to views of the Santa Marguerita Mountains to the north, as well as a relaxing downhill ride to Oceanside Blvd.

BICYCLE RIDES: SAN DIEGO COUNTY

What goes down must come up! (Or something like that.) Next on the agenda is a steep 3/4-mile uphill which tops out near Old Grove Rd. The continued Class II road roller-coasts through the massive tract developments and reaches a high point at Mission Ave. All that remains is to retrace the route back to Guajome Regional Park (20.6).

CONNECTING TRIPS: 1) Connection with the Vista City Tour (Trip #25) - at College Blvd. and Olive Dr., turn east onto the latter street; 2) connection with the Loop O' the Lagoons (Trip #26) - at the Fire Mountain Rd./Avocado Rd. intersection, follow the latter street south across State Hwy. 78 to Jefferson St.; 3) connection with the El Camino Real tour (Trip #28) - at either El Camino Real crossing, turn either north or south; 4) connection with the Fallbrook Countryside Tour (Trip #39) - at the trip origin, bike east on State Hwy. 76 to Bonsall.

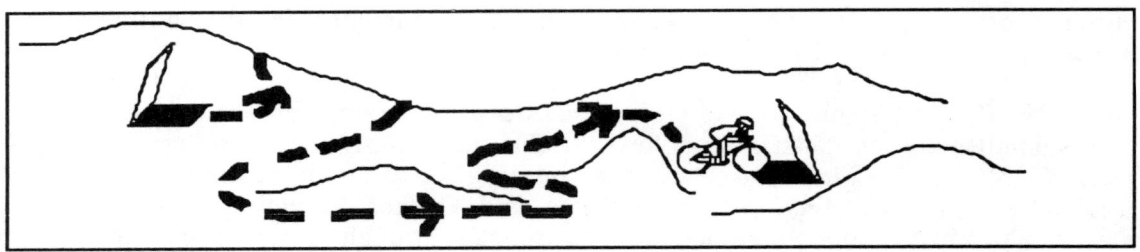

TRIP #30 - OCEANSIDE AT OCEANSIDE

GENERAL LOCATION: Oceanside

LEVEL OF DIFFICULTY: Round trip - easy
Distance - 7.6 miles
Elevation gain - essentially flat

GENERAL DESCRIPTION: Where else in this grand country can a biker enjoy a beachside spin in 89-degree weather in late November but Southern California? We were treated to these superb conditions on a day where Oceanside registered the country's high temperature. However, on any day of the year, bikers can enjoy this easy and scenic coastal loop. The trip highlights are the peripheral Oceanside Harbor tour and the short spin on The Strand near Oceanside Pier. There are also several interesting and unique parks to investigate along the way. Take this tour and work on a tan!

TRAILHEAD: From Interstate Hwy. 5, exit west at the Oceanside Blvd. turnoff and drive 3/4 mile to Pacific St. Turn left and continue 1/4 mile to Buccaneer Beach Park. This unforgettable park has it's very own small lagoon, children's play areas, picnic benches and restrooms For braver souls, an option is to park at more heavily-used City Park near the Oceanside Pier.

Save this trip for other than hot summer days unless your forte is dodging automobile, bike and foot traffic!

TRIP DESCRIPTION: **Northbound.** From Buccaneer Beach Park, bike northwest on Class II Pacific St., enjoying the ocean views. In 3/4 mile at Wisconsin Ave. is the southern edge of Pacific Street Linear Park. At the park's northern edge and below

NORTH COUNTY

highway level on the ocean side is City Park, while the AMTRAK station is on the inland side. Continue another 3/4 mile and pass both 6th St. and a large condominium complex (North Coast Village) before reaching the road which crosses the San Luis Rey River (2.0). (Note the "Proceed at Own Risk" sign which warns motorists about potential flooding in this low-lying area.)

View South from Oceanside Pier

Turn left and follow the road alongside Harbor Beach at the western edge of yacht-packed Oceanside Harbor. There are excellent views of both the inner harbor and the harbor entrance jetties at road's end. Return to Pacific St. and bike the 1-1/2-miles on Class III Harbor Dr. to enjoy the full harbor tour. In order, some of the points of interest are: Cape Cod Village (a collection of eateries and little specialty shops), the elegant Chart House Restaurant (this really is Don's favorite), varied yachts docked throughout the harbor, the Jolly Roger Restaurant complex, and the Villa Marina Hotel at the street terminus on the harbor's north side (5.4).

Southbound. Return to Pacific St. and backtrack to 6th St., just south of North Coast Village. Bike a short distance to The Strand, pass through the automobile entry barriers, and follow this beachside roadway south to the Oceanside Pier, one of the longest ocean piers on the West Coast. Stop and enjoy the views from the pier, including those from the restaurant at the rotunda at pier's end.

Pass The Strand Pier Plaza with its outdoor theater, then continue alongside Tyson St. Park and several other attractions, all within what is referred to as City Park. After a 1.2-mile cruise on The Strand, the road ends at Wisconsin Ave. Bike a short distance up to Pacific St. and return to Buccaneer Beach Park (7.6).

CONNECTING TRIPS: 1) Connection with the Coastal County Tour (Trip #21) - southbound bikers should follow the route described in (2) below, while northbound travelers should bike on Harbor Dr. under Interstate Hwy. 5 to Vandergrift Blvd.; 2) connection with the Loop O' the Lagoons (Trip #26) - bike south from the trip origin, turn inland on Cassidy St., and proceed to Hill St. south which becomes County Hwy. S21; 3) connection with the Oceanside City Tour (Trip #29) - at Oceanside Blvd., bike inland to Crouch St.

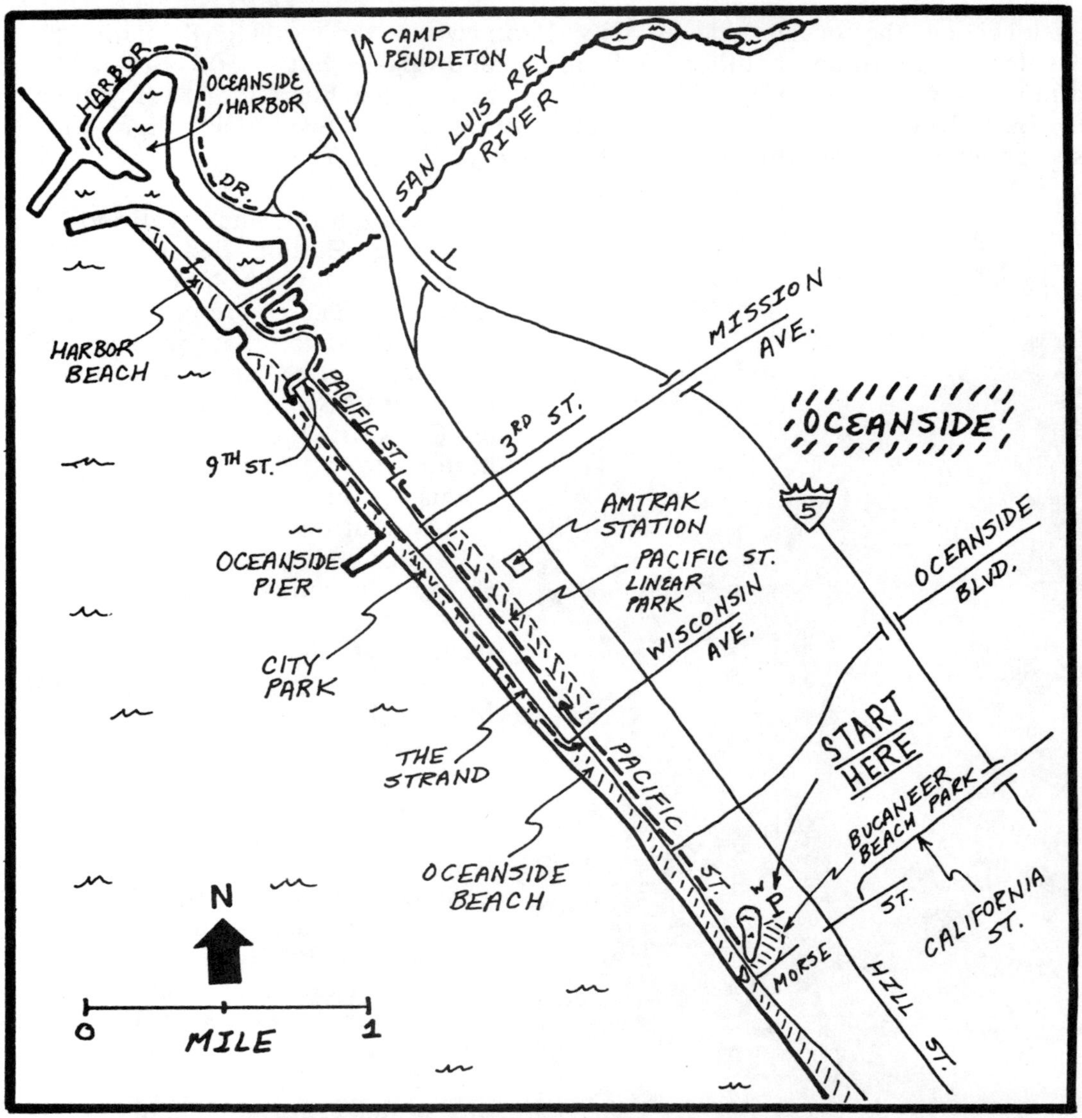

BICYCLE RIDES: SAN DIEGO COUNTY

TRIP #30 - OCEANSIDE AT OCEANSIDE

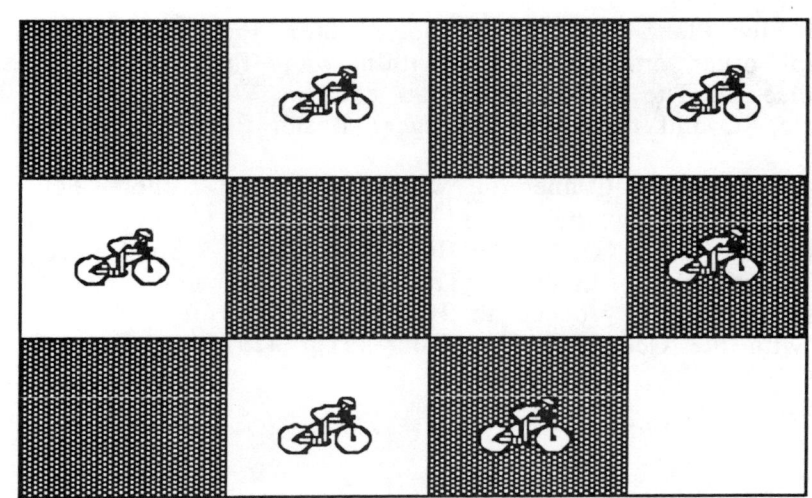

110

INLAND

Moosa Canyon from above Pamoosa Lane

BICYCLE RIDES: SAN DIEGO COUNTY

TRIP #31 - EL CAJON BIKEWAY SYSTEM

GENERAL LOCATION: El Cajon

LEVEL OF DIFFICULTY: Loop - moderate
Distance - 14.6 miles
Elevation gain - single steep grade on Fletcher Pkwy. north of Cuyamacha St.

GENERAL DESCRIPTION: The City of El Cajon is developing an extensive bikeway system. The peripheral route described is but one of many options to tour the city on generally flat roadway. Most of the routes are Class III (or assumed Class III on a couple of long, unmarked roadway stretches, based on the El Cajon city biking map). The described tour leaves the rural east side of El Cajon and continues through mixed residential/light-commercial areas to the base of Fletcher Hills. A workout upgrade leads to Westwind Dr. where the biker is treated to a generally downhill coast past Harry Griffen Regional Park near the trip's mid point. The five-mile return segment steps its way north and east through more residential/light-commercial territory. The east-facing section of this trip provides many interesting mountain views.

TRAILHEAD: From Interstate Hwy. 8, exit at State Hwy. 54. In 1/4 mile, turn left at Madison Ave. and drive one mile to 4th St. John F. Kennedy Park is just south of this intersection. This grassy-knolled park has tree shade, tennis courts, and restrooms.

TRIP DESCRIPTION: **North Segment.** Pedal east on Madison Ave. 0.8 mile to Greenfield Dr., just below the striking Linde Vista Bible College and Seminary on the hillside. This is the rural eastern edge of the trip. Follow Greenfield Dr. north and then west as it returns to increasingly dense residential areas, passes below I-8, then beelines through mixed residential/light-commercial areas to First St. (3.5). There are several mini-markets and gas stations along this segment. A 1-1/2-mile Class II spin includes a passage over State Hwy. 67 and a head-on view of the Fletcher Hills.

The road becomes Vernon Wy. for a short stretch before it ends at Cuyamacha St. A short stint on this street leads to a one-mile, 270-foot climb on busy Fletcher Pkwy. The ascent into the Fletcher hills starts modestly, then gives way to a wind-sucking stretch which passes must-see Hillside Park (bike trails), then levels near Westwind Dr. (6.8). A 1.1-mile twisting, generally downhill, residential segment on this road leads to Main St. where the road name changes to Blackthorne Ave. There are scattered views directly south to Mt. Helix and the surrounding hills. At road's end, the biker turns left onto Murray Dr., then follows a steep downhill to El Cajon Blvd.

South Segment. This elevated roadway passes under I-8 and meets Chase St. just beyond. The flat 5.1-mile return segment follows a northeast stair-step pattern through predominantly residential areas on a Class III bikeway. (Bikepath signs are sporadic on this stretch, although there is generally adequate bike shoulder.) On the east-facing segments, there are views into the colorful local mountains; these are captivating near sunset. There are several markets and gas stations along the route. The final section along Granite Hills Dr. is particularly impressive with its widely scattered classy homes, complete with horse corrals (14.6).

CONNECTING TRIPS: 1) Connection with the Lake Murray ride (Trip #16) - at Fletcher Pkwy. and Westwind Dr., continue west on the former street, turn right at

URBAN

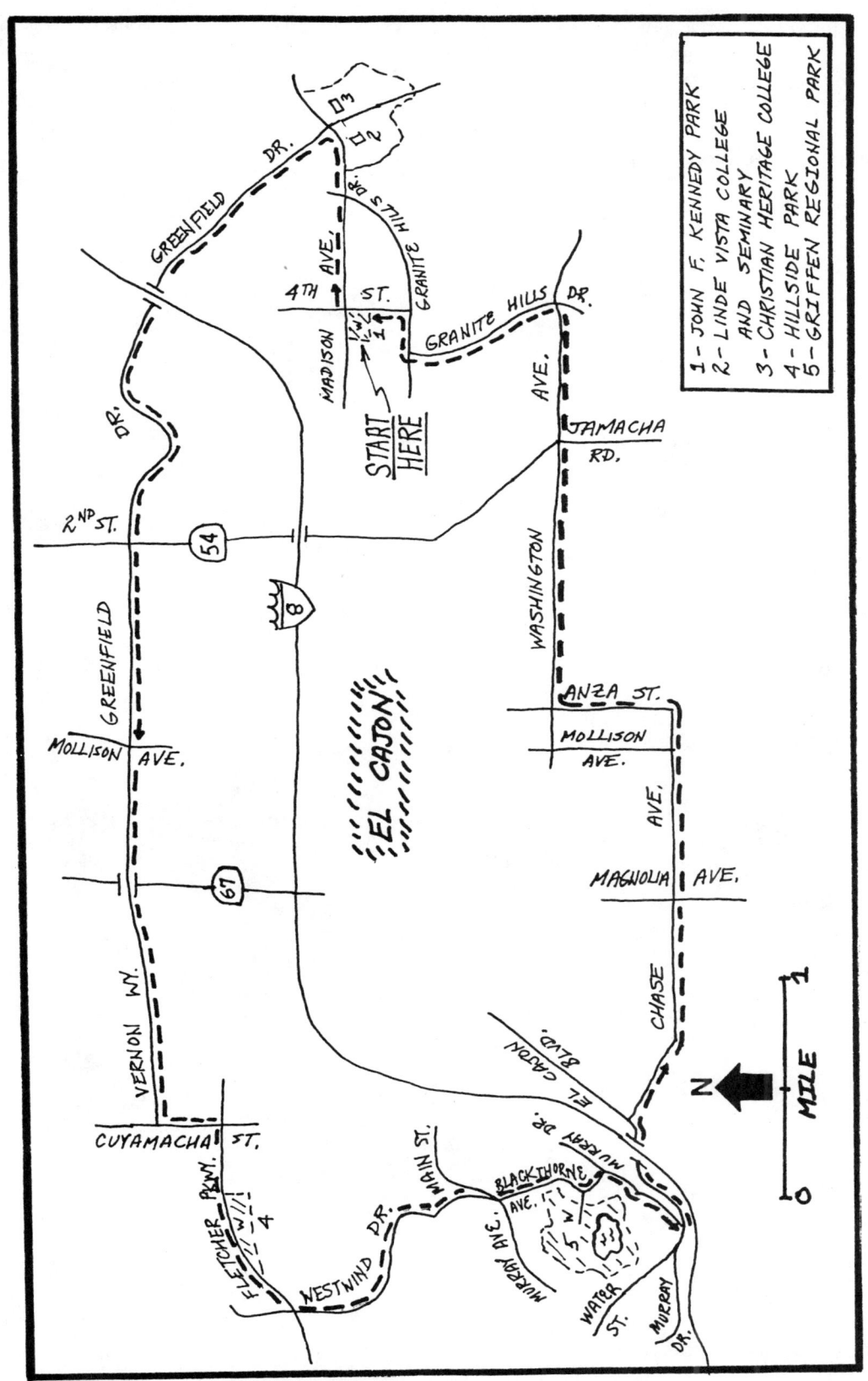

TRIP #31 - EL CAJON BIKEWAY SYSTEM

BICYCLE RIDES: SAN DIEGO COUNTY

Navajo Rd. then left at Lake Murray Blvd.; 2) connection with the Santee Lakes tour (Trip #32) - at Cuyamacha St. and Vernon Wy., bike north on the former street, turn left at Mission Gorge Rd., and right at Carlton Hills Blvd.; 3) connection with the Mt. Helix tour (Trip #44) - at Chase Ave. and Avocado Blvd. turn south on the latter road, then west on Fuerte Dr.; 4) connection with the Crest-Dehesa Valley Loop (Trip #53) - the trips share a common segment on Granite Hills Dr.

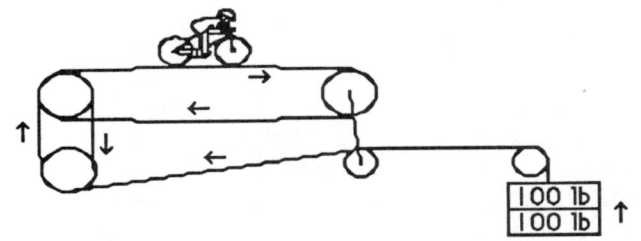

TRIP #32 - SANTEE LAKES

GENERAL LOCATION: Santee

LEVEL OF DIFFICULTY: Loop - easy
Distance - 3.8 miles
Elevation gain - essentially flat

"Duck Pond #5"

DESCRIPTION: Another of a series of family lakeside excursions (also see the Lake Miramar and Lake Murray trips), this ride plies the seven Santee Lakes, with the northern campground area thrown in as a bonus. The 1.1-mile tour on the east side of the lakes passes numerous treed picnic and fishing areas (bass, blue gill and channel cats) as well as the General Store/Arcade/Laundry/Boat Rental/Park Registration (areas between Lakes #4 and #5).

URBAN

Just beyond these two lakes (our favorites) is the Lakeshore (Camping) loop alongside Lake #6. Beyond Lake #7 is the main campground area and a further option to pedal around the three northern loops. Returning south, take the road between Lakes #5 and #6 to begin the westside tour. Here is hard-packed dirt suitable for all types of bikes. The biker returns to the east bank between Lakes #2 and #3 (an overpass was being constructed over Lake #2, causing this detour when we passed through in Winter 1991). The mileage noted is for a route which returns to the park entrance.

TRAILHEAD: From State Hwy. 67 northbound, exit west at Prospect Ave. in Santee. In a short distance, veer left onto Magnolia Ave. and drive 1/2 mile to Mission Gorge Rd. Continue west on that road for 1-3/4 miles, turning right at Carlton Hills Blvd., and left in 1/3 mile at Carlton Oaks Dr. Drive west 1/2 mile to the Santee Lakes Regional Park entrance. From State Hwy. 67 southbound, take the Woodside Ave. off-ramp 1/2 mile, veering right onto Mission Gorge Rd. Continue as described above.

CONNECTING TRIPS: 1) Connection with the San Diego River Run (Trip #17) - bike south to Mission Gorge Rd.; 2) connection with the El Cajon Bikeway System (Trip #31) - return to Mission Gorge Rd. and turn right (south) at Cuyamacha St.

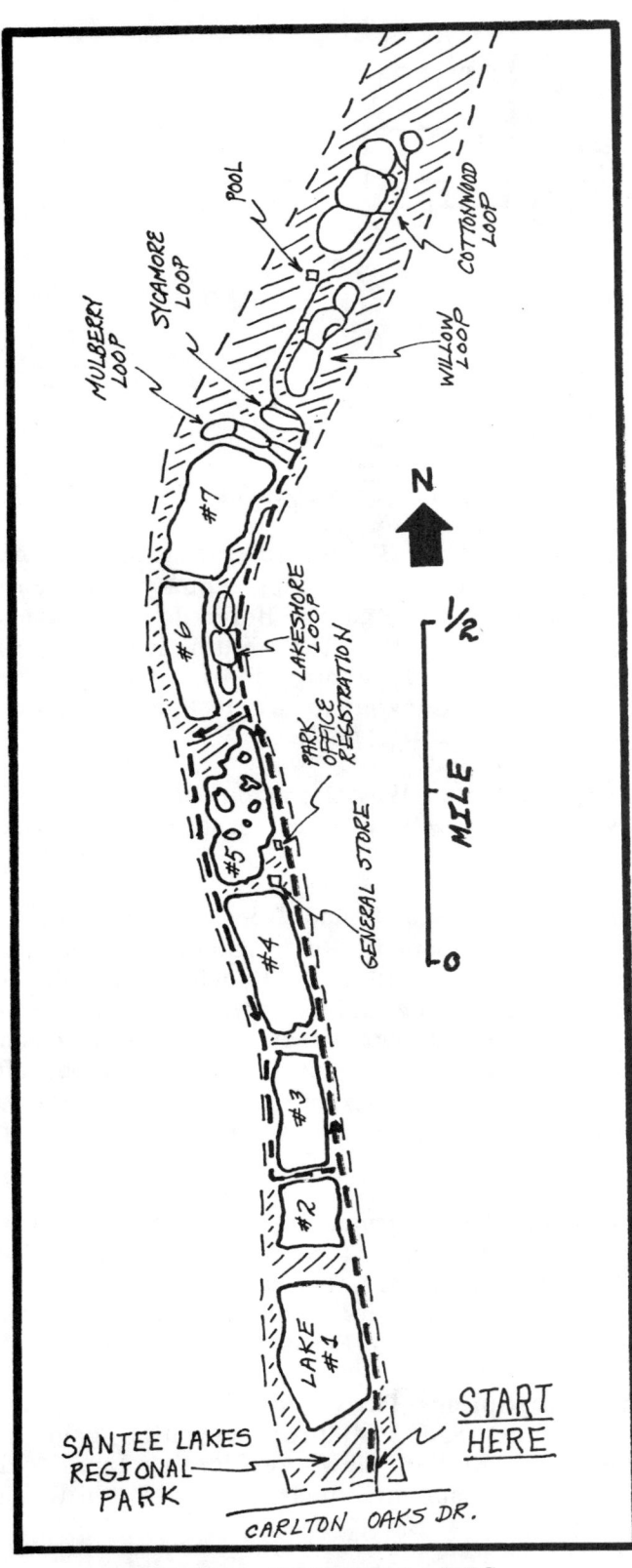

TRIP #32 - SANTEE LAKES

115

BICYCLE RIDES: SAN DIEGO COUNTY

TRIP #33 - RANCHO BERNARDO

GENERAL LOCATION: Rancho Bernardo

LEVEL OF DIFFICULTY: Two loops - moderate
Distance - 20.5 miles
Elevation gain - frequent moderate grades

GENERAL DESCRIPTION: This predominantly Class II mini-roller-coaster tour takes the bicyclist through the heart of Rancho Bernardo, another county residential "boom town." The initial north-to-south leg explores Rancho Bernardo and Rancho Penasquitos in the hilly sections west of the Interstate. The return leg follows a quiltwork series of streets past several golf courses and country clubs. That segment involves a 400-foot climb out of Los Penasquitos Canyon to a crest near Bernardo Heights Pkwy., followed by an easy return to the starting point.

TRAILHEAD: From Interstate Hwy. 15, exit west onto West Bernardo Dr. Continue 3/4 mile to Rancho Bernardo Community Park. The park has water, scattered tree shade, recreation fields and picnic benches.

TRIP DESCRIPTION: Western Segment. Bike southbound from the park on West Bernardo Dr., turning right at the first street, Aguameil Rd. Continue through a residential area, following a patchwork of streets 2.2 miles to Rancho Bernardo Rd. The 200-foot elevation just gained typifies the climbs spread throughout this tour. The reward is a milder series of rolling hills on another street maze which reaches the Interstate, then proceeds on a nifty uphill, cresting in about 0.7 mile. Soon, after a right turn onto Carmel Mountain Rd. (5.5), the biker passes a shopping center and stares into "Condo City." Newly-constructed residences are scattered all over the horizon.

The route crosses back over I-15, passes the lush Carmel Highlands Country Club, then proceeds on a workout 0.5-mile upgrade which peaks at Stoney Creek Rd. There is a spectacular view of the valley below from this area. The next two miles see a general downgrade as the biker passes shopping centers, plush residential areas, recrosses I-15 and reaches a segment low point above Los Penasquitos Canyon (11.0).

Eastern Segment. After a turn on Sabre Springs Pkwy., the cyclist is treated to four miles of variable upgrade (nothing strenuous) and a 400-foot elevation gain. In that segment, the route continues through another new residential area with scattered shopping centers. Just beyond the summit near Calle Pueblito are panoramic views into Rancho Bernardo.

URBAN

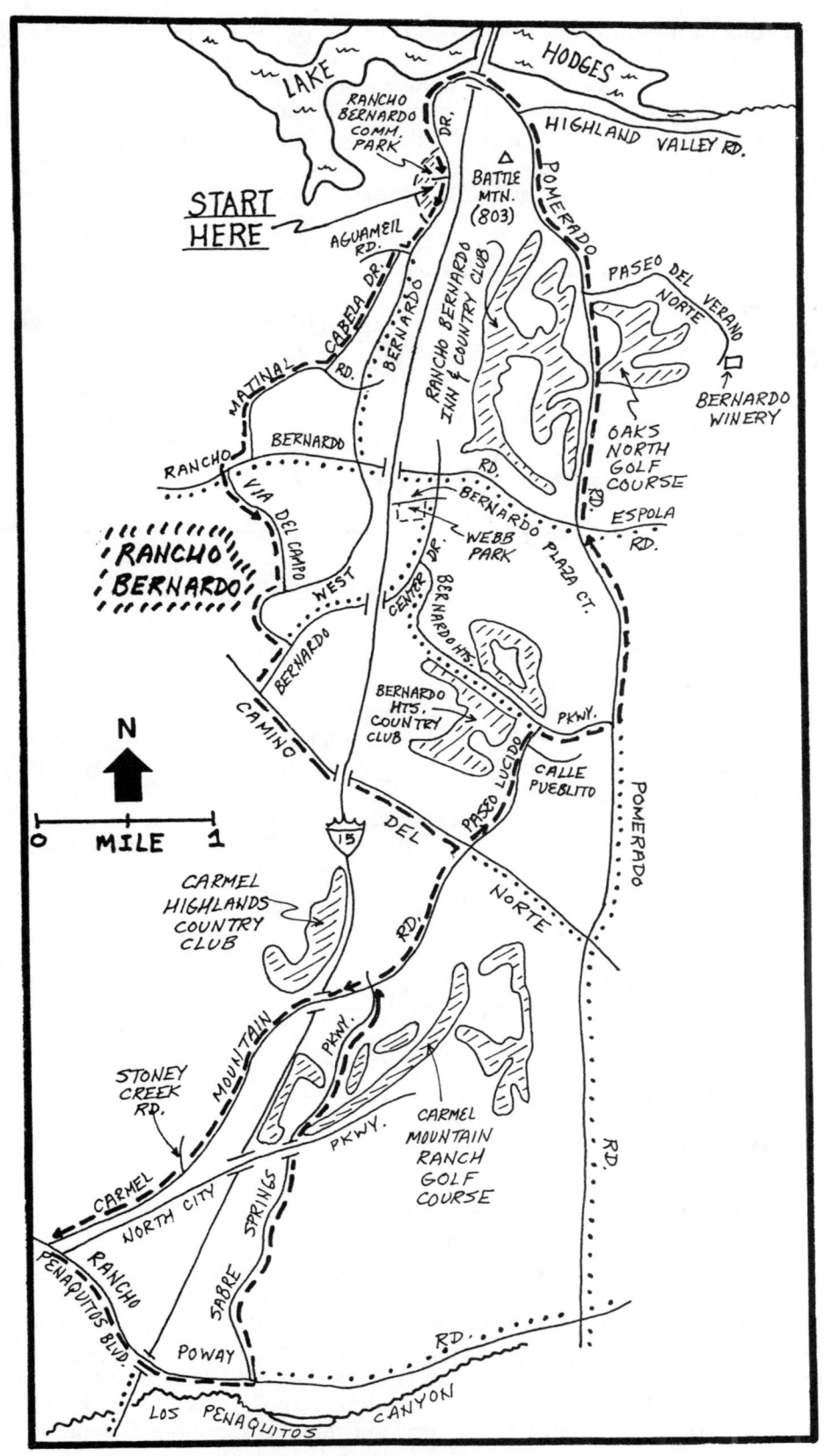

TRIP #33 - RANCHO BERNARDO

BICYCLE RIDES: SAN DIEGO COUNTY

A short segment on Bernardo Heights Pkwy. (15.2) follows, then a steep downhill on Pomerado Rd. which moderates, but continues to Rancho Bernardo Rd./Espola Rd. This is a 320-foot drop in just less than two miles. The remaining segment is on mild rolling roads. The return route passes Paseo Del Verano Norte (the route to the Bernardo Winery), cruises beneath "historic" Battle Mountain (see Trip #36), then makes a 180-degree slow turn as it crosses over the freeway and becomes West Bernardo Dr. In a few foot-pedals is the entrance to the park and the trip's end (20.5).

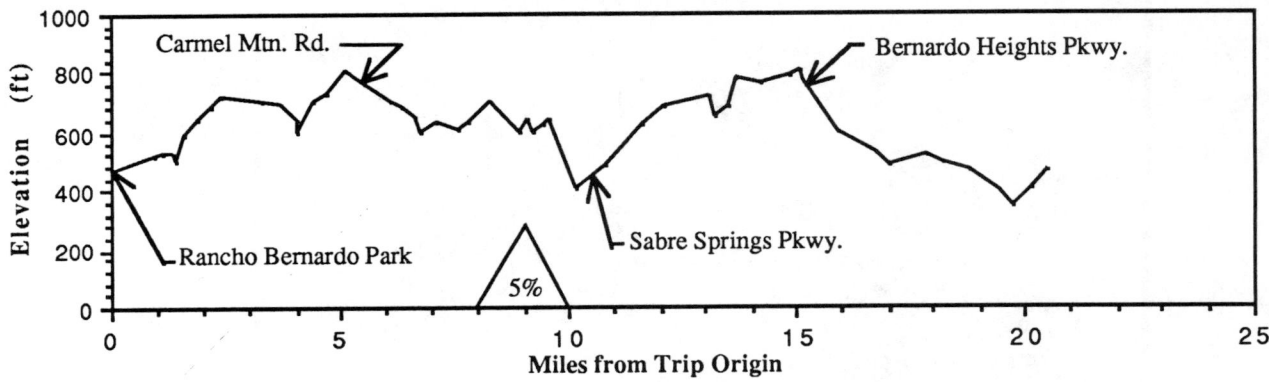

CONNECTING TRIPS: 1) Connection with the Lake Miramar Meander (Trip #20) - follow the Class I bike path on the south side of Poway Rd. (just East of I-15) into Los Penasquitos Canyon; 2) connection with the Escondido City Tour (trip #35) - enter Interstate Hwy. 15 at Pomerado Rd., exiting at Via Rancho Pkwy.; 3) connection with the Poway "Picnic" (Trip #34) - the tours share a common segment on Pomarado Rd.; 4) connection with the San Pasqual Valley ride (Trip #36) - at Pomerado Rd. and Highland Valley Rd., turn right onto the latter road; 5) connection with Old Hwy 395 (Trip #38) - both trips share a common segment on Poway Rd. and Pomerado Rd.

TRIP #34 - POWAY "PICNIC"

GENERAL LOCATION: Poway

LEVEL OF DIFFICULTY: Loop - easy to moderate
Distance - 14.1 miles
Elevation gain - periodic moderate grades

GENERAL DESCRIPTION: The toughest part of this tour is deciding which of the two delightful parks will be the trip's starting point. Our described route leaves goodie-packed Poway Community Park in South Poway and follows a Class II loop. The tour visits the base of Twin Peaks, passes the entrance to gorgeous Lake Poway, skirts Valle Verde Park, then makes a southerly return via highly developed Pomerado Rd.

URBAN

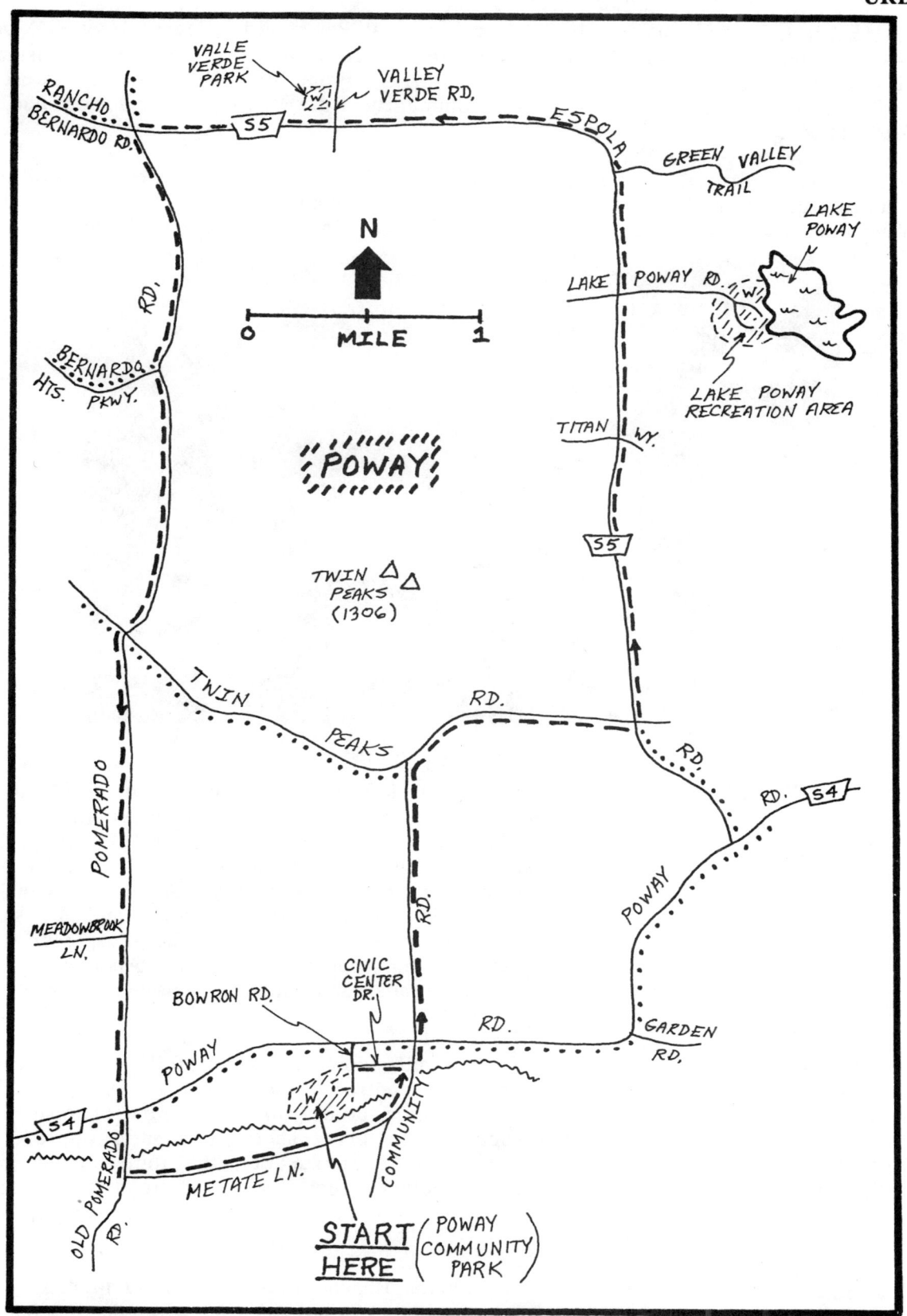

TRIP #34 - POWAY "PICNIC"

BICYCLE RIDES: SAN DIEGO COUNTY

TRAILHEAD: From Interstate Hwy. 15, exit east at Poway Rd. (County Hwy. S4), and drive 4-1/2 miles to Community Rd. Turn right, then right again in a short distance at Civic Center Dr. Follow this road into the park. From State Hwy. 67, turn west at Poway Rd. and continue 5-1/2 miles to Community Rd. Turn left and continue as described above.

Poway Community Park has tree cover, picnic facilities, restrooms, children's playgrounds, recreation fields, tennis courts and a swimming pool. There are also numerous bikeable roads and paths within the park for family entertainment.

Lake Poway

TRIP DESCRIPTION: Leave the park, turn left onto Community Rd. and make a beeline for Poway's centerpiece landmark, Twin Peaks. Bike 1.3 miles through an older residential area ("older" in this territory sometimes equates to 15-20 years), turn left on Espola Rd., and bike a slight, steady two-mile upgrade which peaks near Titan Wy. In 0.9 mile is the turnoff to Lake Poway Recreation Area. If you are willing to pay the modest entry fee, this classy park of grassy knolls and a fishing lake offers restrooms, shade from a wide variety of trees, picnic facilities, recreation fields, children's playgrounds and summer evening concerts to boot! Also, there are several generally hilly walkways/bikeways (roads and surfaced paths) within the park for cycling.

Beyond Lake Poway Rd. is a casual three-mile downhill which follows a sweeping westward turn beyond Green Valley Trail and continues on a line to Pomerado Rd. (7.5). Turning south, the biker follows a 5.0-mile cruise through a mix of residential and commercial areas with numerous shopping centers There is a mild upgrade on this segment which peaks at Twin Peaks Rd. At Metate Ln., the route swings left, sandwiched between Poway Creek and the southern foothills. The road veers north in 0.7 mile, becoming Community Rd. In a short distance is Civic Center Dr. and the return route to the park (14.1).

CONNECTING TRIPS: 1) Connection with the Rancho Bernardo tour (Trip #33) - the tours share a common segment on Pomerado Rd.; 2) connection with the Escondido

City Tour (Trip #35) - bike north on Pomerado Rd., enter I-15 and exit at Via Rancho Pkwy.; 3) connection with the San Pasqual Valley ride (Trip #36) - bike north on Pomerado Rd. and turn at Highland Valley Rd.; 4) connection with Old Hwy. 395 (Trip #38) - the trips share a common segment on Pomerado Rd.

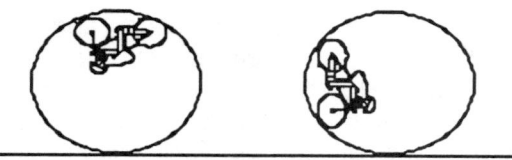

TRIP #35 - ESCONDIDO CITY TOUR

GENERAL LOCATION: Escondido, San Marcos

LEVEL OF DIFFICULTY: Loop - moderate (strenuous if Dixon Lake included)
Distance - 29.9 miles
Elevation gain - periodic moderate grades

GENERAL DESCRIPTION: Gleaned from the Escondido Chamber of Commerce's "Escondido Bike Routes," this is only one of a large number of sanctioned city routes which the biker may ride. We chose this peripheral route to maximize the amount of the trip which is outside busy central-city areas and also to provide a high mileage workout. Highpoints of the tour are the scenic San Pasqual Valley segment, the plush Escondido Country Club residential area, and the rural ride along Country Club Dr. and Harmony Grove Rd. This trip might stretch the limits of the "moderate" label on extremely hot days. Note that all roads on the city's route map were not signed as bikeways, thus we had some difficulties assessing whether some segments were Class X or Class III (we arbitrarily labeled them Class X).

The Ostrich Farm

BICYCLE RIDES: SAN DIEGO COUNTY

TRAILHEAD: From Interstate Hwy. 15, exit west at Via Rancho Pkwy. Drive 1-1/4 miles to Felicita Rd. and turn right. In about 1/2 mile on the left, turn into the Felicita County Park entrance. This enticing, well-treed park offers restrooms, covered and uncovered picnic areas and several biking trails.

TRIP DESCRIPTION: **East Side.** Bike back to I-15, continuing on Via Rancho Pkwy, passing the North County Fair (an enclosed mall), and then the entrance to Kit Carson Park. At San Pasqual Rd., turn right and pedal past the San Pasqual Vineyards/Thomas Jaeger Winery; then follow the road down into the San Dieguito River drainage. In another mile is an ostrich farm (supposedly these critters are low in fat and cholesterol), followed by a 1.5-mile spin through the northern edge of San Pasqual Valley.

Turn left at busy San Pasqual Valley Rd. (State Hwy. 78) (6.1) and start a sometimes winding 1.1-mile general upgrade. The crest is reached at Old Pasqual Rd. A right turn at Citrus Ave. takes the biker on a tour of the outskirts of Escondido. After 3.5 miles on this road, the cyclist meets La Honda Dr. (11.7). There is a diversion route for hearty, well-conditioned bikers to visit Dixon Lake at this point (see description below); however, our reference tour continues on the road now called El Norte Pkwy. Just beyond El Norte Park is a turn to the north at Ash St. The biker follows a circuitous route from this intersection which travels at the base of the less-developed surrounding hillsides and reaches Rincon Ave. in 1.7 miles.

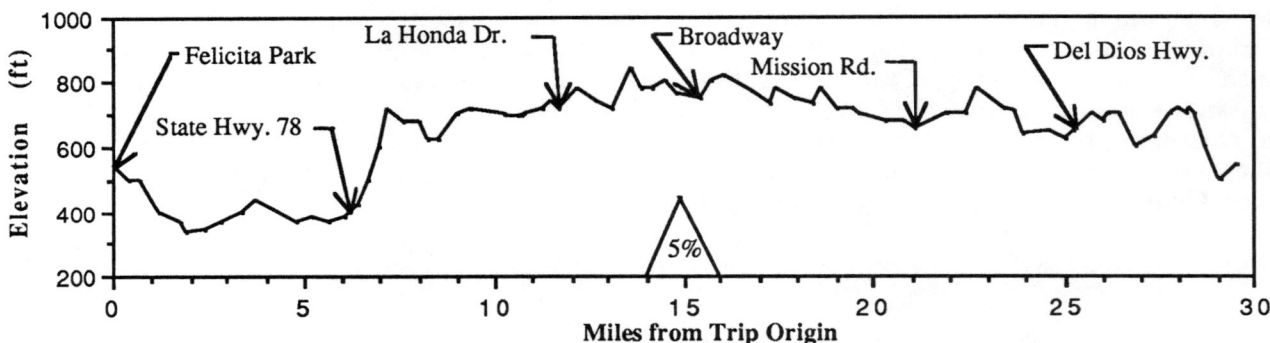

West Side. Bike past Broadway into a more affluent and newly-developed residential area, pass under I-15, then enjoy a nice downhill on Country Club Ln. Pass through the posh Escondido Country Club and surrounding residential areas, veering left to remain on Country Club Ln.

Turn left at El Norte Pkwy. (17.4) and follow a 4-5 mile circuit through the City of San Marcos, primarily through light density residential areas on rolling hills. Pass under State Hwy. 78 on Mission Rd., turn right at Citracado Pkwy. (A very clever name mix for two very predominant crops!) and make another sharp right at Ross Dr. Follow what is now Country Club Dr. through a valley chock full of ranches and horse farms, but look out for unleashed doggies! Next, turn at Kuana Loa Dr. (23.7) and follow a maze of roads through a more densely-populated area, reaching Del Dios Hwy. in 1.5 miles.

Follow this Class II highway south 1.7 miles to Via Rancho Pkwy. and turn left (east). Immediately pass Lake Dr. (there is a spur trip off this road as described below) and pedal on the two-lane highway that follows a general uphill to Kershawn Pl. before heading steeply downhill to Felicita Rd. Turn left and return to the park (29.9).

URBAN

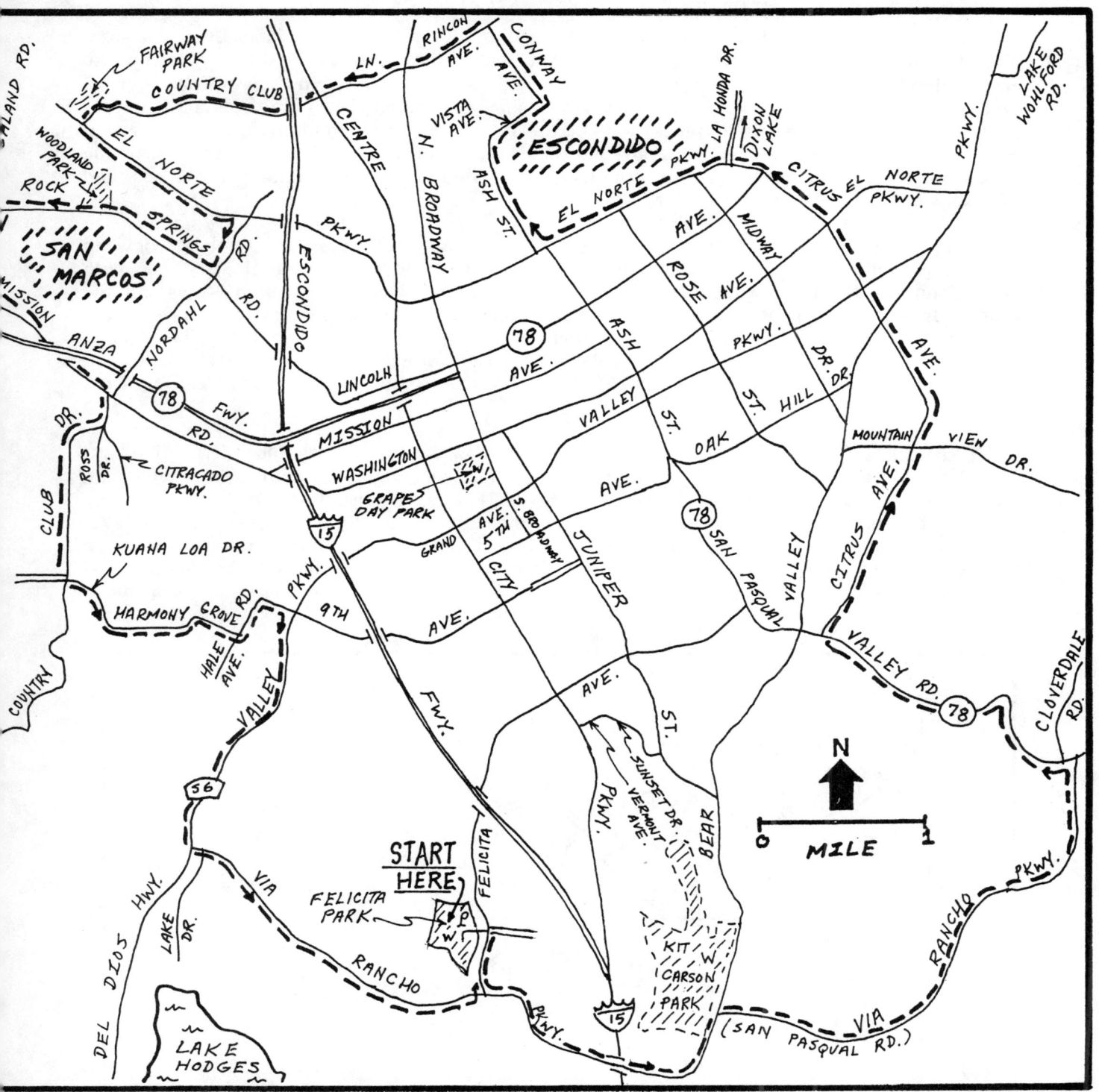

Note: All roads shown, except freeways, are CALTRANS-specified bikeways.

TRIP #35 - ESCONDIDO CITY TOUR

BICYCLE RIDES: SAN DIEGO COUNTY

Dixon Lake Side Tour. It is one grizzly uphill mile to the Dixon Lake entrance. This is over a six percent <u>average</u> grade with sections marked as 10-14%. If you are in excellent biking shape, this is a great workout! Otherwise, you may find yourself walking your bike (it's worth it!). Once inside the gate, there are numerous scenic lake views. Cycling right takes the biker 1.1 miles through individual and group picnic areas, past a concession stand and boat ramp, then to a camping area near the road's end. A left leads to the primitive area where there are hiking trailheads and Catfish Cove at the end of the line (0.5).

Lake Hodges Side Tour. Turn south onto Lake Dr., enjoying the lake view in the foreground with distant mountains beyond. Bike downhill through an area with scrub and small trees which transitions into thick tree cover on both sides of the road. In 0.7 mile near Elm St. is a small center with a country store and Maxine's Restaurant. In another 0.2 mile, the road bottoms out 200 feet below Via Rancho Pkwy. at Juniper Ln. At Tamarack Lake Dr., pass Herman's Hideaway (restaurant) and continue another 0.6 mile with a 165-foot elevation gain before reaching Del Dios Hwy.

<u>**CONNECTING TRIPS**</u>: 1) Connection with the San Pasqual Valley loop (Trip #36) - at Via Rancho Pkwy. and I-15, turn south on the freeway; 2) connection with the Escondido to the Sea---and Back tour (Trip #37) - at Kuana Loa Dr. and Harmony Grove Rd., turn south on the latter road; 3) connection with Old Hwy. 395 (Trip #38) - at the intersection of Country Club Ln. and City Centre Pkwy., turn north or south on the latter street. At Via Rancho Pkwy. and Interstate 15, bike south on the freeway; 4) connection with the Bear Ridge Loop (Trip #56) - same as above except turn north onto City Centre Pkwy.

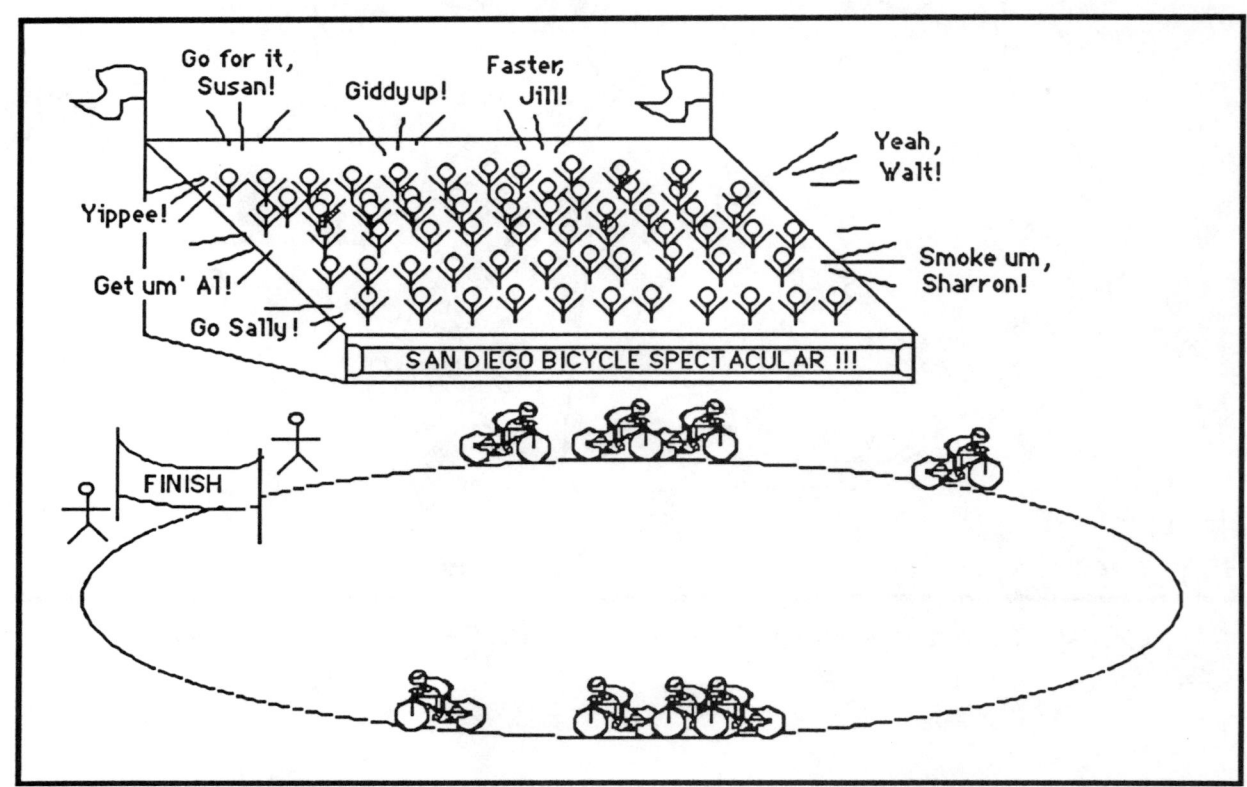

URBAN

TRIP #36 - SAN PASQUAL VALLEY

GENERAL LOCATION: Escondido, Rancho Bernardo

LEVEL OF DIFFICULTY: Loop - strenuous
Distance - 22.9 miles
Elevation gain - periodic moderate-to-strenuous grades
(sheer grade below Bandy Canyon Rd.)

GENERAL DESCRIPTION: This predominantly rural countryside tour visits the Highland Valley plateau and nearly encircles scenic San Pasqual Valley. The biker is treated to splendid views from above and within the valley. Though mainly Class X, this dandy spin is generally on quiet, lightly-traveled roads removed from the big city. One stretch of the tour has 18 lovely miles with only a few stop signs and no signals. Key attractions are Kit Carson Park at the origin and the San Pasqual Battlefield State Historic Park near the mid point. There is a sheer, one-mile upgrade below Bandy Canyon Rd. and a very scenic downgrade into San Pasqual Valley.

TRAILHEAD: From Interstate Hwy. 15, exit west at Via Rancho Pkwy. Drive 1-1/2 miles to the northern Kit Carson Park entry at Las Palmas Ave. Turn left and drive about 1/4 mile to the small parking area near the playground and restrooms.

Explore the park and consider a rewarding picnic at the trip's end. Kit Carson Park has all the goodies: trees, restrooms, recreation fields, children's playgrounds, picnic facilities, walking trails, a duck pond and tennis courts. We watched several model enthusiasts flying gasoline-powered helicopters while in the park, and were surprised with the contrast of seeing a hawk riding the winds off the foothills in the background. Also while there, take advantage of the dandy in-park riding, as well as the Class I bike trail along the park periphery.

The single reliable water source that we found on the tour route was at the park. This is a one-or-two quart trip on hot days.

San Pasqual Valley Backdrop from Bandy Canyon Road

BICYCLE RIDES: SAN DIEGO COUNTY

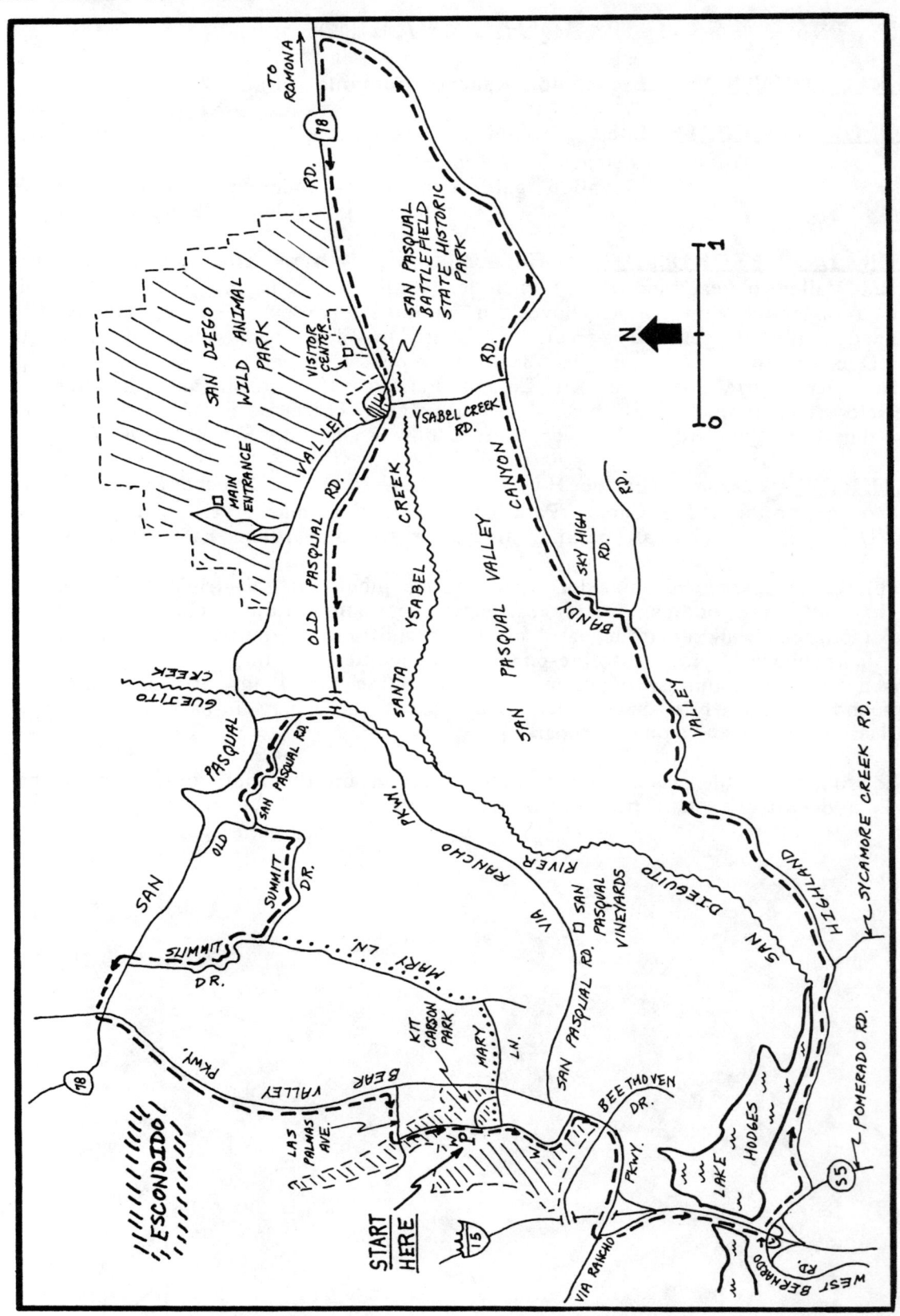

TRIP #36 - SAN PASQUAL VALLEY

URBAN

TRIP DESCRIPTION: Eastbound. Bike to the park's southern exit and continue south on Class II Bear Valley Pkwy. past the I-15 overpass. Just beyond, turn from the left lane onto the freeway and hug the generous Class II bike shoulder as the road passes over the eastern finger of Lake Hodges. After enjoying the elevated lake view, follow the first exit off the freeway (bikers are <u>required</u> to exit at this point). Turn left at Pomerado Rd. and continue east on the overpass. In a short distance to the south is Battle Mountain with its hiking trails to the cross-adorned summit. The cone-shaped peak was mistakenly named assuming that it was a key piece of real estate in the Battle of San Pasqual (the actual battle site is about five miles to the northeast). Just beyond the "historic" mountain is Highland Valley Rd. and the entry to 18 enjoyable rural-highway miles without so much as a stop light (and only a few stop signs) (2.8).

Along this road, the biker is treated to a pleasant flat tour of the Santa Ysabel Creek drainage. There are excellent views of the surrounding hillsides and distant mountains. Beyond Sycamore Creek Rd. (6.2) the route skirts "nurseryland," where pine, eucalyptus and palm seedlings are grown and many cultivated flowers abound. The winding road leaves the bottomland and starts on a 1.4-mile upgrade, a quarter mile of enjoyable workout followed by over a mile "pumperama" (average 6.5% grade). This short breath-grabber, which tops out near Bandy Canyon Rd., provides numerous opportunities to view the nurseries left behind earlier and is easily the toughest segment of this trip.

After turning onto Bandy Canyon Rd., the pedaler can now enjoy the Highland Valley plateau. This pedaling is followed by an exhilarating downhill which hugs the hillside wall forming the south boundary of scenic San Pasqual Valley. Once on the valley floor, the tour passes Ysabel Creek Rd. and continues through citrus groves, reaching San Pasqual Valley Rd. in a couple of miles (13.2).

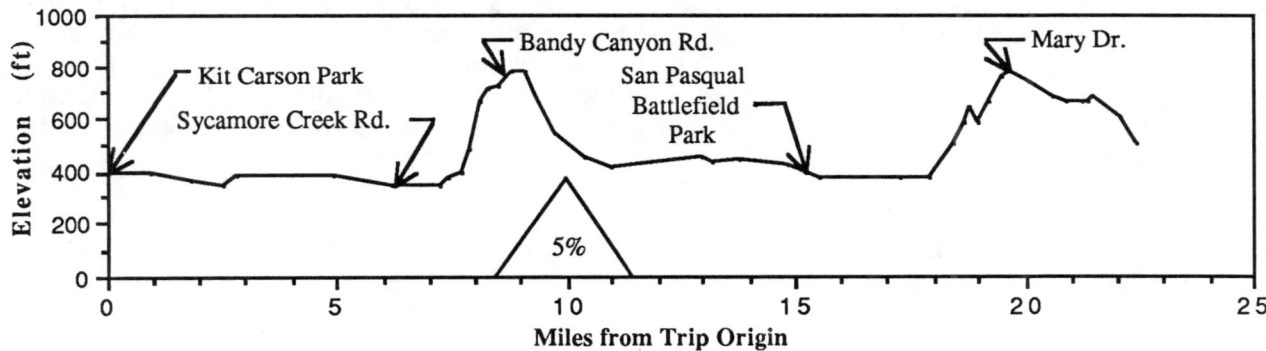

Westbound. Follow this scenic, but busy, road past the San Pasqual Battlefield Visitor Center, reaching the state park itself in another 1/4 mile. This historic site recognizes the men who fought in the Battle of San Pasqual on December 6, 1846 during the Mexican-American War. This indecisive skirmish, the bloodiest armed military conflict in California history, resulted in 22 deaths and numerous casualties.

Another mile west on State Hwy. 78 is the entrance to the San Diego Wild Animal Park. Sometimes referred to as the modern day "Noah's Ark," this 1800-acre wildlife preserve has over 2500 animals from Africa, Asia, and Arabian deserts. Visitors can wander through an Australian rain forest, a Nairobi village with an aviary, a gorilla grotto, or take a photo caravan or monorail tour of the park.

BICYCLE RIDES: SAN DIEGO COUNTY

Local Scenery from San Pasqual Valley Road

However, our reference tour leaves Hwy. 78 soon, following Old Pasqual Rd. and Old San Pasqual Rd. (17.9) through farmland to the base of the northern foothills. A short and steep uphill pedal on the latter road leads to Summit Dr. Turn left and continue uphill, passing the well-kept residences on mini-farm size lots and ever-present orange and avocado groves. There are several nice peeks into San Pasqual Valley on the ascent. Beyond the crest at Mary Ln., the biker turns right (north) and is treated to an excellent view of the northern array of rolling hills and the outskirts of Escondido.

A one-mile downhill spin returns the biker to busy State Hwy. 78. A quarter mile beyond is Bear Valley Rd., where the route heads left onto a Class II bikeway. All that remains is to cruise through the residential-spotted rolling hills 1.8 miles to Las Palmas Ave. Turn into Kit Carson Park and return to the trip origin (22.9).

Flatlander's Option. Spend a couple of hours just in San Pasqual Valley itself, entering from Via Rancho Pkwy. and meandering about on Old Pasqual Rd., Ysabel Creek Rd., the flat portion of Bandy Canyon Rd. and San Pasqual Valley Rd. The trip should allow time to visit the San Pasqual Battlefield State Historic Park and at least one of the local fruit stands.

<u>CONNECTING TRIPS</u>: 1) Connection with the Rancho Bernardo ride (Trip #33) and Poway "Picnic" (Trip #34) - at Highland Valley Rd. and Pomerado Rd., bike south on the latter street; 2) continuation with the Escondido City Tour (Trip #35) - at the park's southern entrance, turn left on Bear Valley Pkwy., then right in a short distance at San Pasqual Rd.; 2) connection with the Escondido to the Sea---and Back ride (Trip #37) - at the park's southern entrance, turn right on Bear Valley Pkwy. and continue 4-1/2 miles to Del Dios Hwy. (County Hwy. S6).

URBAN

TRIP #37 - ESCONDIDO TO THE SEA---AND BACK

GENERAL LOCATION: Escondido, Del Mar, Leucadia, Rancho Santa Fe

LEVEL OF DIFFICULTY: Round trip - strenuous
Distance - 39.4 miles
Elevation gain - periodic moderate-to-steep grades

GENERAL DESCRIPTION: This 40-mile workout loop samples some of the coastal foothills of the North County, as well as one of its most delightful seaside segments. The outbound loop offers a pleasant canyon tour, as well as a refreshing and scenic downhill to the ocean. However, the return leg on Hwy. S6 is the highlight, providing the tourer with a route high in scenic contrast. The 17.8-mile inbound pedal starts at the scenic seaside, traverses two serene valleys, visits the heavily-wooded periphery of Rancho Santa Fe, follows a series of open rolling hills into a large canyon above Lake Hodges, and ends in the bustling City of Escondido. For bikers who enjoy a less strenuous ride, limit the trip to the Hwy. S6 segment and consider starting from Escondido.

TRAILHEAD: From Interstate Hwy. 15, exit west at 9th Ave. in Escondido. Drive 3/4 mile, cross Del Dios Hwy. (County Hwy. S6) and park in the shopping center. Load up on carbos at one of several eateries in the area. We enjoyed stuffing our faces at the Soup Exchange.

The only reliable public water sources that we found are at the beachside parks. On hot days, bring a couple of quarts of aqua pura.

TRIP DESCRIPTION: **Escondido to the Sea.** From the shopping center, follow the route to Harmony Grove Rd. and turn right. A quarter mile after a sharp jog in the road, turn left to remain on this street (Kuana Loa Dr. intersection). Almost immediately, the biker leaves the Escondido metropolis and is immersed in countryside serenity. In a mile, the route passes little Harmony Grove proper, the last "major" community development for many miles.

BICYCLE RIDES: SAN DIEGO COUNTY

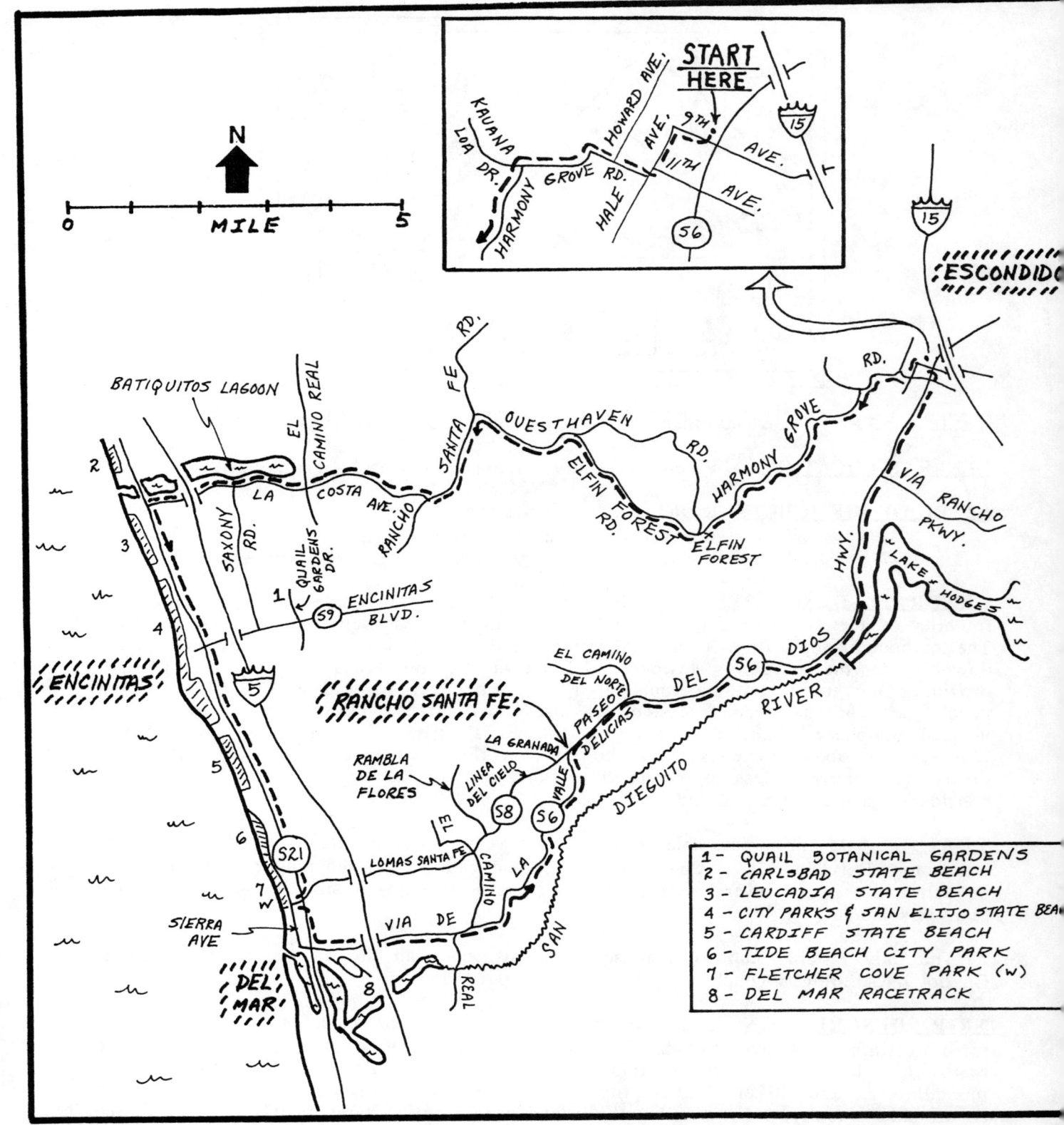

TRIP #37 - ESCONDIDO TO THE SEA---AND BACK

URBAN

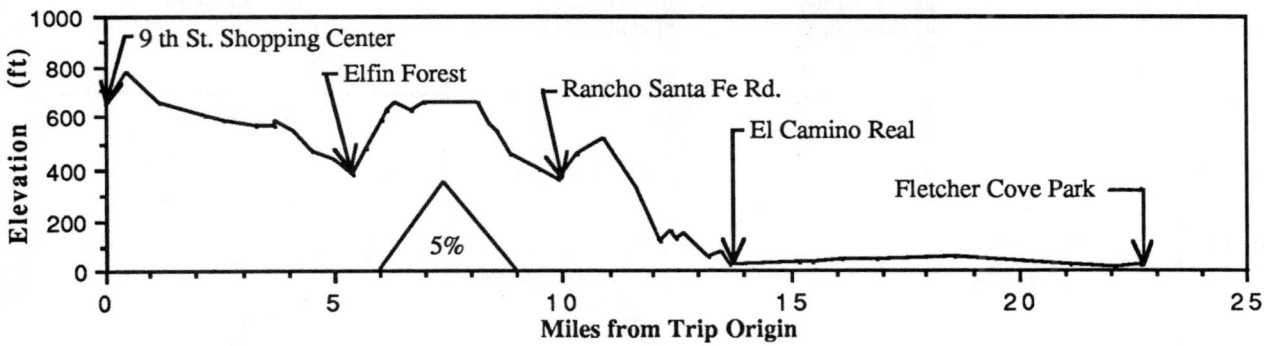

From Country Club Dr. to Elfin Forest, bicyclists are within ever-narrowing San Elijo Canyon with its scattered residences, citrus groves, and eucalyptus-shaded Escondido Creek. The winding and narrow two-lane country road is typical of what the biker will traverse until the Questhaven Rd. intersection with Rancho Santa Fe Rd.

At Elfin Forest is the Elfin Forest store (groceries, deli), Elfin Forest resort (park and campground), and a forest station (5.4). Elfin Forest you say!? The name is a poetic interpretation of the dense patches of low-lying brush and chaparrel scattered around the local hillsides. In a mile of continual rolling hills, the views to the surrounding world reopens, a clear indication that the route has left the canyon. In 2.7 miles from Elfin Forest, after passing scattered residences in the increasingly barren hills, the route turns left (west) at Questhaven Rd. Continuing to pedal through 1.8 miles more of this barren, hilly terrain brings the biker to Rancho Santa Fe Rd. (9.9). A left here and the biker is treated to a 0.4-mile steep upgrade which levels and then peaks in another 0.6 mile. At the crest is an exceptional view westward which overlooks La Costa, the Batiquitos Lagoon and the expansive Pacific Ocean. Coast to La Costa Ave. and turn right onto that Class II roadway, returning to a highly-developed and ritzy-residential area. Continue the downhill through La Costa, cross El Camino Real, cruise along the lagoon and reach County Hwy. S21 in 16.1 miles from the starting point.

Beachside Traverse. Linkage between the interior route segments is provided by a 6.5-mile seaside link which travels south from Leucadia to Solana Beach on S21. On this flat segment, the road passes near several superb beaches, a couple of pleasant parks and the San Elijo Lagoon. A fine place for a rest is Fletcher Cove Park. This park has picnic benches, outdoor shower, vista points atop the surrounding bluffs and several nearby eateries, including the Solana Beach Cafe. The plentiful coastal views are exceptional! A short diversion at Encinitas Blvd. leads to the Quail Botanical Gardens, where there are 30 acres of flowers and blooming plants ranging from the common to the exotic.

--- And Back. Bike 0.7 mile on residential Sierra Ave., turning left at road's end at Border Ave. Cross S21 and continue on what is now Class II Via De La Valle (County Hwy. S6), which the biker will follow into Escondido. Pass the Del Mar Racetrack and, after biking under Interstate Hwy. 5, cruise through San Dieguito Valley with its scattered farms and nurseries. For the next several miles, this flat and scenic roadway follows near the San Dieguito River, meandering near a well-groomed set of country clubs and passing under periodic mammoth overhanging cypress stands. At

BICYCLE RIDES: SAN DIEGO COUNTY

the departure from Osuna Valley, the biker is treated to a 0.7-mile workout upgrade which crests near tree-surrounded Paseo Delicias (29.7).

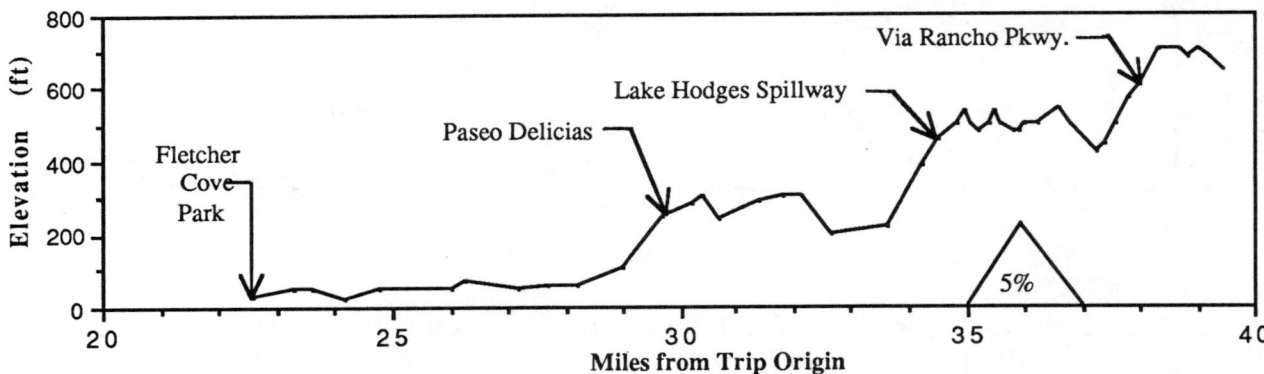

Turn right (northeast) on that busier Class II road and observe the diminishing level of development with each passing mile. Beyond Rancho Del Rio, the pedaler looks out to rolling hills with scattered tree cover while heading directly toward Mt. Israel. About four miles from the Via De La Valle intersection, the hillsides pinch inward and the pedaler finds himself/herself within a canyon with the San Dieguito River to the right and below.

Lake Hodges Dam from Del Dios Highway

On the steady uphill segment at the dam, the cyclist is treated to the first of many views of Lake Hodges far below (34.2). Within this large canyon is a refreshing downhill which bottoms out near Rancho Rd. Another upgrade lurks beyond, as the biker leaves the reservoir behind, followed by a long downhill to Elm Ln. A final uphill pull takes the cyclist past Via Rancho Pkwy. (and the first stoplight in 15 miles!) and into the City of Escondido. The continued Class II highway traverses residential area, then returns to an industrial setting near the trip origin (39.4).

CONNECTING TRIPS: 1) Connection with the Coastal County Tour (Trip #21) - at Hwy. S21 continue north or south and remain on that highway; 2) connection with Riding the "Ranch" (Trip #22) - at Del Dios Hwy. and El Camino Del Norte, turn north onto the latter street; 3) connection with the La Costa tour (Trip #23) - at Rancho Santa Fe Rd. and Cadencia St., turn west onto the latter street; 4) connection with the Lake San Marcos ride (trip #24) - at Questhaven Rd. and Rancho Santa Fe Rd., turn north onto the latter street; 5) connection with the Loop O' the Lagoons (Trip #26) - turn north at El Camino Real; 6) connection with El Camino Real (Trip #28) - at the street of the same name, turn north or south from either La Costa Ave. or Via De La Valle; 7) connection with the Escondido City Tour (Trip #35) - at Del Dios Hwy. and Via Rancho Hwy., turn east onto the latter roadway.

TRIP #38 - OLD HIGHWAY 395

GENERAL LOCATION: San Diego, Escondido, Temecula

LEVEL OF DIFFICULTY: One way - strenuous
Distance - 56.7 miles
Elevation gain - periodic moderate-to-steep grades

GENERAL DESCRIPTION: Being beach people, the coastal tour of San Diego County (Trip #21) is a definite favorite. However, the inland version of this cross-country trek rivals it by providing a more secluded adventure through the continuous chains of hills and mountains. This is particularly characteristic of the roller-coaster workout segment between North Escondido and Temecula. Sightseeing starts at the trip origin at Jack Murphy Stadium and continues as the route passes Miramar Naval Air Station, enters scenic Los Penasquitos Canyon, passes over Lake Hodges, skirts the Lawrence Welk Resort and ends in classic Old Town Temecula. The mostly Class II trip can be extended 26 miles into Corona in Riverside County by criss-crossing Interstate Hwy. 15 all the way from Temecula through Temescal Canyon.

TRAILHEAD: From Interstate Hwy. 15/State Hwy. 15, exit west at Friars Rd. and drive 1/3 mile to the entrance of Jack Murphy Stadium. Park in the stadium lot. From other freeways, transition onto Interstate Hwy. 8 and take the northbound Hwy. 15 exit. Continue as described above.

Bring one to two quarts of water for the more isolated stretches in the North County.

TRIP DESCRIPTION: San Diego to Escondido. Bike to the northeast corner of the parking lot to an asphalt path that begins just below the Friars Rd. overpass. In 0.9 mile, this path fuses into Murray Canyon Rd. and follows that road 4.6 Class II-miles along Interstate Hwy. 15 to Claremont Mesa Blvd. In between is a passage through business and shopping complexes and beneath the busy small-plane traffic of Montgomery Field. A series of turns brings the biker to the somewhat confusing intersection (the road name both to the left and directly ahead is Kearney Villa Rd.). Continue straight ahead and cross State Hwy. 52 onto Kearny Mesa. The next 4.4 flat

BICYCLE RIDES: SAN DIEGO COUNTY

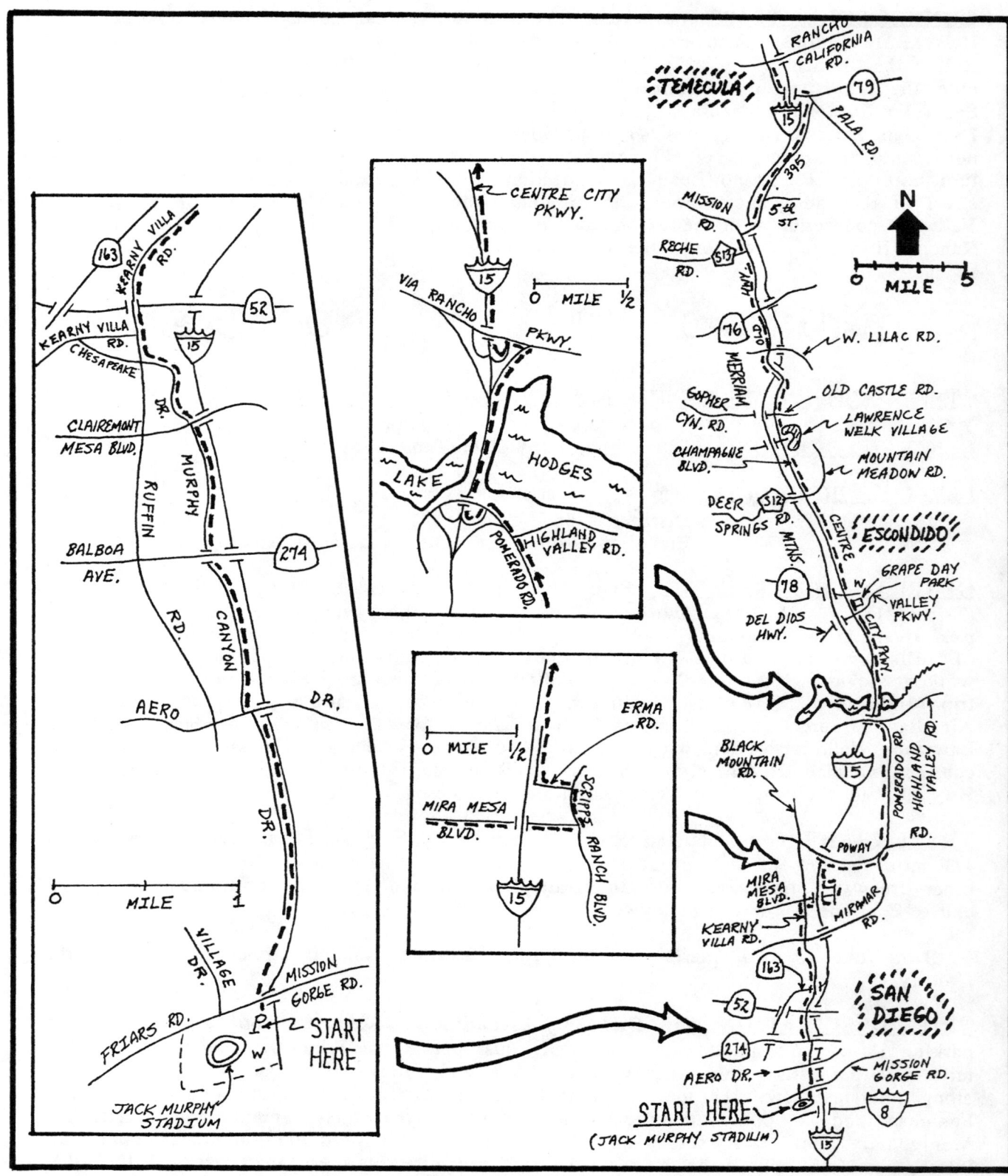

TRIP #38 - OLD HIGHWAY 395

miles is across a mesa with unobstructed views of the surrounding hills, followed by a crossing under the Miramar Naval Air Station flight path (holy shrieking jets!!) and passage into Mira Mesa.

Military Fan Club at Jack Murphy Stadium

A jog east on Mira Mesa Blvd. (10.0) is followed by a sequence of turns which places the cyclist at the entrance to a small path along I-15 (at the end of Erma Rd. at the tennis court). The two miles which follow on Class I path include a drop of several hundred feet into scenic Los Penasquitos Canyon and a short uphill to Poway Rd. The subsequent 6.7-mile segment on Class II Pomerado Rd. passes through Poway/Rancho Bernardo and alongside Battle Mountain (see Trip #36 for a bit of humor on this subject) just before reaching the Interstate. Bike onto the right-hand shoulder of the freeway, cross over the eastern arm of Lake Hodges, and exit at the next off-ramp (Via Rancho Pkwy.). <u>Do not</u> try to cross the off-ramp! At this street, follow the cross-walk to the northbound on-ramp and take the 180-degree loop back onto I-15 (23.2).

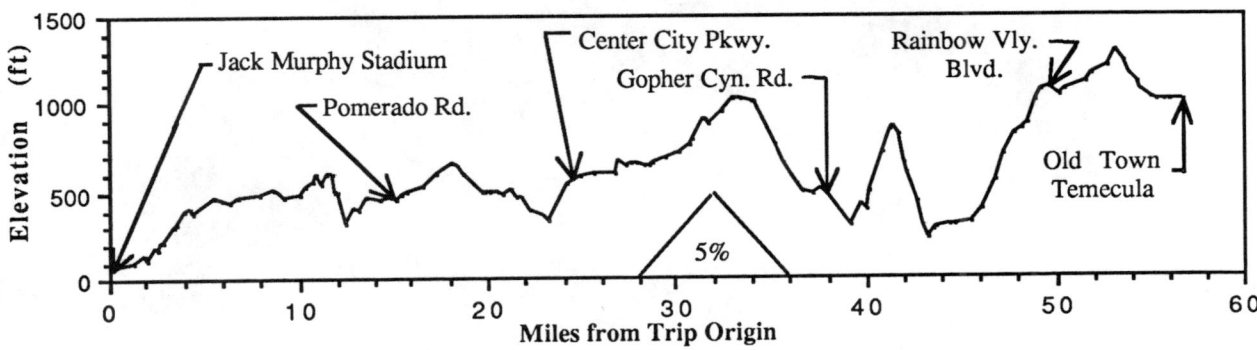

Escondido to Rainbow. Exit at the next off-ramp at Center City Pkwy. and follow that road 6.7 miles on the western edge of Escondido. In this flat stretch are

BICYCLE RIDES: SAN DIEGO COUNTY

commercial business offices, hotels, motels, fast-food centers, shopping malls, etc. At Country Club Ln., however, the route returns to less-developed countryside and follows the first of several challenging upgrades that the biker will face on the way into Rainbow. The route is sandwiched between the Merriam Mountains to the west and a series of steep bluffs to the east as the road meets Jesmond Dean Rd. and a high point (33.4).

In 3/4 mile at Deer Springs Rd./Mountain Meadows Rd., North Center City Pkwy. becomes Champagne Blvd. The biker is free to enjoy an excellent view further into the canyon as he/she coasts downhill, passing the Lawrence Welk Resort Village at Lawrence Welk Dr. (gas station). Still enclosed by the barren and rocky slopes, the highway passes a cafe near Gopher Canyon Rd. and reaches a low point at the southern edge of Moosa Canyon. The road is now named Old Highway 395.

A 2-1/2-mile upgrade takes the tourer over the Interstate into an area of scattered residences and citrus orchards peppered over the steep hillsides. The subsequent reward is a very scenic downgrade which leads past Keys Canyon, the San Luis Rey River, State Hwy. 76 (gas station) (43.7), a mini-mart and La Estancia Inn (a classy old favorite "hideaway" of ours). Four miles and several hundred feet elevation gain later, the road recrosses I-15, then continues another 1.3 miles to a crest near Rainbow Valley Blvd. A half-mile beyond at 5th St. is the Rainbow Oaks Restaurant, a place to load up on "pedaling fuel," if the intent is to continue beyond Temecula.

Rainbow to Temecula. The highway passes a series of tree and flower nurseries, crosses the Riverside County Line (51.9), then passes through a narrow opening between two high ridges. At the summit, and for the next mile, the biker can enjoy a winding downgrade with views into the Pauba and Temecula Valleys and beyond. The road cruises through the golf course of the Temecula Creek Inn, follows Pala Rd. west, then passes under Interstate 15 before reaching the outskirts of Old Town Temecula (56.7). Browse the old restored commercial area of town and enjoy a meal at any one of many varied and enticing eateries.

Class I Bikeway in Los Penasquitos Canyon

URBAN

... And Beyond. The route can be extended about 26 mostly flat miles into Corona. This destination is reached by biking north 15-1/2 miles alongside the Interstate to the outskirts of Lake Elsinore at Railroad Canyon Rd. (North of Winchester Ave. in Temecula is mainly farm and cattle country.) Skirt Lake Elsinore to the east and follow Lake St. north into the little burg of Alberhill. The grand finale is an extremely pleasant and generally downhill 15-mile ride through scenic Temescal Canyon to the outskirts of Corona.

CONNECTING TRIPS: 1) Connection with the San Diego River Run (Trip #17) - from Jack Murphy Stadium, bike east on Friars Rd.; 2) connection with the Lake Miramar Meander (Trip #20) - at Mira Mesa Blvd. and Scripps Ranch Blvd., turn right (south) on the latter street; 3) connection with the Poway "Picnic" (Trip #34) or Rancho Bernardo city tour (Trip #33) - the tours share a common segment on Pomerado Rd.; 4) connection with the Escondido City Tour (Trip #35) - turn east or west onto Country Club Ln. or Via Rancho Pkwy.; 5) connection with the San Pasqual Valley tour (Trip #36) - at Pomerado Rd. and Highland Valley Rd., turn east on the latter road; 6) connection with the Fallbrook Countryside Tour (Trip #39) - at the junction where Old Hwy. 395 crosses eastward over I-15, veer left onto Mission Rd.; 7) connection with the Tierrasanta Tour (Trip #43) - at Murphy Canyon Dr. and Aero Dr. or Tierrasanta Blvd., turn east on either of the latter two roads; 8) connection with the Pala Mission Loop (Trip #49) - at Rainbow Valley Blvd., turn east onto that road; 9) connection with the Canyons N' Citrus Tour (Trip #52) - turn east or west at any intersection between Old Castle Rd. and W. Lilac Rd.

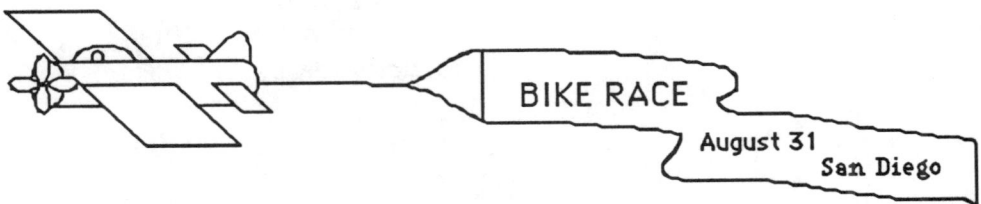

TRIP #39 - FALLBROOK COUNTRYSIDE TOUR

GENERAL LOCATION: Fallbrook, Bonsall

LEVEL OF DIFFICULTY: Round trip - moderate to strenuous
Distance - 23.8 miles
Elevation gain - periodic moderate-to-steep grades

GENERAL DESCRIPTION: This is country biking at its best! Trees, orchards, scenic views and serene two-lane country roads in the Fallbrook area. Over hill and dale, the biker can ride a 20-mile plus "double looper" with a fiendishly clever loop intersection at the inviting Live Oak Creek Park. Bikers will particularly enjoy the "Green Arches," an extremely scenic wooded portion of Live Oak Park Rd. The tour is predominantly Class X, with some high-speed traffic, particularly on State Hwy. 76.

TRAILHEAD: From Interstate Hwy. 15, exit west onto Mission Rd. (County Hwy. S13) and drive about 3/4 mile to Live Oak Park Rd. Turn onto that road and continue 2-3/4 miles to Live Oak Park. From coastal areas, follow State Hwy. 76 in Oceanside about 15 miles to Gird Rd. Turn left and continue four miles to the park's entrance. This

BICYCLE RIDES: SAN DIEGO COUNTY

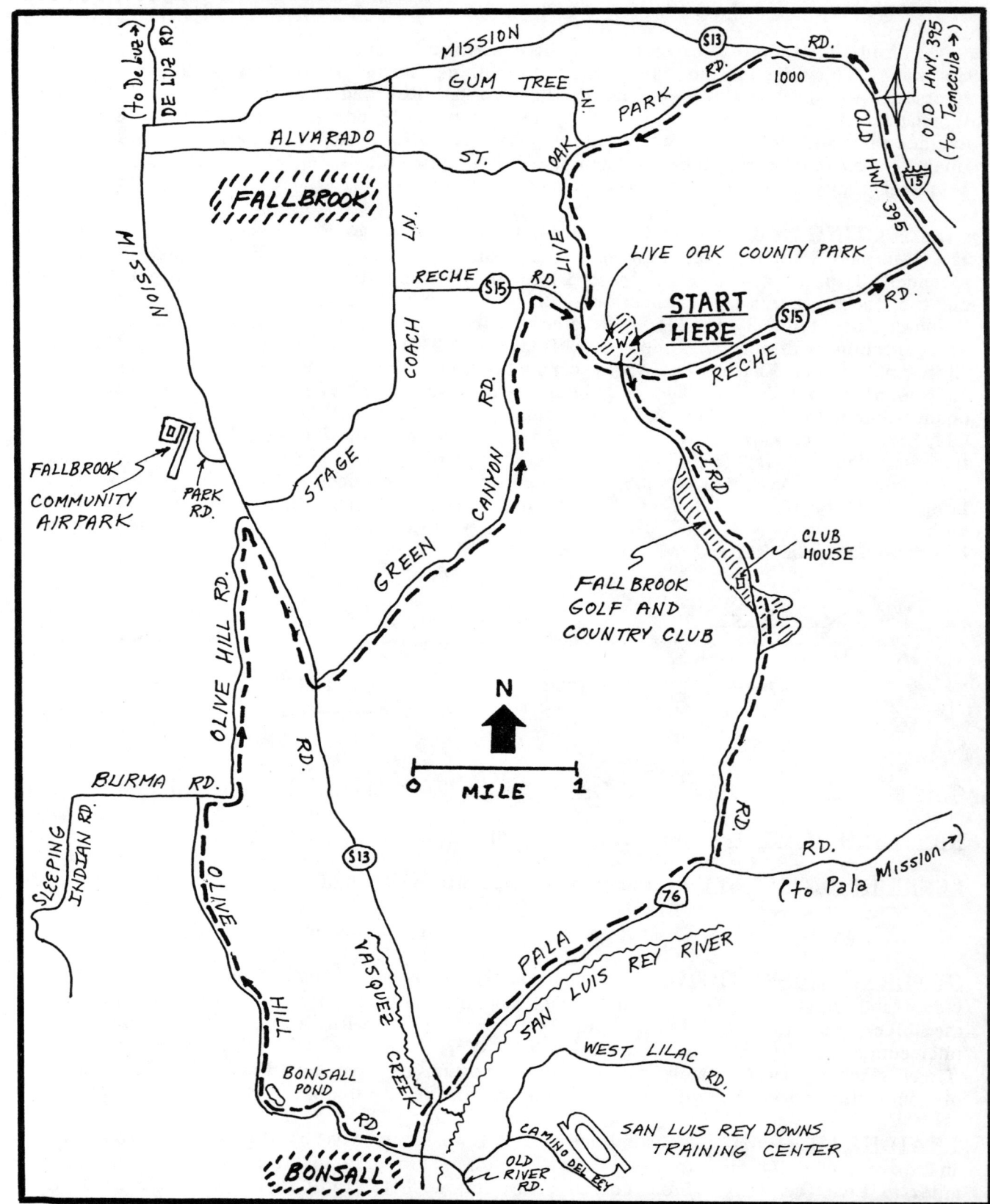

TRIP #39 - FALLBROOK COUNTRYSIDE TOUR

excellent and shady day-use park has water, restrooms, full picnic facilities, recreation fields, and a creek running through its center.

Bring a quart of water or two quarts on hot days. The single reliable water source is at Live Oak Park.

TRIP DESCRIPTION: **Western Loop.** Leave the serenity of Live Oak Park and bike downhill on Live Oak Park Rd. in a high-density traffic area. At Gird Rd., turn right (south) and cruise mainly downhill four miles to Pala Rd. (State Hwy. 76). The route is rural with periodic tree cover and scattered residences. The biker passes the Fallbrook Golf Course near the half-way point and one of the few open meadows on the trip in three miles.

Turn right onto Pala Rd. and bike on this busy highway through gentle rolling hills with mixed evergreens and seasonal trees scattered about the roadway. After 1.8 miles, the road passes a new shopping center and continues through an older developed commercial area which spreads to Mission Rd. In 0.6 mile, at the trip's low-elevation point, is Olive Hill Rd. and a gas station (6.7).

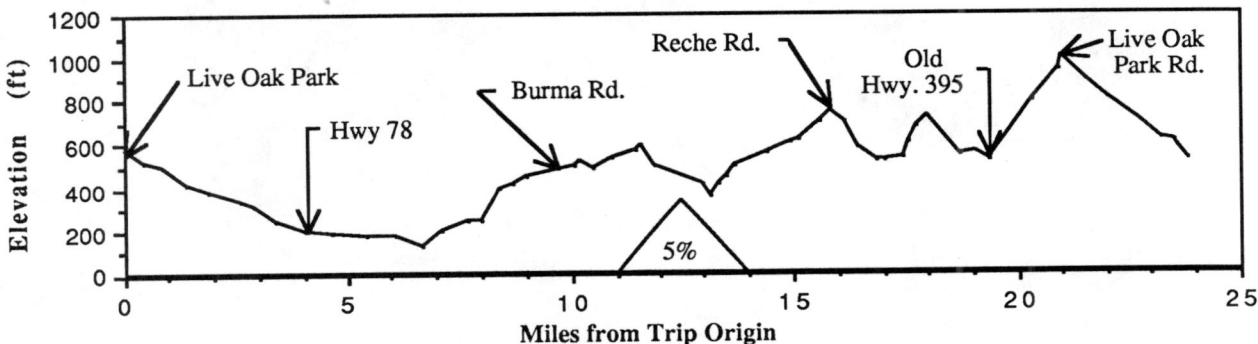

Turn right (north) and prepare to suck it in! (You knew that this trip could not stay this easy!) Bike over two miles of upgrade of varying degrees of steepness to a flat near Rancho Camino Rd. This segment is on a two-lane country road with periodic overhanging tree cover and pleasant little Bonsall Pond at the one-mile point. Turn right at the Burma Rd. intersection and continue on the agriculturally-rich plateau with light rolling hills. Olive Hill Rd. passes large complexes of hot houses, Barlow's Flower Farm and reaches a summit near Elm Tree Ln. Next is a refreshing 0.3-mile downhill with views of the southern Fallbrook area and the Mission Rd. intersection (11.9).

After a sharp right turn, bike 1.1 miles in a heavier traffic zone under a water storage tank that totally dominates the hill upon which it sits. A left on Green Canyon Rd. returns the biker to a little two-lane, tree-shadowed country road. In a short distance is one of the stately local residences; however, it is unique in the sense of its duck-filled pond and the sign near the road which reads, "Caution, Duck Crossing." For the next three miles, this generally uphill roadway passes scattered residences, each seemingly with its own citrus grove -- this is definitely orange and avocado country. A short downgrade leads the biker to Reche Rd. near the Live Oak Park area (16.5).

Eastern Loop. Pass the Live Oak Restaurant, then Live Oak Creek Park again, and stay to the left on Reche Rd. The country roadway passes a number of "gentleman-farmer" residences on Reche Rd. in the next 1/2 mile, then begins an

BICYCLE RIDES: SAN DIEGO COUNTY

uphill stretch which crests in the next 1/2 mile at Colina Vista. Just beyond, the rider is treated to both a fine eastward view, as well as a rewarding downhill to Old Hwy. 395.

Just as the biker is congratulating himself, he/she is faced with a northbound 1-1/2-mile steady and grueling uphill in one of the few somewhat-exposed sections of this trip. Just before the peak of this Class II segment, Old Hwy. 395 crosses eastward over Interstate Hwy. 15 and our reference tour continues on what is now Mission Rd. (Hwy. S13). Pass an extensive area of citrus groves, Ranger Rd. and reach the trip's highpoint at the Live Oak Park Rd. fork (21.0). The generally downhill two-mile segment that follows will bring tears to your eyes! We refer to this scenic stretch as the "Emerald Arches." Live Oak Park Rd. is a quiet two-lane country path that cruises along Live Oak Creek. The road passes a tree-covered archway which allows only highly filtered sunlight to penetrate in some sections. Below Los Alisos Rd., the roadway is merely reduced to serene and naturally scenic. In another 1/2 mile, the tour reaches its terminus at the now-familiar Live Oak Park (23.8).

Live Oak Park Road

Trip Options: Note that there are also spur trips off the described route: Pala Mission can be reached by continuing east on Pala Rd.; Temecula and the wine country are accessible by continuing on Old Hwy. 395 across Interstate Hwy. 15; the City of Fallbrook is a short distance west of Live Oak Park Rd. on Mission Rd.; and the torturous uphill to De Luz can be reached via De Luz Rd. in northwestern Fallbrook.

<u>**CONNECTING TRIPS**</u>: 1) Connection with the Oceanside City Tour (Trip #29) - at Bonsall (State Hwy. 76 and Olive Hill Rd.), continue west on Hwy. 76 to Oceanside; 2) connection with Old Hwy. 395 (Trip #38) - the tours share a common segment between Reche Rd. and Mission Rd.; 3) connection with the Canyons N' Citrus ride (Trip #52) - at the same intersection, bike southwest across State Hwy. 76 on Olive Hill Rd.

URBAN

TRIP #40 - RAMONA/SAN VICENTE VALLEY

GENERAL LOCATION: Ramona

LEVEL OF DIFFICULTY: Ramona Loop - moderate to strenuous;
San Vicente Valley - easy to moderate
Distance - 17.5 miles (loop); 9.8 miles (valley, one way)
Elevation gain - periodic moderate-to-steep grades (loop);
periodic moderate grades (valley)

GENERAL DESCRIPTION: The Ramona area loop provides a back country tour on little used Old Julian Hwy. This rural road takes the biker through lightly-developed rolling hills and up a steep switchback to busier Julian Rd. The return leg on that road passes through Santa Teresa Valley, then follows a small canyon essentially downhill back to Ramona city proper. An added, relatively-flat, extended mileage option is to continue the trip from Collier Park into the deep recesses of the moderately-developed San Vicente Valley.

TRAILHEAD: From the west county, follow either State Hwys. 78 or 67 into the City of Ramona. At the intersection of these two highways is a street now named Main St. Follow that road east 1/4 mile to 6th St. and turn south. Continue 1/4 mile to "F" St. and Collier County Park. The park has scattered tree cover, restrooms, tennis courts and children's play area. From the east, follow Hwy. 78 into Ramona and follow the numbered streets to 7th St. Turn south and continue as above.

Bring at least a quart of water on hot days. We found public water sources only near Ramona proper.

TRIP DESCRIPTION: Ramona Loop - Old Julian Hwy. Bike east on "E" St. 1/2 mile to 3rd St. and turn right (south). Almost immediately, the cyclist finds an old country road passing through a setting more characteristic of the 1950's. This is Old Julian Hwy., which takes the biker through six curving miles of countryside with scattered small ranches and residences before reaching Ballena Valley.

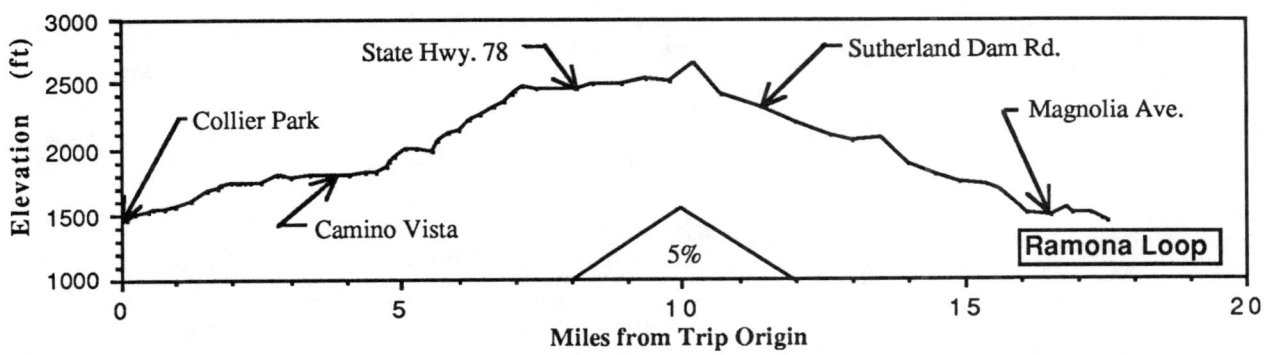

On the way there, cyclists explore a region of rocky scrub-laden rolling hills for 3-1/2 miles before encountering a solid 3/4-mile upgrade one-half mile beyond Camino Vista. A short flat pedal gives way to a rugged one-mile upgrade on a long switchback, which lets out at a flat farming area within Ballena Valley. Another 1-1/4 miles of easy pedaling leads to State Hwy. 78 (8.4).

BICYCLE RIDES: SAN DIEGO COUNTY

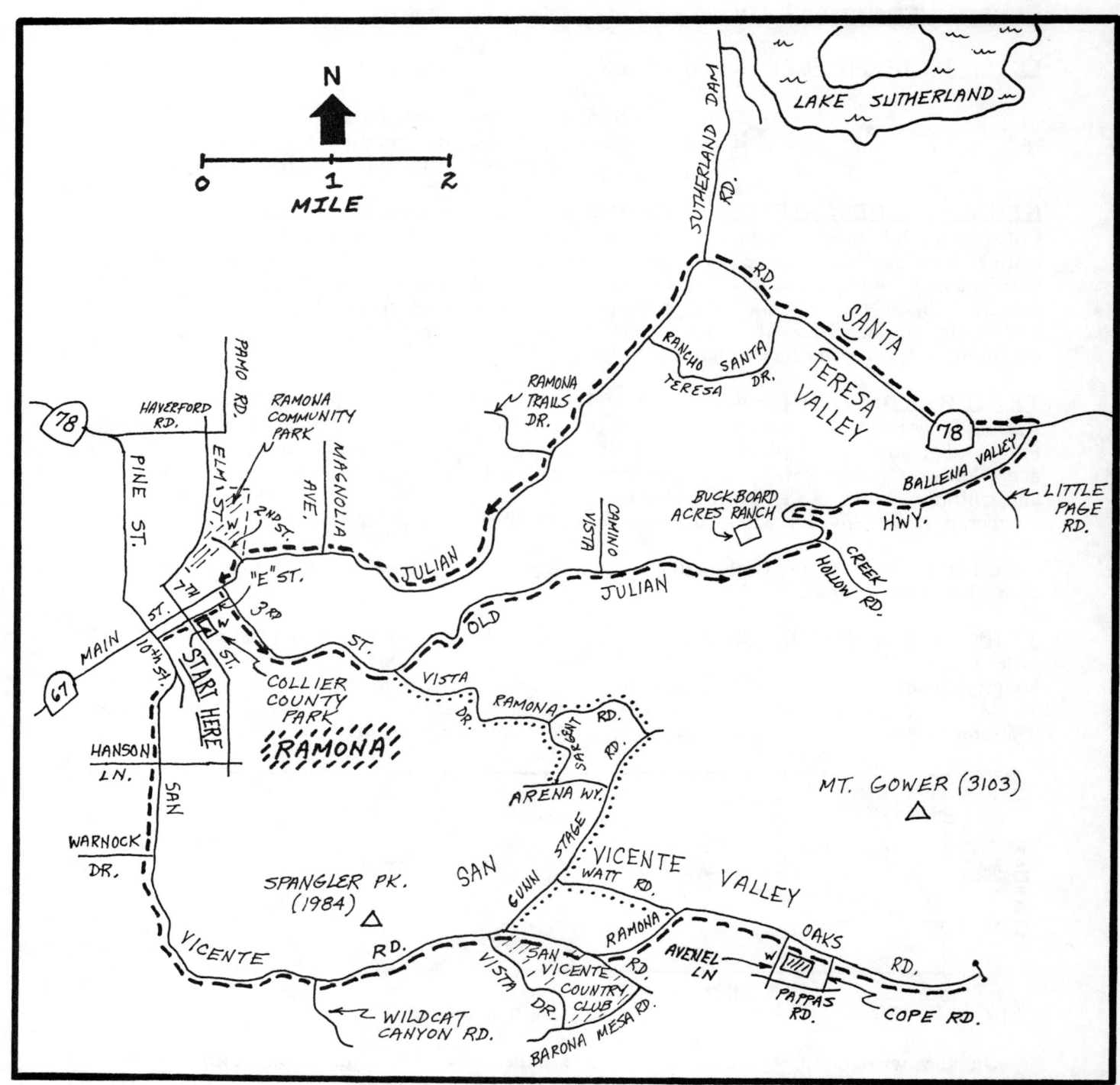

TRIP #40 - RAMONA/SAN VICENTE VALLEY

URBAN

Don with Like-minded Friend

Julian Rd. A left turn onto Julian Rd. (Hwy. 78) returns the biker to higher speed- and more frequent-traffic. After a 1/2-mile easy cruise between the scrub-laden rolling hills, pedal a 1-1/4 mile upgrade and be treated to a nifty downhill which passes Rancho Santa Teresa Dr. in one-half mile. Next is a flat ride through Santa Teresa Valley. The next five miles is essentially another downgrade on a sinuous path through a still lightly-populated small canyon area.

At Julian Rd.'s most northern reach is the turnoff to Sutherland Lake (11.4), a large body of water nestled in a beautiful canyon with mountains on all sides (fishing, camping, lake concession). Also, 1-1/4 miles beyond that turnoff is a resort with a general store. As the road nears Ramona proper, the biker tackles a short grade which is on the northern flank of a ridge that looks down into Goose and Santa Maria Valleys. Just beyond is 3rd St. within the City of Ramona, where the biker turns left, cruises a short distance to "F" St. and returns to the park (17.5).

San Vicente Valley Tour. From Collier Park, bike southwest on "E" St. to 10th St. and turn south. After 2-1/2 miles of flat roadway in the residential Ramona outskirts, the road climbs over a modest ridge and drops into a small, relatively-undeveloped valley. Another flat stretch in open country leads past Wildcat Canyon Rd. (5.2) where the road pulls up alongside San Vicente Creek and enters San Vicente Valley. The road follows the valley, which is wedged between the surrounding rock- and brush-laden peaks, another 4.6 miles to a gated road's end at Shalom Rd. (9.8). Along the way, the basically flat road passes interspersed areas of development and open space, a shopping plaza near Gunn Stage Rd., and a lovely park about 1-1/2 miles east of the junction of San Vicente Valley Rd. and Ramona Oaks Rd.

<u>**CONNECTING TRIPS**</u>: 1) Connection with Wildcat Canyon (Trip #54) - at San Vicente Rd. and Wildcat Canyon Rd., turn south on the latter highway; 2).connection with the Mussey Grade Rd. tour (Trip #55) - at State Hwy. 67, turn northeast toward Ramona.

BICYCLE RIDES: SAN DIEGO COUNTY

TRIP #41 - EUCALYPTUS HILLS

GENERAL LOCATION: Eucalyptus Hills

LEVEL OF DIFFICULTY: Loop - moderate
Distance - 5.0 miles
Elevation gain - periodic moderate grades

Lindo Lake County Park

DESCRIPTION: So named because of the extensive Australian tree plantings in this hilly terrain, Eucalyptus Hills is a cyclist's territorial delight. Take any road in this tucked-away hamlet and enjoy the low-key rural setting. The city aura is that of a large ranch which has been subdivided and settled 30-40 years past, and remains relatively unchanged. The route described provides the biker with a long paved city loop. The trip starts in the San Diego River Plain and follows a 2.3-mile, 500-foot, general uphill which explores the wooded glens and quiet and quaint residential areas. Beyond the crest near Manzanita Rd. and Valle Vista Rd., the biker is treated to a refreshing downhill return via Oak Creek Dr. There are several interesting farms and residences to "inspect" on this easy return. A side note: Keep an eye out for unfriendly, unleashed dogs in this territory!

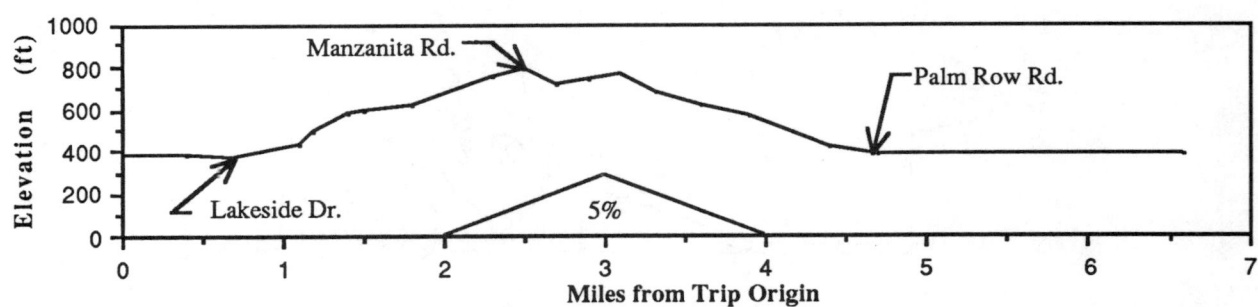

URBAN

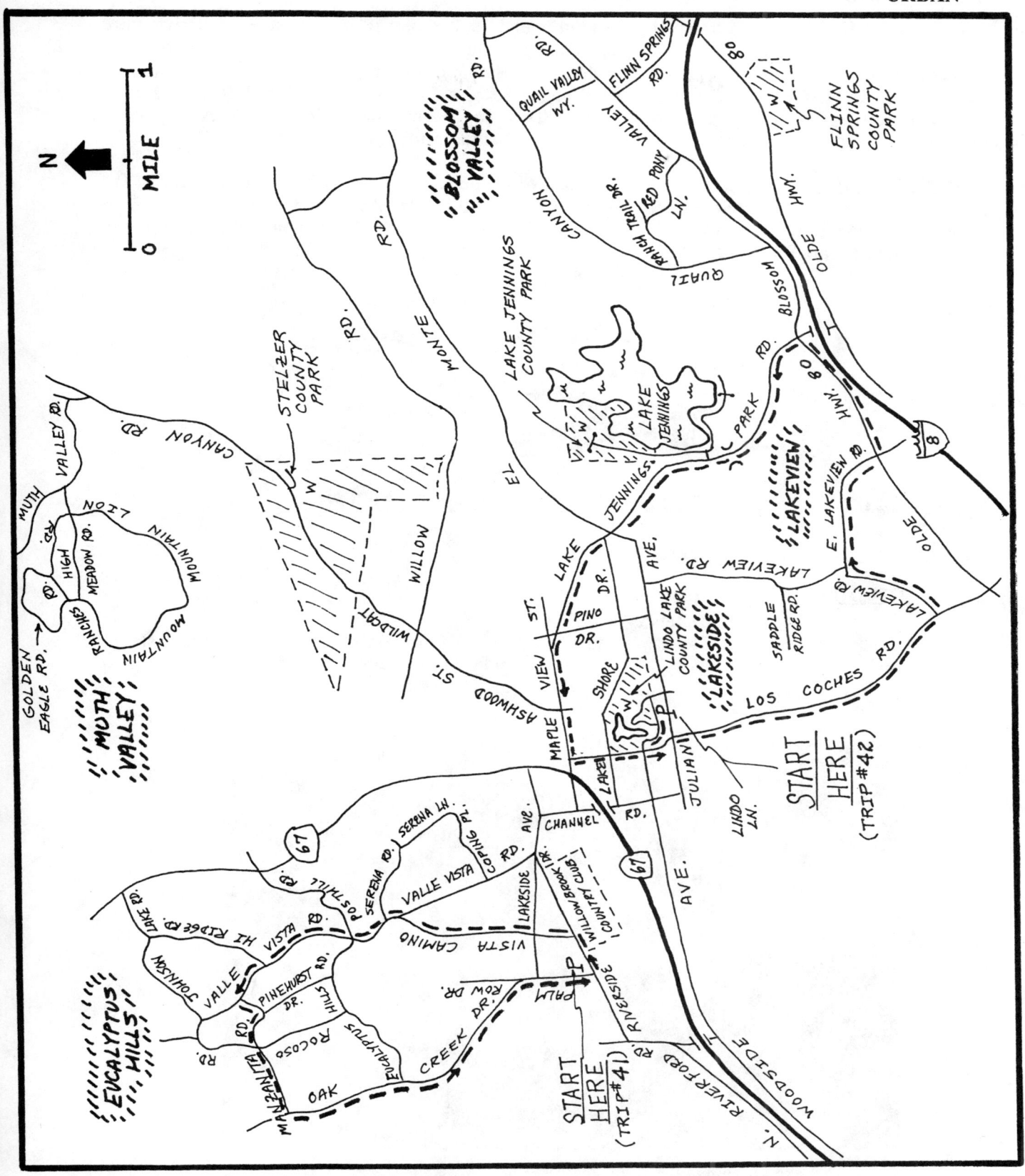

TRIP #41 - EUCALYPTUS HILLS   TRIP #42 - LAKESIDE-LAKEVIEW LOOP

BICYCLE RIDES: SAN DIEGO COUNTY

TRAILHEAD: From State Hwy. 67 southbound, exit west at Riverford Rd. Drive north 1/2 mile to Riverside Dr., turn right, and park near the Palm Row intersection near the convenience store. From the northbound Hwy. 67, exit at Maple View, turn left (west) and, in 1/4 mile, turn right on Channel Rd. In 1/4 mile, turn left at Lakeside Ave. and left again in 1/3 mile to Riverside Dr. In 3/4 mile is Palm Row. An option is to start the trip from Lindo Lake County Park in Lakeside (see Trip #42).

CONNECTING TRIPS: 1) Connection with the San Diego River Run (Trip #17) - follow Riverford Ave. south under Hwy. 67 to Woodside Ave. and turn either left or right; 2) connection with the Lakeside-Lakeview Loop (Trip #42) - as above, but turn left (northeast) at Woodside Ave.

TRIP #42 - LAKESIDE-LAKEVIEW LOOP

GENERAL LOCATION: Lakeside, Lakeview

LEVEL OF DIFFICULTY: Loop - moderate
Distance - 7.3 miles
Elevation gain - periodic moderate grades; moderate-steep grade below Lake Jennings

Lake Jennings

URBAN

DESCRIPTION: This short-distance rural road trip leaves Lakeside's pleasing Lindo Lake County Park, follows Class X Los Coches Rd. along the Los Coches Creek drainage 2-1/4 miles, then turns east and follows Lakeview Rd. through the small town of Lakeview. A 3/4-mile spin on Olde Highway 80 (now an Interstate Hwy. 8 frontage road) leads to Class II Lake Jennings Park Rd., where the cyclist pedals north under the distant imposing structure of El Cajon Mountain. In about a mile is Lake Jennings and a park of the same name. A short diversion at this turnoff leads to a fine lake overlook. The cyclist can pedal 1/2 mile to the left (west side of the lake) to the county park/campground entrance or 2/3 mile to the right to the boat launch/boat rental fishing areas (no biking is allowed beyond either entrance). However, our reference route follows a steep downgrade 1.3 miles past El Monte Rd. to Pino Dr. The remaining 1.3-mile Class X portion of the route plies the residential Lakeside area and returns along the north edge of Lindo Lake Country Park.

Blossom Valley and El Cajon Mountain above Lake Jennings

TRAILHEAD: From State Hwy. 67, exit west at Maple View St., drive a short distance to Vine St. and turn right. In 1/2 mile at Woodside Ave./Lindo Ln., turn left and either park in the first parking area alongside Lindo Lake County Park or continue onto the more scenic parking area off Lindo Ln. From Interstate Hwy. 8, exit north at Los Coches Rd. and drive three miles to Woodside Ave. Turn right and continue as above.

This restful shaded park includes scenic Lindo Lake, a community center, picnic and barbecue facilities, children's play area, restrooms, a peripheral walkway/bikeway, and a large and friendly duck population.

CONNECTING TRIPS: 1) Connection with the San Diego River Run (Trip #17) - from Lake Jennings Park Rd. and El Monte Rd., take the latter street in either direction; 2) connection with the Eucalyptus Hills tour (Trip #41) - return to Woodside Ave. and take Riverford Rd. north; 3) connection with the Hills and Dales ride (Blossom Valley) (Trip #45) and the Crest-Dehesa Valley Loop (Trip #53) - bike east on Olde Hwy. 80 and follow the I-8 frontage roads.

BICYCLE RIDES: SAN DIEGO COUNTY

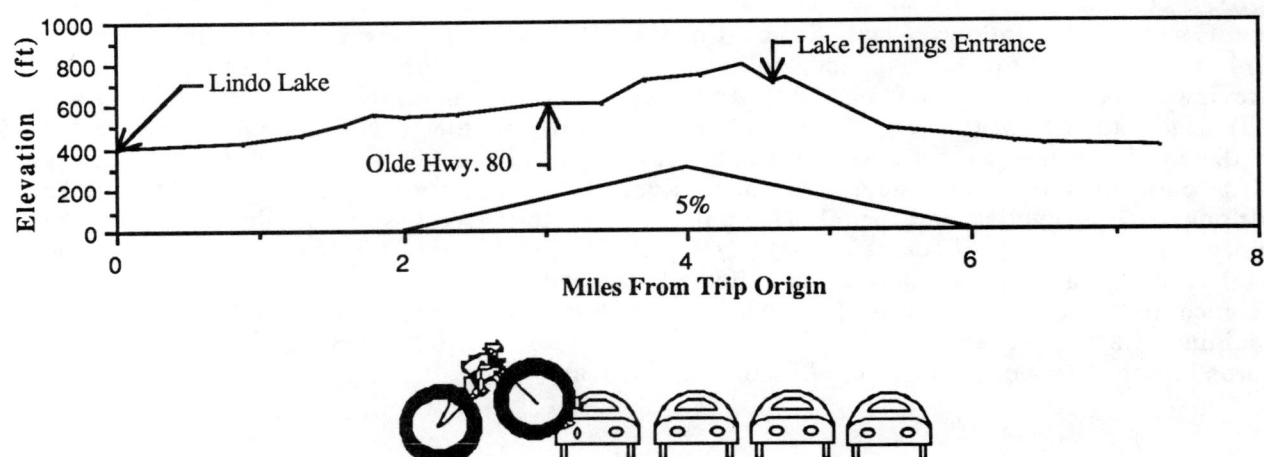

TRIP #43 - TIERRASANTA TOUR

GENERAL LOCATION: Tierrasanta

LEVEL OF DIFFICULTY: Loop - moderate
Distance - 5.0 miles
Elevation gain - periodic moderate grades;
steep grade on Colina Dorada Dr.

DESCRIPTION: This five-mile mesa tour is in lightly-trafficked Tierrasanta, a city with several westside entries, but blocked to the east by the mountain barrier of Mission Trails Regional Park. The mixed Class II/Class X tour is through mostly new residential development. The route leaves well-equipped Tierrasanta Park and Recreation Center (unlike most of our trips, we start near the trip summit), travels 0.9 mile downhill to Santo Rd., then heads south 0.4 mile to busy Tierrasanta Blvd. The entire spin is Class II, followed by more Class II biking eastward on the latter road. From the trip's low point at Rueda Dr. to the trip's end, there is little traffic and the biker can enjoy the upscale residential territory. Take the extension of Tierrasanta Blvd. a short distance beyond Colina Dorada Dr.; there are excellent views of Mission Valley and the Mission Gorge Naval Golf Course below. Return to Colina Dorada Dr. and follow the very steep half-mile uphill on Class X road (the grade is short and walking the bike is convenient, if necessary). Beyond this grade, which peaks near Petirrojo Ct., the biker follows little rolling hills on a zig-zag return path which abuts the natural slopes of Mission Trails Regional Park.

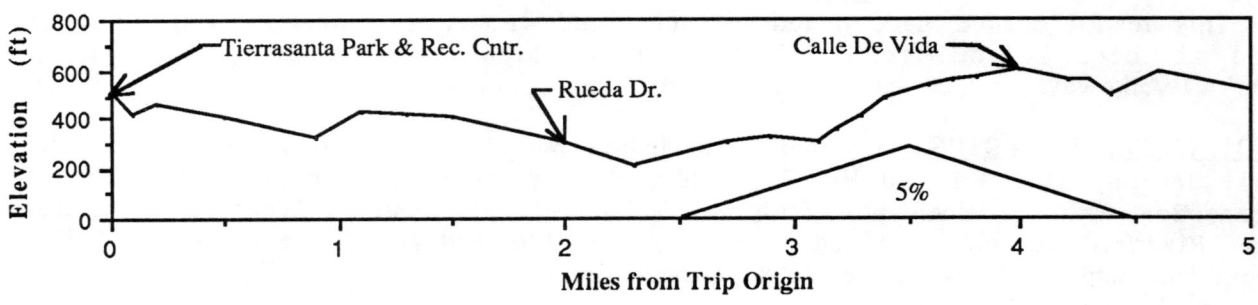

URBAN

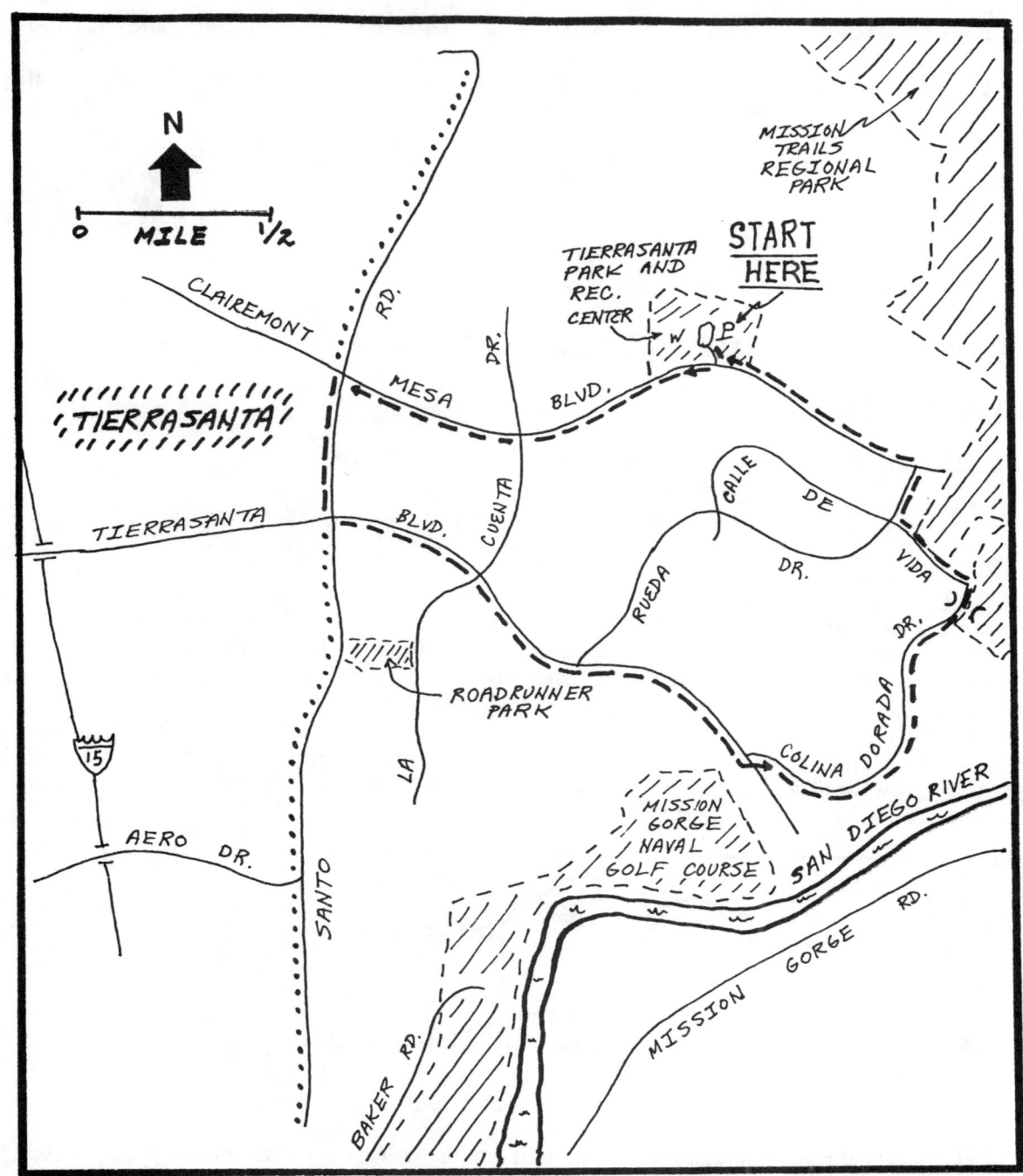

TRIP #43 - TIERRASANTA TOUR

Options. There is an option to add mileage to the tour by continuing either north or south along Class II Santo Rd. beyond the bounds of the described route. The southern option is a flat 1.5 miles (one-way) which ends at a dirt berm; the northern add-on segment is a modestly hilly 1.3 miles (one-way) which ends at the State Hwy. 52 entry. The biker can freewheel through other parts of this hilly area; bring a roadmap if you are bothered by deadend streets or getting temporarily lost.

BICYCLE RIDES: SAN DIEGO COUNTY

TRAILHEAD: From Interstate Hwy. 15, exit east at Clairemont Mesa Blvd. and drive 2-1/4 miles to Tierrasanta Park and Recreation Center. The park has picnic tables, tennis courts, basketball courts, baseball fields, children's playground and restrooms.

CONNECTING TRIPS: 1) Connection with Old Hwy. 395 (Trip #38) - follow Tierrasanta Blvd. west across Interstate Hwy. 15.

TRIP #44 - MOUNT HELIX

GENERAL LOCATION: La Mesa, Mt. Helix

LEVEL OF DIFFICULTY: Loop - strenuous
Distance - 6.1 miles
Elevation gain - steep-to-sheer grades on Alto Dr. and Mt. Helix Dr.

GENERAL DESCRIPTION: A "peak bagger's" special, this is a hilly residential loop with an ascent of Mt. Helix, from which one can enjoy some of the finest unobstructed metropolitan vistas in the county! The Mt. Helix climb is reserved for aggressive, in-shape bikers willing to negotiate a steep, narrow roadway for about 1-3/4 miles. (Don walked some of the sheer grades and was still nervous about the passing traffic.) An option is to follow the basic loop, but to bypass the Alto Dr./Mt. Helix Dr. segment. There are still many hilly challenges without the Mt. Helix pumpathon (now a "moderate" tour, however), and the biker still has the option to extend the route in several directions.

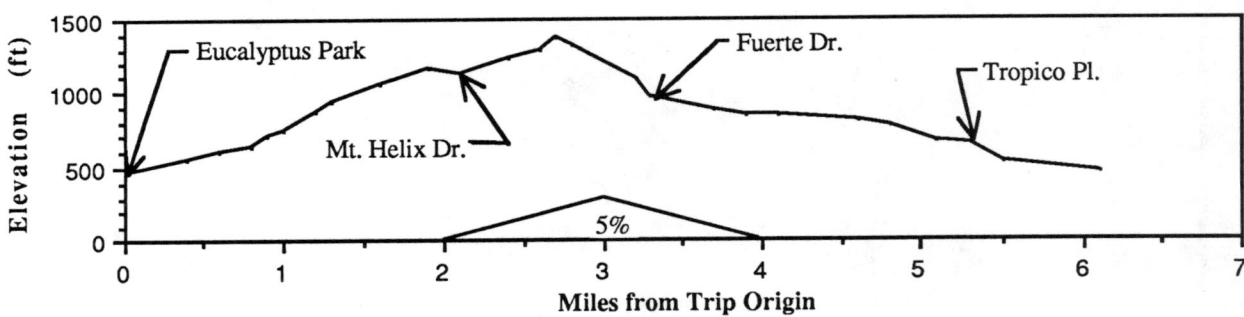

TRAILHEAD: From Interstate Hwy. 8, exit south at Jackson Dr. in La Mesa, drive 1/2 mile south to street's end at Lemon Ave. Follow that street 1/4 mile under State Hwy. 125, and turn right at the first street, Bancroft Dr. In one mile, just beyond Edgewood Dr., is the entrance to Eucalyptus County Park. From State Hwy. 125 northbound, exit at Lemon Ave. Make a hard right onto Bancroft Dr. and proceed south to the park. Southbound traffic should exit at Grossmount Blvd., turn east on that street, drive under State Hwy. 125 to Bancroft Dr., and continue 1-1/4 miles south. Eucalyptus County Park lies on a shaded hillside and has a children's play area, picnic benches and restrooms.

URBAN

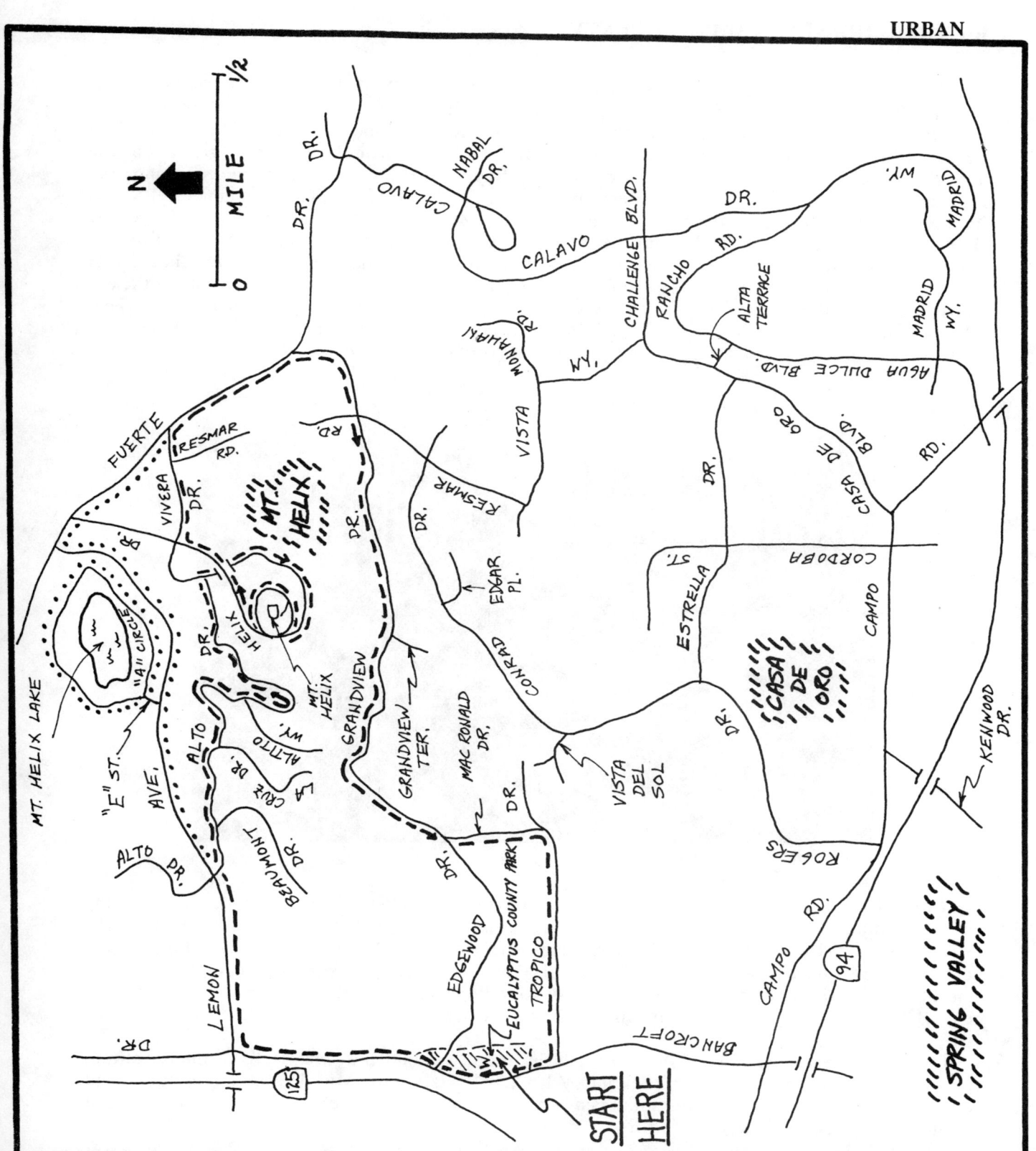

Note: All unmarked roadways, except freeways, are viable alternate bike routes.

TRIP #44 - MOUNT HELIX

BICYCLE RIDES: SAN DIEGO COUNTY

TRIP DESCRIPTION: The Ascent. Follow busy Class II Bancroft Dr. on a modest uphill to Lemon Ave. The next increasingly inclined uphill 0.4 mile through treed residential areas is preparation for the turn onto Alto Dr. and the "killer" ascent. The first 0.4 mile attacks the mountain "head on," with a particularly sheer grade on the straight stretch of road near La Cruz Dr. Beyond, the road switchbacks along the mountain contour, and the grade lessens to simply "painful." The distant city vistas on the uphill climb are extremely rewarding. At Mt. Helix Dr., the cyclist veers to the right and follows the signed route to Mt. Helix. The route to the summit follows a steep, half-helical (one-way) contour where there is a parking area at the lower edge of the outdoor Mt. Helix Amphitheater. A short foot climb up the amphitheater steps leads to the Easter Cross and the dedication marker to Mary Carpenter Yawkey, whose family deeded this lady's favorite meditation place to the county. The view from near the cross on a clear day is awe-inspiring!

View from the Amphitheater Stage

The Descent. The return down the mountain on Mt. Helix Dr. completes the helical contour. At Vivera Dr., the biker turns right, connects with busy Fuerte Dr. (3.3), then follows Grandview Dr. 1.6 miles through a posh, well-landscaped neighborhood with interesting views of the Mt. Helix summit directly above. Another mile of cruising in a similar surroundings ends with a stair-step downgrade near Bancroft Dr. A short segment north returns the biker to the park (6.1).

Optional Routes. To follow the basic loop without the Mt. Helix summit climb, continue east on Lemon Ave. beyond Alto Dr., visit the Mt. Helix Lake loop and continue to Fuerte Dr. Bike southeast on that road 0.8 mile to Grandview Dr. and continue as described above (6.6).

There are numerous other hills and dales to investigate in the Mt. Helix/Casa De Oro/Spring Valley areas. A sample of the potential scenic connector routes from our reference trip are shown on the tour map.

URBAN

CONNECTING TRIPS: 1) Connection to the El Cajon Bikeway System (Trip #31) - at Fuerte Dr. and Grandview Dr., continue southeast on the latter street and turn north on Avocado Blvd.

TRIP #45 - HILLS N' DALES

GENERAL LOCATION: Blossom Valley

LEVEL OF DIFFICULTY: Loop - moderate
Distance - 11.6 miles
Elevation gain - periodic moderate grades

GENERAL DESCRIPTION: We thought about Hills and Bales (of money), but settled on a more benign trip title. This is a snooper's tour through one of the newest and most exclusive residential developments of inland San Diego. Situated in Blossom Valley above Lake Jennings, the area is peppered with half-million dollar-and-up homes with their attendant large lots, white-wood fencing and horse stables. There are views aplenty of the mountains to the north and the low frontal ranges southward, along with scattered looks down Quail Canyon to Lake Jennings. As the landscaping develops, the views across the valley will be even more spectacular.

Bikers leave Flinn Springs County Park, cross under Interstate Hwy. 8, and enter Blossom Valley via Oak Creek Rd. off Olde Hwy. 80. The sample route mapped primarily uses Oak Creek Rd., Blossom Valley Rd. and Quail Canyon Rd. (4.7), while the best Lake Jennings vistas are found on Sleepy Creek Rd. and Quail Canyon Rd. near the upper reaches of Quail Canyon (8.0). Olde Hwy. 80 and part of Blossom Valley Rd. are Class II, while the remainder of the trip traverses Class X, lightly-traveled, residential roads.

TRAILHEAD: From Interstate Hwy. 8, exit south at Lake Jennings Park Rd. Turn left at Olde Hwy. 80 and drive 1-1/3 miles to the Flinn Springs County Park entrance. The park has picnic benches/barbecue facilities, restrooms, children's playground, tree-shaded grassy fields and several small bridges which cross over serene Coches Creek.

Bring a filled water bottle as there are no public water sources in Blossom Valley.

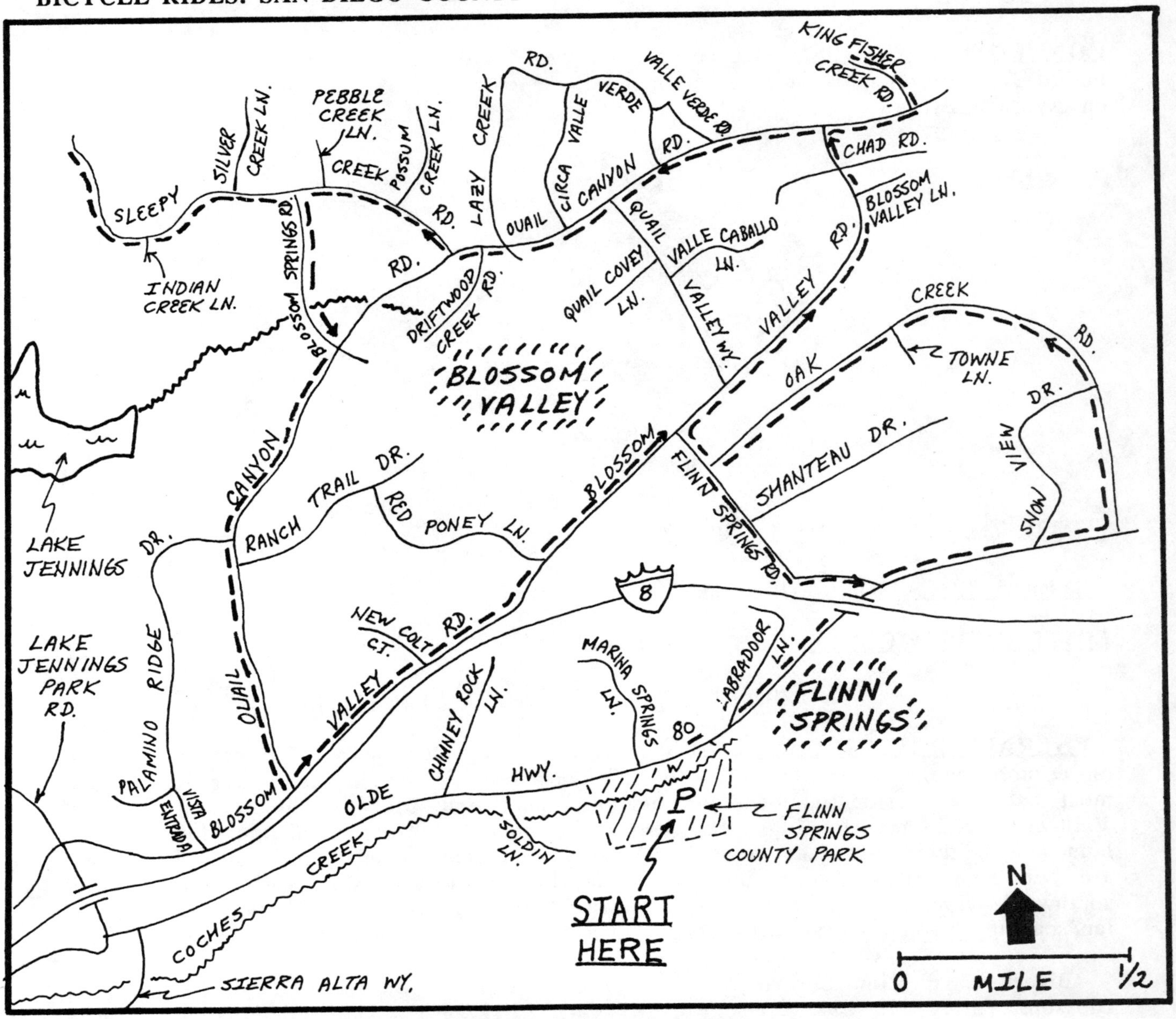

BICYCLE RIDES: SAN DIEGO COUNTY

TRIP #45 - HILLS N' DALES

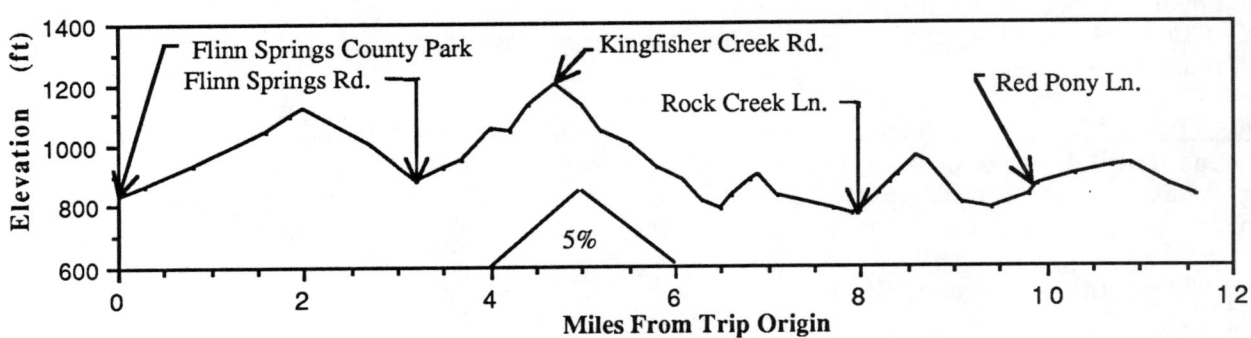

MOUNTAINS/BACKCOUNTRY

CONNECTING TRIPS: 1) Connection with the Lakeside-Lakeview Loop (Trip #42) - return to Lake Jennings Park Rd. from the park or from Blossom Valley Rd.; 2) connection with the Crest-Dehesa Valley Loop (Trip #53) - follow Olde Hwy. 80 east and continue along the I-8 frontage roads.

Blossom Valley Residences

TRIP #46 - PALOMAR MOUNTAIN

GENERAL LOCATION: Palomar Mountain

LEVEL OF DIFFICULTY: Up and back - moderate
Distance - 22.0 miles
Elevation gain - periodic moderate-to-steep grades

GENERAL DESCRIPTION: The trip described concentrates on biking the Palomar Mountain crest. From Palomar Mountain County Park, the tour works its way six miles through this stunning portion of the Cleveland National Forest and visits the Palomar Observatory. Along the way are the Observatory Campground and Fry Creek Campground. A return on the "Highway to the Stars" is punctuated with a visit to the primo Palomar Mountain State Campground, one of our longstanding favorite camping areas, nestled in the woods with scenic Doane Pond and Upper Doane Valley nearby. There are options to bike up to the Boucher Hill fire lookout and to take an 11.6-mile ridgeline spin (one way) to serene Dyche Valley on East Grade Rd. Finally, there is an "Experts Only" alternative to take a "barn-burner," very strenuous 27-mile loop which includes a cruise of the San Luis Rey River canyon, a rugged East Grade Rd. upgrade and a screaming, switchback-filled seven-percent downgrade on South Grade Rd. This is refered to as the Palomar Mountain Loop.

BICYCLE RIDES: SAN DIEGO COUNTY

Lake Henshaw from East Grade Road

TRAILHEAD: From the west, take State Hwy. 76 five miles east beyond Rincon Springs. Turn left (north) at South Grade Rd. (County Hwy. S6) and drive seven steep, winding uphill miles to the County Hwy. S7 intersection. Turn left, then left again in 1/4 mile at Crestline Rd. and drive 3/4 mile to Palomar Mountain County Park. From the east, follow State Hwy. 76 northwest 9-1/2 miles beyond the State Hwy. 79 junction. Turn right at South Grade Rd. and continue as above. The day-use park has generous tree cover, water, picnic tables and restrooms.

Note that there are no gasoline stations on Palomar Mountain.

TRIP DESCRIPTION: Palomar Observatory. Coast down to East Grade Rd. and turn right, biking the South Grade Rd. and following the Palomar Observatory sign northbound. Pass State Park Rd., a general store, restaurant, post office and lawyer's office (say what??), and follow the pleasant tree-shaded downhill for about two miles and a 400-foot elevation loss. This is the "Highway to the Stars." A curving return uphill takes the cyclist past the Observatory Campground (overnight camping, hiking trails) and, in 0.3 mile, past the turnoff to the Fry Creek Campground. In another workout mile, the grade lessens and the cyclist is treated to a quick peek to the left (west) and below of Doane Pond in Palomar Mountain State Park.

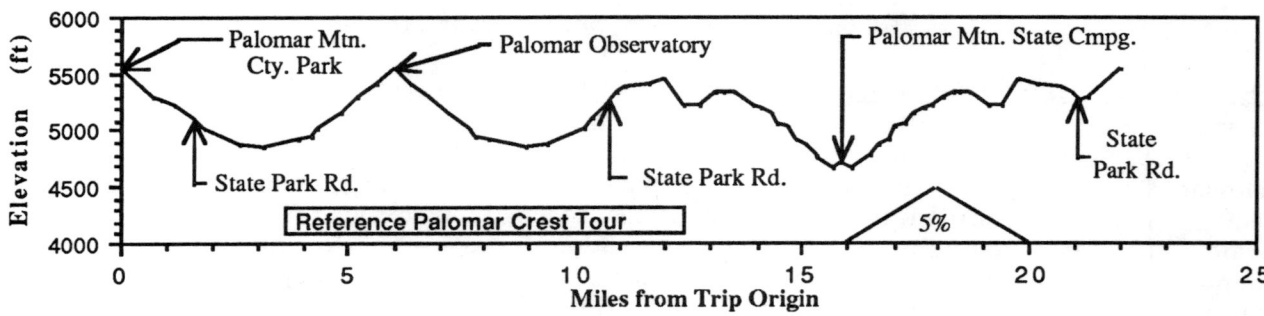

Another 0.8 mile of renewed workout includes a passage by the observatory fire station and road's end at the Palomar Observatory parking lot (6.0). Here is a hiking path to the large dome containing the enormous 200-inch Hale Telescope. On the way is a gift shop (with restrooms) and nearby is the mellow Gus Weber Picnic Area.

MOUNTAINS/BACKCOUNTRY

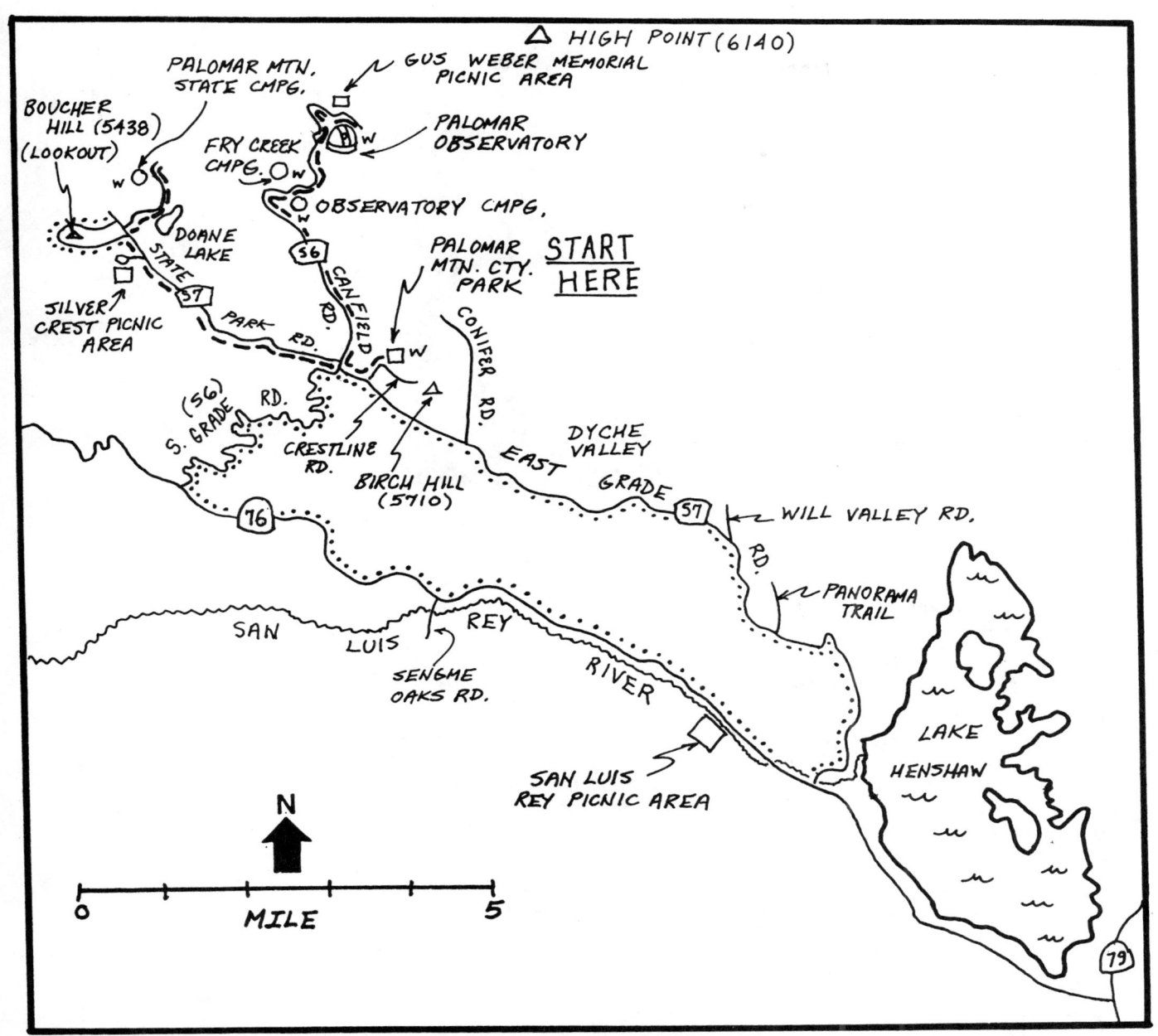

TRIP #46 - PALOMAR MOUNTAIN

After a walking tour of the flat Palomar Observatory area (there are also separate 18-inch and 52-inch telescope facilities nearby), enjoy the scenic views (including the High Point Lookout to the east) and return to State Park Rd. (10.7).

Palomar Mountain State Park. Follow that road northwest, passing several roads which lead east to the little burg of Palomar Mountain. A several-mile pedal through the tree-shaded area leads to a junction where a left turn leads to Boucher Hill with its fire lookout, and a right turn leads to Palomar Mountain State Park. Our reference tour proceeds right and drops moderately into the Upper Doane Valley area, with Doane Pond at the edge of the valley nearest the road.

157

At the upper paved reaches of this lovely sea of green is Palomar Mountain State Campground (15.9), one of our old, long-time favorites. The public campground offers restrooms, water, camp sites and barbecue facilities, gorgeous scenery and numerous hiking trails. What remains is the backtrack to East Grade Rd. and the short, steep upgrade back to Palomar Mountain County Park (22.0).

Palomar Obsevatory

Boucher Hill Fire Lookout. At the previously mentioned junction, the cyclist can take a gut-busting 0.7-mile ride to the summit of Boucher Hill and coast the loop return as a reward. At the summit is a fire lookout and the incumbent unobstructed views of the surrounding mountains and beyond.

Dyche Valley Option. From Crestline Rd., the cyclist can pedal southeast 11.6 miles along the Palomar Mountain ridgeline to serene Dyche Valley. This is a large, plat piece of lightly-treed real estate buried within a green segment of the Cleveland National Forest. To get there, the biker drops about 400 feet through decreasing density forest before transitioning into the rolling hills and pastureland of the high valley. The modest uphill return provides an interesting and alternate tour perspective.

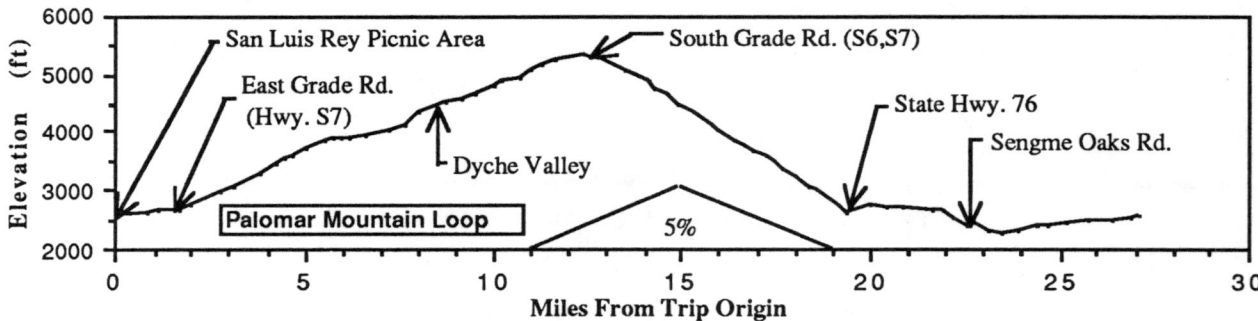

Palomar Mountain Loop. Cyclists in excellent shape, with bikes in top-fight working order, and with a willingness to share steep, switch-backed roadway with auto traffic can try a very strenuous 27-mile, 3000-foot elevation gain loop (we did not!). Save this one for a weekday when traffic is minimal. San Luis Rey Picnic Area might be used as a starting point. A mile beyond the start point, the cyclist turns north on Hwy. S7 and soon begins a four-mile, 1220-foot elevation gain pumpathon, which moderates near the southern edge of Will Valley.

MOUNTAINS/BACKCOUNTRY

Observatory Campground Visitor

For the next seven miles, the route transits the ridgeline on lesser grades, passing Dyche Valley and reaching the loop crest near the South Grade Rd. junction. The bottom falls out on that switchback-packed road (Hwy. S6) as the cyclist bombs down down a seven-mile, seven-percent grade highway before returning to State Hwy. 76. Eight miles of less testy cycling on this scenic, high-traffic road returns the biker to the starting point.

TRIP #47 - JULIAN 'JUNKET'

GENERAL LOCATION: Julian, Pine Hills

LEVEL OF DIFFICULTY: Round Trip - moderate to strenuous (trip altitude)
Distance - 19.7 miles
Elevation gain - periodic short moderate-to-steep grades

GENERAL DESCRIPTION: This invigorating wooded-area workout at 4000-feet plus elevation explores the countryside around the tourist mecca of Julian. The nice change-of pace trip explores the scenic back roads where there are mixed stretches of flat and inclined roadway, as well as varied mountain scenery. The Class X double-looper starts at woodsy, well laid out, William Heise County Park. A forested, generally downhill span, followed by a workout climb on busy Hwy. 78/79, sends the biker through the painstakingly restored town of Julian. Just beyond is a quiet countryside tour through rolling hills, followed by a serious downhill on Wynola Rd. via a sloped, high-meadow path which transitions to a shaded canyon. An uphill pedal on Hwy. 78/79 returns the biker to Pine Hills Rd., followed by a circuitous, wooded stretch and a "back door" entry to the park.

Come for the ride and stay for the peripheral goodies. Two suggestions: 1) ride in the morning hours before the tourist onslaught; and 2) come in the fall when the foliage is changing color and the apples are being harvested (Julian Apple Days is in October). However, anytime of year is a good time to see this quaint town. Julian, a product of an 1870's gold rush, has a little something for everybody. The town boasts

BICYCLE RIDES: SAN DIEGO COUNTY

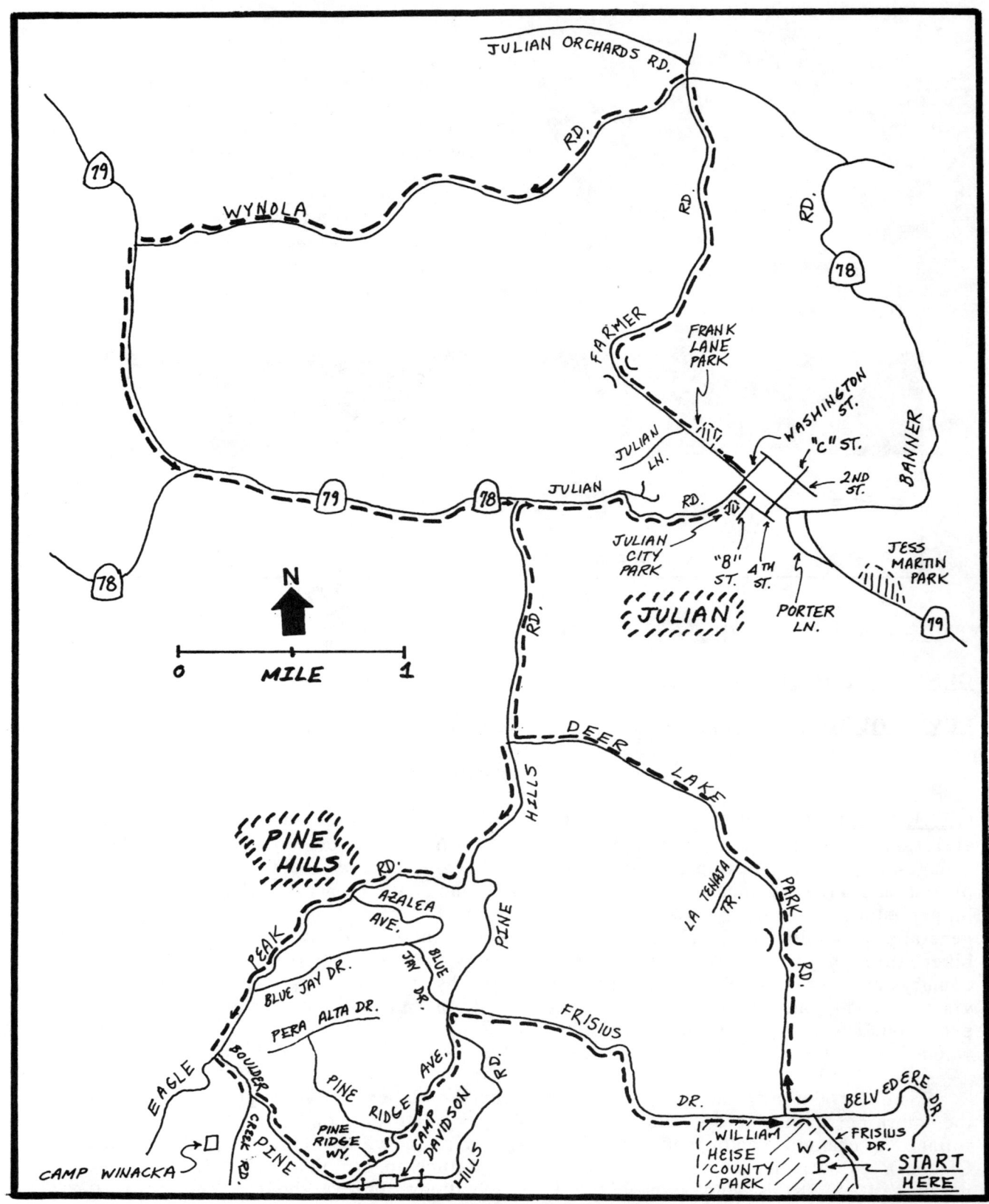

TRIP #47 - JULIAN JUNKET

MOUNTAINS/BACKCOUNTRY

the Eagle Gold Mine, Julian Pioneer Museum, Menghine Winery, 30 bed-and-breakfast establishments, 15 restaurants, three bakeries and several antique shops.

TRAILHEAD: From the west and north (Escondido), follow State Hwys. 78 and 79, respectively, through Santa Ysabel. Continue on the combined Hwy. 78/79 and turn right (south) at Pine Hills Rd. Follow the signs to Heise County Park.

From the south (San Diego, El Centro), exit Interstate Hwy. 8 north onto State Hwy. 79. Drive through Julian and turn at Pine Hills Rd., a little over one mile from the town center. From the east (Borrego Springs, Salton Sea), follow State Hwy. 78 west through Julian and turn as noted above on Pine Hills Rd.

Heise Park is a true gem, particularly for overnight campers. The forested park provides numerous, well-spaced and scenic campsites with benches, firepits, water, and firewood (paid for on the honor system!). There are numerous hiking and riding trails in the park. The park has snow cover for limited periods, although the roads are generally open.

TRIP DESCRIPTION: **Heise County Park to Julian.** Bike out of the pine- and oak- filled park on well-shaded, rural two-lane Frisius Dr. to Deer Lake Park Rd. Follow this road 2.2 miles through a tantalizing rolling meadow with scattered ranches before reaching Pine Hills Rd. A right here and a one-mile transit through a mix of shaded and open two-lane roadway leads to State Hwy. 78/79. Heading east, the biker is treated to a varying moderate-to-steep, one-mile upgrade on this busy highway, which levels near the heart of Julian at Farmer Rd. (4.6).

Farmer Road Meadowland

Northern Loop. Follow quaint and wood-shaded Farmer Rd. on a steep, short upgrade, part of the 2.2 miles of rolling meadowland tour that preceeds the junction with Wynola Rd. A left turn here takes the biker on a refreshing 3.1-mile, 450-foot downgrade. This cozy two-lane road now snakes through the meadow's western edge before slowly sinking into a wooded canyon on a series of mildly graded switchbacks. A mile and a half of this sunlight-filtered segment gives way to a straight, flatter road with scattered gentleman-farmer properties. At the end of the meadow is Hwy. 79. Pass Tom's Chicken Snacks (double-yummy chicken) and prepare to pay for the prior "downhill sins." Just beyond Calico Ranch Rd. on this fast-moving highway is a serious 1.3-mile upgrade which levels off within another gorgeous meadow. Just beyond is Pine Hills Rd. (12.5).

Pine Hills. Continuing south on Pine Hills Rd., return to Deer Lake Park Rd. Bike through open meadowland with scattered tree cover, veering right at Eagle Peak Rd. Bike on the winding uphill road through a heavily wooded glen, cross a small

BICYCLE RIDES: SAN DIEGO COUNTY

(normally dry) creek spillway, and continue through an area with alternating dense tree cover and open views to the west. Pass Azalea Ave. and continue another uphill pedal through scattered residential area before reaching Boulder Creek Rd. (15.8).

Veer left at Boulder Creek Rd. and follow this little road under increasingly thick tree cover through scattered rural residences. In 0.2 mile, veer left again at Pine Hills Rd. (Boulder Creek Rd. heads south to Camp Winacka and a fire station). There are periodic looks at nearby North Peak and more distant Cuyamaca, Japacha, and Stonewall Peaks as the road meanders upward. Follow a sharp left at Pine Ridge Wy. and power uphill through a series of tight curves. Continue through heavy tree cover and, in a short distance, turn right onto Pine Ridge Ave.

In 0.6 mile of continued delightful cycling under the the solid tree mantle, we wind our way back to the Pine Hills Rd. intersection. The route steers left (north) onto that road and meets Friscius Dr. just beyond. There is a grand view from the roadway of the Camp Martson area, complete with mountain backdrop, just beyond the intersection. Continue another 1.6 miles through rolling meadows and coast the last 0.4 mile as the tour ends at the Heise County Park entrance (19.7).

Frisius Dr. Overlooking Camp Martson

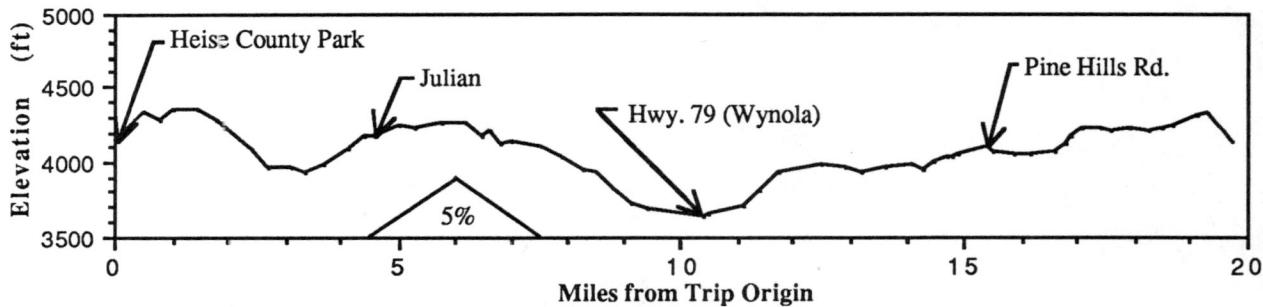

CONNECTING TRIPS: Connection with the Laguna Mountains Crest tour (Trip #48) - from the center of Julian, follow Hwy. 79 south.

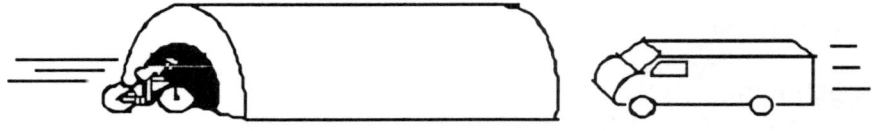

MOUNTAINS/BACKCOUNTRY

TRIP #48 - LAGUNA MOUNTAINS CREST

GENERAL LOCATION: Laguna Mountains

LEVEL OF DIFFICULTY: Up and back - moderate to strenuous
Distance - 20.4 miles (up and back)
Elevation gain - periodic moderate grades

GENERAL DESCRIPTION: This is the "cheater" way to ride the Laguna Mountains, a tour that serves up the most scenic portion of the Sunrise Hwy., without having to bike the gut-busting south grade. The views are plentiful with particularly spectacular vistas from the Desert View Picnic Area, continuing to the trip's end. The focus of these scenic points is the Anza-Borrego Desert and the snake-like thread of Hwy. S2, the Great Overland Stage Route, far below. Most of the route is on moderately-traveled two-lane roads through dense pine forest. There are several overnight camping areas, as well as resorts, which could serve as base camps for this tour.

There are two trip extention options, one to continue to Julian, the other to bike south on the steep Sunrise Hwy. downgrade.

TRAILHEAD: From the south and Interstate Hwy. 8, exit at County Hwy. S1 (just beyond Pine Valley) and continue 5-1/2 miles to the Meadows Information Center (a generally unattended kiosk). From State Hwy. 79 in Julian, drive south six miles to a junction near Lake Cuyamaca. Take the left fork (County Hwy. S1) and continue 8-1/2 miles to the Pioneer Mail Trail Picnic Area. (The termination point of the trip described. From here, bike the reference trip in reverse.)

Check the weather first, since this area can easily become a snowy playground or come under a significant downpour (the area collects 40-50 inches of the wet stuff per year). Depending on your mental and physical makeup, plan accordingly. Preferred times to bike this area are weekdays and mornings, if periodically heavy tourist traffic is to be avoided. The 1200-foot plus up-and-back elevation gain, combined with the mile-high altitude, pushes this trip classification toward "strenuous."

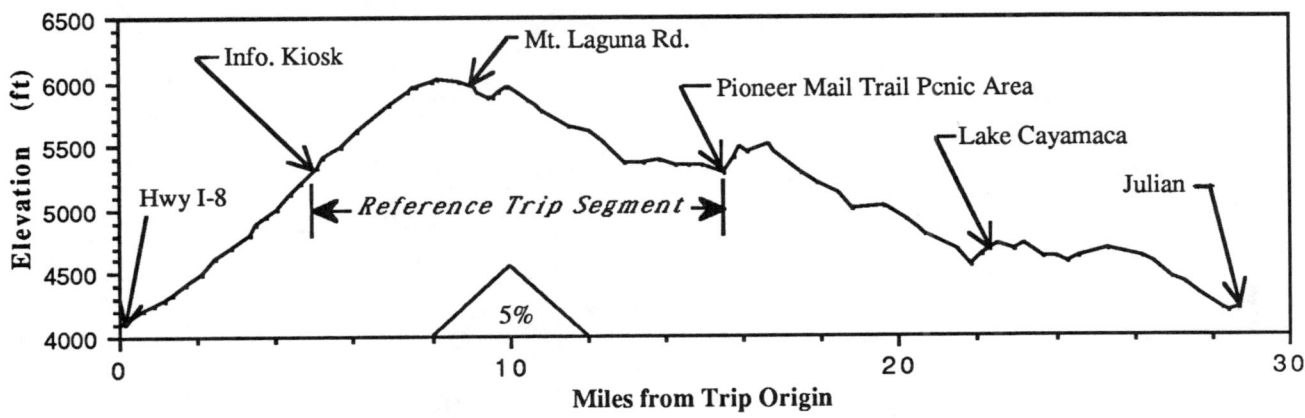

BICYCLE RIDES: SAN DIEGO COUNTY

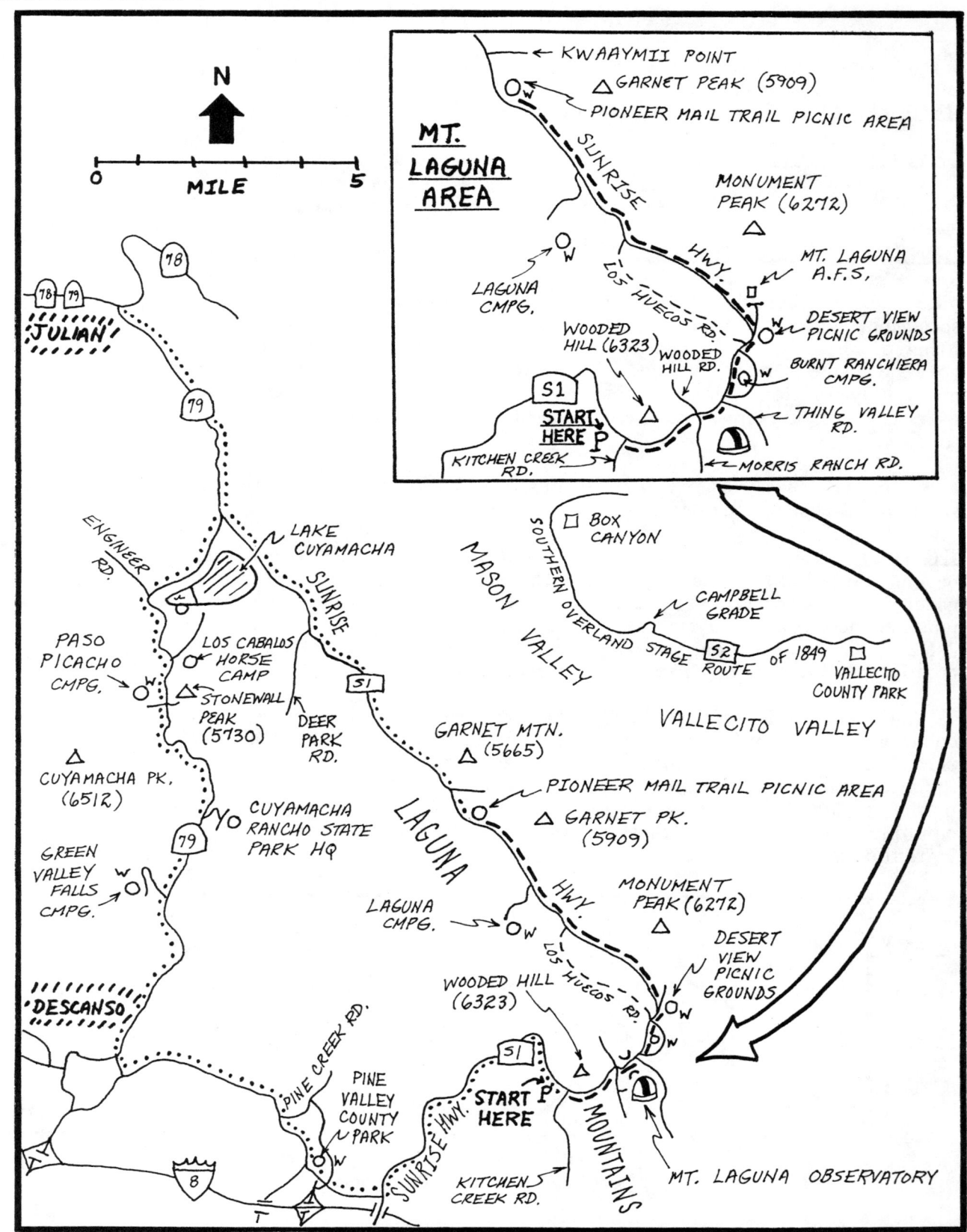

TRIP #48 - LAGUNA MOUNTAINS CREST

MOUNTAINS/BACKCOUNTRY

TRIP DESCRIPTION: Follow the pine-tree lined, two-lane road on a grade past an automobile turnout with a grand view of the north-south ridgelines of the frontal peaks and of the encompassed valleys to the south. A short flat stretch gives way to another climb past the turnoffs to Mt. Laguna Observatory and Wooded Hill. The roadway flattens (2.5), continuing through the generously tree-populated area, passes the Mt. Laguna Fire Department, and reaches the Burnt Ranchiera Campground, Sunrise Cafe and a resort village at Mt. Laguna Rd. Just beyond is the Desert View Picnic Grounds (3.8), where there is an award-winning view down the ridgelines of the Sawtooth Mountains and The Potrero into the Great Overland Stage Route (County Hwy. S2) (see Trip #60). Another fine perspective is found by following the nearby access road to the Mt. Laguna Air Force Station radar facility.

Desert View Picnic Grounds Overlook

In a short distance, the cyclist follows a mild downgrade, then traverses a series of small rolling hills in this densely-treed area and passes the Forest Fire Station. The downhill continues in earnest just beyond, passing the turnoff to the Laguna El Prado Campground (7.3) and entering an area where the sporadic breaks in the tree cover allow spectacular views down to the desert region below. Hwy. S1 continues on mild rolling terrain through treed meadows, passes another information booth and breaks out of the tree line. Just beyond is the Pioneer Mail Trail Picnic Area and the trip's turnaround point (10.2).

CONNECTING TRIPS: Trip Extensions: 1) At the picnic area, continue north on Hwy. S1 and State Hwy. 79 14 miles and 1000-foot elevation loss to Julian; 2) from the trip's starting point, return south down the Sunrise Hwy. 5.4 miles and about 1600 feet to the Pine Valley turnoff. (Think long and hard about this option if you are not "turned on" by both exciting downhills and a 5-1/2 mile, six-percent <u>average</u> grade on the return uphill!)

BICYCLE RIDES: SAN DIEGO COUNTY

Helmet  No Helmet

TRIP #49 - PALA MISSION LOOP

GENERAL LOCATION: Rainbow, Temecula, Pala

LEVEL OF DIFFICULTY: Loop - strenuous
Distance - 25.0 miles
Elevation gain - periodic moderate-to-steep grades

GENERAL DESCRIPTION: This Class X country tour starts in nursery-filled Rainbow Valley, drops down through the southeastern edge of Temecula into Wolf Valley, then follows Pala-Temecula Rd. through a forested, precipitous canyon to Pala Mission. Next, a short stretch along the San Luis Rey River plain is followed by the trip's highlight segment into Rice Canyon. This workout return upgrade on a small country road takes the biker past citrus farms, pony farms, and into lush forested areas with trees mantling the roadway. The Pala-Temecula Rd. segment is not for bikers who are squeamish about dealing with impatient automobile drivers (traffic is light, however); if in doubt, at least bike Rice Canyon.

Pala Mission

TRAILHEAD: From Interstate Hwy. 15, exit at the Mission Rd. turnoff (County Hwy. S13) and turn east at the first stop sign. Turn left onto the Frontage Rd. and continue 2-1/2 miles to 5th St. in Rainbow. Turn right and park in the generous oak-tree shade near the Rainbow Oaks Restaurant. Also near this wooded glen are a general store and a fruit stand.

Bring a couple quarts of water for hot days. We found no public water sources on this route.

TRIP DESCRIPTION: **Rainbow to Pala.** Pedal east on 5th St., pass a small market on Huffstatler St., and turn left in 1.1 miles at Rainbow Valley Blvd. This is flat, treed Rainbow Valley, which is chock full of nurseries, hot houses and citrus farms. Soon, the road veers right and, in 1.5 miles from the 5th Ave./Rainbow Valley Blvd. junction, reaches another junction. To the left is a frontage road, while our route turns right onto Rainbow Canyon Rd. (the road signs are confusingly canted). Follow

MOUNTAINS/BACKCOUNTRY

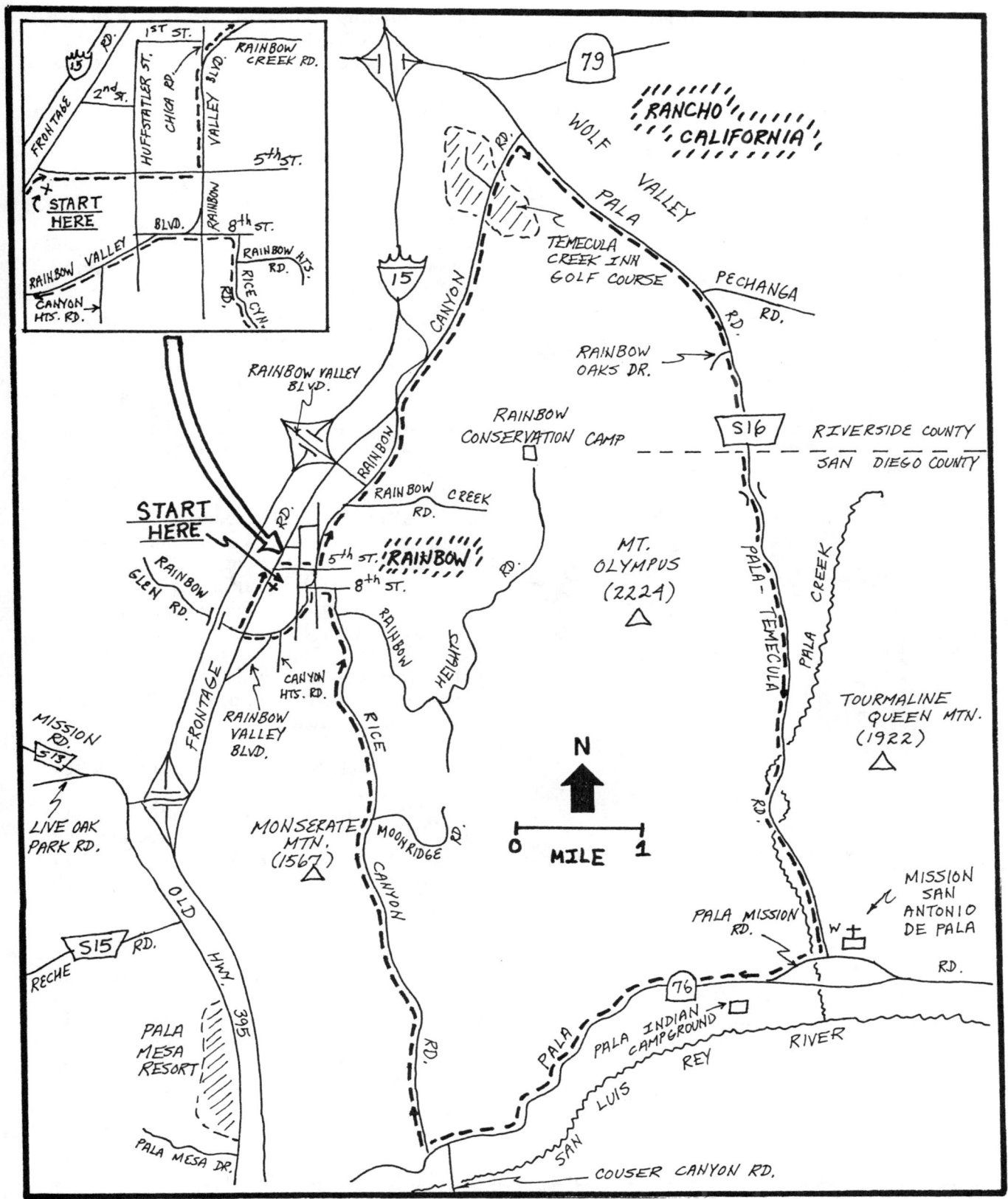

TRIP #49 - PALA MISSION LOOP

BICYCLE RIDES: SAN DIEGO COUNTY

this more exposed road through rolling hills to a winding downhill section with an overlook of Wolf and Temecula Valleys. In the far distance, Mt. San Gorgonio and Mt. San Jacinto peaks are clearly visible. The route reaches valley level and passes through the lush golf course surrounding upscale Temecula Creek Inn (a great sports and lounging retreat that has delectable dining).

Burned-out Structure above Rice Cyn. Rd.

Turn right at Pala Rd. (County Hwy. S16 - if you reach State Hwy. 79, you've gone too far), pass a mini-mart, then cruise through wide-open and flat Wolf Valley. This area is the home of the "instant lawn," with sod farms dotted along the road. After about three miles, the highway narrows, then enters the tree-covered landscape near Rainbow Oaks Dr.

Just beyond is the trip's highest elevation point near the San Diego County Line (with Rancho Heights Rd. just beyond) and a winding five-percent downgrade over the next several miles. Now called Pala-Temecula Rd., this asphalt ribbon overlooks a canyon with Pala Creek at its bottom, then plummets downward through scattered tree cover to creek level in a couple miles. To the east is Tourmaline Queen Mountain, which our topo map and a couple of rock hound friends tell us is spotted with active and inactive mines. Hwy. S16 flattens and deadends near a small general store in a short distance. A short diversion to the left leads to the Pala Mission, built in 1816, and still in use by the Pala Indians as both a school and a place of worship. Here are the classic Mission Chapel, an Indian artifact-filled museum and cemetery (14.3).

The Return Leg. Follow Pala Mission Rd. westward 0.7 mile until it rejoins State Hwy. 76. The next 3-1/2 miles is on the wide San Luis Rey River plain, nestled between mountain ranges. Keep an eye out for the fast-moving traffic while enjoying the ranchos with their prize quarterhorses and cattle. After a few serious roadway twists, the highway passes Couser Canyon Rd. and, just beyond, meets Rice Canyon Rd.

This is time to "pay the piper" for the easy incoming tour segment. What better way than on this little gem of a tucked away country road, which has to be the trip highlight! Follow the narrow two-lane road 0.7 mile through flat farming country, then enter Rice Canyon with its attendant steep winding upgrade. Pass an avocado farm, Pala Mesa Heights Dr., and a pony farm as the tree cover steadily builds around

MOUNTAINS/BACKCOUNTRY

the road. Above Moonridge Rd. (22.2) on a hilltop is an interesting burned out circular structure.

Rice Canyon Road

Continue puffing another 1/2-mile to a crest, then coast past orange and avocado groves and the serene homesteads alongside the canyon creek. The tree cover totally engulfs the road as the biker navigates rolling hills, then reaches a high and more-open plateau. The road leaves the canyon and returns to a higher density residential area, then makes a sharp turn to the west on 8th St. Follow this road directly west past more nurseries as it becomes Rainbow Valley Blvd., then pedal the I-15 frontage road back to the origin (25.0).

Side Trip. Three miles east of Pala Mission on State Hwy. 76 is the Wilderness Gardens Preserve. This oak woodland has walk-in campsites, fishing ponds, a picnic area and nature trails. Motor vehicles (and, thus, many of their attendant modern "conveniences") must be left in the parking area. (Hooray!)

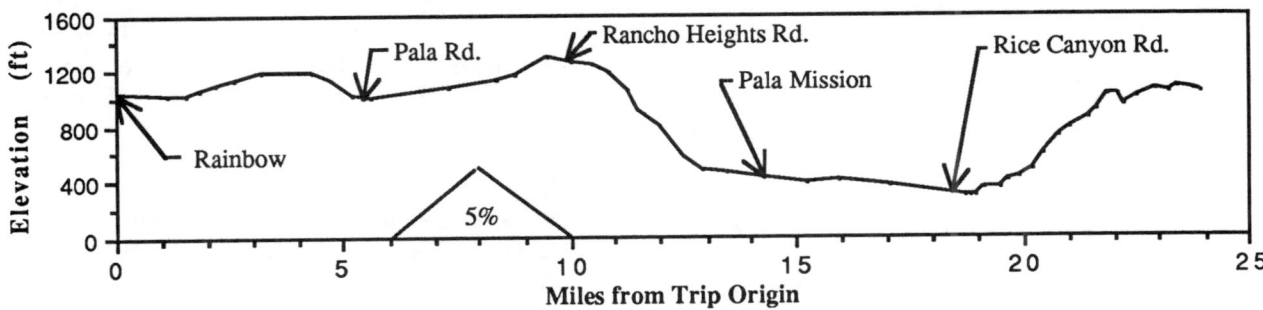

CONNECTING TRIPS: 1) Connection with Old Hwy. 395 (Trip #38) - the tours share a common segment between Rainbow Valley Rd. and Pala Rd.; 2) connection with the Fallbrook Countryside Tour (Trip #39) - return to the I-15 Mission Rd. exit and cross over the Interstate.

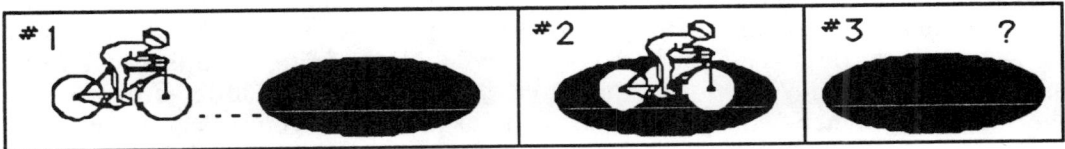

BICYCLE RIDES: SAN DIEGO COUNTY

TRIP #50 - JAMUL-BRAYTON VALLEY LOOP

GENERAL LOCATION: Jamul - Brayton Valley - Lyons Valley

LEVEL OF DIFFICULTY: Loop - very strenuous
Distance - 25.2 miles
Elevation gain - strenuous eight-mile upgrade on Honey Springs Rd.

GENERAL DESCRIPTION: A short distance from the bustling San Diego area metropolis is a ride into what seems to be the "middle of nowhere." Beyond the starting point in Jamul, the cyclist is treated to a warm-up stretch on Campo Rd. before disappearing into the mountain country outback of Honey Springs Rd. Traffic is light, developed land is minimal, the rock-strewn mountain scenery is interesting, and the upgrade is close to torturous. After eight-plus miles and an 1850-foot elevation gain (an <u>average</u> 4-1/2% grade), the bicyclist is treated to a well-deserved downhill, a cruise through serene, tree-covered Lyons Valley, and a short, steep climb to Lee Valley. Beyond the valley is a steep scenic 3.7-mile runout on Kimbal Grade, which takes the cyclist through North Jamul and returns to the trip origin at Simpson Country Park.

TRAILHEAD: From the San Diego area, follow State Hwy. 94 as it transitions from freeway to become Campo Rd. Continue 1-1/2 miles, staying to the right at Jamacha Junction. In 5-1/2 miles, turn left (northeast) on Lyons Valley Rd., then veer off to the right at Olive Vista Dr. Just beyond is Jefferson Rd.; Simpson County Park is just south on that street. From the east, exit south at State Hwy. 54 (Jamacha Rd.) and continue to its terminus at Jamacha junction. Turn left onto State Hwy. 94 and continue as described above. Bring 2-3 quarts of water. The only reliable water sources are in Jamul and Lyons Valley.

TRIP DESCRIPTION: **The Warmup (Campo Rd.).** Return to Campo Rd. via Jefferson Rd. south, passing through the commercial section of Jamul. The 5-1/2 miles on Campo Rd. is on gentle rolling hills. On the way, there are distant views of the San Ysidro Mountains, a close-up of the Jamul Mountains backdrop to the right, and a pleasant cruise through a successive chain of small valleys. About 1/2 mile beyond the scattered development of Indian Springs and to the north is St. Francis Xavier Cemetery--more about that later!

The Test (Honey Springs Rd.). At Honey Springs Rd., bike into the scrub-covered hills and enjoy the immediate drop in traffic flow. Pass a stand of trees, noting that the few scattered stands prior to Lyons Valley will be the only sensible rest spots on the way up. Within a short distance, the cyclist encounters a grade which grows from modest to steep, then passes the heart of Honey Springs with its horse corrals and scattered trees in about 2-1/2 miles (8.4). The rugged, boulder-strewn mountains, so characteristic of this segment, surround the biker on the ascent.

The road hugs the hillside while climbing above the valley. The seemingly endless upgrade causes one some thought as to who is buried in the Xavier Cemetery (ha ha!). An isolated tree stand and a couple miles later brings the biker into Bratton Valley and the Deerhorn Valley Rd. junction. The next 1/2 mile provides time to eyeball the scattered ranch-like properties, and to admire Lyons Peak, the dominant

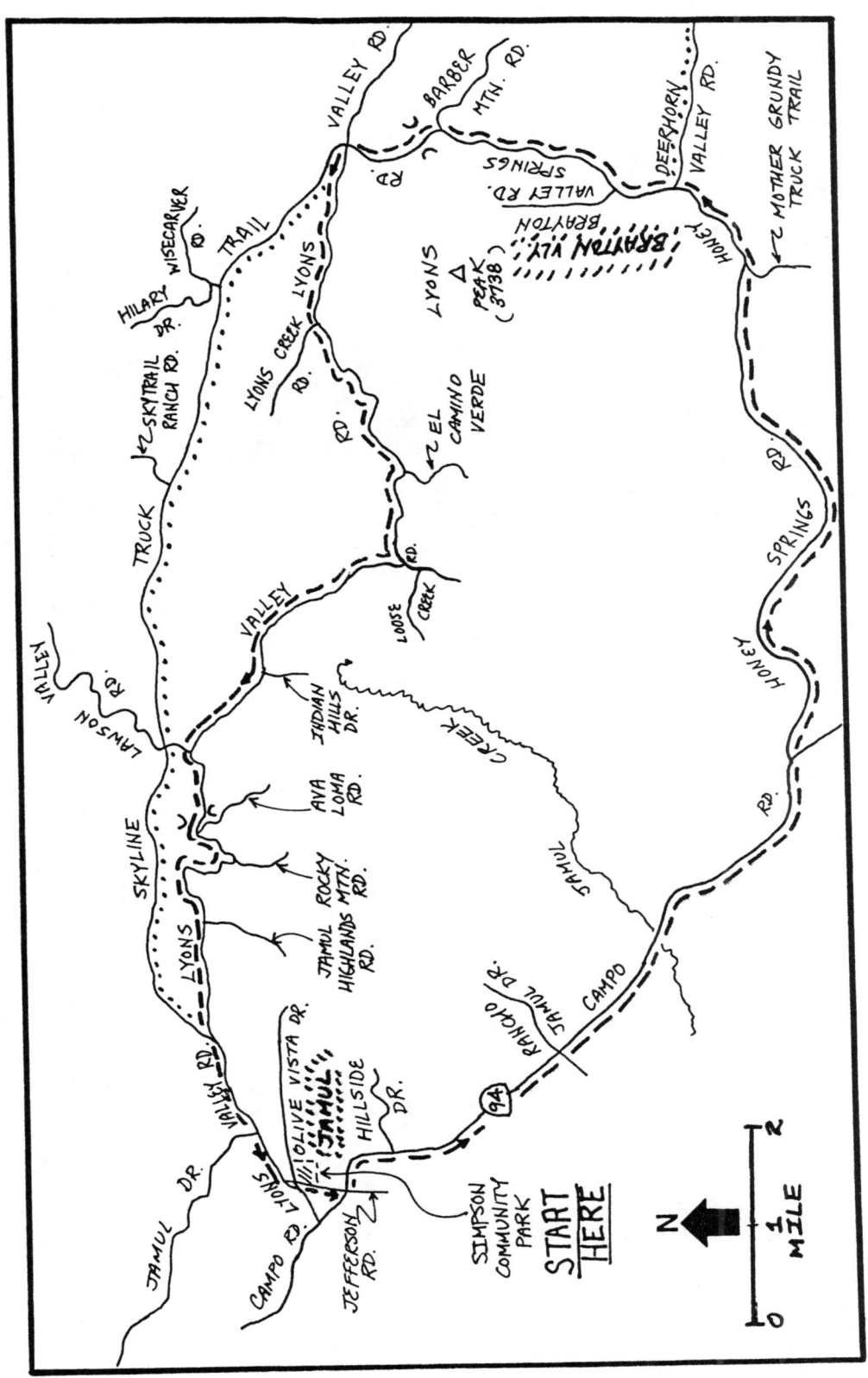

TRIP #50 - JAMUL - BRAYTON VALLEY LOOP

BICYCLE RIDES: SAN DIEGO COUNTY

feature in the landscape for miles to come. In three more predominantly uphill miles is the Honey Springs Rd. crest and the trip's high point. In just less than a mile of truly refreshing downgrade, the cyclist reaches Lyons Valley Rd.

The Crossroads - Deerhorn Valley Road

Natural Beauty -- and the Last Upgrade (Lyons Valley Rd.) This is a major decision point. Continuing straight ahead leads to Skyline Truck Trail with an early, steep 300-foot climb and six miles of general downgrade. This is the easier route, but less scenic than the route we take. For the next 1.3 miles before reaching the rustic Lyons Valley Trading Post (15.9), the road transits an extended shaded glen on a small, rural road and passes a comfy ranch with a tennis court. (We could live here!) In less than a mile, the road stairsteps downhill on a winding course, passing several small valleys, and reaching a low point near the entrance to Hollenback Canyon.

A one-mile, testy, winding upgrade takes the biker out of the valley below (a spectacular view looking back) and lets out at broad, wide-open Lee Valley. On this elevated plateau are Jamul Creek, nearby rocky peaks to the east, and the typical scattered farming and residential properties. Lyons Valley Rd. veers left at Lawson Valley Rd. Just beyond is a curving road marker, and near Ave. Loma Rd. (21.4), begins the steep, switch-backed Kimbal Grade. Immediately, there are frequent superb views down into North Jamul, as the road dives down to meet the valley floor. In 2.3 miles from Ava Loma Rd., our route fuses with the Skyline Truck Trail and continues through this more densely developed area. In 3.7 miles and almost 900-foot elevation loss below Ava Loma Rd., Lyons Valley Rd. meets Jefferson Rd. Turn south here and bike the short distance to Simpson Community Park (25.1).

Deerhorn Valley Spur. At Deerhorn Valley Rd., the biker can explore an even more remote area of scattered ranches, farms and residences. Wander through the area and contemplate the laid-back lifestyle that emanates from these surroundings. The diversion will add 2.9 miles and about 500-foot elevation gain or loss, one way.

MOUNTAINS/BACKCOUNTRY

Beyond the end of the paved highway are little-used dirt roads that could provide some interesting riding for "off-road" bikers.

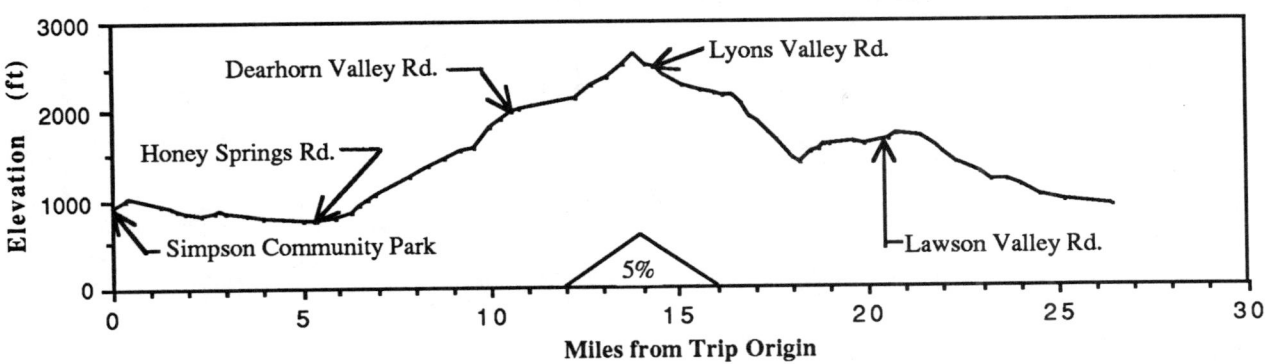

CONNECTING TRIPS: Lyons Peak? Ironman Triathlon? Mt. Everest? (Just kidding!)

TRIP #51 - LAKE MORENA-LIVE OAK SPRINGS LOOP

GENERAL LOCATION: Lake Morena, Campo, Live Oak Springs

LEVEL OF DIFFICULTY: Loop - strenuous
Distance - 41.7 miles
Elevation gain - periodic moderate-to-steep grades

GENERAL DESCRIPTION: Would you expect oak-covered slopes a few miles from the Mexican Border? What are the chances of finding such refreshing territory, just off of an Interstate, which is only lightly developed? Plan to do a lot of sightseeing and exploring natural delights just off the main route. This sometimes thumper-pumper hilly tour boasts two dandy parks, Lake Morena County Park and Boulder Oaks Campground. The mountain views throughout the tour are terrific and the periodic tree cover along the highway is welcome. The passage near and under the San Diego-Imperial Valley Railroad trestle is a grabber. Take this dynamite country tour before the big developers find this territory.

TRAILHEAD: From Interstate Hwy. 8, turn south at Buckman Springs Rd., drive four miles to Oak Dr., then three miles west to Lake Morena Dr. Turn right and continue to the Lake Morena County Park entrance. The park has restrooms, showers, fishing, overnight camping areas, abundant tree cover and a nearby general store. For hiking buffs, the Pacific Crest Trail passes near the lake.

TRIP DESCRIPTION: **Southern Segment.** Leave the camp serenity and bike past the ranger station following Lake Morena Dr. southward. Cruise through Morena Village (grocery store and other amenities), then follow an upgrade to a wide plateau and enjoy the views of nearby Hauser Mountain and the more distant In-Ko-Pah Mountains. Over the next three miles, the cyclist enjoys a 500-foot downgrade,

BICYCLE RIDES: SAN DIEGO COUNTY

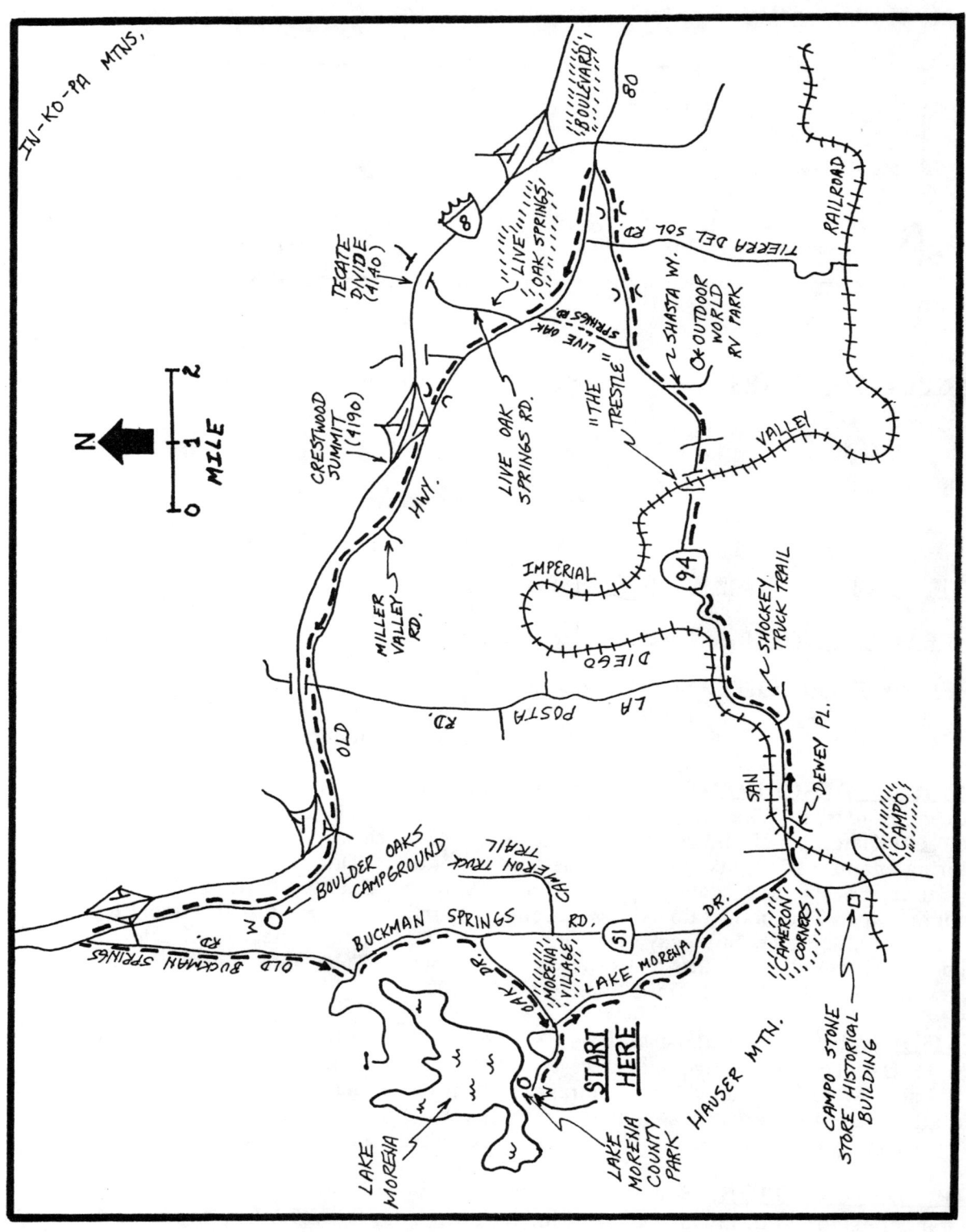

TRIP #51 - LAKE MORENA - LIVE OAK SPRINGS LOOP

primarily through a hilly ranching area with abundant scrub brush and scattered tree cover. At the foot of the downgrade is the trip's low point at Cameron Corners, where there is a restaurant (6.0). To the right and 1-1/2 miles south is the Campo Stone Store and a railroad museum, plus the Campo Stone Store County Park.

However, our reference tour turns left at State Hwy. 94. This road was only slightly busier in mid-week than the two-lane rural byways that characterize the other parts of this tour. The road hugs the northern edge of a large valley of ranches and farms, then starts upward along Campo Creek onto a rocky hillside just beyond Shockey Truck Trail. The workout subsides in a flat area near La Posta Rd. (9.3), then returns to a winding upgrade, where the cyclist is rewarded with a view back to the valley below. In a short distance looms a high bridge suspended between two massive rock outcroppings. A few rolling hills later, the road passes directly beneath that structure, a San Diego-Imperial Valley Railroad trestle.

The bridge-viewing euphoria subsides and the biker returns to a steep climb, passing Outdoor World RV Park and continuing another two uphill miles to Tierra Del Sol Rd. In another 0.6 mile, the route crests and the biker gets a well deserved downhill spin into the town of Boulevard (17.7).

Lake Morena

Northern Segment. Turn left onto Old Hwy. 80, pass a delicatessen, then follow a hefty 0.7 mile upgrade onto a high plateau. While observing Hill Valley to the left (west) and below, navigate the rolling hills into Live Oak Springs. Just beyond town, follow a two-step steep upgrade, one 0.3-mile and the other a 0.4-mile incline, with a little breathing space in between. There are mountain views in this area near Crestwood Summit, where Old Hwy. 80 nestles up to I-8 (22.5).

Just below the underpass, turn left and parallel I-8, biking a cooling descent, then continuing through rolling hills for about 2-1/2 miles. Next is a 4.2-mile general downgrade; in this interval, the road passes La Posta Rd. (and a small cafe), then settles into picturesque Cameron Valley with its peaceful meadows and scattered tree

BICYCLE RIDES: SAN DIEGO COUNTY

stands. As the highway swings northward, pass the Boulder Oaks Campground (restrooms, picnic areas, trees, overnight camping and nearby general store) (30.4).

Continue three miles and make a hard left on Old Buchman Springs Rd. (County Hwy. S1). This smaller country road passes a large grove of trees, a school, a firehouse and makes its way through rolling hills to Oak Dr. (39.1). An immediate uphill takes the cyclist onto a plateau. Scattered residences give way to more dense housing in the Morena Village area. Near Molchan Rd. is a combined grocery/deli/soda fountain/gas station. (Ah, the '50s still live in some parts of the state!) In 1.6 miles from the Hwy. S1 junction, Oak Dr. fuses into Lake Morena Dr., and another mile returns the biker to the trip's starting point (41.7).

Shortcut. The trip can be shortened by using La Posta Rd. and doing either the east or west loops (21 and 23-1/2 miles respectively). The eastern loop is at a lower elevation and has the lesser total elevation gain.

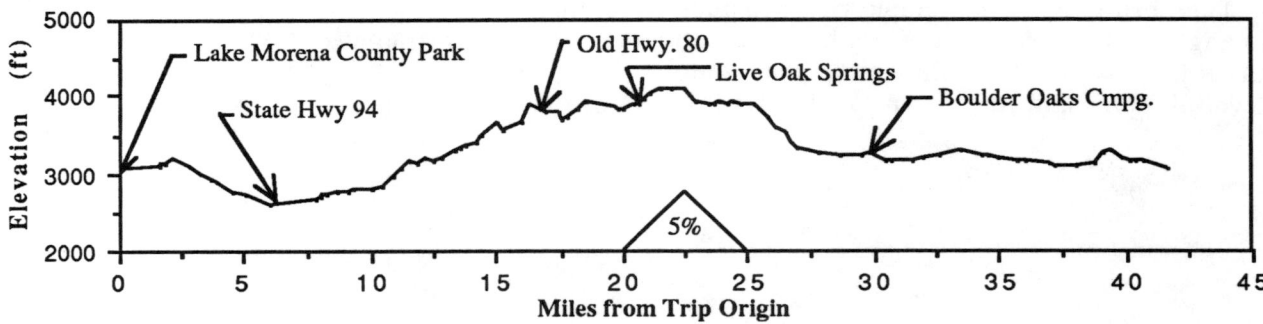

CONNECTING TRIPS: For true torture addicts, bike north on S1, cross over I-8 and go for the Sunrise Hwy. upgrade to Mt. Laguna (see Trip #48).

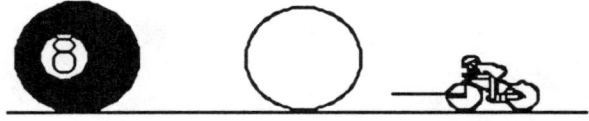

TRIP #52 - CANYONS N' CITRUS

GENERAL LOCATION: Bonsall

LEVEL OF DIFFICULTY: Loop - strenuous
Distance - 24.5 miles
Elevation gain - periodic moderate-to-strenuous grades

GENERAL DESCRIPTION: The reference tour plies Gopher and Moosa Canyons and the Southern California world of citrus and avocado orchards. The interesting Class X loop leaves Bonsall and continues east at a mild pace before climbing steeply out of Moosa Canyon. The segment beyond is a circuitous tour through the citrus-covered hills east of Interstate Hwy. 15. Just beyond the eastside, view-studded crest is a pleasurable 8.6-mile general downhill return to Bonsall. An alternate loop option is also provided which is 6.6 miles shorter and which substitutes a lesser traveled southern tour segment for Gopher Canyon Rd.-Old Castle Rd.

MOUNTAINS/BACKCOUNTRY

TRAILHEAD: From I-15, exit west at State Hwy. 76 (Pala Rd.) and drive 5-1/2 miles to Olive Hill Rd. Park in the post office parking lot, which is a short distance east of the intersection on Olive Hill Rd.

The strenuous rating is earned by the steep grade on Old Castle Rd. when exiting Moosa Canyon, and for the optional route presented by the climb just beyond Circle R Ranch on Circle R Dr. Bring a couple quarts of water on hot days; the only replenishment stops that we found outside of Bonsall were near the Champagne Blvd./Circle R Dr. area (all are private enterprises).

TRIP DESCRIPTION: **Gopher Canyon Rd./Old Castle Rd.** Cross the San Luis Rey River, turn right on Old River Rd. (for the Camino Del Rey loop option, turn left), and pedal 2.2 miles along that waterway to Gopher Canyon Rd. A flat 1.5-mile segment on this farm- and ranch- dotted road skirts the northern tip of the San Marcos Mountains and leads the biker to the Ormsby St. intersection. Just beyond is a one-mile upgrade into a wider section of Gopher Canyon, followed by a 1.7-mile resting segment. A steady upgrade beyond leads to a "let-it-out" nine-percent downgrade in the Wild Acres Rd. area which levels near I-15.

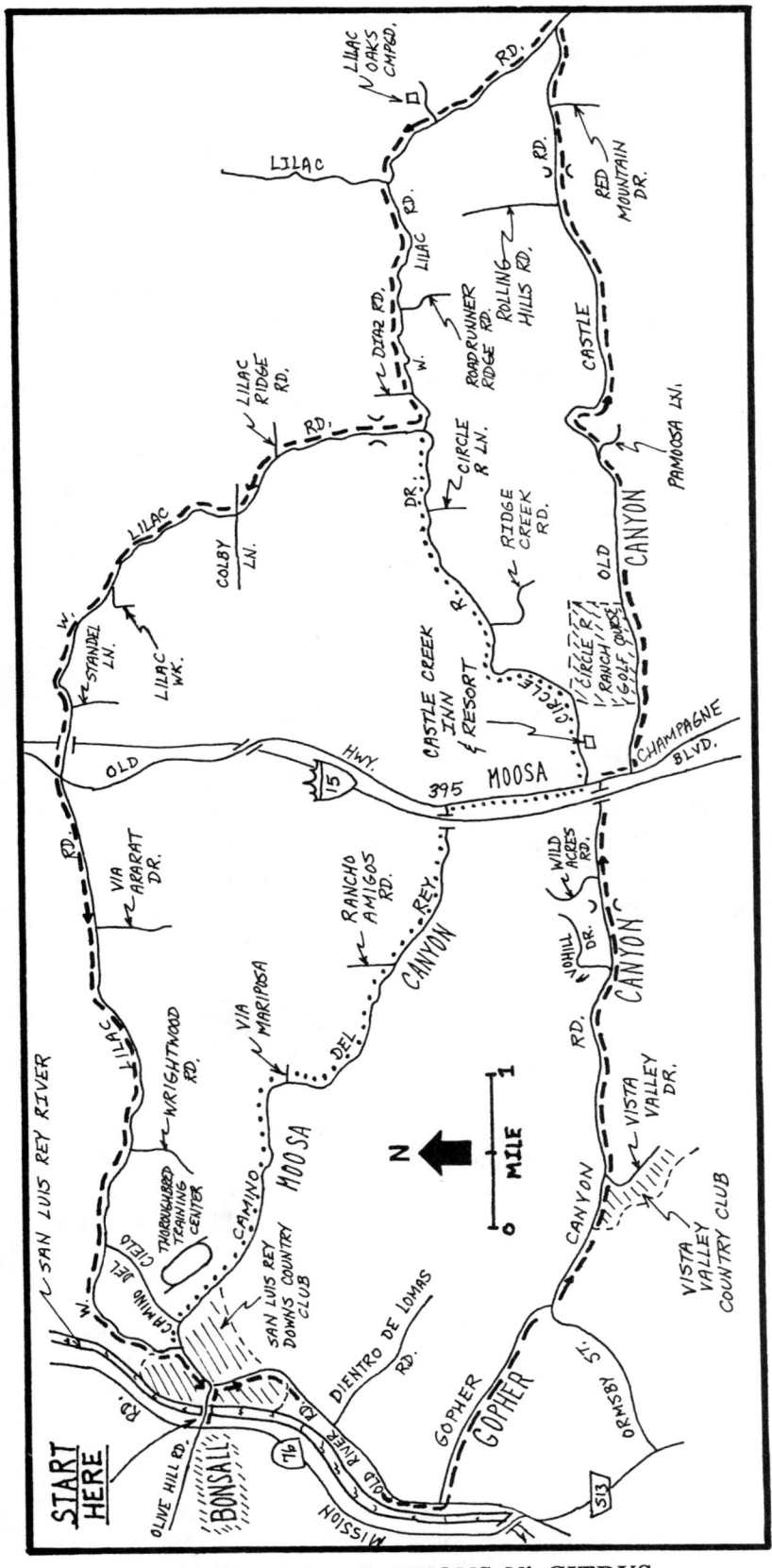

TRIP #52 - CANYONS N' CITRUS

BICYCLE RIDES: SAN DIEGO COUNTY

Continue to Old Hwy. 395/Champagne Blvd. (the Lawrence Welk Resort Village is a couple of miles south) and turn into Old Castle Rd. Pass Old Castle Pl. with its Trading Post and gas station and follow the road as it transitions from the southern to northern edges of wide Moosa Canyon. The road narrows, then heads uphill past scattered ranch-like properties with their attendant gorgeous homes. Beyond Pamoosa Ln., climb steeply out of the canyon on a 2.6-mile huff-and-puff trip leg. The view back into the canyon is spectacular in the early climb segment. At the climb's end, the biker finds a plateau covered with expansive "gentleman-farmer" properties (citrus groves, ranches). A steep downgrade just beyond Red Mountain Dr. leads to Lilac Rd.

The Lilac Roads. The two-lane, meandering country road follows a general downgrade past private Lilac Oaks Campground (fishing, recreation, picnicking) and soon reaches W. Lilac Rd. Turn west and follow the snakelike road along the citrus-covered hillsides. Just beyond Diaz Rd. is the intersection with Circle R Rd., where W. Lilac Rd. takes a sharp turn north and follows a short upgrade to a local summit. While enjoying the vistas in this area, contemplate the pleasure of the long and general downhill beyond. The road continues to meander through less-developed hillsides, then wanders downward to I-15 and the architectually-pleasing W. Lilac Rd. overpass (20.8).

West Lilac Road East of Old Highway 395

Continue a mile through an exposed area surrounded by scrub-filled hills, then navigate downward as the road hugs the hillsides on the north side of a small valley. Cruising through this valley of farms, ranches and more citrus groves, the cyclist reaches the Camino Del Rey intersection 4.1 miles from I-15. Keep right and return across the San Luis Rey River to the starting point (24.5).

Camino Del Rey Loop Option. From Bonsall, turn left onto W. Lilac Rd., then turn east (right) onto Camino Del Rey. Pass the San Luis Rey Downs Thoroughbred Training Center and several adjacent horse ranches, then cycle through wide Moosa Canyon on reasonably-flat terrain. Follow the road as it transitions from north to south canyon edges, all the while pedaling through "citrusville." The road skirts the hillsides for several miles before passing under I-15 (4.6).

A right on Champagne Rd. takes the biker past an RV campground and coffee shop to Circle R Rd. An eastward turn here leads to Briarwood Restaurant, part of the lush Castle Creek Inn and Resort. Soon, the road starts upward out of Moosa Canyon and greets the biker with 2-1/2 "sweet" miles of variable moderate-to-steep grades.

MOUNTAINS/BACKCOUNTRY

The route crests at Reden Ln., which is on a citrus orchard-filled plateau. A short and steep downgrade leads to the intersection with West Lilac Rd. (8.4). The return to the trip origin is as described in the reference trip above.

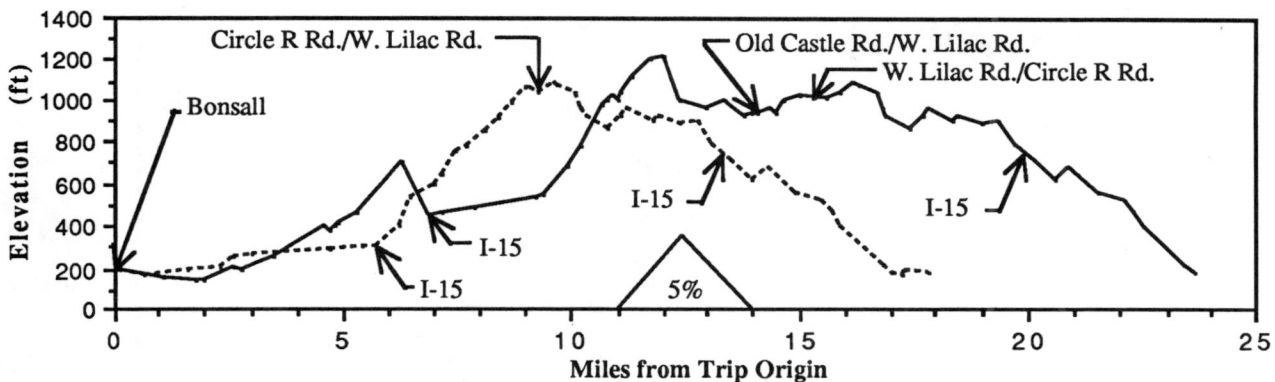

(Note: The dashed line in the elevation contour above is for the **Camino Del Rey Loop Option**.)

CONNECTING TRIPS: 1) Connection with Old Hwy. 395 (Trip #38) - the tours share a common segment between Old Castle Rd. and W. Lilac Rd. alongside Interstate Hwy. 15; 2) connection with the Fallbrook Countryside Tour (Trip #39) - at the trip origin, bike west across State Hwy. 76 on Olive Hill Rd.

TRIP #53 - CREST-DEHESA VALLEY LOOP

GENERAL LOCATION: Alpine, Crest, El Cajon, Dehesa Valley

LEVEL OF DIFFICULTY: Loop - strenuous
Distance - 26.7 miles
Elevation gain - steep grades from Harbison Canyon to Crest and Dehesa Rd. beyond Dehesa Valley

GENERAL DESCRIPTION: This could just as well have been called the Alpine-El Cajon Loop; however, we named the trip for its highlight rural areas. We also stepped out of our normal mode and developed a trip with the hard work at the end (for the sake of an easy starting point access). A leisurely cruise from Alpine leads to a short tour at the upper edge of Harbison Canyon. A long steady pull from the canyon takes the cyclist by several interesting vista points and a crest near the little town of Crest (Surprise, surprise!). A fast-paced downhill and short tour along the El Cajon periphery returns the biker to the rural environs of Dehesa Rd. This roadway leads through pleasant Dehesa Valley, then navigates a four-mile, 1000-foot upgrade to reach Alpine Heights. What remains is a refreshing two-mile breath-catching return to Alpine.

BICYCLE RIDES: SAN DIEGO COUNTY

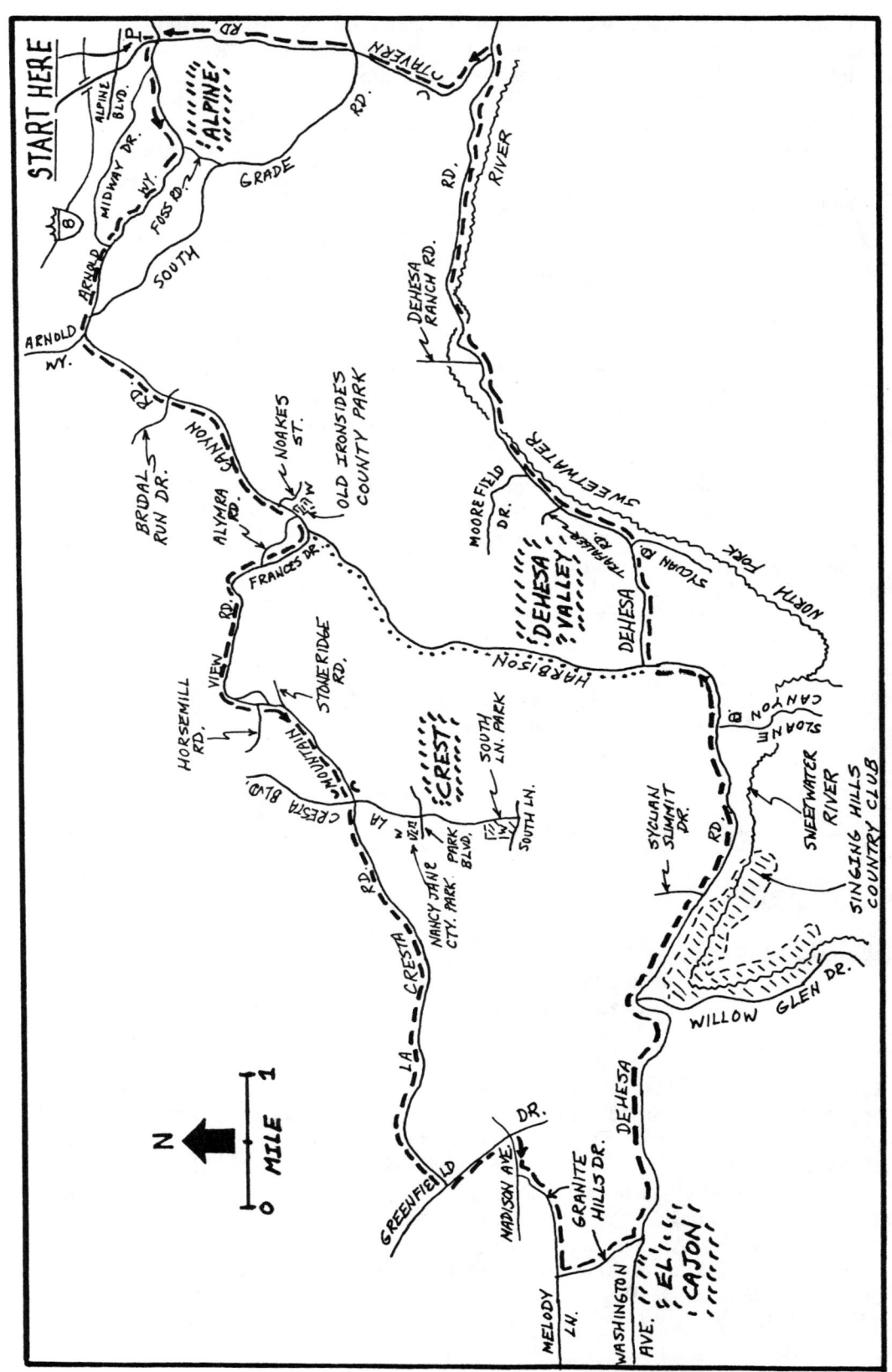

TRIP #53 - CREST - DEHESA VALLEY LOOP

MOUNTAINS/BACKCOUNTRY

TRAILHEAD: From Interstate Hwy. 8 at Alpine, exit south at Tavern Rd. and park at the Park and Ride hear the Alpine Shopping Center. Bring a filled water bottle or two. We found no reliable water sources on the El Cajon-to-Alpine segment.

TRIP DESCRIPTION: **Alpine to El Cajon.** Turn west at Arnold Wy., biking through a thicket of apartments and condominiums. The development soon thins as the route transits an area surrounded by small scattered hills and canyons. Near Midway Dr. on the downhill is the first look at Galloway Valley below. In 2-1/2 miles, after a 450-foot elevation loss, is Harbison Canyon Rd. Two miles on this road leads past contrasting developments, scattered older homesteads to the right and new housing tracts to the left. The transition from open valley to tree-studded canyon is increasingly evident after the first mile. Just beyond Noakes St. (4.3) is shady Old Ironsides County Park, a "last chance" rest stop before tackling the first major upgrade.

Turn onto Frances Dr. and start an upgrade on this tiny rural road. The grade transitions from moderate to steep and winds its way below scattered plush hillside residences; in this area, the road name changes to Mountain View Rd. This gyrating pumpathon continues up to a high plateau beyond Ryan Ridge Rd. where there are more impressive residences, then resumes uphill another mile before leveling at La Cresta Blvd. (7.4). On this upgrade, there are superb views both westward beyond Horsemill Rd. and eastward near Stoneridge Rd. Explore the hamlet of Crest or simply take La Cresta Blvd. 1/2-mile south for a refreshing break at Nancy Jane County Park.

Pass a convenience store, then gaze at the 20-25 miles distant Pacific Ocean just before starting a serious downgrade. Mt. Helix comes into view as the cyclist follows undulating Forrester Creek. In 3.4 miles and over a 1000-foot elevation loss is Greenfield Dr. (10.2) on the edge of El Cajon.

El Cajon to Dehesa Valley. On the way to Granite Hills Dr., enjoy the more close-up view of Mt. Helix, then follow that multi-directional Class II road over to Dehesa Rd. (13.2). The route immediately transitions back to a rural, tree-rich setting, climbs 100 feet to a crest near Singing Hills Dr., then plunges to Wilson Glen Dr. on a short, ten-percent downgrade. The road steers along the northern edge of the Singing Hills Country Club, passes a riverbed quarry in the Sweetwater River, and follows that river for 2-1/2 miles before it transitions south near Sloane Canyon Rd. The road bows sharply left (north), then enters the southern edge of enclosed Dehesa Valley. A modest upgrade leads to a junction with Harbison Canyon Rd. just beyond (18.7).

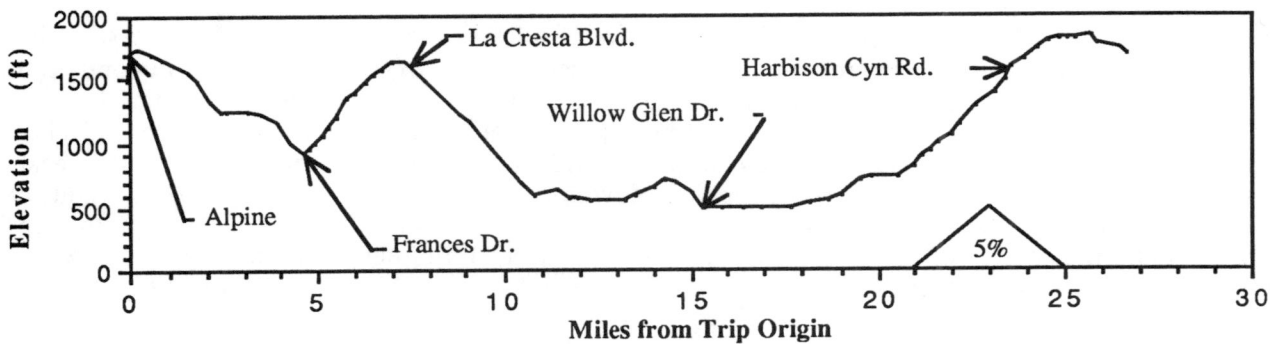

BICYCLE RIDES: SAN DIEGO COUNTY

Return to Alpine. Stay to the right and start a steady uphill in 1/4 mile, passing through an elevated valley surrounded by low rocky peaks. Just as the visual enjoyment of the horse ranches and oak-filled valley is reaching a high, the road passes Starr Park Ranch and begins a challenging upgrade. The road makes one of several crossings of the Sweetwater River's North Fork in this area. We leave the valley and the attendant development, hugging the southern hillside wall. The road winds into the hills, entering a distinct canyon area, and transitions to the north canyon face. Three miles from Starr Park Ranch, the highway reaches the Tavern Rd. junction (23.6).

A hard left here leads steeply uphill on a switchback carved into the canyon hillside (unlike our standard form, we saved the "best" part of the trip until last!). A one-mile climb leads to a plateau and the southern outskirts of Alpine Heights. In 0.3 mile is South Grade Rd., followed by a more relaxing straight-line route back to the starting point (26.7). In this area is a nice, clear-day view of distant El Cajon Mountain.

The Shortcut. An option to cut the trip mileage in half is to pass Frances Dr. and continue south through Harbison Canyon. This is 2.5 miles of mostly downgrade (350-foot elevation loss) through ranch country and beneath the steep canyon walls.

<u>CONNECTING TRIPS</u>: 1) Connection with the El Cajon Bikeway System (Trip #31) - the trips have a common segment on Granite Hills Dr.; 2) connection with the Lakeside-Lakeview Loop (Trip #42) - bike west on Alpine Blvd. and follow the I-8 frontage roads to Lake Jennings Rd.; 3) connection with Hills and Dales (Blossom Valley) (Trip #45) - from the trip origin, bike west as above to Flinn Springs Rd.

TRIP #54 - WILDCAT CANYON

<u>GENERAL LOCATION</u>: Lakeside, Barona Valley, San Vicente Canyon

<u>LEVEL OF DIFFICULTY</u>: One-way - strenuous; up and back - strenuous
Distance - 15.1 miles (one way)
Elevation gain - lengthy steep upgrade beyond Willow Rd.

<u>GENERAL DESCRIPTION</u>: This is a trip of mixed rewards and punishments. The early three-mile uphill segment is short, but steep, and exposed. Once beyond the initial crest, the cyclist is treated to a dandy six-mile rest segment in scenic Barona Valley. In addition to the natural scenery, the cyclist is presented with such delights as the Barona Casino, Barona Indian Mission and a motorized glider port at the east valley edge. Next is an extremely scenic downhill with distant mountain vistas and a bird's-eye view of San Vicente Valley. A strenuous two-mile climb back up to the valley puts the biker in the position of enjoying a 13-mile easy return trip. There is also the option to arrange a car shuttle for a pick-up at either San Vicente Rd. or further north in Ramona (refer to Trip #40).

MOUNTAINS/BACKCOUNTRY

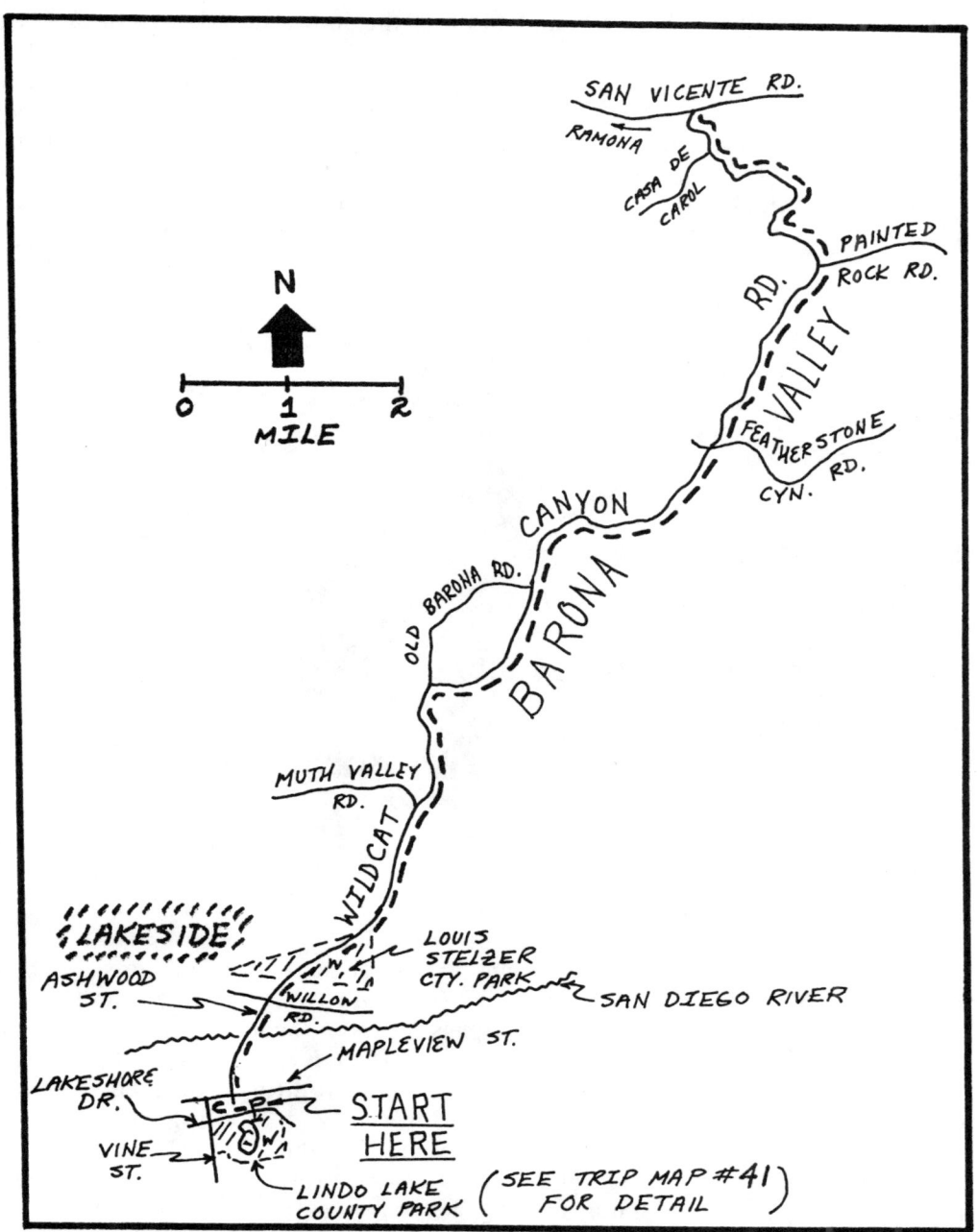

TRIP #54 - WILDCAT CANYON

TRAILHEAD: From State Hwy. 67, exit south on Winter Gardens Rd. Turn left (east) at Woodside Ave. and drive 3/4 mile to Vine St. Turn north, then east again at Lake Shore Dr. Soon is the entrance to Lindo Lake County Park. The delightful, shaded park includes scenic Lindo Lake, a community center, picnic and barbecue facilities, children's play area, restrooms and a peripheral walkway/bikeway.

Bring 1-2 water bottles. There are no public facilities along the described route.

BICYCLE RIDES: SAN DIEGO COUNTY

TRIP DESCRIPTION: The Workout. Follow the 0.8-mile zig-zag route to the Mapleview St./Ashwood St. intersection. A one-mile relatively-flat stretch leads past Castle County Park and the Pony League Baseball Park. A look around confirms the mountains and hills encirclement. Next is a San Diego River crossing. Just beyond Willow Rd., the road changes names to Wildcat Canyon Rd. and the grade becomes a "tiger" (wildcat? tiger? --- oh forget it!). After a short workout, we reach a flat near Stelzer County Park, a nicely treed park with water, restrooms, barbecue facilities and playground, with enticing Wildcat Canyon Creek passing through.

Barona Valley Landmark

Wind upward on an unshaded road through the canyon which is pressed between adjacent, rocky, scrub-filled slopes. There are few and only meager letups as the route meets Muth Valley Rd. (4.1). The road passes under scattered residences on the ridges above, then enters the El Capitan Open Space Preserve. In a short distance, a lovely end-on valley view opens up in the area of lightly-developed Whispering Pines, just before we reach a crest. This is followed by a cooling downhill within Barona Valley (the upgrade beyond Willow Rd. averages about 6-1/2 percent for 3.3 miles). The cattle guards on the valley roadway can be a nuisance (but not dangerous); keep an eye peeled or stand by for a bumpy surprise!

Barona Valley. The next six miles through this lovely hill-surrounded valley is the trip's highlight. Coast mildly downhill for about 2.3 miles in this elevated valley of scattered oaks crossing the Barona Indian Reservation, passing the Barona Casino and Barona Indian Mission. The view about the valley is both scenic and serene. However, we did note the paint blobs and bullet holes in the "Caution, Cattle on or Near Roadway" signs and thanked our lucky stars that these weren't "Bike Route" markers. Just beyond the Barona Trading Post (8.3), the road works its way to the elevated eastern side of the valley, climbing modestly to a peak near a motorized glider port just to the right of the road.

MOUNTAINS/BACKCOUNTRY

The Scenic Cruise. No this is not a luxury liner cruise, but a picture postcard, back-country downhill that provides views of successive mountain ranges to the east, then leaves the valley on a 10-percent downgrade. A couple miles beyond the start of the grade is a striking view of San Vicente Valley below and to the south. Continue the downward spin between the rocky ridges, pass through a tree-rich area along the Klondike Creek drainage, then barrel by a new housing development. All that is left is to follow the bridge over the creek, which leads to the trip's terminus, or turnaround point, at San Vicente Rd. (15.1).

Action at the Glider Port

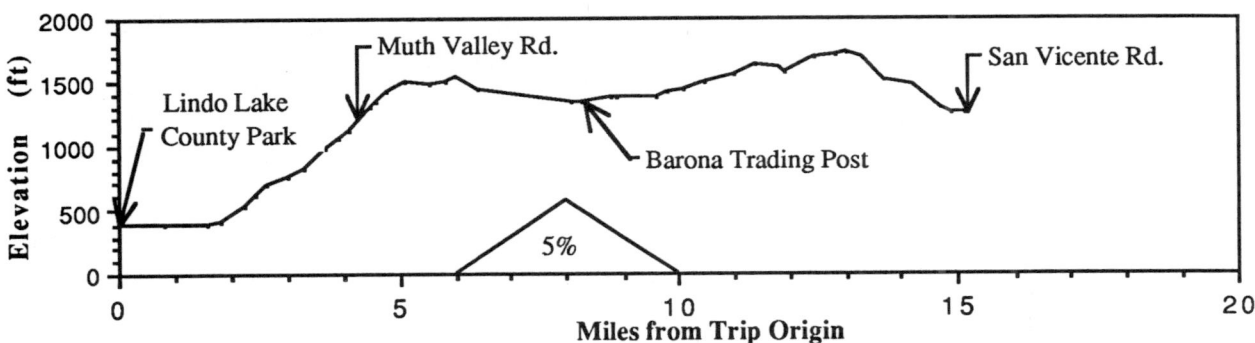

CONNECTING TRIPS: 1) Connection with the San Diego River Run (Trip #17) - follow Mapleview St. east and continue to El Monte Rd.; 2) connection with the Ramona/San Vicente Valley ride (Trip #40) - at San Vicente Rd., turn in either direction; 3) connection with the Lakeside-Lakeview Loop (Trip #42) - from the trip origin, turn south on Vine St.

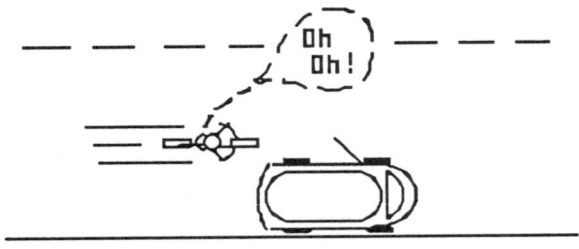

BICYCLE RIDES: SAN DIEGO COUNTY

TRIP #55 - MUSSEY GRADE ROAD

GENERAL LOCATION: Ramona, San Vicente Reservoir

LEVEL OF DIFFICULTY: Up and back - moderate
Distance - 5.1 miles (one way)
Elevation gain - steady, modest upgrade (return segment)

DESCRIPTION: We visualize a T-shirt that says, "*I Biked Mussey Grade Rd.*" This out-of-the-way rural road leads from the busy thoroughfares of Ramona to the quiet isolation of a shady and scenic overlook of San Vicente Reservoir. It's not so much a "survival" challenge as it is a pleasant out-of-the-way ride, unknown to most. Our described route starts at the Dos Picos County Park Rd. intersection and climbs back to State Hwy. 67. (To earn the T-shirt you must do the entire road!)

Turn back south and leave the "big city" noise behind, recrossing Dos Picos Park Rd. and the park, cycling beneath the filtered shade of the overhanging trees. Keep an eye on the pleasant creek which accompanies us on the downhill journey. The winding, "sneaky" downgrade passes several distinct little valleys, a small cafe near Laurel Ln., and meets Kimball Valley Rd. (5.2). The trees thin, and in 0.3 mile, the road reaches an area with an open view of the surrounding hills and mountains. In another 0.4 mile is the locked gate at Stone Meadow where there is scattered tree shade for taking in the San Vicente Reservoir view and contemplating the four-mile moderate return ride.

TRAILHEAD: From State Hwy. 67 in Ramona, turn southwest at Mussey Grade Rd. (about 2-1/2 miles southwest of the Ramona City Center) and continue 1.1 miles to Dos Picos Park Rd. Turn west and continue about 3/4 mile to the park area. The park has picnic facilities, hiking trails, children's play area and camping sites. Add about 3/4 mile and about 100-foot elevation change (one way) if starting from the tree-shaded park.

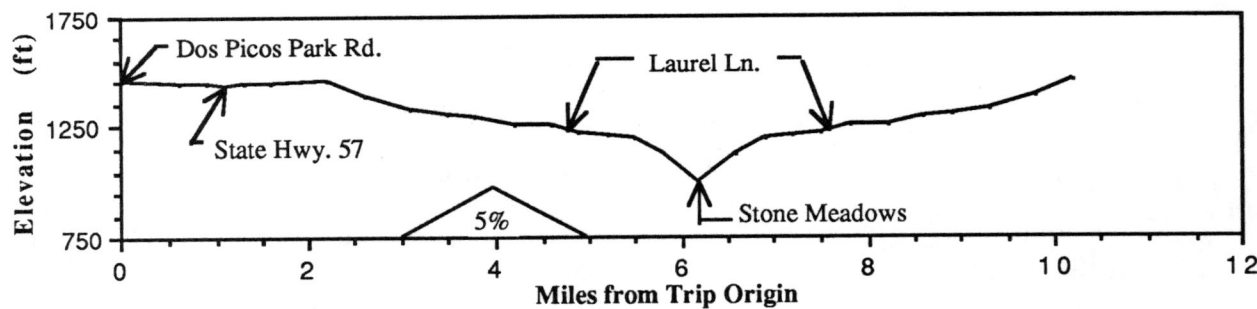

CONNECTING TRIPS: Connection with the Ramona/San Vicente Valley tour (Trip #40) - at State Hwy. 67, turn right toward Ramona.

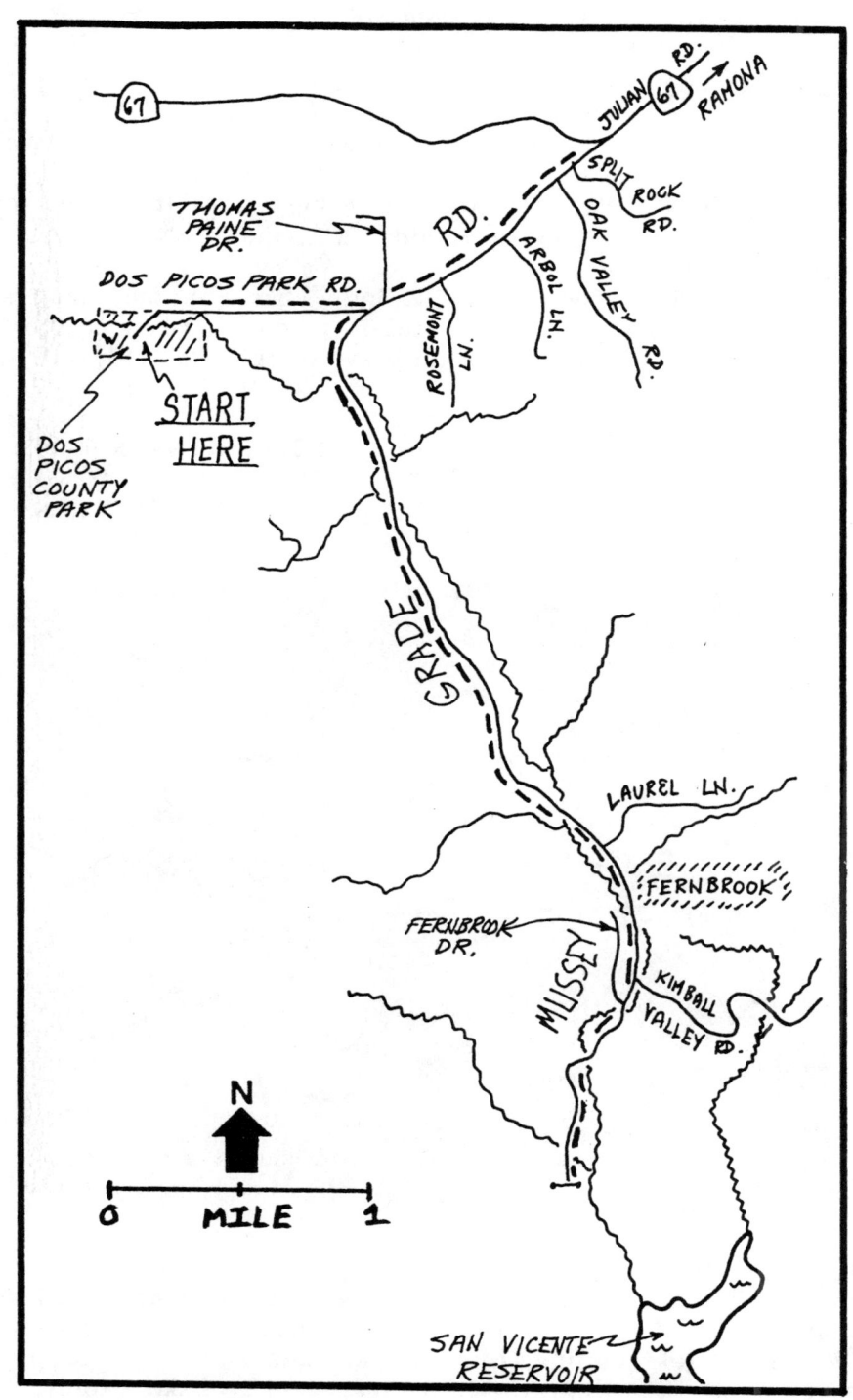

TRIP #55 - MUSSEY GRADE ROAD

BICYCLE RIDES: SAN DIEGO COUNTY

TRIP #56 - BEAR RIDGE LOOP

GENERAL LOCATION: Escondido, Lake Wohlford

LEVEL OF DIFFICULTY: Loop - strenuous
Distance - 14.3 miles
Elevation gain - steady steep upgrade on Lake Wohlford Rd.

GENERAL DESCRIPTION: This outdoorsey adventure takes the cyclist on a super-scenic short mountain climb, passes alongside a fisherman's "heaven" at Lake Wohlford, and visits the emerald greenery of Woods Valley. In the valley is a "must visit" to Bates Nut Farm. The route is Class X but, other than the initial segment on Valley Center Rd., is on lightly-traveled rural roads. What makes the tour additionally interesting is that this out-of-the-way delight is only 10-15 minutes away from the heart of Escondido.

TRAILHEAD: From Interstate Hwy. 15, exit east at El Norte Pkwy. and follow that road five miles to its terminus at Valley Pkwy. Turn left and drive 1/2 mile to Valley Center Rd., turn left again, then continue 5-1/2 miles to Woods Valley Rd. Find parking in the small commercial center.

Petting Zoo at "The Farm"

TRIP DESCRIPTION: **On to Lake Wohlford.** Turn south onto wide, busy County Hwy. S6, enjoying both the speedy downhill and the tremendous view into the Escondido Creek drainage. The raw, powerful, unnamed peak directly ahead and a view of Lake Wohlford Rd. cutting into the mountainside are additional visual delights. Just beyond the Escondido Creek overcrossing is Lake Wohlford Rd. (3.6) and the end of a euphoric downhill. Pass the valley's citrus groves, then pedal on a two-lane countrylike road with overhanging trees before hitting the first upgrade in 1/4 mile. Our route follows the exposed, winding roadway as it climbs out of, and

MOUNTAINS/BACKCOUNTRY

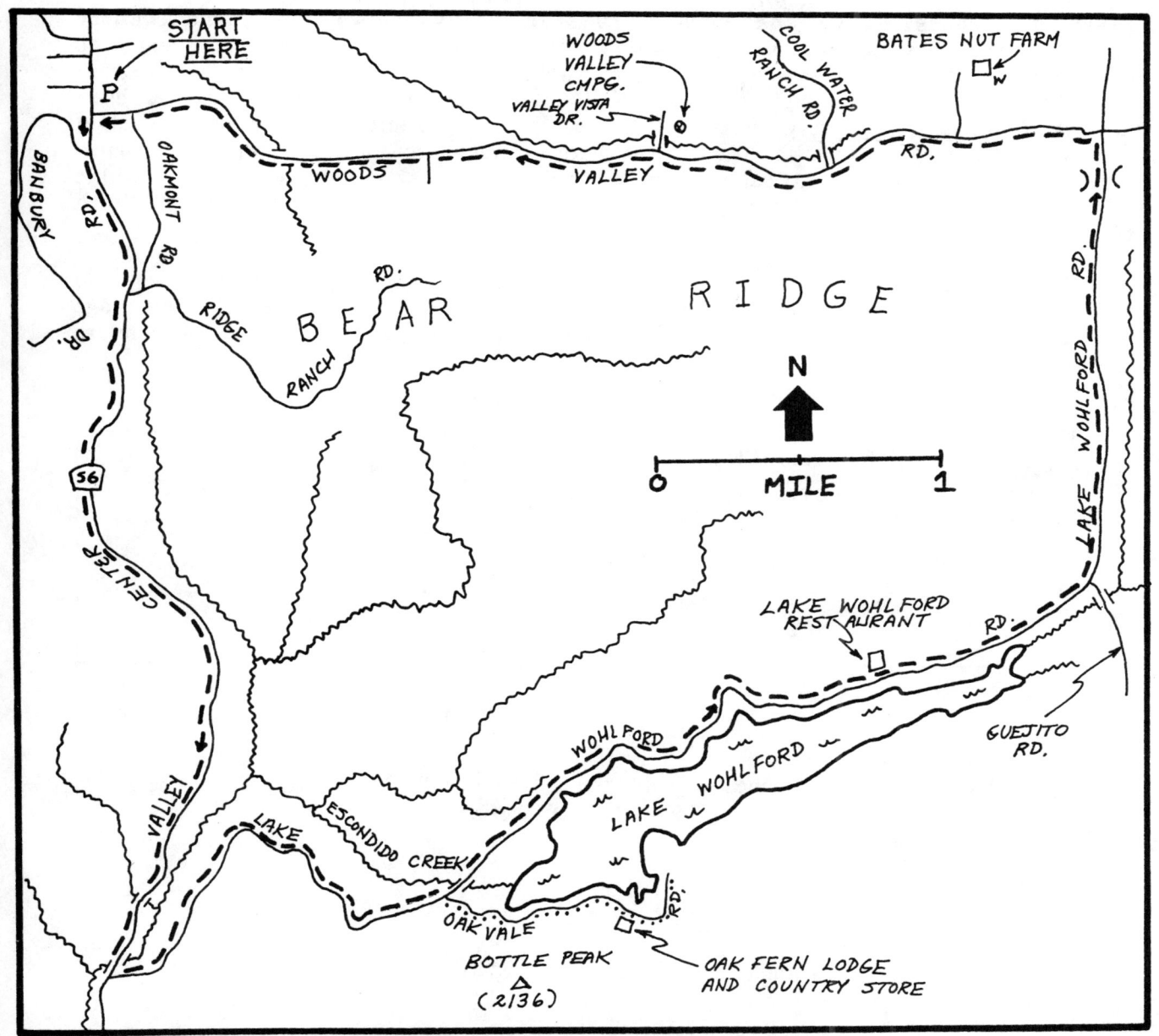

TRIP #56 - BEAR RIDGE LOOP

steadily above the Escondido Creek drainage. The view of the valley and of the thread of Valley Center Rd. below, as they become more distant figures, is captivating!

  Two miles of gutsy pedaling leads to the Oakvale Rd. intersection, where there is a nice 1.9-mile (up and back) diversion on the south shore of Lake Wohlford (tree-shade, lake views, Oakvale Park, Oak Fern Lodge and Country Store). A bridge takes the cyclist across the upper reaches of Escondido Creek onto a flat road where there are numerous lake and mountain backdrop views. Pass the small community surrounding the rustic Lake Wohlford Restaurant (catfish dinners from the lake's catch), then continue beyond the lake's end into Bear Valley and Guejito Rd. (8.2).

BICYCLE RIDES: SAN DIEGO COUNTY

On to Woods Valley and Beyond. Pass a massive nursery area, then continue north as the valley shrinks in width and winds its way slowly between the unnamed mountains to the east and Bear Ridge westward. In 1-1/2 miles of modest upgrade alongside the Escondido Canal is Woods Valley Rd. A turn westward sends the biker through farming and nursery areas with citrus groves scattered throughout. A short distance down the road is the Bates Nut Farm ("Nuts from all over the world meet here!") with several specialty shops and a small children's petting zoo. Also within this beautiful valley, in the early Spring, were numerous species of brightly-colored birds.

After leaving the farm, the road continues east through dense tree cover and visits connecting strands of the valley. To the south is the steep face of Bear Ridge with citrus groves planted in the foothills. Pass Oakmont Rd. and, in 0.2 mile, return to the trip origin (14.3).

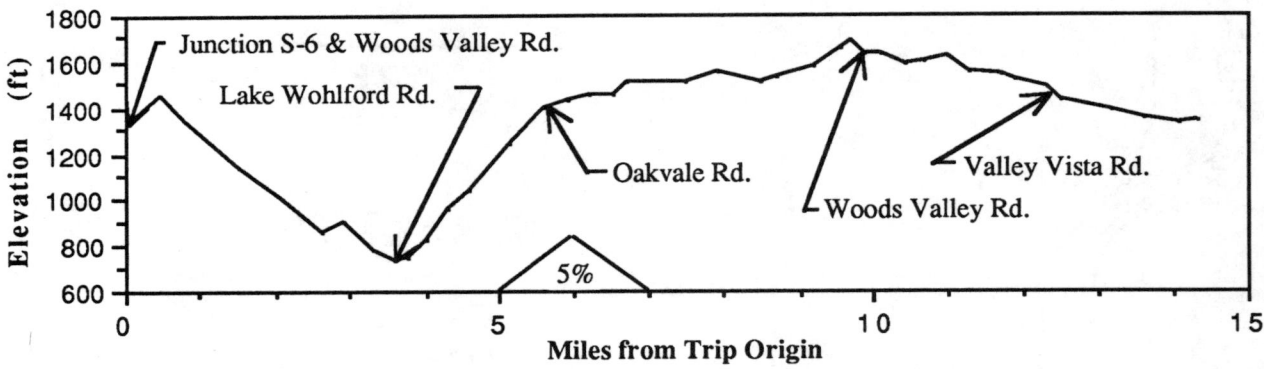

CONNECTING TRIPS: Connection with the Escondido City Tour (Trip #35) - return to El Norte Pkwy. as described in the 'TRAILHEAD' section.

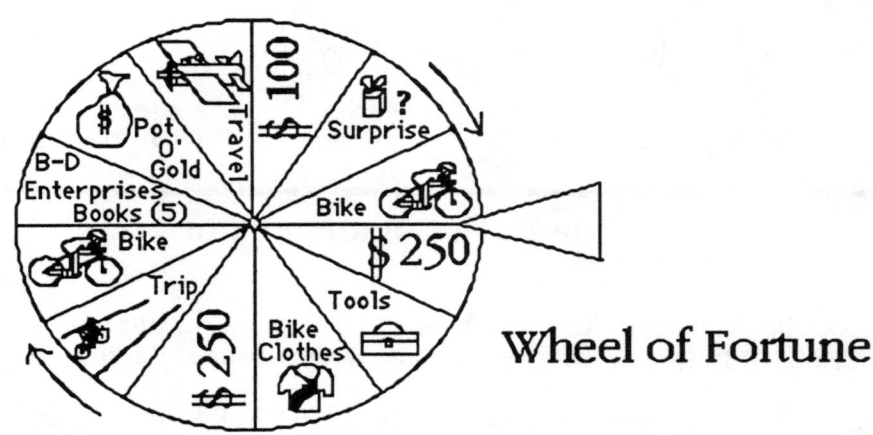

Wheel of Fortune

DESERT

TRIP #57 - EL CENTRO CITY TOUR

GENERAL LOCATION: El Centro

LEVEL OF DIFFICULTY: Loop - easy
Distance - 5.6 miles
Elevation gain - flat

GENERAL DESCRIPTION: El Centro has a planned set of predominantly Class III roadways which criss-cross the city. This 100 percent below-sea-level tour is a chance to get a close-up look at the city ranging from the older commercial section on the northern leg to the cozy residential areas on the southern segment. The route described is one of many city tour options that the cyclist might explore, as is evident from the trip map provided. There are also side-attractions such as Sunbeam Lake County Park, Wiest Park, Cattle Call Park and the spectacular Algodones Dunes.

TRAILHEAD: From the south, exit Interstate Hwy. 8 at State Hwy. 86 and proceed north 1/3 mile, turning left (west) on Aurora Dr. Continue 1/2 mile to Bucklin Park. From the north, follow State Hwy. 86 southbound into El Centro. At Adams Ave. (County Hwy. S80), where Hwy. 86 makes a sharp jog eastward, continue south on Imperial Ave. 2-1/4 miles to Ross Ave. Turn left and proceed 1/3 mile to the park. The park has little grassy knolls, scattered tree shade, pond, children's playground, recreational fields, picnic facilities, water and restrooms.

TRIP DESCRIPTION: **El Centro.** The tour routing is fairly straightforward, as provided in the trip map. Highlights of the tour are Bucklin Park, the two statuesque, domed churches on Orange Ave., the contrasting commercial areas on Main St. and Broadway (where old transitions to new as the cyclist heads westward), and the pleasant residential areas near Ross Ave. Excursions beyond the city are noted below.

Algodones Dunes

BICYCLE RIDES: SAN DIEGO COUNTY

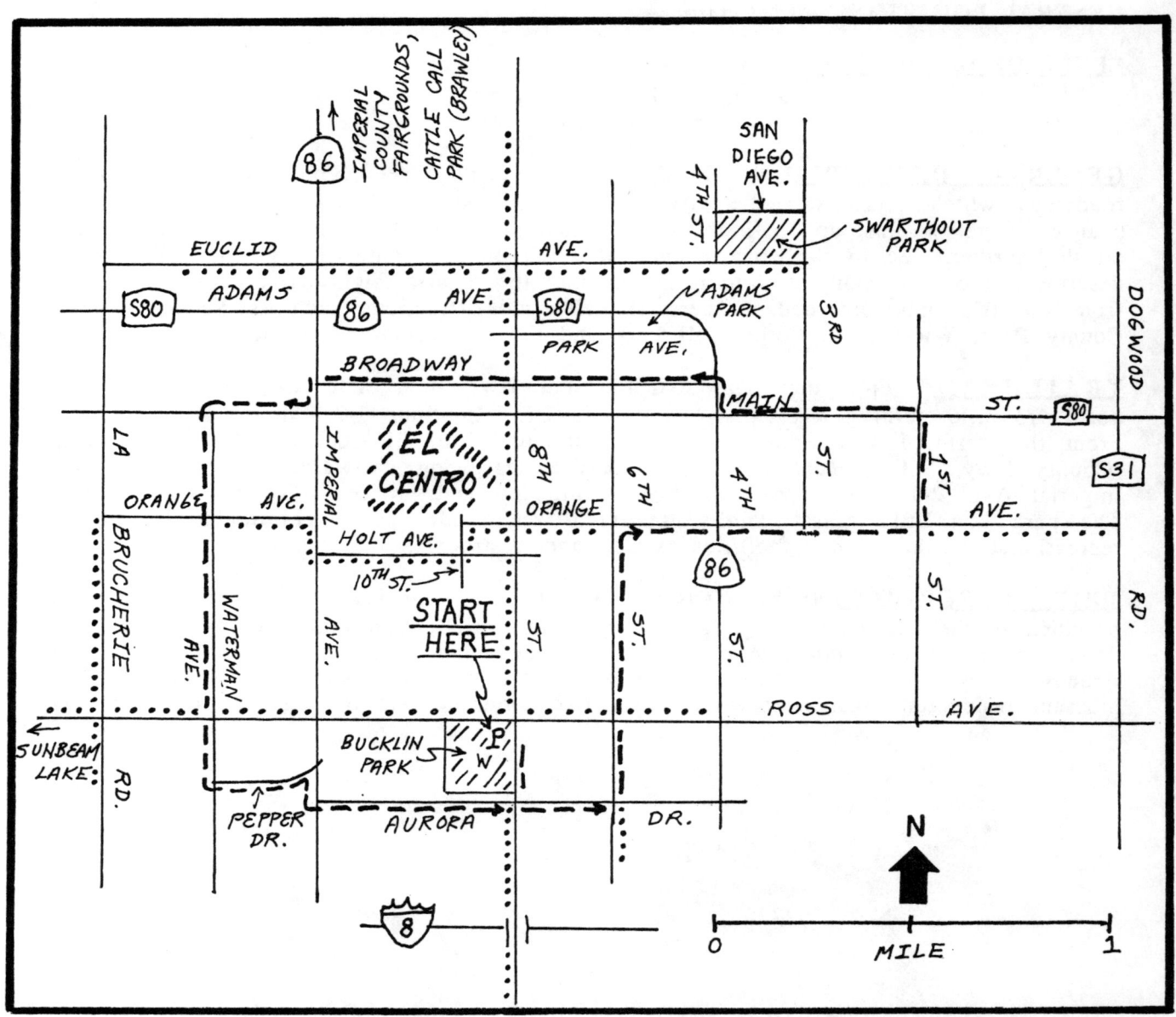

TRIP #57 - EL CENTRO CITY TOUR

Sunbeam Lake. Follow Ross Ave. west 3-1/2 miles to Sunbeam Lake County Park. This set of pleasant reed-lined lakes are open year-round for swimming, fishing and sailboarding. There is also an excellent picnic area here.

Cattle Call Park. Cycle or drive seven miles north on busy Hwy. 86 just past the O' Connell Airport in Brawley. Turn left at Cattle Call Dr. (Malan St. to the right) and continue 0.3 mile to the park. November is the month for the famous Cattle Call, a

DESERT

two-day extravaganza that includes a rodeo, parades, cook-off, and both mariachi and bluegrass music.

Wiest Lake. From Cattle Call Park, continue north on Western Ave. five miles and turn right (east) at Rutherford Rd. In about three miles is the lake entry. The brush-lined lake offers the same amenities as Sunbeam Lake County Park and a small campground to boot.

Algodones Dunes. Bike 25 miles east from Cattle Call Park on State Hwy. 78. Beyond State Hwy. 111, the route leaves Brawley and enters an agricultural area. Just beyond the Highline Canal, the biker is treated to a low-desert tour through the middle of the U.S. Naval Aerial Gunnery Range. Pedal beyond Hugh Osbourne County Park to get the best view of the shifting dunes, which reach up to 300 feet in height.

The dunes are a product of ancient Lake Cahuilla's windblown beach sand. The generally westward wind creates a shallow buildup on the west or windward side and a sharp, steep face on the leeward side. A limited area south of State Hwy. 78 is marked and set aside for off-road vehicle enthusiasts, while the remaining dune area has been left in its normal state.

CONNECTING TRIPS: Connection with the Border Run (Trip #61) - bike south seven miles on La Brucherie Rd. or Dogwood Rd. to State Hwy. 98.

TRIP #58 - SALTON SEA SURVEY

GENERAL LOCATION: Salton Sea

LEVEL OF DIFFICULTY: Loop - very strenuous (one day); strenuous (two days)
Distance - 118 miles
Elevation gain - essentially flat

GENERAL DESCRIPTION: Take the opportunity to bike a 100-plus mile loop around one of California's great landmarks, the 229-foot below-sea-level saline sea. Why? Circumnavigate this large body of water surrounded by mountains and desert and enjoy the thrill of seeing these landmarks from a thousand different perspectives. This flat, high-mileage workout provides a rare feeling of accomplishment at its completion. A tour saved for the cooler seasons, the highlights of this Class X bikeathon include the plush gardens of the northern shore, the comfortable state

BICYCLE RIDES: SAN DIEGO COUNTY

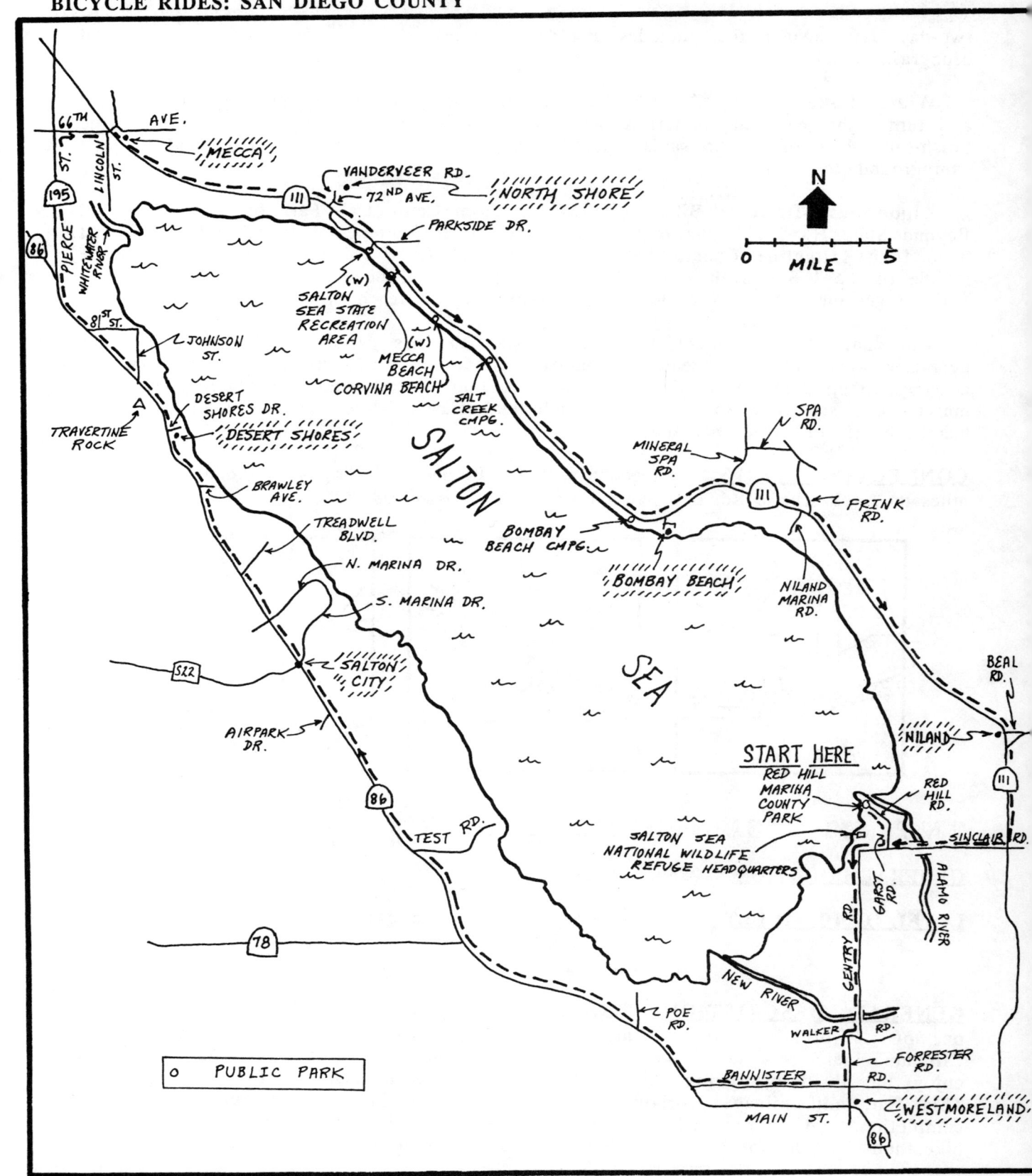

TRIP #58 - SALTON SEA SURVEY

DESERT

recreation areas of the eastern beaches, and the wildlife refuges of the southern beachfront. The Salton Sea provides nesting grounds for over 200 species of birds.

Ride the more scenic east shore if your group doesn't choose to do the full loop.

TRAILHEAD: From Interstate Hwy. 8, exit north at State Hwy. 111 and continue past the city of Calipatria, turning left (west) on Sinclair Rd. Drive 5-1/2 miles to Garst Rd., turn right and follow the dirt road to Red Hill Rd. Turn left and continue across the land bridge to road's end at the Red Hill Marina County Park. The park has restrooms, including showers, fire rings, picnic areas and a boat marina. Forget shade! Walk the shoreline in this area and enjoy the egrets, herons, ducks and geese.

Load up with at least two quarts of wet stuff at the trip origin. We found no public facilities on the west shore.

TRIP DESCRIPTION: The sea was formed in 1905-1907 when a temporary cut in the banks of the Colorado River was made to irrigate the Imperial Valley. High water conditions forced a breech in the cut and the river diverted north into the Salton Sink, an ancient lake bed. With no natural outlet and being fed by the irrigation runoff from three rivers, the sea is now saltier than the ocean.

Western Segment. Return to Sinclair St. on mixed packed dirt and asphalt and follow a 13-mile generally-southwest tack on several roadways to Bannister Rd. The territory is heavily agricultural with geothermal power plants. Follow that road through continued agriculture for as far as the eye can see to State Hwy. 86 and turn north (18.5). Ahead in the distance are the Fish Creek Mountains, while to the west are the Sand Sculptures (wind-shaped sand figures) and part of the Salton Sea National Wildlife Refuge, respectively.

Salton Sea Recreation Area

BICYCLE RIDES: SAN DIEGO COUNTY

In a little over a mile, the Salton Sea returns to view, while the desert scrub surrounding the road appears endless. For the first ten miles on Hwy. 86, only the palms of Kane Spring and the State Hwy. 78 junction disturb the pedaling routine. From here, both the Fish Creek Mountains to the west and Chocolate Mountains to the east are readily viewable. The contrast of colors, desert floor tans and browns, faded green shrubbery, the blue sea, and purple mountains will "grab" you. Roughly 12 miles further is the Borrego Salton Seaway and the faltering remains of Salton City to the west (40.3). There were great growth expectations here in times past, as evidenced by the numerous roadway "stubs" built along the road which were never extended.

Ten miles further up the road near Desert Shores is a small commercial patch consisting of a gas station, market and the Salty Sea Restaurant. Shortly, the road skirts the edge of the Santa Rosa Mountains at a massive complex of naturally-stacked boulders known as Travertine Rock. This landmark has regretably become a spray-painter's canvas. Hwy. 86 begins to pull away from the Salton Sea, crosses the Riverside County Line (52.0), and enters a man-made desert oasis consisting of palm trees and citrus groves (not surprisingly, at the small hamlet named Oasis).

In the next few miles, the biker passes a mini-mart and general store, numerous roadside fruit/vegetable stands, and reaches the State Hwy. 195 junction. After a several-mile continuation of the date palm, citrus and general agricultural tour, a right turn (east) at Ave. 66, and a little bit more pedaling puts the cyclist smack dab at the outskirts of the town of Mecca (64.8). On that segment are over-the-shoulder views of Thomas Mountain, as well as forward-looking views to the more distant Orocopia and Chocolate Mountains.

Eastern Segment. Turn right at State Hwy. 111 and continue past Grant St., where there are produce stands, a restaurant and grocery store. About six miles down the line, views of the Salton Sea return. Nearby is Vander Veer Rd. with a gas station and grocery store. A right turn here takes the bicyclist on a seaside diversion past the North Shore Beach and Yacht Club and a boat launch area.

After returning to Hwy. 111, continue several more miles through this scrub-dotted giant sandpile before reaching State Park Rd./Parkside Dr. and the Salton Sea State Recreation Area (75.6). Probably the finest camping spot on the sea, this area sports a sandy beach, restrooms with showers, picnic areas, boat launch and a breakwater fishing area. The park itself has a couple of miles of roadway for families wishing to cruise off the main highway.

Continuing south on small rolling hills, the road passes alongside a 14-mile stretch of recreation area that contains the unimproved sites (restrooms and open space) of Corvina Beach and Salt Creek Campgrounds. Near the recreation area mid-point is Bob's Playa Riviera (RV campground, restaurant, marina), while Bombay Beach is near its terminus (Bombay Beach Campground, market, motel, marina) (90.4). A comforting thought is that Bombay Beach is nestled near an aerial mine-laying area and the Chocolate Mountains live bombing area. (Okay, "nestled" is an overstatement!)

Hwy. 111 pulls away from the coastline and heads directly for the Chocolate Mountains, then veers back to the southeast before passing Hot Mineral Spa Rd. (Several commercial spas are 2-4 miles up this road, such as the Fountain of Youth Spa.) Several miles beyond is Frink Rd., the last major side road until Niland. In this

DESERT

continued sandy, scrub-covered stretch, we amused ourselves by reading off the names of the washes we crossed (Bug Wash and Z Drane Wash, to name a few). Beyond the small metropolis of Niland (gas station) (106.9), the tour returns to agricultural area.

Keep an eye peeled for small Sinclair Rd. (about 4-1/2 miles from Niland) and turn west onto that tractor-filled road, following a rural beeline through more agricultural environs. In 4.4 miles, after passing two large geothermal plants, is Garst Rd. Follow this road north and return to Red Hill Marina County Park (118.0).

CONNECTING TRIPS: Connection with the Borrego Springs tour (Trip #59) - bike west on the Borrego-Salton Seaway (County Hwy. S22) at Salton City.

TRIP #59 - BORREGO SPRINGS

GENERAL LOCATION: Borrego Springs

LEVEL OF DIFFICULTY: Borrego Springs Loop - moderate;
   Yaqui Pass Loop - strenuous
   Distance - 35.0 miles (Borrego Springs); 59.7 miles (2-loops)
   Elevation gain - essentially flat; periodic moderate grades
      with steep grade to Yaqui Pass

GENERAL DESCRIPTION: Nestled between the Santa Rosa and San Ysidro Mountains and Pinyon Ridge is San Diego County's desert playground, Borrego Springs. This resort center within the Anza-Borrego Desert lies within Borrego Valley, a pleasant setting for a flat, scenic bike ride. The described route provides a Borrego Springs city tour, together with some pedaling on the barren outskirts of this sunny mecca. The tour starts at the Borrego Palm Canyon Campground, then proceeds on a Class X valley loop on wide roads past such sights as the De Anza Country Club, Pegleg Smith Monument and the Borrego Sink.

There is an option to extend the tour by biking southeast into Lower Borrego Valley and returning via Yaqui Pass. The steep dip into San Felipe Creek is exciting, and the Yaqui Pass transit is both scenic and exhilarating. This adds close to 25 miles plus 1300-feet elevation gain and turns the total tour into a strenuous adventure.

There are also several off-road sight-seeing tours available to "fat-tire" bikers from both tour segments described.

TRAILHEAD: From the west and south, follow State Hwy. 78 into the Anza Borrego Desert and turn north at County Hwy. S3 (Yaqui Pass Rd.). Follow the guidelines of this tour's bicycle map north and west into Borrego Springs to the Borrego Palm Canyon Campground.

Southbound motorists should find their way to State Hwy. 79 and turn southeast at County Hwy. S2 (San Felipe Rd.), turn left (east) at County Hwy. S22 (Montezuma Valley Rd.), then follow the exciting Montezuma downgrade beyond Ranchita into Borrego Valley. At Palm Canyon Dr., turn left and continue to the campground.

BICYCLE RIDES: SAN DIEGO COUNTY

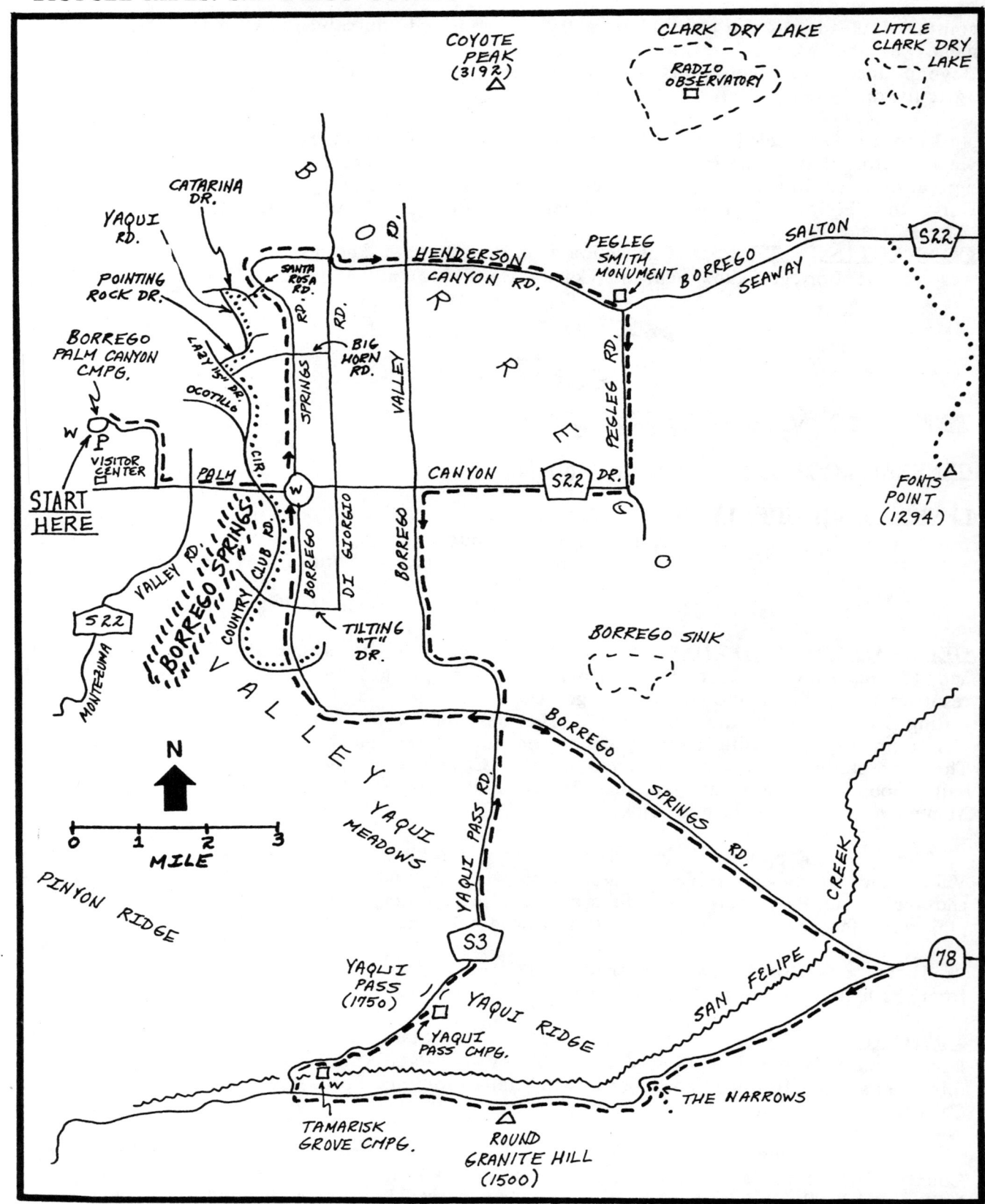

TRIP #59 - BORREGO SPRINGS

DESERT

Visitors from the Riverside County area should enter Borrego Springs from either Hwy. 78 or Hwy. S22. State Hwy. 78 drivers should turn northeast at Borrego Springs Rd.

This is a Fall-through-Spring ride which could be exceedingly uncomfortable on hot days. When planning this trip, note that the desert wild flowers are in bloom mid-March through mid-April. Bring two quarts of water for safety if taking the Yaqui Pass extension route.

Borrego Palm Canyon Campground has both R.V. sites and campsites, fireplaces, showers and a nearby grocery store. While in the campground, take time to explore the Borrego Palm Canyon Nature Trail. From the west edge of the campground, the trail extends 1-1/2 miles up the impressive canyon. Signs providing information on desert plants and Native American life are posted along the route.

<u>**TRIP DESCRIPTION**</u>: **Borrego Springs Loop.** Return to County Hwy. S22, pausing to look back at the imposing group of peaks which surround Borrego Palm Canyon. Consider turning right to visit the Anza Borrego Desert State Park Visitor Center. This partly-underground building has numerous exhibits which focus on the desert flora and fauna, geography and Native American history. However, our reference route heads left (east) and continues through the heart of the commercial/resort city area to Christmas Tree Circle.

Pegleg Smith Monument

Follow the circle and turn north on Borrego Springs Rd. While on this quiet 3.3-mile stretch, observe the ranges which encapsulate Borrego Valley on three sides. The road fuses into Henderson Canyon Rd. and makes a beeline toward the lower ridgeline of Coyote Peak, passing several palm tree nurseries along this otherwise baron route. The road veers right and passes alongside the Pegleg Smith Monument (13.8). Pegleg was a miner, adventurer and Indian fighter (so he claimed!) whose prolific storytelling about his lost "motherlode" earned him a local reputation (and a few free drinks). In honor of Pegleg, visitors are admonished by a sign reading, "Let him who seeks Pegleg Smith's gold add 10 rocks to this monument." We did!!

BICYCLE RIDES: SAN DIEGO COUNTY

Turn onto Pegleg Rd. and bike through open desert, enjoying the partial view of the Borrego Badlands to the left, then make a hard right at Palm Canyon Dr. (The road signs were out of kilter when we passed through, with the result that we continued straight ahead to a deadend!) A short pedal through this open area (great views of the San Ysidro Mountains, Yaqui Pass and Borrego Springs). and a left (south) on Borrego Valley Rd. leads to a sharp curve, where the byway becomes Yaqui Pass Rd. Continue to the Borrego Springs Rd. intersection, where there is a gas station, and ponder a major decision (25.0). A left turn leads to the Yaqui Pass loop, while the reference route heads right.

For Borrego Springs "loopers," turn right and bike directly toward the San Ysidro Mountains, then follow a wide curve which takes the cyclist into increasingly developed residential areas. Pass Country Club Rd. and enjoy the view into Borrego Springs proper. In a short distance is Christmas Circle, followed by a short return segment to the campground (35.0).

Yaqui Pass Loop. The basic tour can be extended by adding a southern loop which visits Lower Borrego Valley and returns via vista-packed Yaqui Pass. This route through relatively-untamed desert adds nearly 25 miles and 1300 feet elevation gain, bumping the tour into the strenuous category. Early highlights of the added segment are the exciting steep "bathtub" ride through San Felipe Creek and Lower Borrego Valley. Next the biker is treated to a scenic undulating tour along the creek, including a passage through the aptly-named Narrows, and a passby of shaded Tamarisk Campground which is directly off Yaqui Pass Rd. Following, the tour offers a rugged switch-back-laden workout up to Yaqui Pass with scenic views of the local Yaqui Ridge and of the Borrego Valley well below. Finally, the biker is treated to a sensory transition from the stark pass area down to relatively lush, well-developed Borrego Springs.

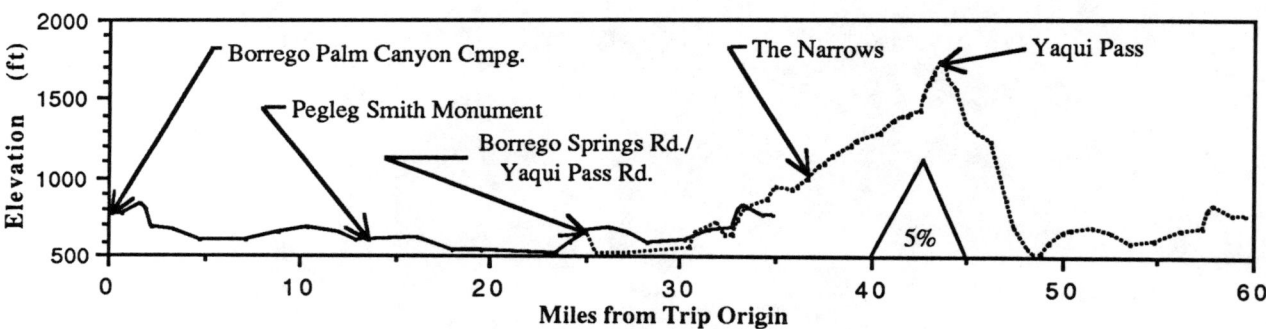

CONNECTING TRIPS: 1) Connection with the Great Overland Stage Route (Trip #60) - at the intersection of Hwy. 78 and Yaqui Pass Rd., continue west six miles to Hwy. S2.; 2) **Font's Point Excursion** - the turnoff to this scenic overlook point of the forbidding Borrego Badlands is about 3-1/2 miles east from the Pegleg Smith Monument on S22. The viewpoint is 3-1/2 unpaved-road miles from the turnoff; 3) **Narrow Earth Trail** (Yaqui Pass Loop) - about three miles from the junction of Hwy. 78 and Borrego Springs Rd. at the Narrows is a 1/2-mile dirt loop trail which displays such interesting park geological features as an alluvial fan that joins ancient granite rocks with a visible earthquake fault.

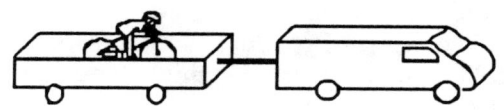

DESERT

TRIP #60 - GREAT OVERLAND STAGE ROUTE

GENERAL LOCATION: Scissor's Crossing, Agua Caliente Springs, Ocotillo

LEVEL OF DIFFICULTY: One way - strenuous
Distance - 47.9 miles
Elevation gain - major upgrade to Campbell Grade Summit and Sweeney Pass Summit

GENERAL DESCRIPTION: The trip described follows the treacherous Overland Stage Route used by Los Angeles-bound travelers crossing the vast southern desert from Yuma. Officially, the Great Southern Overland Stage Route of 1849, the Butterfield Overland Mail stagecoaches, immigrants and gold miners alike used the dreaded corridor to reach the coast. Remnants of the old stage system still exist along what is now a paved roadway traversed by high-speed traffic.

This Fall-through-Spring tour takes advantage of the chiefly-downhill topography between the starting point at Scissor's Crossing and the trip's end at Ocotillo. There are two serious grades on the trip which could be very soul-sapping on warm days. County Hwy. S2 has light traffic and reasonable biking shoulder. The general tour setting is one of transiting a desolate desert corridor through successive ranges of hills and mountains. There are many impressive natural sights and man-made landmarks interspersed between long uninterrupted miles reserved for "desert daydreaming." Trip highlights are the remnant stage stations, Box Canyon, Agua Caliente Springs, the mystic Sweeney Pass area and the joyous initial sighting of Ocotillo!

TRAILHEAD: Scissors Crossing is at the junction of State Hwy. 78, and County Hwy. S2. This junction is 21 miles south of Warner Springs, 11 miles east of Julian, 18 miles southwest of Borrego Springs, and 48 miles north of Ocotillo. The preferred option is to find a friend who will both drop you off and pick you up. The alternative is to plan a car shuttle, leaving one car in Shelter Valley and the other at Ocotillo.

Bring two to three quarts of water for safety and <u>avoid</u> biking this tour on hot days. There are long stretches between the towns and campgrounds along Hwy. S2, so load up at "pit stops" if you have any doubts.

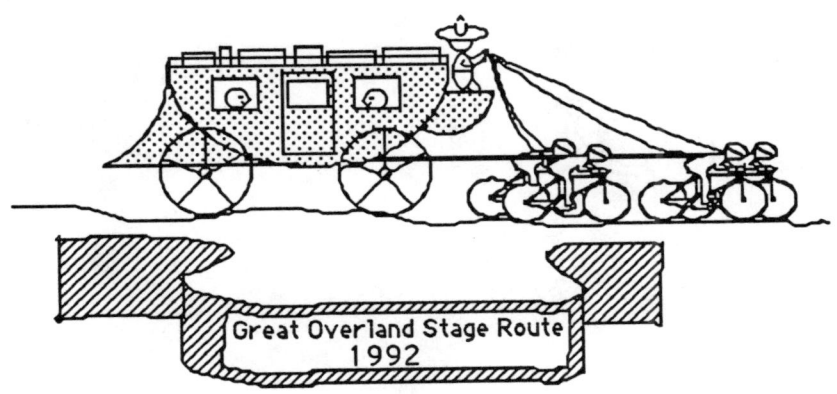

201

BICYCLE RIDES: SAN DIEGO COUNTY

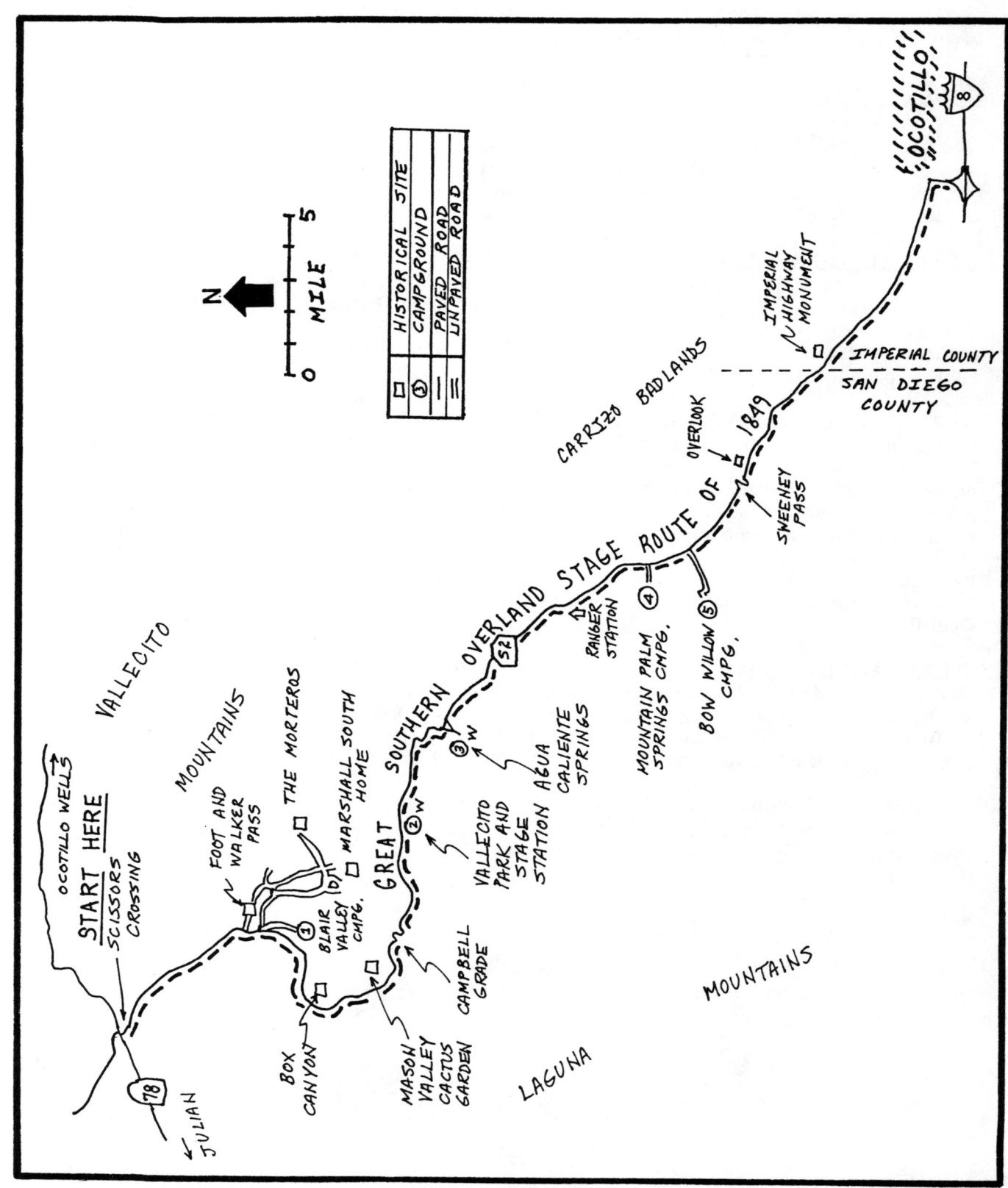

TRIP #60 - GREAT OVERLAND STAGE ROUTE

DESERT

TRIP DESCRIPTION: Earthquake Valley to Agua Caliente Springs. Just beyond aptly named Scissors Crossing, the cyclist navigates on lightly-traveled two-lane "outback" highway between the North Pinyon Mountains (left) and Granite Mountain. In a short distance is the small settlement of Shelter Valley (located within Earthquake Valley, faults and all!) with its scattered farmland. Beyond the valley, a limited upgrade leads the biker to the upper reaches of scenic Blair Valley. Another upgrade and a constructed passage through the rugged hills guides the biker to a signed point just above Foot and Walker Pass (5.7). This is the steep 150-foot pass where the Old Butterfield Overland Stage passengers frequently were required to walk, or to help push the stage in dire circumstances! Dirt road-crossed Blair Valley also hosts the Morteros (Indian grinding holes) and the remains of the isolated hillside homestead of the reclusive Marshall South family.

In three miles, the road descends steeply above the northern rim of Box Canyon. Here is the historical monument commemorating the Mormon Battalion's successful efforts to hack a crude road bypassing a dead-end canyon in 1847. An overlook here allows visitors to view the road remnants and canyon and to envision the stagecoaches working their way up the tortuous canyon. The steep and winding downhill brings the traveler into sweeping Mason Valley with its impressive Laguna Mountains backdrop (the view of Hwy. S2 from the top of those mountains is even more impressive - see Trip #48). Here is the large, natural Mason Valley Cactus Garden with its mix of teddybear cholla, prickly pear, hedgebog, fishhook, barrel and buckhorn cacti.

The route passes the Butterfield Ranch Resort with a store and swimming pool (11.9) at the valley's south end, rises to a small summit, then follows a short and steep uphill pitch to a pass. Just beyond, the steep and refreshing Campbell Grade downhill takes the cyclist to wide-open Vallecito Valley. Hwy. S2 holds to the western valley edge, then winds down the center of the mountain-surrounded valley past Vallecito County Park and Stage Station (16.7). The park area, an oasis at the edge of the great Colorado Desert, has served as an Indian campsite, an army outpost and later as one of the historic Butterfield Stage Stations. Here is a weathered sod stage station, ranger station, play area, hiking trails and overnight camping. (The park is open from November to June, which should hint at the maximum cycling window!)

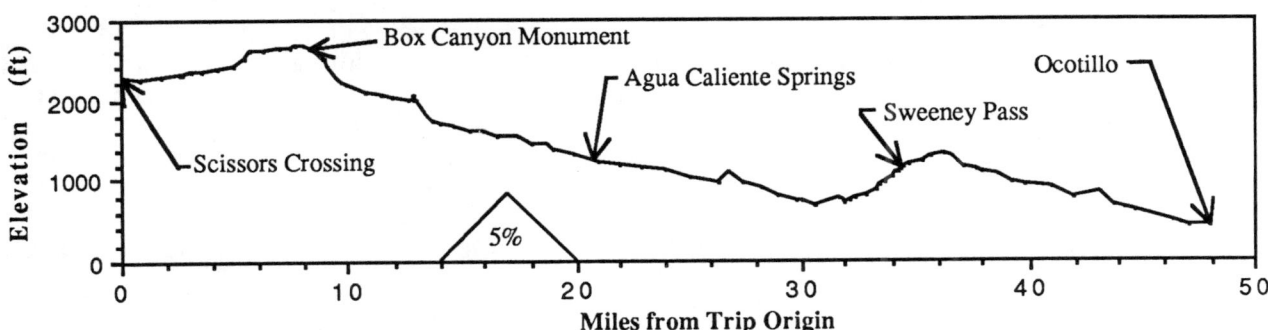

Agua Caliente Springs to Ocotillo. Several downhill miles beyond is Agua Caliente Park (21.1) with its four natural hot springs and Agua Caliente County Park, providing picnic facilities, bath house, recreation building, hiking trails, overnight campsites and a general store. Beyond is the forbidding spread of low desert with scattered low scrub and cacti, only briefly interrupted by palm oases such as Palm Spring, Well of Eight Echos, Mountain Palm Springs and Bow Willow (31.9). After crossing Carrizo Canyon Wash, the highway enters Sweeney Canyon, then works its

BICYCLE RIDES: SAN DIEGO COUNTY

way on a winding upgrade to the northern flank of the Jacuba Mountains. In a rugged uphill mile, after a steep switchback, there is a reprieve at Sweeney Pass. Take a short break and enjoy the panoramic view of surrounding mountains, as well as the vista back down into Sweeney Canyon. Continue the workout onto the eerie desert plateau, then slow down and take a gander at the tortured dirt and rock canvas from the Corrizo Badlands Overlook (35.3).

Follow the high plateau to a summit, then observe the grand "see-forever" view of the low desert plain land out between and beneath the Coyote and Jacumba Mountains. Coast through a pass with a side road leading to the West Dolomite Mine, cross the Imperial County Line (39.8), then continue to the top of a small rise for the first look at civilization in a spell. In the distance is Mexico's Signal Mountain. Several more miles of downhill put the biker at the first stop sign of the trip, in Ocotillo at Shell Canyon Rd. A sharp curve leads the cyclist into Ocotillo proper with a gas station and market near County Hwy. S80 and Interstate Hwy. 8 (47.9).

CONNECTING TRIPS: 1) Continuation with the Borrego Springs tour (Trip #59) - at Scissors Crossing, bike east on State Hwy. 78; 2) continuation with the Border Run (Trip #61) - at Ocotillo, follow Imperial Hwy. (Hwy. S2) under Interstate Hwy. 8.

TRIP #61 - BORDER RUN

GENERAL LOCATION: Ocotillo, Calexico

LEVEL OF DIFFICULTY: One way - moderate to strenuous (strenuous on hot days)
Distance - 55.2 miles
Elevation gain - essentially flat

GENERAL DESCRIPTION: This "Desert Dandy" follows State Hwy. 98 along the U.S.A.-Mexico border, remaining within 2-3 miles of that demarcation line for most of this one-way trip. The trip departs Ocotillo and wanders 20 miles through the Yuha Desert before transiting another 20 miles of predominantly-agricultural area. A short visit to Calexico is included in this segment. Outside the city limits, the road follows the All-American Canal to the road's terminus at Interstate Hwy. 8. The desert segments provide a multitude of looks at Ocotillo cactus, miles of desert scrub, scenic long-distance views into the mountainous regions across the border, and a special brand of solitude. There is an option to couple this tour with a less-scenic return leg and create a very strenuous "century" ride.

TRAILHEAD: From I-8, "The Friendship Highway," exit north at Imperial Hwy. and drive a short distance to the town of Ocotillo. There is a delicatessen and gas station here. The ride as described requires a car shuttle. A good pickup point is on Evan Hewes Hwy. just north of Hwy. 8 at the State Hwy. 98 junction.

There is also an option to do a Century-plus (110 miles) loop by returning via the Evan Hewes Hwy. This return offers a nice 15-mile stretch of desert solitude east of

DESERT

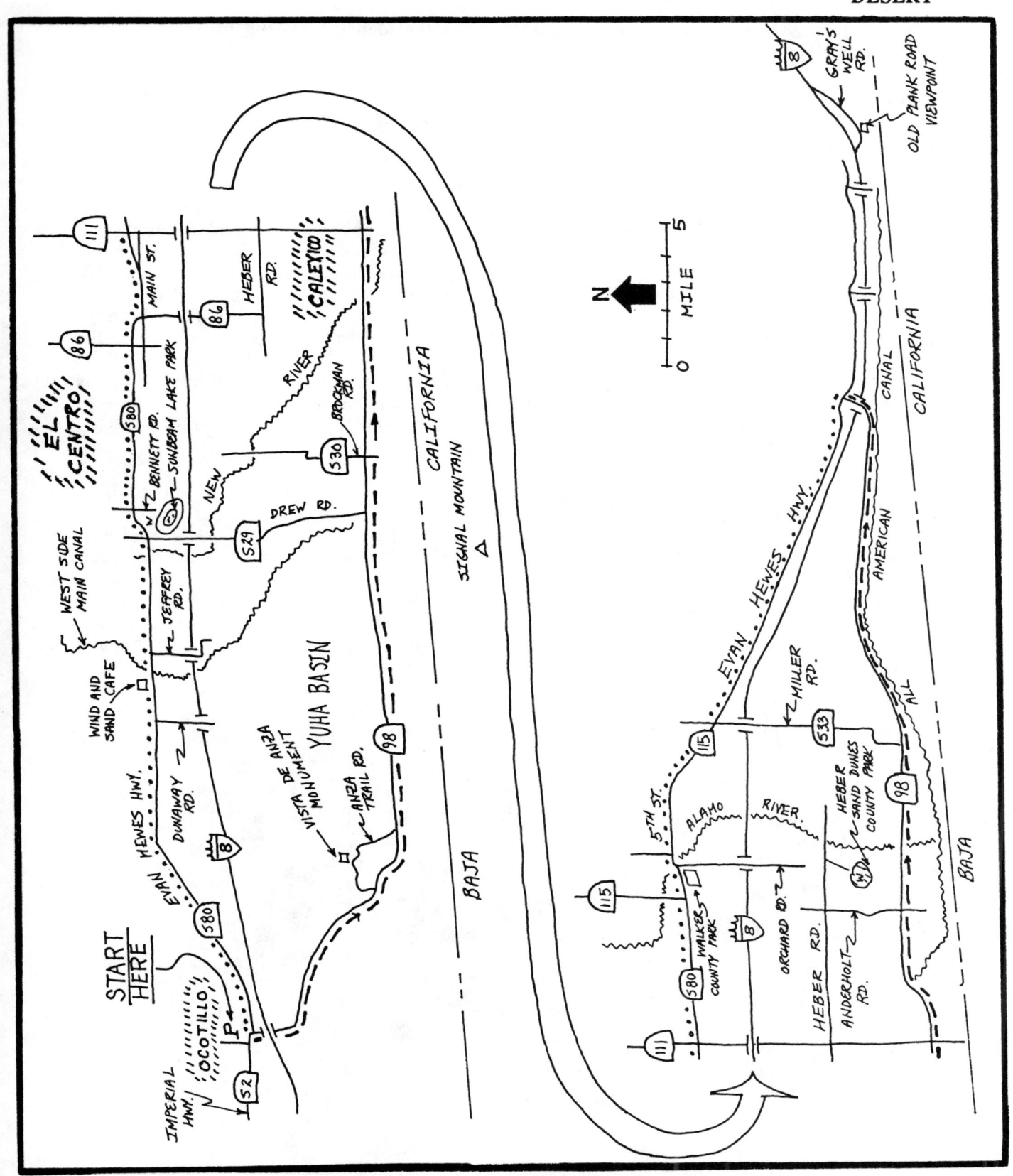

TRIP #61 - BORDER RUN

BICYCLE RIDES: SAN DIEGO COUNTY

Ocotillo, but also has a 15-20 mile segment of higher-density traffic in the Holtville and El Centro areas.

Bring at least a couple quarts of water for safety. The first 20 miles and last ten miles of the State Hwy. 98 trip are isolated and waterless. Check the weather first to ensure avoiding both hot weather and high winds.

TRIP DESCRIPTION: **Yuha Basin.** Bike under the Interstate, pass a gas station (last water source that we saw in the next 23.2 miles), and turn left (east) on Hwy. 98. Follow this two-lane highway (wide, with sometimes rough shoulder and limited, but high-speed traffic) through wide expanses covered with spring-blooming Ocotillo cactus and desert scrub. There are interesting views into Davis Valley, nestled between the mountain ranges to the south. In several miles, the cyclist stares directly into a dome-shaped peak rising directly out of the desert floor, which is covered with a sand-like surface on one flank. At 6.5 miles from the trip origin, the road passes the western and eastern intersections of the Anza Trail Rd. loop (the Vista De Anza Monument is near the mid-point of that dirt road). Near the 20-mile point is the onset of typical Imperial Valley agriculture, and there is an unobstructed view of imposing Signal Mountain in Mexico, complete with the huge water pipes passing over the mountain's lower northern ridge.

Calexico. Just beyond, the road passes County Hwy. S30, where there is a restaurant and store (23.2). In seven more miles of riding through varied pockets of agriculture, the biker encounters the first stoplight at State Hwy. 111! For the next couple of miles, the biker visits part of the Calexico business district, with its mini-marts, shopping centers, gas stations and eateries. A mile further, the city influence fades almost as quickly as it built up on the incoming leg. Returning to an agricultural setting, Hwy. 98 passes Barbara Worth Rd. (35.5) (Heber San Dunes County Park is northeast of this intersection) and reenters the desert world beyond Highline Canal (45.3).

Eastern Segment of Highway 98

DESERT

End Segment. The highway passes through aptly-named Creosote Flats and begins to parallel the All-American Canal. Clear evidence of the canal are the periodic hydroelectric plants and the associated power lines. After a few miles of continued low-desert traverse, I-8 suddenly looms to the left and State Hwy. 98 comes to an end on the freeway overpass; the short upgrade proves a pleasant change of pace. In 9.3 miles (just to the north of the freeway) is Evan Hewes Hwy., where your car shuttle is waiting (55.5).

Evan Hewes Hwy. Return Leg. The 55-mile return leg follows alongside Interstate Hwy. 8 for 13.5 miles, visits farmland for 4.5 miles, then laboriously works its way through Holtville and El Centro for 15 miles. Beyond this point, the route returns to agricultural and desert domains (also known as "the land of few stop signs"). Beyond Seely is the most interesting part of this return leg: 1) Trucker's "heaven" at the Wind N' Sand Cafe (41.5); 2) visible remnants of the ancient Lake Cahuilla beachline (43.0); and 3) Plaster City, a huge industrial complex that makes nothing but plaster products (surprise!) (45.0). The end of the line is Ocotillo.

Calexico's Historic Hotel

CONNECTING TRIPS: 1) Continuation with the Great Overland State Route (Trip #60) - at the trip origin, bike north on Imperial Hwy. (Hwy. S2); 2) **Old Plank Road** - drive ten miles east on Interstate Hwy. 8 or bike east on Evan Hewes Rd. to Gordon's Well and bike 1-1/2 miles east on the interstate, exiting at Gray's Well Rd. An automobile railroad, consisting of four-inch thick planks attached to cross ties and bound with steel straps, was used in the early 1900's to allow motor transport across the shifting Algodones Dunes. Sections of the road, used for ten years, are visible from Gray's Well Rd.; 3) **De Anza Hotel** - on East 4th St. in Calexico, about 0.7 mile off the reference route, this landmark hotel was a center of activity for the wealthy in the Prohibition Era. Fallen into disrepair when that era ended, this magnificent hotel was restored in the late 1960's and includes many of the original furnishings.

BICYCLE RIDES: SAN DIEGO COUNTY

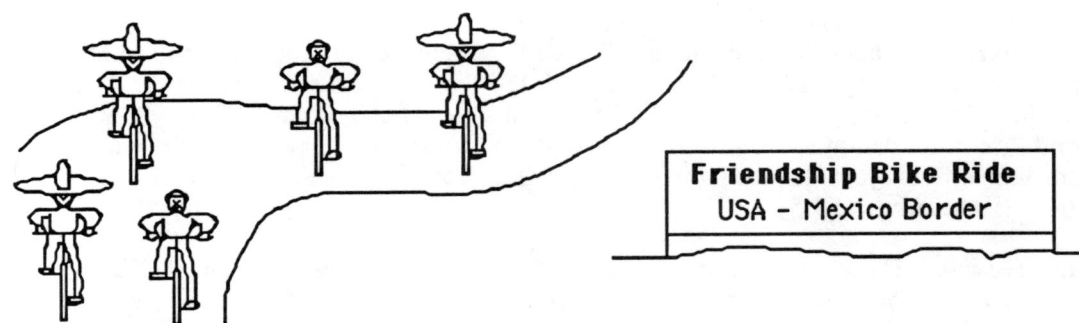

TRIP #62 - WINTERHAVEN WORKOUT

GENERAL LOCATION: Winterhaven, Bard, Yuma

LEVEL OF DIFFICULTY: Winterhaven-Bard Loop - easy
Loop + Colorado River up and back - moderate to strenuous
Distance - 44.5 miles (loop + up and back)
Elevation gain - moderate grade (Senator Wash area)

GENERAL DESCRIPTION: Every now and then, we stumble across a relatively-unknown ride that is a real winner. This three-season, basically flat workout in the agricultural region of southeast California along the Colorado River is one of them. Most of the tour is on rural roads (some rough pavement) with very little traffic. There are excellent views of the Cargo Muchacho Mountains, a variety of farms to inspect (citrus, palm trees, hay) and local sights such as the Dome Roadside Market to keep the trip interesting. After completing the Winterhaven-Bard Loop, the cyclist is then treated to an optional (but highly recommended) transit along the Colorado River, which terminates at scenic Senator Wash Reservoir.

There is an additional option to extend this tour by crossing into the Yuma Proving Grounds (Duck!!) and returning via Yuma, Arizona. Tour distance from the reservoir to the trip origin is 26.2 miles. Finally, our book reviewer Sally also surmised that this tour has potential as a "bike up-float down" experience!

TRAILHEAD: From Interstate Hwy. 8, exit at the Winterhaven turnoff, turn north and cross the Colorado River. Turn right and follow County Hwy. S24 across the Yuma Main Canal, left under an old railroad bridge, and left again to Picacho Rd. A short distance and to the right is Quechan Community Center and the trip starting point.

TRIP DESCRIPTION: Winterhaven-Bard Loop (21.9 miles). The tour route starts in Winterhaven and follows a counterclockwise maze as shown on the map, passing through Bard and returning via a 6.3-mile final loop on Indian Rock Rd./Arnold Rd. Of particular interest are the geodesic domes at York Rd. and Colby Rd. which house the Bard Valley Date Farms and Citrus Market, and the Imperial Date Gardens store just south of Bailey Rd. on York Rd. We also enjoyed seeing such sights as a small isolated "crackerbox house" with a giant satellite dish in the front yard on eastern Arnold Rd. Note that there is a market at Ross Corner.

Senator Wash Reservoir (22.6 miles up and back). At the northernmost point of the Winterhaven-Bard Loop, continue north on York Rd., turning right on

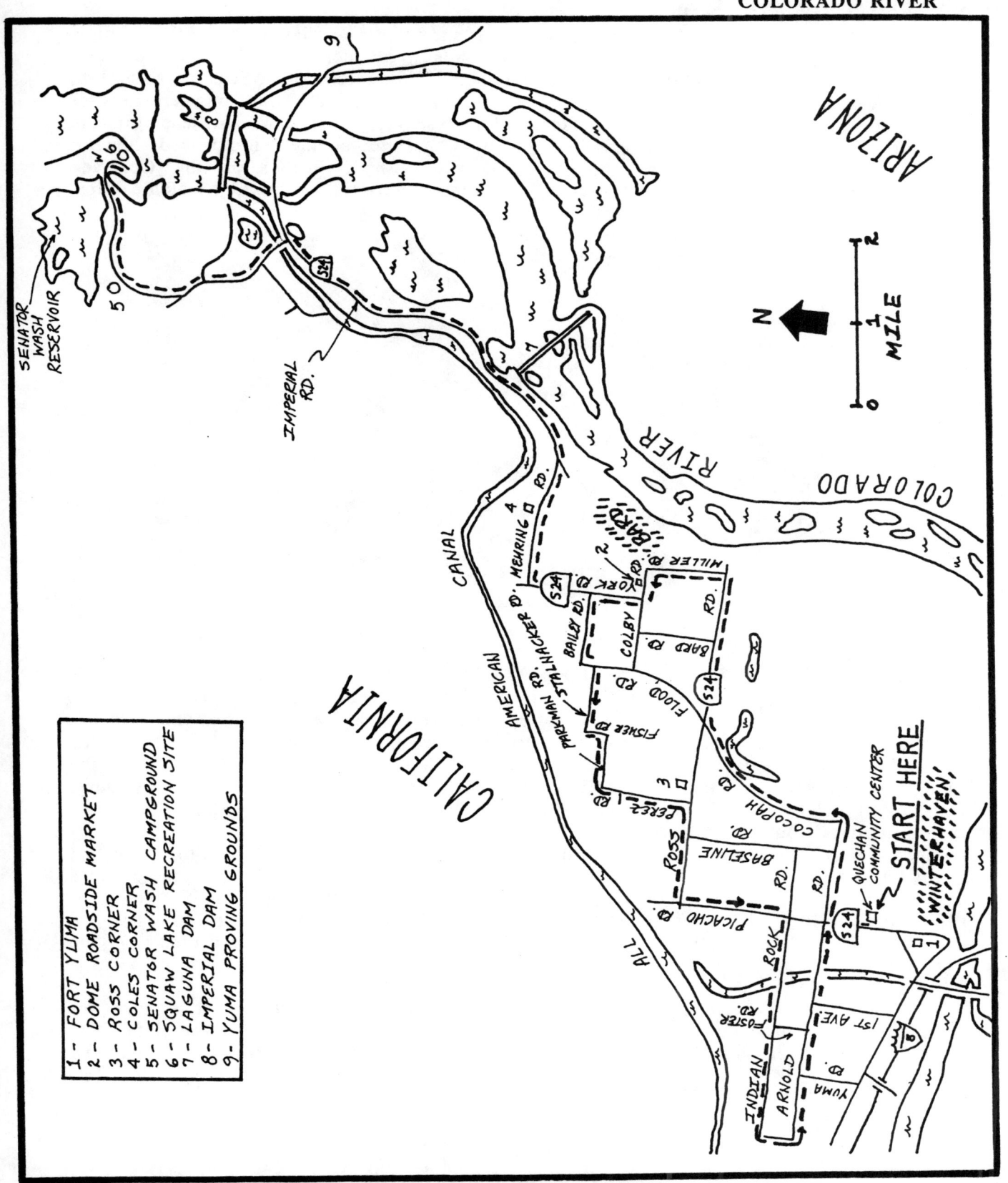

TRIP #62 - WINTERHAVEN WORKOUT

BICYCLE RIDES: SAN DIEGO COUNTY

Mehring Rd. Pass Cole's Corner with its fruit and other goodies market, then follow the curving road northward along the lush bottomland of the Colorado River to small Laguna Dam. In 1.9 miles on what is now Imperial Rd., turn left at Senator Wash Rd., pass McKenley Rd. and follow a testy 0.3-mile upgrade to the flat long-term visitor area. There is a panoramic vista of the Colorado River, Senator Wash Reservoir and the surrounding territory from this area. In 0.3 mile is the unimproved Senator Wash Campground (picnic area, boat launch) and a mile further on the Colorado River is the Squaw Lake Recreation Site (toilets, showers, swimming, picnic area, boat ramp and overnight camping).

Senator Wash Reservoir

CONNECTING TRIPS: Arizona Loop (26.2 miles). An option to extend the trip is to complete the loop through Yuma. Return 4.7 miles to Imperial Rd. (County Hwy. S24) and turn north. The roadway crosses "The River" and enters the Yuma Proving Grounds, where tanks, mobile artillery and other weapon systems are tested in this harsh desert environment. In 7.3 miles from the Senator Wash Rd./S24 junction, the route reaches Arizona State Hwy. 95. There is a reasonable shoulder on this busy, fast-moving highway, which crosses along some desolate foothills before reentering the agricultural outskirts of Yuma. The road crosses the Gila River and, after 5.7 miles on Hwy. 95, passes Miner's Camp Cafe and Walt and Sally's Pit Stop. In 8.2 additional flat miles is a light commercial area with a mini-mart, and five more miles brings the first stoplight of the trip near Interstate 8. Continuing to 4th Ave., turn right and follow that very busy Yuma street 2-1/2 miles to the Interstate 8 overcrossing. Then retrace the route to the trip origin as described in the "Trailhead" section above.

Lazyperson's Option. With a little clever planning, cyclists might arrange for a car shuttle to pick up the bikes at the Squaw Lake Recreation Site (accessible from Senator Wash Reservoir), then float down the Colorado to Yuma. Greater love hath no car shuttler!!

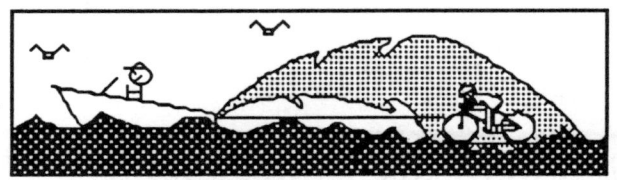

OTHER BICYCLING INFORMATION SOURCES

SOURCE	PHONE NUMBER	COMMENT(S)
Emergency	911	
Other traffic and accident reporting	(619) 268-2276	
GENERAL SOURCES:		
American Youth Hostels (S.D. Chapter)	(619) 239-2644	Members only (some events). General info., rides.
AMTRAK Train (from L.A. or San Diego)	(800) 872-7245	Bikes allowed aboard on selected trains.
Automobile Club of So. Calif. (S.D. Office)	(619) 233-1000	Members only. Contact Bicycle Tour Counselor.
Fire Department	(619) 533-4300	Bicycle registration (state law) - $2.00 for two years.
Northeast Rural Bus System (Julian)	(619) 765-0145	Room for two bikes; make advanced reservations.
San Diego Regional Transit	(619) 233-3004	Bikes allowed aboard on selected days.
Southwest Coaches	(619) 232-7579	Route 901 - downtown San Diego to Coronado to Imperial Beach - can accommodate up to four bikes.
Tourist/Visitor Info. (City of San Diego)	(619) 236-1212	
Weather Report	(619) 225-9492	General information dispensed.
BICYCLE TOURING CLUBS & ORGANIZATIONS:		
Sierra Club (San Diego)	(619) 299-1743	Store with books and other touring information.
California Bicyclist	(213) 478-2840	Cycling incl. club list & cycling events calendar.
Competitor	(619) 793-2711	Running, cycling, triathlon. Events calendar.
Southwest Cycling	(818) 247-9384	Cycling incl. club list & cycling events calendar.
CITY CYCLING INFORMATION:	Contact city.	City Hall, Public Works, or Parks & Recreation.
RECREATION AND PARKS DEPARTMENTS:		
City of San Diego	(619) 236-5555	Bicycle coordinator.
Cleveland National Forest	(619) 232-3769	Camping information.
County of San Diego	(619) 694-3049	Maps, brouchures.
State of California/S.D. City Parks Dept.	(619) 565-3600	Maps, brochures, camping information.
U.S. Government National Park Service	(619) 226-6311	National park information.
TRANSPORTATION/OTHER DEPARTMENTS:		
Caltrans (State of California) - Bike info	(619) 231-2453	Maps, safety tips, Park & Ride locations.
Commuter Computer	(619) 237-7665	Bicyclist information.
San Diego Transit	(619) 233-3004	Route and schedule info.; bikes ok on several routes.

INDEX: SAN DIEGO COUNTY

ATTRACTION, POINT OF INTEREST	PAGE NUMBER(S)
Anderson's Pea Soup Restaurant	98
Agua Caliente Springs/Agua Caliente County Park	201,203
Agua Hedionda Lagoon (Carlsbad)	83,97,101
AMTRAK	81,84,109
Anza Borrego Desert	163,197
Anza Borrego Desert State Park Visitor Center	199
Balboa Park	21,43,52
Barona Casino, Barona Mission (Barona Valley)	182,184
Bates Nut Farm (Woods Valley)	188,190
Batiquitos Lagoon (Carlsbad, Leucadia)	83,88,97,98,104,131
Battle Mountain	118,127,135
Bayside Park (San Diego Harbor)	27
Bear Ridge	188,190
Bernardo Winery	118
Bicentennial Bike Route	18,36
Blossom Valley	147,153,182
Bonita Cove Park (Mission Bay)	18,19,81
Borrego Badlands	200
Borrego Palm Canyon Campground/Nature Trail	197,199
Borrego Springs	197,199,200
Boucher Hill Fire Lookout	155,158
Boulder Oaks Campground	173,176
Box Canyon	201
Brengle Terrace Park (Vista)	96
Broadway Pier (San Diego Harbor)	25
Bucaneer Beach Park (Oceanside)	83,108,109
Buddy Todd Memorial Park (Oceanside)	105
Butterfield Overland Mail/Stagecoach	201,203
Buena Vista Lagoon (Oceanside, Carlsbad)	83,97
Cabrillo Bridge (Balboa Park)	21,24
Cabrillo Monument (Point Loma)	29
Campo Stone Store, Railroad Museum	175
Camp Pendleton	78,83,84,110
Cape Cod Village (Oceanside Harbor)	109
Car Country Park (Carlsbad)	97
Carrizo Badlands Overlook	204
Centennial Park (Coronado)	28
Clairemont Park and Recreation Center	56,59
Coast Blvd. Park (La Jolla)	36
Coronado Bridge	25
Coronado Ferry	25,28
Crown Point Shores Park (Mission Bay)	19
Crystal Pier (Mission Beach)	18
Dehesa Valley	179,181
Del Mar Race Track	83,131
Desert View Picnic Grounds (Mt. Laguna)	163,165
Dos Picos County Park (Ramona)	186
Dixon Lake	121,122,124

INDEX: SAN DIEGO COUNTY

ATTRACTION, POINT OF INTEREST	PAGE NUMBER(S)
Dog Beach	67
Eagle Gold Mine (Julian)	161
El Cajon Mountain	69,147,182,
El Camino Real (The King's Highway)	87,88,90,91,98,100, 102,104,107,108
El Capitan Reservoir	66
Elfin Forest	131
Embarcadero Marina Park (San Diego Harbor)	25,29,42,43,81
"Emerald Arches" (Fallbrook)	140
Eucalyptus County Park (Mt. Helix)	150
Eucalyptus Hills	144
Fiesta Island (Mission Bay)	18,19,29
Firehouse Museum (Downtown San Diego)	42
Fletcher Cove Park (Solana Beach)	131
Flinn Springs County Park	153
Florida Canyon	21,22
Font's Point (Anza Borrego Desert)	200
Foot and Walker Pass (Great Overland Stage Route)	203
Fort Stockton	44,45,48
Fuerte Park (La Costa)	90
Gas Lamp Quarter (Downtown San Diego)	42
Great Overland Stage Route	163,165,201
Griffen Regional Park (El Cajon)	112
Guajome Regional Park (Oceanside/Vista)	108
Harbison Canyon	179
Harbor Island (San Diego Bay)	31
Heise County Park (Julian)	159,161
Heritage Park (Old Town)	45
Hilltop Park (Chula Vista)	71,74
Hillside Park (El Cajon)	112
Honey Springs Road ("The Test")	170
Hotel Del Coronado	25,27,28
Imperial Beach Naval Station	59,61
Jack Murphy Stadium	69,133
Julian	159,161,163,201
Julian Apple Days	159
Kellogg Park (La Jolla)	38
Kennedy Park (El Cajon)	112
Kensington Park	47,49
Kit Carson Park (Escondido)	125,128
La Costa Country Club	90,98
Laguna Mountains	163,203
La Jolla Caves	36,38
La Jolla Shores Beach	36,38
Lake Henshaw	156
Lake Hodges	124,127,129,132,133
Lake Elsinor	137
Lake Jennings	147,153
Lake Miramar	77
Lake Morena	173

ATTRACTION, POINT OF INTEREST	PAGE NUMBER(S)
Lake Murray	65,112
Lake Poway Recreation Area	120
Lake San Marcos	91,93
Lake San Marcos Country Club and Dining Room	93
Lake Wohlford	188,189
Lawrence Welk Resort	133,136,178
Lindo Lake County Park (Lakeside)	70,144,146,147,183
Live Oak Park (Fallbrook)	137,139
Los Penaquitos Canyon	116,118,133,136
Lower Otay Lake/Lower Otay Park	74-76
Lyons Peak/Lyons Valley, Lyons Valley Trading Post	170,172
Marian Bear Park (San Clemente Canyon)	32,33,59
Marina View Park (San Diego Harbor)	25,27
Mason Valley Cactus Garden	203
Mexico/Mexican Border	39,59,61,63,75,206
Miramar Naval Air Station	133,135
Mission Bay	18,19,38,39,41,52,59,70
Mission Bay Visitor's Center	19
Mission Hills Park	44,45,47
Mission Gorge	48,69
Mission Point (Mission Bay)	18
Mission San Luis Rey	104,105,107
Mission Trails Regional Park	65,66,148
Mission Valley	45,47,48,66,69,70,148
Moosa Canyon	136,176-178
Morley Field Sports Complex (Balboa Park)	21,22
Mt. Helix/Mt. Helix County Park	112,150,152,181
Mt. Helix Lake	152
Mt. Laguna Observatory	165
Mt. Soledad/Mt. Soledad Easter Cross	39,52
Mussey Grade Road	186
Nancy Jane County Park (Crest)	181
National Steel and Shipbuilding Yard (San Diego Harbor)	25
Ocean Beach Park Athletic Area	29,32,67,81
Ocean Beach Pier	18,32
Ocean Front Walk (Mission Beach)	18,81
Oceanside Pier	108
Old Highway 395	70,77,118,133,136,140,150,178
Old Ironsides County Park (Harbison Canyon)	181
Old Julian Hwy.	141
Old Town (San Diego)	44,47,52
Old Town Temecula	133,136
Pacific Coast Bicentennial Bike Route	18,78
Pacific Crest Trail	173
Pala Mission	166,168,169
Palomar Mountain State Park	155,156,158
Palomar Observatory	155-157
Paradise Hills Park and Recreation Center	63

INDEX: SAN DIEGO COUNTY

ATTRACTION, POINT OF INTEREST	PAGE NUMBER(S)
Pegleg Smith Monument (Borrego Springs)	197-199
Point Loma	29,31,43,52,70,81
Poopout Hill (Techolote Canyon)	55,56,58
Poway Community Park	120
Presidio Park	44,45,48,52
Rainbow Oaks Restaurant	136,166
Rice Canyon	166
Quivera Basin (Mission Bay)	18,20
Quail Botanical Gardens (Encinitas)	131
Rancho Santa Fe ("The Ranch")	85,87,88
Rohr Park (Chula Vista)	74
Rose Canyon	33,35
San Clemente Canyon	32
San Diego 59-Mile Scenic Drive	52,70
San Diego International Airport	18,47,81
San Diego River	18,19,29,32,48,52,66,67, 69,70,81,184
San Diego Wild Animal Park	127
San Diego Zoo	22
San Dieguito Park (Lomas Santa Fe)	85,102
San Dieguito River	102,122,132
San Elijo Lagoon	131
San Felipe Creek	197,200
San Luis Rey River	107,109,136,155,166,178
San Marcos Creek	88
San Onofre State Beach	84
San Pasqual Valley	121,122,125,127,128
San Pasqual Vineyards (Escondido)	122
Santee Lakes Regional Park	114
San Vicente Valley	141,143,182,185,186
Scripps Park (La Jolla)	36,38
Scripps Institute of Oceanography	36,38,52,82
Seaport Village (San Diego Harbor)	25,29,42,43
Sea World (Mission Bay)	18,19
Serra Museum	44,48
Sessions Park (La Jolla)	39
Shelter Island (San Diego Bay)	29,31
Silver Strand Beach/Silver Strand Bikepath	25,27,62
South Bay Park and Recreation Center (Imperial Beach)	60
South Carlsbad State Beach	83,99
South Mission Beach Park (Mission Bay)	18
Spanish Landing Park (San Diego)	29,31,81
Standley Park and Recreation Center (University City)	33
Star of India (San Diego Harbor)	42
Stelzer County Park (Wildcat Canyon)	184
Sunset Cliffs Park (Point Loma)	29,31
Sunrise Highway	163,165
Swamis County Park (Encinitas)	83
Sweetwater Park (Chula Vista)	71,74-76
Sweetwater River	71,74,181,182

ATTRACTION, POINT OF INTEREST	PAGE NUMBER(S)
Techolote Canyon/Techolote Park and Recreation Center	35,55,56
Temecula Creek Inn	168
Temescal Canyon	133,137
Thibodo Hills Park	100,101
Tidelands Park (Coronado)	25,27
Tierrasanta Park and Recreation Area	148,150
Tijuana, Bullring-by-the-Sea	61
Tijuana River	61
Tijuana Slough National Wildlife Area	59,61
Torrey Pines State Beach/Torrey Pines State Preserve	38,82
Tourmaline Creek Mountain	168
Trestle Beach/San Mateo Point	84
University of California, San Diego	38,50,52,53,56,82
Vallecito County Park	203
Western Salt Evaporators (San Diego Bay)	27
Wildcat Canyon	182
Wildwood Park (Vista)	94,96
Wilderness Gardens Preserve (Pala Valley)	169
Woods Valley	188

INDEX: IMPERIAL COUNTY

ATTRACTION, POINT OF INTEREST	PAGE NUMBER(S)
Algodones Dunes	191,193
Bombay Beach (Salton Sea)	196
Bucklin Park (El Centro)	191
Cattle Call Park (Brawley)	191,193
Colorado River	208,210
De Anza Hotel (Calexico)	207
Dome Roadside Market (Bard)	208
Evan Hewes Highway	204,207
Fountain of Youth Spa (Salton Sea)	196
Heber Sand Dunes County Park (El Centro)	206
Old Plank Road (Algodones Dunes)	207
Red Hill Marina County Park (Salton Sea)	195
Salton Sea	193-196
Salton Sea National Wildlife Refuge	195
Senator Wash Reservoir	208,210
Signal Mountain-Mexico	204,206
Squaw Lake Recreation Site	210
Sunbeam Lake County Park (El Centro)	192,193
Travertine Rock (Desert Shores)	196
USA-Mexico Border	204
Wind N' Sand Cafe (Seely)	207
Yuma Proving Grounds	210

ODDs N' ENDS

Bye Bye Bicycle Rack!
(low overhead)

Penasquitos Canyon

San Diego AMTRAK Station

Navy Pier/Embarcadero

"Sea Watch"
(Susan Cohen Photo)

"Sailing San Diego Bay"